Kali Linux Revealed

Mastering the Penetration Testing Distribution

Kali Linux Revealed

Mastering the Penetration Testing Distribution

by Raphaël Hertzog, Jim O'Gorman, and Mati Aharoni

OFFSEC
PRESS

Kali Linux Revealed

Offsec Press
19701 Bethel Church Road, #103-253
Cornelius NC 28031
USA
www.offensive-security.com

Library of Congress Control Number: 2017905895

Printed in the United States of America.

Table of Contents

8. Debian Package Management

Preface

You have no idea how good you have it.

In 1998, I was an up-and-coming hacker, co-founding one of the earliest professional white hat hacking teams. We were kids, really, with dream jobs, paid to break into some of the most secure computer systems, networks, and buildings on the planet.

It sounds pretty sexy, but in reality, we spent most of our time hovering over a keyboard, armed with the digital tools of our trade. We wielded a sordid collection of programs, designed to map networks and locate targets; then scan, exploit, and pivot through them. In some cases, one of us (often Jim Chapple) would write custom tools to do wicked things like scan a Class A network (something no other tool could do, at the time), but most often we would use or modify tools written by the hacker community. In those pre-Google days, we frequented BugTraq, AstaLaVista, Packet Storm, w00w00, SecurityFocus, X-Force, and other resources to conduct research and build our arsenal.

Since we had limited time on each gig, we had to move quickly. That meant we couldn't spend a lot of time fiddling with tools. It meant we had to learn the core tools inside and out, and keep the ancillary ones on tap, just in case. It meant we had to have our tools well-organized, documented, and tested so there would be few surprises in the field. After all, if we didn't get in, we lost face with our clients and they would take our recommendations far less seriously.

Because of this, I spent a lot of time cataloging tools. When a tool was released or updated, I'd go through a routine. I had to figure out if it would run on the attack platform (some didn't), and whether it was worthwhile (some weren't); I had to update any scripts that relied on it, document it, and test it, including carrying over any changes made to the previous version.

Then, I would shake out all the tools and put them in directories based on their purpose during an assessment. I'd write wrapper scripts for certain tools, chain some tools together, and correlate all that into a separate CD that we could take into sensitive areas, when customers wouldn't let us take in attack machines or remove media from their labs.

This process was painful, but it was necessary. We knew that we had the ability to break into any network—if we applied our skills and expertise properly, stayed organized, and worked efficiently. Although remaining undefeated was a motivator, it was about providing a service to clients who *needed* us to break into networks, so they could plug gaps and move money toward critical-but-neglected information security programs.

We spent years sharpening our skills and expertise but we wouldn't have been successful without organization and efficiency. We would have failed if we couldn't put our hands on the proper tool when needed.

That's why I spent so much time researching, documenting, testing, and cataloging tools, and at the turn of the 21st Century, it was quickly becoming an overwhelming, full-time job. Thanks to the Internet, the worldwide attack surface exploded and the variety and number of attack tools increased exponentially, as did the workload required to maintain them.

Starting in 2004, the Internet exploded not only as a foundation for business but also as a social platform. Computers were affordable, more consumer-friendly and ubiquitous. Storage technology expanded from megabytes to gigabytes. Ethernet jumped from hundreds of kilobits to tens of megabits per second, and Internet connections were faster and cheaper than ever before. E-commerce was on the rise, social media sites like Facebook (2004) and Twitter (2006) came online and Google (1998) had matured to the point that anyone (including criminals) could find just about anything online.

Research became critical for teams like ours because we had to keep up with new attacks and toolsets. We responded to more computer crimes, and forensic work demanded that we tread lightly as we mucked through potential evidence. The concept of a *live CD* meant that we could perform live forensics on a compromised machine without compromising evidence.

Now our little team had to manage attack tools, forensic tools, and a sensitive area tool distribution; we had to keep up with all the latest attack and exploit methodologies; and we had to, you know, actually do what we were paid for—penetration tests, which were in high demand. Things were spinning out of control, and before long, we were spending less time in battle and much more time researching, sharpening our tools, and planning.

We were not alone in this struggle. In 2004, Mati "Muts" Aharoni, a hacker and security professional released "WHoppiX" (White Hat Knoppix), a live Linux CD that he billed as "the ultimate pen testing live CD," It included "all the exploits from SecurityFocus, Packet Storm and k-otik, Metasploit Framework 2.2, and much, much more."

I remember downloading WHoppiX and thinking it was a great thing to have around. I downloaded other live CDs, thinking that if I were ever in a real pinch, live CDs could save my bacon in the field. But I wasn't about to rely on WHoppiX or any other CD for real work. I didn't trust any of them to fulfill the majority of my needs; none of them felt right for my workflow; they were not full, installable distributions; and the moment I downloaded them they were out of date. An aged toolset is the kiss of death in our industry.

I simply added these CD images, despite their relatively massive size, to our arsenal and kept up the painful process of maintaining our "real" toolkit.

But despite my personal opinions at the time, and perhaps despite Muts' expectations, WHoppiX and its descendants had a seismic impact on his life, our industry, and our community.

In 2005, WHoppiX evolved into WHAX, with an expanded and updated toolset, based on "the more modular SLAX (Slackware) live CD." Muts and a growing team of volunteers from the hacker community seemed to realize that no matter how insightful they were, they could never anticipate all the growth and fluctuation of our industry and that users of their CD would have varied needs in the field. It was obvious that Muts and his team were actually using WHAX in the field, and they seemed dedicated to making it work. This was encouraging to me.

In 2006, Muts, Max Moser, and their teams consolidated Auditor Security Linux and WHAX into a single distribution called BackTrack. Still based on SLAX, BackTrack continued to grow, adding more tools, more frameworks, extended language support, extensive wireless support, a menu structure catering to both novice and pro users, and a heavily modified kernel. BackTrack became the leading security distribution, but many like me still used it as a backup for their "real tools."

By early 2009, Muts and his team had extended BackTrack significantly to BackTrack 4. Now a full-time job for Muts, BackTrack was no longer a live CD but a full-blown Ubuntu-based distribution leveraging the Ubuntu software repositories. The shift marked a serious evolution: BackTrack 4 had an update mechanism. In Muts' own words: "When syncing with our BackTrack repositories, you will regularly get security tool updates soon after they are released."

This was a turning point. The BackTrack team had tuned into the struggles facing pen testers, forensic analysts and others working in our industry. Their efforts would save us countless hours and provide a firm foundation, allowing us to get back into the fight and spend more time doing the important (and fun) stuff. As a result, the community responded by flocking to the forums and wiki; and by pitching in on the dev team. BackTrack was truly a community effort, with Muts still leading the charge.

BackTrack 4 had finally become an industrial-strength platform and I, and others like me, breathed a sigh of relief. We knew firsthand the "pain and sufferance" Muts and his team were bearing, because we had been there. As a result, many of us began using BackTrack as a primary foundation for our work. Yes, we still fiddled with tools, wrote our own code, and developed our own exploits and techniques; and we researched and experimented; but we did not spend all our time collecting, updating, validating, and organizing tools.

BackTrack 4 R1 and R2 were further revisions in 2010, leading to the ground-up rebuild of Back-Track 5 in 2011. Still based on Ubuntu, and picking up steam with every release, BackTrack was now a massive project that required a heroic volunteer and community effort but also funding. Muts launched Offensive Security (in 2006) not only to provide world-class training and penetration testing services but also to provide a vehicle to keep BackTrack development rolling, and ensure that BackTrack remained open-source and free to use.

BackTrack continued to grow and improve through 2012 (with R1, R2, and R3), maintaining an Ubuntu core and adding hundreds of new tools, including physical and hardware exploitation tools, VMware support, countless wireless and hardware drivers, and a multitude of stability improvements and bug fixes. However, after the release of R3, BackTrack development went relatively, and somewhat mysteriously, quiet.

There was some speculation in the industry. Some thought that BackTrack was getting "bought out", selling its soul to a faceless evil corporate overlord for a massive payout. Offensive Security was growing into one of the most respected training companies and a thought leader in our industry, and some speculated that its success had gobbled up and sidelined the key BackTrack developers. However, nothing could be farther from the truth.

In 2013, Kali Linux 1.0 was released. From the release notes: "After a year of silent development, Offensive Security is proud to announce the release and public availability of Kali Linux, the most advanced, robust, and stable penetration-testing distribution to date. Kali is a more mature, secure, and enterprise-ready version of BackTrack."

Kali Linux was not a mere rebranding of BackTrack. Sporting more than 600 completely repackaged tools, it was clearly an amazing toolset, but there was still more to it than that. Kali had been built, from the ground up, on a Debian core. To the uninformed, this might not seem like a big deal. But the ripple effects were staggering. Thanks to a massive repackaging effort, Kali users could download the source for every single tool; they could modify and rebuild a tool as needed, with only a few keystrokes. Unlike other mainstream operating systems of the day, Kali Linux synchronized with the Debian repositories four times a day, which meant Kali users could get wickedly current package updates and security fixes. Kali developers threw themselves into the fray, packaging and maintaining upstream versions of many tools so that users were constantly kept on the bleeding edge. Thanks to its Debian roots, Kali's users could bootstrap an installation or ISO directly from the repositories, which opened the door for completely customized Kali installations or massive enterprise deployments, which could be further automated and customized with preseed files. To complete the customization trifecta, Kali Users could modify the desktop environment, alter menus, change icons, and even replace windowing environments. A massive ARM development push opened the door for installation of Kali Linux on a wide range of hardware platforms including access points, single-board computers (Raspberry Pi, ODROID, BeagleBone, and CubieBoard, for example), and ARM-based Chromebook computers. And last but certainly not least, Kali Linux sported seamless minor and major upgrades, which meant devotees would never have to re-install customized Kali Linux setups.

The community took notice. In the first five days, 90,000 of us downloaded Kali 1.0.

This was just the beginning. In 2015, Kali 2.0 was released, followed by the 2016 rolling releases. In summary, "If Kali 1.0 was focused on building a solid infrastructure, then Kali 2.0 is focused on overhauling the user experience and maintaining updated packages and tool repositories."

The current version of Kali Linux is a rolling distribution, which marks the end of discrete versions. Now, users are up to date continuously and receive updates and patches as they are created. Core tools are updated more frequently thanks to an upstream version tagging system, groundbreaking accessibility improvements for the visually impaired have been implemented, and the Linux kernels are updated and patched to continue wireless 802.11 injection support. Software Defined Radio (SDR) and Near-Field Communication (NFC) tools add support for new fields of security testing. Full Linux encrypted disk installation and emergency self-destruct options are available, thanks to LVM and LUKS respectively, USB persistence options have been added, allowing USB-based Kali installs to maintain changes between reboots, whether the USB drive is encrypted or not. Finally, the latest revisions of Kali opened the door for NetHunter, an open-source world-class operating system running on mobile devices based on Kali Linux and Android.

Kali Linux has evolved not only into the information security professional's platform of choice, but truly into an industrial-grade, world-class, mature, secure, and enterprise-ready operating system distribution.

Through the decade-long development process, Muts and his team, along with the tireless dedication of countless volunteers from the hacker community, have taken on the burden of streamlining and organizing our work environment, freeing us from much of the drudgery of our work and providing a secure and reliable foundation, allowing us to concentrate on driving the industry forward to the end goal of securing our digital world.

And interestingly, but not surprisingly, an amazing community has built up around Kali Linux. Each and every month, three to four hundred thousand of us download a version of Kali. We come together on the Kali forums, some forty-thousand strong, and three to four hundred of us at a time can be found on the Kali IRC channel. We gather at conferences and attend Kali Dojos to learn how to best leverage Kali from the developers themselves.

Kali Linux has changed the world of information security for the better, and Muts and his team have saved each of us countless hours of toil and frustration, allowing us to spend more time and energy driving the industry forward, together.

But despite its amazing acceptance, support, and popularity, Kali has never released an official manual. Well, now that has changed. I'm thrilled to have come alongside the Kali development team and specifically Mati Aharoni, Raphaël Hertzog, Devon Kearns, and Jim O'Gorman to offer this, the first in perhaps a series of official publications focused on Kali Linux. In this book, we will focus on the Kali Linux platform itself, and help you understand and maximize the usage of Kali from the ground up. We won't yet delve into the arsenal of tools contained in Kali Linux, but whether you're a veteran or an absolute n00b, this is the best place to start, if you're ready to dig in and get serious with Kali Linux. Regardless of how long you've been at the game, your decision to read this book connects you to the growing Kali Linux community, one of the oldest, largest, most active, and most vibrant in our industry.

On behalf of Muts and the rest of the amazing Kali team, congratulations on taking the first step to mastering Kali Linux!

Johnny Long

February 2017

Foreword

The sixteen high-end laptops ordered for your pentesting team just arrived, and you have been tasked to set them up—for tomorrow's offsite engagement. You install Kali and boot up one of the laptops only to find that it is barely usable. Despite Kali's cutting-edge kernel, the network cards and mouse aren't working, and the hefty NVIDIA graphics card and GPU are staring at you blankly, because they lack properly installed drivers. You sigh.

In Kali *Live mode*, you quickly type `lspci` into a console, then squint. You scroll through the hardware listing: "PCI bridge, USB controller, SATA controller. Aha! Ethernet and Network controllers." A quick Google search for their respective model numbers, cross referenced with the Kali kernel version, reveals that these cutting-edge drivers haven't reached the mainline kernel yet.

But all is not lost. A plan is slowly formulating in your head, and you thank the heavens for the *Kali Linux Revealed* book that you picked up a couple of weeks ago. You could use the Kali Live-Build system to create a custom Kali ISO, which would have the needed drivers baked into the installation media. In addition, you could include the NVIDIA graphics drivers as well as the CUDA libraries needed to get that beast of a GPU to talk nicely to hashcat, and have it purr while cracking password hashes at blistering speeds. Heck, you could even throw in a custom wallpaper with a Microsoft Logo on it, to taunt your team at work.

Since the hardware profiles for your installations are identical, you add a preseeded boot option to the ISO, so that your team can boot off a USB stick and have Kali installed with no user interaction—the installation takes care of itself, full disk encryption and all.

Perfect! You can now generate an updated version of Kali on demand, specifically designed and optimized for your hardware. You saved the day. Mission complete!

With the deluge of hardware hitting the market, this scenario is becoming more common for those of us who venture away from mainstream operating systems, in search of something leaner, meaner, or more suitable to our work and style.

This is especially applicable to those attracted to the security field, whether it be an alluring hobby, fascination, or line of work. As newcomers, they often find themselves stumped by the environment or the operating system. For many newcomers Kali is their first introduction to Linux.

We recognized this shift in our user base a couple of years back, and figured that we could help our community by creating a structured, introductory book that would guide users into the world of security, while giving them all the Linux sophistication they would need to get started. And so, the Kali book was born—now available free over the Internet for the benefit of anyone interested in entering the field of security through Kali Linux.

As the book started taking shape, however, we quickly realized that there was untapped potential. This would be a great opportunity to go further than an introductory Kali Linux book and explore some of the more interesting and little-known features. Hence, the name of the book: *Kali Linux Revealed*.

By the end, we were chuffed with the result. The book answered all our requirements and I'm proud to say it exceeded our expectations. We came to the realization that we had inadvertently enlarged the book's potential user base. It was no longer intended only for newcomers to the security field, but also included great information for experienced penetration testers who needed to improve and polish their control of Kali Linux—allowing them to unlock the full potential of our distribution. Whether they were fielding a single machine or thousands across an enterprise, making minor configuration changes or completely customizing down to the kernel level, building their own repositories, touching the surface or delving deep into the amazing Debian package management system, *Kali Linux Revealed* provides the roadmap.

With your map in hand, on behalf of myself and the entire Kali Linux team, I wish you an exciting, fun, fruitful, and "revealing" journey!

Muts, February 2017

Introduction

Kali Linux is the world's most powerful and popular penetration testing platform, used by security professionals in a wide range of specializations, including penetration testing, forensics, reverse engineering, and vulnerability assessment. It is the culmination of years of refinement and the result of a continuous evolution of the platform, from WHoppiX to WHAX, to BackTrack, and now to a complete penetration testing framework leveraging many features of Debian GNU/Linux and the vibrant open source community worldwide.

Kali Linux has not been built to be a simple collection of tools, but rather a flexible framework that professional penetration testers, security enthusiasts, students, and amateurs can customize to fit their specific needs.

Why This Book?

Kali Linux is not merely a collection of various information security tools that are installed on a standard Debian base and preconfigured to get you up and running right away. To get the most out of Kali, it is important to have a thorough understanding of its powerful Debian GNU/Linux underpinnings (which support all those great tools) and learning how you can put them to use in your environment.

Although Kali is decidedly multi-purpose, it is primarily designed to aid in penetration testing. The objective of this book is not only to help you feel at home when you use Kali Linux, but also to help improve your understanding and streamline your experience so that when you are engaged in a penetration test and time is of the essence, you won't need to worry about losing precious minutes to install new software or enable a new network service. In this book, we will introduce you first to Linux, then we will dive deeper as we introduce you to the nuances specific to Kali Linux so you know exactly what is going on under the hood.

This is invaluable knowledge to have, particularly when you are trying to work under tight time constraints. It is not uncommon to require this depth of knowledge when you are getting set up, troubleshooting a problem, struggling to bend a tool to your will, parsing output from a tool, or leveraging Kali in a larger-scale environment.

Is This Book for You?

If you are eager to dive into the intellectually rich and incredibly fascinating field of information security, and have rightfully selected Kali Linux as a primary platform, then this book will help you in that journey. This book is written to help first-time Linux users, as well as current Kali users seeking to deepen their knowledge about the underpinnings of Kali, as well as those who have used Kali for years but who are looking to formalize their learning, expand their use of Kali, and fill in gaps in their knowledge.

In addition, this book can serve as a roadmap, technical reference, and study guide for those pursuing the Kali Linux Certified Professional certification.

General Approach and Book Structure

This book has been designed so that you can put your hands on Kali Linux right from the start. You don't have to read half of the book to get started. Every topic is covered in a very pragmatic manner, and the book is packed with samples and screenshots to help make the explanations more concrete.

In chapter 1, "About Kali Linux" [page 2], we define some basic terminology and explain the purpose of Kali Linux. In chapter 2, "Getting Started with Kali Linux" [page 14], we guide you step-by-step from the download of the ISO image to getting Kali Linux running on your computer. Next comes chapter 3, "Linux Fundamentals" [page 48] which supplies the basic knowledge that you need to know about any Linux system, such as its architecture, installation process, file system hierarchy, permissions, and more.

At this point, you have been using Kali Linux as live system for a while. With chapter 4, "Installing Kali Linux" [page 66] you will learn how to make a permanent Kali Linux installation (on your hard disk) and with chapter 5, "Configuring Kali Linux" [page 104] how to tweak it to your liking. As a regular Kali user, it is time to get familiar with the important resources available to Kali users: chapter 6, "Helping Yourself and Getting Help" [page 124] gives you the keys to deal with the unexpected problems that you will likely face.

With the basics well covered, the rest of the book dives into more advanced topics: chapter 7, "Securing and Monitoring Kali Linux" [page 150] gives you tips to ensure that your Kali Linux installation meets your security requirements. Next, chapter 8, "Debian Package Management" [page 170] explains how to leverage the full potential of the Debian packaging ecosystem. And in chapter 9, "Advanced Usage" [page 222], you learn how to create a fully customized Kali Linux ISO image. All those topics are even more relevant when you deploy Kali Linux at scale in an enterprise as documented in chapter 10, "Kali Linux in the Enterprise" [page 252].

The last chapter, chapter 11, "Introduction to Security Assessments" [page 280], makes the link between everything that you have learned in this book and the day-to-day work of security professionals.

Acknowledgments of Raphaël Hertzog

I would like to thank Mati Aharoni: in 2012, he got in touch with me because I was one out of dozens of Debian consultants and he wanted to build a successor to BackTrack that would be based on Debian. That is how I started to work on Kali Linux, and ever since I have enjoyed my journey in the Kali world.

Over the years, Kali Linux got closer to Debian GNU/Linux, notably with the switch to Kali Rolling, based on Debian Testing. Now most of my work, be it on Kali or on Debian, provides benefits to the entire Debian ecosystem. And this is exactly what keeps me so motivated to continue, day after day, month after month, year after year.

Working on this book is also a great opportunity that Mati offered me. It is not the same kind of work but it is equally rewarding to be able to help people and share with them my expertise of the Debian/Kali operating system. Building on my experience with the *Debian Administrator's Handbook*, I hope that my explanations will help you to get started in the fast-moving world of computer security.

I would also like to thank all the Offensive Security persons who were involved in the book: Jim O'Gorman (co-author of some chapters), Devon Kearns (reviewer), Ron Henry (technical editor), Joe Steinbach and Tony Cruse (project managers). And thank you to Johnny Long who joined to write the preface but ended up reviewing the whole book.

Acknowledgments of Jim O'Gorman

I would like to thank everyone involved in this project for their contributions, of which mine were only a small part. This book, much like Kali Linux itself was a collaborative project of many hands making light work. Special thanks to Raphaël, Devon, Mati, Johnny, and Ron for taking on the lion's share of the effort. Without them, this book would not have come together.

Acknowledgments of Mati Aharoni

It has been a few years since Kali Linux was first released, and since day one, I have always dreamt of publishing an official book which covers the Kali operating system as a whole. It is therefore a great privilege for me to finally see such a book making it out to the public. I would like to sincerely thank everyone involved in the creation of this project—including Jim, Devon, Johnny, and Ron. A very special thanks goes to Raphaël for doing most of the heavy lifting in this book, and bringing in his extensive expertise to our group.

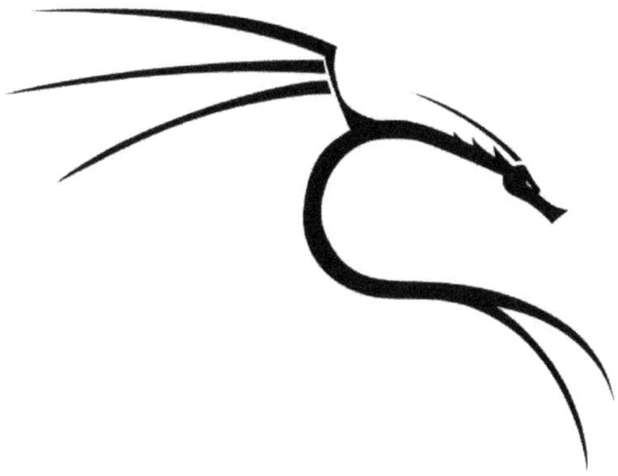

Keywords

Linux distribution
Debian derivative
Purpose
Features
Policies

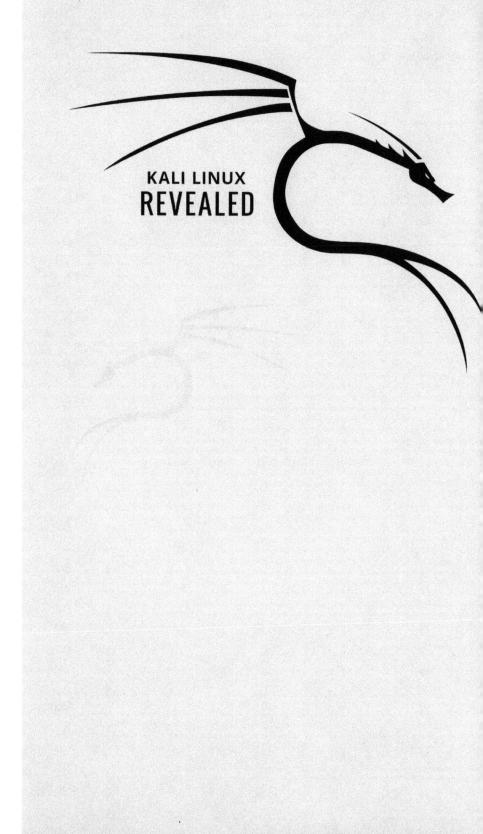

About Kali Linux

Kali Linux[1] is an enterprise-ready security auditing Linux distribution based on Debian GNU/Linux. Kali is aimed at security professionals and IT administrators, enabling them to conduct advanced penetration testing, forensic analysis, and security auditing.

What is a Linux Distribution?	Although it is commonly used as a name for the entire operating system, Linux is just the name of the kernel, a piece of software that handles interactions between the hardware and end-user applications.
	The expression *Linux distribution*, on the other hand, refers to a complete operating system built on top of the Linux kernel, usually including an installation program and many applications, which are either pre-installed or packaged in an easily installable way.
	Debian GNU/Linux[2] is a leading generic Linux distribution, known for its quality and stability. Kali Linux builds on the work of the Debian project and adds over 300 special-purpose packages of its own, all related to information security, particularly the field of penetration testing.
	Debian is a free software project providing multiple versions of its operating system and we often use the term *distribution* to refer to a specific version of it, for example the Debian Stable or Debian Testing distributions. The same also applies to Kali Linux—with the Kali Rolling distribution, for example.

1.1. A Bit of History

The Kali Linux project began quietly in 2012, when Offensive Security decided that they wanted to replace their venerable BackTrack Linux project, which was manually maintained, with something that could become a genuine Debian derivative[3], complete with all of the required infrastructure and improved packaging techniques. The decision was made to build Kali on top of the Debian distribution because it is well known for its quality, stability, and wide selection of available software. That is why I (Raphaël) got involved in this project, as a Debian consultant.

The first release (version 1.0) happened one year later, in March 2013, and was based on Debian 7 "Wheezy", Debian's stable distribution at the time. In that first year of development, we packaged hundreds of pen-testing-related applications and built the infrastructure. Even though the number of applications is significant, the application list has been meticulously curated, dropping applications that no longer worked or that duplicated features already available in better programs.

During the two years following version 1.0, Kali released many incremental updates, expanding the range of available applications and improving hardware support, thanks to newer kernel releases. With some investment in continuous integration, we ensured that all important packages

---

[1]https://www.kali.org
[2]https://www.debian.org
[3]https://wiki.debian.org/Derivatives/Census

were kept in an installable state and that customized live images (a hallmark of the distribution) could always be created.

In 2015, when Debian 8 "Jessie" came out, we worked to rebase Kali Linux on top of it. While Kali Linux 1.x avoided the GNOME Shell (relying on GNOME Fallback instead), in this version we decided to embrace and enhance it: we added some GNOME Shell extensions to acquire missing features, most notably the Applications menu. The result of that work became Kali Linux 2.0, published in August 2015.

GNOME is Kali Linux's Default Desktop Environment	A desktop environment is a collection of graphical applications that share a common graphical toolkit and that are meant to be used together on user workstations. Desktop environments are generally not used in servers. They usually provide an application launcher, a file manager, a web browser, an email client, an office suite, etc.
	GNOME[4] is one of the most popular desktop environments (together with KDE[5], Xfce[6], LXDE[7], MATE[8]) and is installed on the main ISO images provided by Kali Linux. If you dislike GNOME, it is easy to build a custom ISO image with the desktop environment of your choosing. Instructions to do so are covered later in this book in chapter 9, "Advanced Usage" [page 222].

In parallel, we increased our efforts to ensure that Kali Linux always has the latest version of all pen-testing applications. Unfortunately, that goal was a bit at odds with the use of Debian Stable as a base for the distribution, because it required us to backport many packages. This is due to the fact that Debian Stable puts a priority on the stability of the software, often causing a long delay from the release of an upstream update to when it is integrated into the distribution. Given our investment in continuous integration, it was quite a natural move to rebase Kali Linux on top of Debian Testing so that we could benefit from the latest version of all Debian packages as soon as they were available. Debian Testing has a much more aggressive update cycle, which is more compatible with the philosophy of Kali Linux.

This is, in essence, the concept of Kali Rolling. While the rolling distribution has been available for quite a while, Kali 2016.1 was the first release to officially embrace the rolling nature of that distribution: when you install the latest Kali release, your system actually tracks the Kali Rolling distribution and *every single day you get new updates*. In the past, Kali releases were snapshots of the underlying Debian distribution with Kali-specific packages injected into it.

A rolling distribution has many benefits but it also comes with multiple challenges, both for those of us who are building the distribution and for the users who have to cope with a never-ending flow of updates and sometimes backwards-incompatible changes. This book aims to give you the knowledge required to deal with everything you may encounter while managing your Kali Linux installation.

---

[4]https://www.gnome.org
[5]https://www.kde.org
[6]http://www.xfce.org
[7]http://lxde.org
[8]http://mate-desktop.org

1.2. Relationship with Debian

The Kali Linux distribution is based on Debian Testing[9]. Therefore, most of the packages available in Kali Linux come straight from this Debian repository.

While Kali Linux relies heavily on Debian, it is also entirely independent in the sense that we have our own infrastructure and retain the freedom to make any changes we want.

1.2.1. The Flow of Packages

On the Debian side, the contributors are working every day on updating packages and uploading them to the Debian Unstable distribution. From there, packages migrate to the Debian Testing distribution once the most troublesome bugs have been taken out. The migration process also ensures that no dependencies are broken in Debian Testing. The goal is that Testing is always in a usable (or even releasable!) state.

Debian Testing's goals align quite well with those of Kali Linux so we picked it as the base. To add the Kali-specific packages in the distribution, we follow a two-step process.

First, we take Debian Testing and force-inject our own Kali packages (located in our *kali-dev-only* repository) to build the *kali-dev* repository. This repository will break from time to time: for instance, our Kali-specific packages might not be installable until they have been recompiled against newer libraries. In other situations, packages that we have forked might also have to be updated, either to become installable again, or to fix the installability of another package that depends on a newer version of the forked package. In any case, *kali-dev* is not for end-users.

kali-rolling is the distribution that Kali Linux users are expected to track and is built out of *kali-dev* in the same way that Debian Testing is built out of Debian Unstable. Packages migrate only when all dependencies can be satisfied in the target distribution.

1.2.2. Managing the Difference with Debian

As a design decision, we try to minimize the number of forked packages as much as possible. However, in order to implement some of Kali's unique features, some changes must be made. To limit the impact of these changes, we strive to send them upstream, either by integrating the feature directly, or by adding the required hooks so that it is straightforward to enable the desired features without further modifying the upstream packages themselves.

The Kali Package Tracker[10] helps us to keep track of our divergence with Debian. At any time, we can look up which package has been forked and whether it is in sync with Debian, or if an update

---

[9]https://www.debian.org/releases/testing/
[10]http://pkg.kali.org/derivative/kali-dev/

is required. All our packages are maintained in Git repositories[11] hosting a Debian branch and a Kali branch side-by-side. Thanks to this, updating a forked package is a simple two-step process: update the Debian branch and then merge it into the Kali branch.

While the number of forked packages in Kali is relatively low, the number of additional packages is rather high: in April 2017 there were almost 400. Most of these packages are free software complying with the Debian Free Software Guidelines[12] and our ultimate goal would be to maintain those packages within Debian whenever possible. That is why we strive to comply with the Debian Policy[13] and to follow the good packaging practices used in Debian. Unfortunately, there are also quite a few exceptions where proper packaging was nearly impossible to create. As a result of time being scarce, few packages have been pushed to Debian.

1.3. Purpose and Use Cases

While Kali's focus can be quickly summarized as "penetration testing and security auditing", there are many different tasks involved behind those activities. Kali Linux is built as a *framework*, because it includes many tools covering very different use cases (though they may certainly be used in combination during a penetration test).

For example, Kali Linux can be used on various types of computers: obviously on the laptops of penetration testers, but also on servers of system administrators wishing to monitor their network, on the workstations of forensic analysts, and more unexpectedly, on stealthy embedded devices, typically with ARM CPUs, that can be dropped in the range of a wireless network or plugged in the computer of target users. Many ARM devices are also perfect attack machines due to their small form factors and low power requirements. Kali Linux can also be deployed in the cloud to quickly build a farm of password-cracking machines and on mobile phones and tablets to allow for truly portable penetration testing.

But that is not all; penetration testers also need servers: to use collaboration software within a team of pen-testers, to set up a web server for use in phishing campaigns, to run vulnerability scanning tools, and other related activities.

Once you have booted Kali, you will quickly discover that Kali Linux's main menu is organized by theme across the various kind of tasks and activities that are relevant for pen-testers and other information security professionals as shown in Figure 1.1, "Kali Linux's Applications Menu" [page 6].

---

[11]http://git.kali.org
[12]https://www.debian.org/social_contract
[13]https://www.debian.org/doc/debian-policy/

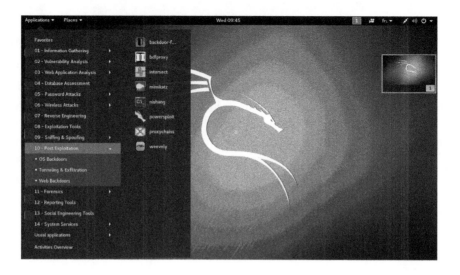

Figure 1.1 *Kali Linux's Applications Menu*

These tasks and activities include:

- Information Gathering: Collecting data about the target network and its structure, identifying computers, their operating systems, and the services that they run. Identifying potentially sensitive parts of the information system. Extracting all sorts of listings from running directory services.

- Vulnerability Analysis: Quickly testing whether a local or remote system is affected by a number of known vulnerabilities or insecure configurations. Vulnerability scanners use databases containing thousands of signatures to identify potential vulnerabilities.

- Web Application Analysis: Identifying misconfigurations and security weaknesses in web applications. It is crucial to identify and mitigate these issues given that the public availability of these applications makes them ideal targets for attackers.

- Database Assessment: From SQL injection to attacking credentials, database attacks are a very common vector for attackers. Tools that test for attack vectors ranging from SQL injection to data extraction and analysis can be found here.

- Password Attacks: Authentication systems are always a go-to attack vector. Many useful tools can be found here, from online password attack tools to offline attacks against the encryption or hashing systems.

- Wireless Attacks: The pervasive nature of wireless networks means that they will always be a commonly attacked vector. With its wide range of support for multiple wireless cards, Kali is an obvious choice for attacks against multiple types of wireless networks.

- Reverse Engineering: Reverse engineering is an activity with many purposes. In support of offensive activities, it is one of the primary methods for vulnerability identification and exploit development. On the defensive side, it is used to analyze malware employed in targeted attacks. In this capacity, the goal is to identify the capabilities of a given piece of tradecraft.

- Exploitation Tools: Exploiting, or taking advantage of a (formerly identified) vulnerability, allows you to gain control of a remote machine (or device). This access can then be used for further privilege escalation attacks, either locally on the compromised machine, or on other machines accessible on its local network. This category contains a number of tools and utilities that simplify the process of writing your own exploits.

- Sniffing & Spoofing: Gaining access to the data as they travel across the network is often advantageous for an attacker. Here you can find spoofing tools that allow you to impersonate a legitimate user as well as sniffing tools that allow you to capture and analyze data right off the wire. When used together, these tools can be very powerful.

- Post Exploitation: Once you have gained access to a system, you will often want to maintain that level of access or extend control by laterally moving across the network. Tools that assist in these goals are found here.

- Forensics: Forensic Linux live boot environments have been very popular for years now. Kali contains a large number of popular Linux-based forensic tools allowing you to do everything from initial triage, to data imaging, to full analysis and case management.

- Reporting Tools: A penetration test is only complete once the findings have been reported. This category contains tools to help collate the data collected from information-gathering tools, discover non-obvious relationships, and bring everything together in various reports.

- Social Engineering Tools: When the technical side is well-secured, there is often the possibility of exploiting human behavior as an attack vector. Given the right influence, people can frequently be induced to take actions that compromise the security of the environment. Did the USB key that the secretary just plugged in contain a harmless PDF? Or was it also a Trojan horse that installed a backdoor? Was the banking website the accountant just logged into the expected website or a perfect copy used for phishing purposes? This category contains tools that aid in these types of attacks.

- System Services: This category contains tools that allow you to start and stop applications that run in the background as system services.

1.4. Main Kali Linux Features

Kali Linux is a Linux distribution that contains its own collection of hundreds of software tools specifically tailored for their target users—penetration testers and other security professionals. It also comes with an installation program to completely setup Kali Linux as the main operating system on any computer.

This is pretty much like all other existing Linux distributions but there are other features that differentiate Kali Linux, many of which are tailored to the specific needs of penetration testers. Let's have a look at some of those features.

1.4.1. A Live System

Contrary to most Linux distributions, the main ISO image that you download is not simply dedicated to installing the operating system; it can also be used as a bootable live system. In other words, you can use Kali Linux without installing it, just by booting the ISO image (usually after having copied the image onto a USB key).

The live system contains the tools most commonly used by penetration testers so even if your day-to-day system is not Kali Linux, you can simply insert the disk or USB key and reboot to run Kali. However, keep in mind that the default configuration will not preserve changes between reboots. If you configure persistence with a USB key (see section 9.4, "Adding Persistence to the Live ISO with a USB Key" [page 239]), then you can tweak the system to your liking (modify config files, save reports, upgrade software, and install additional packages, for example), and the changes will be retained across reboots.

1.4.2. Forensics Mode

In general, when doing forensic work on a system, you want to avoid any activity that would alter the data on the analyzed system in any way. Unfortunately, modern desktop environments tend to interfere with this objective by trying to auto-mount any disk(s) they detect. To avoid this behavior, Kali Linux has a forensics mode that can be enabled from the boot menu: it will disable all such features.

The live system is particularly useful for forensics purposes, because it is possible to reboot any computer into a Kali Linux system without accessing or modifying its hard disks.

1.4.3. A Custom Linux Kernel

Kali Linux always provides a customized recent Linux kernel, based on the version in Debian Unstable. This ensures solid hardware support, especially for a wide range of wireless devices. The kernel is patched for wireless injection support since many wireless security assessment tools rely on this feature.

Since many hardware devices require up-to-date firmware files (found in /lib/firmware/), Kali installs them all by default—including the firmware available in Debian's non-free section. Those are not installed by default in Debian, because they are closed-source and thus not part of Debian proper.

1.4.4. Completely Customizable

Kali Linux is built by penetration testers for penetration testers but we understand that not everyone will agree with our design decisions or choice of tools to include by default. With this in mind, we always ensure that Kali Linux is easy to customize based on your own needs and preferences. To this end, we publish the live-build configuration used to build the official Kali images so you can customize it to your liking. It is very easy to start from this published configuration and implement various changes based on your needs thanks to the versatility of live-build.

Live-build includes many features to modify the installed system, install supplementary files, install additional packages, run arbitrary commands, and change the values pre-seeded to debconf.

1.4.5. A Trustable Operating System

Users of a security distribution rightfully want to know that it can be trusted and that it has been developed in plain sight, allowing anyone to inspect the source code. Kali Linux is developed by a small team of knowledgeable developers working transparently and following the best security practices: they upload signed source packages, which are then built on dedicated build daemons. The packages are then checksummed and distributed as part of a signed repository.

The work done on the packages can be fully reviewed through the packaging Git repositories[14] (which contain signed tags) that are used to build the Kali source packages. The evolution of each package can also be followed through the Kali package tracker[15].

1.4.6. Usable on a Wide Range of ARM Devices

Kali Linux provides binary packages for the armel, armhf, and arm64 ARM architectures. Thanks to the easily installable images provided by Offensive Security, Kali Linux can be deployed on many interesting devices, from smartphones and tablets to Wi-Fi routers and computers of various shapes and sizes.

1.5. Kali Linux Policies

While Kali Linux strives to follow the Debian policy whenever possible, there are some areas where we made significantly different design choices due to the particular needs of security professionals.

---

[14]http://git.kali.org
[15]http://pkg.kali.org

1.5.1. Single Root User by Default

Most Linux distributions encourage, quite sensibly, the use of a non-privileged account while running the system and the use of a utility like sudo when administrative privileges are needed. This is sound security advice, providing an extra layer of protection between the user and any potentially disruptive or destructive operating system commands or operations. This is especially true for multiple user systems, where user privilege separation is a requirement—misbehavior by one user can disrupt or destroy the work of many users.

Since many tools included in Kali Linux can only be executed with root privileges, this is the default Kali user account. Unlike other Linux distributions, you will not be prompted to create a non-privileged user when installing Kali. This particular policy is a major deviation from most Linux systems and tends to be very confusing for less experienced users. Beginners should be especially careful when using Kali since most destructive mistakes occur when operating with root privileges.

1.5.2. Network Services Disabled by Default

In contrast to Debian, Kali Linux disables any installed service that would listen on a public network interface by default, such as HTTP and SSH.

The rationale behind this decision is to minimize exposure during a penetration test when it is detrimental to announce your presence and risk detection because of unexpected network interactions.

You can still manually enable any services of your choosing by running `systemctl enable service`. We will get back to this in chapter 5, "Configuring Kali Linux" [page 104] later in this book.

1.5.3. A Curated Collection of Applications

Debian aims to be the universal operating system and puts very few limits on what gets packaged, provided that each package has a maintainer.

By way of contrast, Kali Linux does not package every penetration testing tool available. Instead, we aim to provide only the best freely-licensed tools covering most tasks that a penetration tester might want to perform.

Kali developers working as penetration testers drive the selection process and we leverage their experience and expertise to make enlightened choices. In some cases this is a matter of fact, but there are other, more difficult choices that simply come down to personal preference.

Here are some of the points considered when a new application gets evaluated:

- The usefulness of the application in a penetration testing context

- The unique functionality of the application's features
- The application's license
- The application's resource requirements

Maintaining an updated and useful penetration testing tool repository is a challenging task. We welcome tool suggestions within a dedicated category (*New Tool Requests*) in the Kali Bug Tracker[16]. New tool requests are best received when the submission is well-presented, including an explanation of why the tool is useful, how it compares to other similar applications, and so on.

1.6. Summary

In this chapter we have introduced you to Kali Linux, provided a bit of history, run through some of the primary features, and presented several use cases. We have also discussed some of the policies we have adopted when developing Kali Linux.

Summary Tips:

- Kali Linux[17] is an enterprise-ready security auditing Linux distribution based on Debian GNU/Linux. Kali is aimed at security professionals and IT administrators, enabling them to conduct advanced penetration testing, forensic analysis, and security auditing.
- Unlike most mainstream operating systems, Kali Linux is a rolling distribution, which means that *you will receive updates every single day.*
- The Kali Linux distribution is based on Debian Testing[18]. Therefore, most of the packages available in Kali Linux come straight from this Debian repository.
- While Kali's focus can be quickly summarized with "penetration testing and security auditing", there are several use cases including system administrators wishing to monitor their networks, forensic analysis, embedded device installations, wireless monitoring, installation on mobile platforms, and more.
- Kali's menus make it easy to get to tools for various tasks and activities including: vulnerability analysis, web application analysis, database assessment, password attacks, wireless attacks, reverse engineering, exploitation tools, sniffing and spoofing, post exploitation tools, forensics, reporting tools, social engineering tools, and system services.
- Kali Linux has many advanced features including: use as a live (non-installed) system, a robust and safe forensics mode, a custom Linux kernel, ability to completely customize the system, a trusted and secure base operating system, ARM installation capability, secure default network policies, and a curated set of applications.

In the next chapter, we will jump in and try out Kali Linux thanks to its live mode.

---

[16]http://bugs.kali.org
[17]https://www.kali.org
[18]https://www.debian.org/releases/testing/

Keywords

Download
ISO image
Live boot

Getting Started with Kali Linux

Contents

Unlike some other operating systems, Kali Linux makes getting started easy, thanks to the fact that its disk images are *live ISOs*, meaning that you can boot the downloaded image without following any prior installation procedure. This means you can use the same image for testing, for use as a bootable USB or DVD-ROM image in a forensics case, or for installing as a permanent operating system on physical or virtual hardware.

Because of this simplicity, it is easy to forget that certain precautions must be taken. Kali users are often the target of those with ill intentions, whether state sponsored groups, elements of organized crime, or individual hackers. The open-source nature of Kali Linux makes it relatively easy to build and distribute fake versions, so it is essential that you get into the habit of downloading from original sources and verifying the integrity and the authenticity of your download. This is especially relevant to security professionals who often have access to sensitive networks and are entrusted with client data.

2.1. Downloading a Kali ISO Image

2.1.1. Where to Download

The only official source of Kali Linux ISO images is the Downloads section of the Kali website. Due to its popularity, numerous sites offer Kali images for download, but they should not be considered trustworthy and indeed may be infected with malware or otherwise cause irreparable damage to your system.

➡ https://www.kali.org/downloads/

The website is available over *HTTPS*, making it difficult to impersonate. Being able to carry out a man-in-the-middle attack is not sufficient as the attacker would also need a www.kali.org certificate signed by a Transport Layer Security (TLS) certificate authority that is trusted by the victim's browser. Because certificate authorities exist precisely to prevent this type of problem, they deliver certificates only to people whose identities have been verified and who have provided evidence that they control the corresponding website.

> **cdimage.kali.org** The links found on the download page point to the cdimage.kali.org domain, which redirects to a mirror close to you, improving your transfer speed while reducing the burden on Kali's central servers.
>
> A list of available mirrors can be found here:
>
> ➡ http://cdimage.kali.org/README.mirrorlist

2.1.2. What to Download

The official download page shows a short list of ISO images, as shown in Figure 2.1, "List of Images Offered for Download" [page 15].

Download Kali Linux Images

We generate fresh Kali Linux image files every few months, which we make available for download. This page provides the links to **download Kali Linux** in its latest official release. For a release history, check our Kali Linux Releases page. Please note: You can find unofficial, untested weekly releases at http://cdimage.kali.org/kali-weekly/.

Image Name	Download	Size	Version	sha256sum
Kali 64 bit	ISO | Torrent	2.6G	2017.1	49b1c5769b909220060dc4c0e11ae09d97a270a80d259e05773101df62e11e9d
Kali 32 bit	ISO | Torrent	2.7G	2017.1	501b3747e5ac7c698217392fe49ec21dacee277404500fc49d4a0ee82625aabe
Kali 64 bit Light	ISO | Torrent	0.8G	2017.1	5c0f6300bf9842b724df92cb20e4637f4561ffc03029cdcb21af3902442ae9b0
Kali 32 bit Light	ISO | Torrent	0.8G	2017.1	6c83101ecf8702c7d93d32562e822b639d5c577314b448e3b8330995e0f07e0f
Kali 64 bit e17	ISO | Torrent	2.4G	2017.1	ae293cf679f38a4f17d090a272ccb13d7619e66d4502374154186c12891fb99c
Kali 64 bit KDE	ISO | Torrent	2.7G	2017.1	839741fec378114ff068df3ec2dbed9d8e4fae613e690d50b25ce9cc1468104b
Kali 64 bit Mate	ISO | Torrent	2.6G	2017.1	3ea748aa8c5f50d80f020acdbca5f0398ee90242bb4413c12985e1865186ca9e
Kali 64 bit Xfce	ISO | Torrent	2.5G	2017.1	8a17c2f54850585760b9d32a22e26df9a28f395b401753fa0a9b298aef4c4593
Kali 64 bit LXDE	ISO | Torrent	2.5G	2017.1	35eae65aaaabba8188dfd963e45b7b4d76e0684e7721c7d232cf18320b7cae3b
Kali armhf	Image | Torrent	0.5G	2017.1	a75199aa8a3d7b64561bc03fcd6e3ff8b94743c8769eecfaa4b719f04f7cbb63
Kali armel	Image | Torrent	0.4G	2017.1	180414422196f0797c1ea5f3c18682bc4b3ced871cb3e874e90de52dd4af877c

Figure 2.1 *List of Images Offered for Download*

All disk images labeled 32- or 64-bit refer to images suitable for CPUs, found in most modern desktop and laptop computers. If you are downloading for use on a fairly modern machine, it most likely contains a 64-bit processor. If you are unsure, rest assured that all 64-bit processors can run 32-bit instructions. You can always download and run the 32-bit image. The reverse is not true, however. Refer to the sidebar for more detailed information.

If you are planning to install Kali on an embedded device, smartphone, Chromebook, access point, or any other device with an ARM processor, you must use the Linux *armel* or *armhf* images.

Is My CPU 32- or 64-bit? Under Windows, you can find this information by running the *System Information* application (found in the Accessories > System Tools folder). On the System Summary screen, you can inspect the System Type field: it will contain "x64-based PC" for a 64-bit CPU or "x86-based PC" for a 32-bit CPU.

Under OS X/macOS, there is no standard application showing this information but you can still infer it from the output of the uname -m command run on the terminal. It will return x86_64 on a system with a 64-bit kernel (which can only run on a 64-bit CPU) and on systems with a 32-bit kernel, it will return i386 or something similar (i486, i586, or i686). Any 32-bit kernel can run on a 64-bit CPU, but since Apple controls the hardware and the software, it is unlikely you will find this configuration.

Under Linux, you can inspect the flags field in the /proc/cpuinfo virtual file. If it contains the lm attribute, then your CPU is a 64-bit; otherwise, it is a 32-bit. The following command line will tell you what kind of CPU you have:

```
$ grep -qP '^flags\s*:.*\blm\b' /proc/cpuinfo && echo 64-bit
➡ || echo 32-bit
64-bit
```

Now that you know whether you need a 32-bit or 64-bit image, there is only one step left: selecting the kind of image. The default Kali Linux image and the Kali Linux Light variant are both live ISOs that can be used to run the live system or to start the installation process. They differ only by the set of pre-installed applications. The default image comes with the GNOME desktop and a large collection of packages found to be appropriate for most penetration testers, while the light image comes with the Xfce desktop, (which is much less demanding on system resources), and a limited collection of packages, allowing you to choose only the apps you need. The remaining images use alternate desktop environments but come with the same large package collection as the main image.

Once you have decided on the image you need, you can download the image by clicking on "ISO" in the respective row. Alternatively, you can download the image from the BitTorrent peer-to-peer network by clicking on "Torrent," provided that you have a BitTorrent client associated with the .torrent extension.

While your chosen ISO image is downloading, you should take note of the checksum written in the sha256sum column. Once you have downloaded your image, use this checksum to verify that the downloaded image matches the one the Kali development team put online (see next section).

2.1.3. Verifying Integrity and Authenticity

Security professionals must verify the integrity of their tools to not only protect their data and networks but also those of their clients. While the Kali download page is TLS-protected, the actual download link points to an unencrypted URL that offers no protection against potential man-in-the-middle attacks. The fact that Kali relies on a network of external mirrors to distribute the image means that you should not blindly trust what you download. The mirror you were directed to may have been compromised, or you might be the victim of an attack yourself.

To alleviate this, the Kali project always provides checksums of the images it distributes. But to make such a check effective, you must be sure that the checksum you grabbed is effectively the checksum published by the Kali Linux developers. You have different ways to ascertain this.

Relying on the TLS-Protected Website

When you retrieve the checksum from the TLS-protected download webpage, its origin is indirectly guaranteed by the X.509 certificate security model: the content you see comes from a web site that is effectively under the control of the person who requested the TLS certificate.

Now you should generate the checksum of your downloaded image and ensure that it matches what you recorded from the Kali website:

```
$ sha256sum kali-linux-2017.1-amd64.iso
49b1c5769b909220060dc4c0e11ae09d97a270a80d259e05773101df62e11e9d  kali-linux-2016.2-amd64.iso
```

If your generated checksum matches the one on the Kali Linux download page, you have the correct file. If the checksums differ, there is a problem, although this does not indicate a compromise or an attack; downloads occasionally get corrupted as they traverse the Internet. Try your download again, from another official Kali mirror, if possible (see "cdimage.kali.org" [page 14] for more information about available mirrors).

Relying on PGP's Web of Trust

If you don't trust HTTPS for authentication, you are a bit paranoid but rightfully so. There are many examples of badly managed certificate authorities that issued rogue certificates, which ended up being misused. You may also be the victim of a "friendly" man-in-the-middle attack implemented on many corporate networks, using a custom, browser-implanted trust store that presents fake certificates to encrypted websites, allowing corporate auditors to monitor encrypted traffic.

For cases like this, we also provide a GnuPG key that we use to sign the checksums of the images we provide. The key's identifiers and its fingerprints are shown here:

```
pub   rsa4096/0xED444FF07D8D0BF6 2012-03-05 [SC] [expires: 2018-02-02]
      Key fingerprint = 44C6 513A 8E4F B3D3 0875  F758 ED44 4FF0 7D8D 0BF6
uid                 [  full  ] Kali Linux Repository <devel@kali.org>
sub   rsa4096/0xA8373E18FC0D0DCB 2012-03-05 [E] [expires: 2018-02-02]
```

This key is part of a global *web of trust* because it has been signed at least by me (Raphaël Hertzog) and I am part of the web of trust due to my heavy GnuPG usage as a Debian developer.

The PGP/GPG security model is very unique. Anyone can generate any key with any identity, but you would only trust that key if it has been signed by another key that you already trust. When you sign a key, you certify that you met the holder of the key and that you know that the associated identity is correct. And you define the initial set of keys that you trust, which obviously includes your own key.

This model has its own limitations so you can opt to download Kali's public key over HTTPS (or from a keyserver) and just decide that you trust it because its fingerprint matches what we announced in multiple places, including just above in this book:

```
$ wget -q -O - https://www.kali.org/archive-key.asc | gpg --import
[ or ]
$ gpg --keyserver hkp://keys.gnupg.net --recv-key ED444FF07D8D0BF6
gpg: key 0xED444FF07D8D0BF6: public key "Kali Linux Repository <devel@kali.org>" imported
gpg: Total number processed: 1
gpg:               imported: 1  (RSA: 1)
[...]
$ gpg --fingerprint 7D8D0BF6
[...]
     Key fingerprint = 44C6 513A 8E4F B3D3 0875  F758 ED44 4FF0 7D8D 0BF6
[...]
```

After you have retrieved the key, you can use it to verify the checksums of the distributed images. Let's download the file with the checksums (SHA256SUMS) and the associated signature file (SHA256SUMS.gpg) and verify the signature:

```
$ wget http://cdimage.kali.org/current/SHA256SUMS
[...]
$ wget http://cdimage.kali.org/current/SHA256SUMS.gpg
[...]
$ gpg --verify SHA256SUMS.gpg SHA256SUMS
gpg: Signature made Thu 16 Mar 2017 08:55:45 AM MDT
gpg:                using RSA key ED444FF07D8D0BF6
gpg: Good signature from "Kali Linux Repository <devel@kali.org>"
```

If you get that "Good signature" message, you can trust the content of the SHA256SUMS file and use it to verify the files you downloaded. Otherwise, there is a problem. You should review whether you downloaded the files from a legitimate Kali Linux mirror.

Note that you can use the following command line to verify that the downloaded file has the same checksum that is listed in SHA256SUMS, provided that the downloaded ISO file is in the same directory:

```
$ grep kali-linux-2017.1-amd64.iso SHA256SUMS | sha256sum -c
kali-linux-2017.1-amd64.iso: OK
```

If you don't get OK in response, then the file you have downloaded is different from the one released by the Kali team. It cannot be trusted and should not be used.

2.1.4. Copying the Image on a DVD-ROM or USB Key

Unless you want to run Kali Linux in a virtual machine, the ISO image is of limited use in and of itself. You must burn it on a DVD-ROM or copy it onto a USB key to be able to boot your machine into Kali Linux.

We won't cover how to burn the ISO image onto a DVD-ROM, as the process varies widely by platform and environment, but in most cases, right clicking on the .iso file will present a contextual menu item that executes a DVD-ROM burning application. Try it out!

Warning   In this section, you will learn how to overwrite an arbitrary disk with a Kali Linux ISO image. Always double-check the target disk before launching the operation as a single mistake would likely cause complete data loss and possibly damage your setup beyond repair.

Creating a Bootable Kali USB Drive on Windows

As a prerequisite, you should download and install *Win32 Disk Imager*:

➡ https://sourceforge.net/projects/win32diskimager/

Plug your USB key into your Windows PC and note the drive designator associated to it (for example, "E:\").

Launch *Win32 Disk Imager* and choose the Kali Linux ISO file that you want to copy on the USB key. Verify that the letter of the device selected corresponds with that assigned to the USB key. Once you are certain that you have selected the correct drive, click the Write button and confirm that you want to overwrite the contents of the USB key as shown in Figure 2.2, "Win32 Disk Imager in action" [page 20].

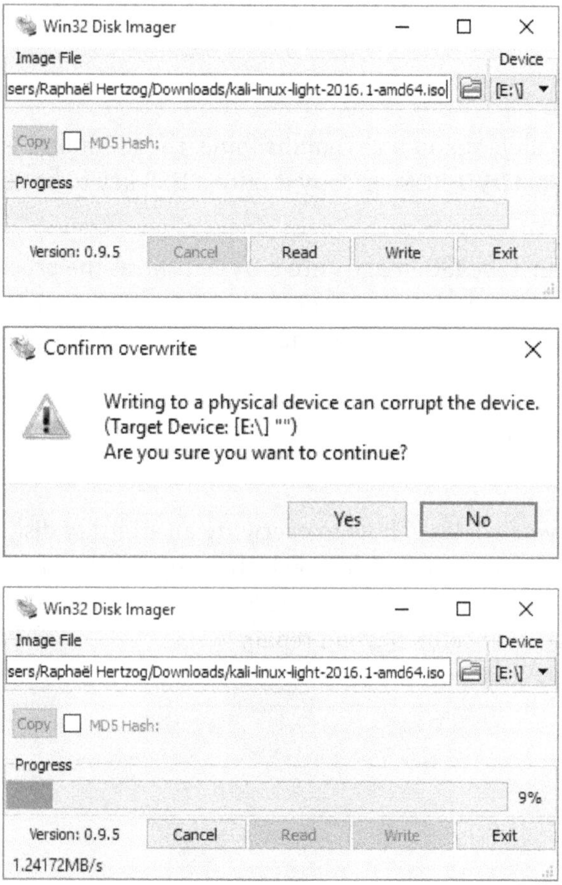

Figure 2.2 *Win32 Disk Imager in action*

Once the copy is completed, safely eject the USB drive from the Windows system. You can now use the USB device to boot Kali Linux.

Creating a Bootable Kali USB Drive on Linux

Creating a bootable Kali Linux USB key in a Linux environment is easy. The GNOME desktop environment, which is installed by default in many Linux distributions, comes with a *Disks* utility (in the *gnome-disk-utility* package, which is already installed in the stock Kali image). That program shows a list of disks, which refreshes dynamically when you plug or unplug a disk. When you select your USB key in the list of disks, detailed information will appear and will help you confirm that you selected the correct disk. Note that you can find its device name in the title bar as shown in Figure 2.3, "GNOME Disks" [page 21].

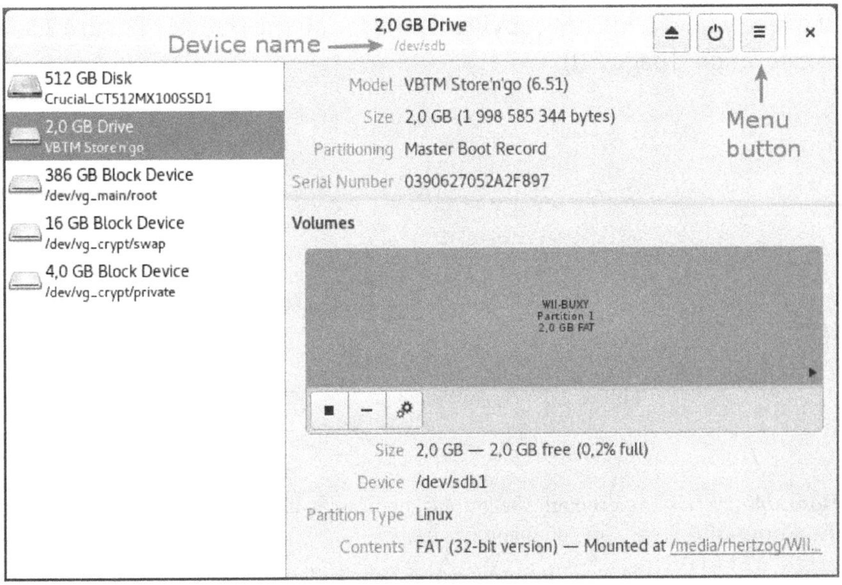

Device name ——→ /dev/sdb

512 GB Disk
Crucial_CT512MX100SSD1

2,0 GB Drive
VBTM Store'n'go

386 GB Block Device
/dev/vg_main/root

16 GB Block Device
/dev/vg_crypt/swap

4,0 GB Block Device
/dev/vg_crypt/private

2,0 GB Drive
/dev/sdb

Model   VBTM Store'n'go (6.51)
Size   2,0 GB (1 998 585 344 bytes)
Partitioning   Master Boot Record
Serial Number   0390627052A2F897

Menu
button

Volumes

WII-BUXY
Partition 1
2,0 GB FAT

Size   2,0 GB — 2,0 GB free (0,2% full)
Device   /dev/sdb1
Partition Type   Linux
Contents   FAT (32-bit version) — Mounted at /media/rhertzog/WII...

Figure 2.3   *GNOME Disks*

Click on the menu button and select Restore Disk Image... in the displayed pop-up menu. Select the ISO image that you formerly downloaded and click on Start Restoring... as shown in Figure 2.4, "Restore Disk Image Dialog" [page 21].

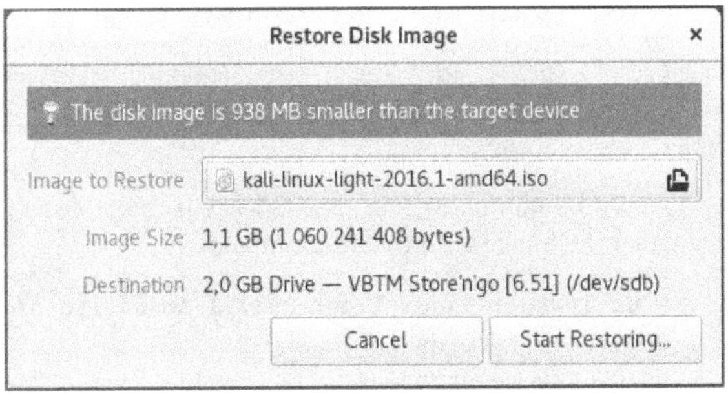

Restore Disk Image

The disk image is 938 MB smaller than the target device

Image to Restore   kali-linux-light-2016.1-amd64.iso
Image Size   1,1 GB (1 060 241 408 bytes)
Destination   2,0 GB Drive — VBTM Store'n'go [6.51] (/dev/sdb)

Cancel   Start Restoring...

Figure 2.4   *Restore Disk Image Dialog*

Enjoy a cup of coffee while it finishes copying the image on the USB key (Figure 2.5, "Progression of the Image Restoration" [page 22]).

Figure 2.5 *Progression of the Image Restoration*

Create the Bootable USB Drive from the Command Line

Even though the graphical process is fairly straightforward, the operation is just as easy for command line users.

When you insert your USB key, the Linux kernel will detect it and assign it a name, which is printed in the kernel logs. You can find its name by inspecting the logs returned by dmesg.

```
$ dmesg
[...]
[234743.896134] usb 1-1.2: new high-speed USB device number 6 using ehci-pci
[234743.990764] usb 1-1.2: New USB device found, idVendor=08ec, idProduct=0020
[234743.990771] usb 1-1.2: New USB device strings: Mfr=1, Product=2,
    ➥ SerialNumber=3
[234743.990774] usb 1-1.2: Product: Store'n'go
[234743.990777] usb 1-1.2: Manufacturer: Verbatim
[234743.990780] usb 1-1.2: SerialNumber: 0390627052A2F897
[234743.991845] usb-storage 1-1.2:1.0: USB Mass Storage device detected
[234743.992017] scsi host7: usb-storage 1-1.2:1.0
[234744.993818] scsi 7:0:0:0: Direct-Access     VBTM     Store'n'go      6.51
    ➥ PQ: 0 ANSI: 0 CCS
[234744.994425] sd 7:0:0:0: Attached scsi generic sg1 type 0
[234744.995753] sd 7:0:0:0: [sdb] 3903487 512-byte logical blocks: (2.00 GB
    ➥ /1.86 GiB)
[234744.996663] sd 7:0:0:0: [sdb] Write Protect is off
[234744.996669] sd 7:0:0:0: [sdb] Mode Sense: 45 00 00 08
[234744.997518] sd 7:0:0:0: [sdb] No Caching mode page found
[234744.997524] sd 7:0:0:0: [sdb] Assuming drive cache: write through
[234745.009375]  sdb: sdb1
[234745.015113] sd 7:0:0:0: [sdb] Attached SCSI removable disk
```

Now that you know that the USB key is available as /dev/sdb, you can proceed to copy the image with the dd command:

```
# dd if=kali-linux-light-2017.1-amd64.iso of=/dev/sdb
2070784+0 records in
2070784+0 records out
1060241408 bytes (1.1 GB, 1011 MiB) copied, 334.175 s, 3.2 MB/s
```

Note that you need root permissions for this operation to succeed and you should also ensure that the USB key is unused. That is, you should make sure that none of its partitions are mounted. The command also assumes that it is run while in the directory hosting the ISO image, otherwise the full path will need to be provided.

For reference, if stands for "input file" and of for "output file." The dd command reads data from the input file and writes it back to the output file. It does not show any progress information so you must be patient while it is doing its work (It is not unusual for the command to take more than half an hour!). Look at the write activity LED on the USB key if you want to double check that the command is working. The statistics shown above are displayed only when the command has completed. On OS X/macOS, you can also press CTRL+T during the operation to get statistical information about the copy including how much data has been copied.

Creating a Bootable Kali USB Drive on OS X/macOS

OS X/macOS is based on UNIX, so the process of creating a bootable Kali Linux USB drive is similar to the Linux procedure. Once you have downloaded and verified your chosen Kali ISO file, use dd to copy it over to your USB stick.

To identify the device name of the USB key, run diskutil list to list the disks available on your system. Next, insert your USB key and run the diskutil list command again. The second output should list an additional disk. You can determine the device name of the USB key by comparing the output from both commands. Look for a new line identifying your USB disk and note the /dev/diskX where X represents the disk ID.

You should make sure that the USB key is not mounted, which can be accomplished with an explicit unmount command (assuming /dev/disk6 is the device name of the USB key):

```
$ diskutil unmount /dev/disk6
```

Now proceed to execute the dd command. This time, add a supplementary parameter — bs for block size. It defines the size of the block that is read from the input file and then written to the output file.

```
# dd if=kali-linux-light-2017.1-amd64.iso of=/dev/disk6 bs=1M
1011+0 records in
1011+0 records out
1060241408 bytes transferred in 327.061 secs (3242328 bytes/sec)
```

That's it. Your USB key is now ready and you can boot from it or use it to install Kali Linux.

Booting an Alternate Disk on OS X/macOS To boot from an alternate drive on an OS X/macOS system, bring up the boot menu by pressing and holding the Option key immediately after powering on the device and selecting the drive you want to use.

For more information, see Apple's knowledge base[1].

---

[1] http://support.apple.com/kb/ht1310

2.2. Booting a Kali ISO Image in Live Mode

2.2.1. On a Real Computer

As a prerequisite, you need either a USB key prepared (as detailed in the previous section) or a DVD-ROM burned with a Kali Linux ISO image.

The BIOS/UEFI is responsible for the early boot process and can be configured through a piece of software called Setup. In particular, it allows users to choose which boot device is preferred. In this case, you want to select either the DVD-ROM drive or USB drive, depending on which device you have created.

Starting Setup usually involves pressing a particular key very soon after the computer is powered on. This key is often Del or Esc, and sometimes F2 or F10. Most of the time, the choice is briefly flashed onscreen when the computer powers on, before the operating system loads.

Once the BIOS/UEFI has been properly configured to boot from your device, booting Kali Linux is simply a matter of inserting the DVD-ROM or plugging in the USB drive and powering on the computer.

Disable Secure Boot While the Kali Linux images can be booted in UEFI mode, they do not support *secure boot*. You should disable that feature in Setup.

2.2.2. In a Virtual Machine

Virtual machines have multiple benefits for Kali Linux users. They are especially useful if you want to try out Kali Linux but aren't ready to commit to installing it permanently on your machine or if you have a powerful system and want to run multiple operating systems simultaneously. This is a popular choice for many penetration testers and security professionals who need to use the wide range of tools available in Kali Linux but still want to have full access to their primary operating system. This also provides them with the ability to archive or securely delete the virtual machine and any client data it may contain rather than reinstalling their entire operating system.

The snapshot features of virtualization software also make it easy to experiment with potentially dangerous operations, such as malware analysis, while allowing for an easy way out by restoring a previous snapshot.

There are many virtualization tools available for all major operating systems, including *VirtualBox®*, *VMware Workstation®*, *Xen*, *KVM*, and *Hyper-V* to name a few. Ultimately, you will use the one that best suits you but we will cover the two most frequently-used in a desktop context: *VirtualBox®* and *VMware Workstation Pro®*, both running on Windows 10. If you don't have corporate policy constraints or personal preference, our recommendation is that you try out VirtualBox first, as it is free, works well, is (mostly) open-source, and is available for most operating systems.

For the next sections, we will assume that you have already installed the appropriate virtualization tool and are familiar with its operation.

Preliminary Remarks

To fully benefit from virtualization, you should have a CPU with the appropriate virtualization features and they should not be disabled by the BIOS/UEFI. Double check for any "Intel® Virtualization Technology" and/or "Intel® VT-d Feature" options in the Setup screens.

You should also have a 64-bit host operating system, such as amd64 architecture for Debian-based Linux distributions, x86_64 architecture for RedHat-based Linux distributions, and Windows ... 64-bit for Windows.

If you lack any of the prerequisites, either the virtualization tool will not work properly or it will be restricted to running only 32-bit guest operating systems.

Since virtualization tools hook into the host operating system and hardware at a low level, there are often incompatibilities between them. Do not expect these tools to run well at the same time. Also, beware that professional versions of Windows come with *Hyper-V* installed and enabled, which might interfere with your virtualization tool of choice. To turn it off, execute "Turn windows features on or off" from Windows Settings.

VirtualBox

After the initial installation, VirtualBox's main screen looks something like Figure 2.6, "Virtual-Box's Start Screen" [page 26].

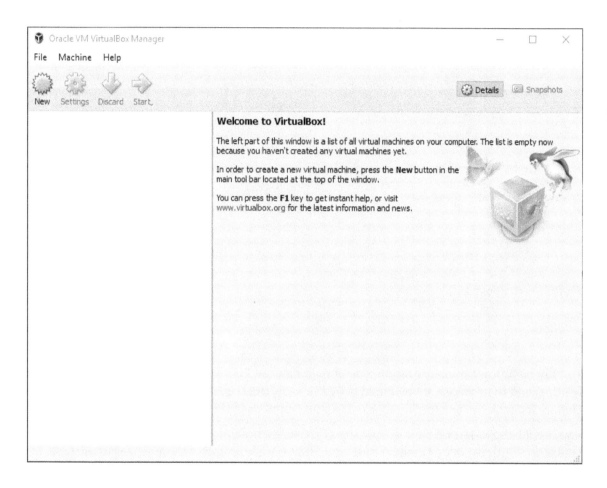

Figure 2.6 *VirtualBox's Start Screen*

Click on New (Figure 2.7, "Name and Operating System" [page 27]) to start a wizard that will guide you through the multiple steps required to input all the parameters of the new virtual machine.

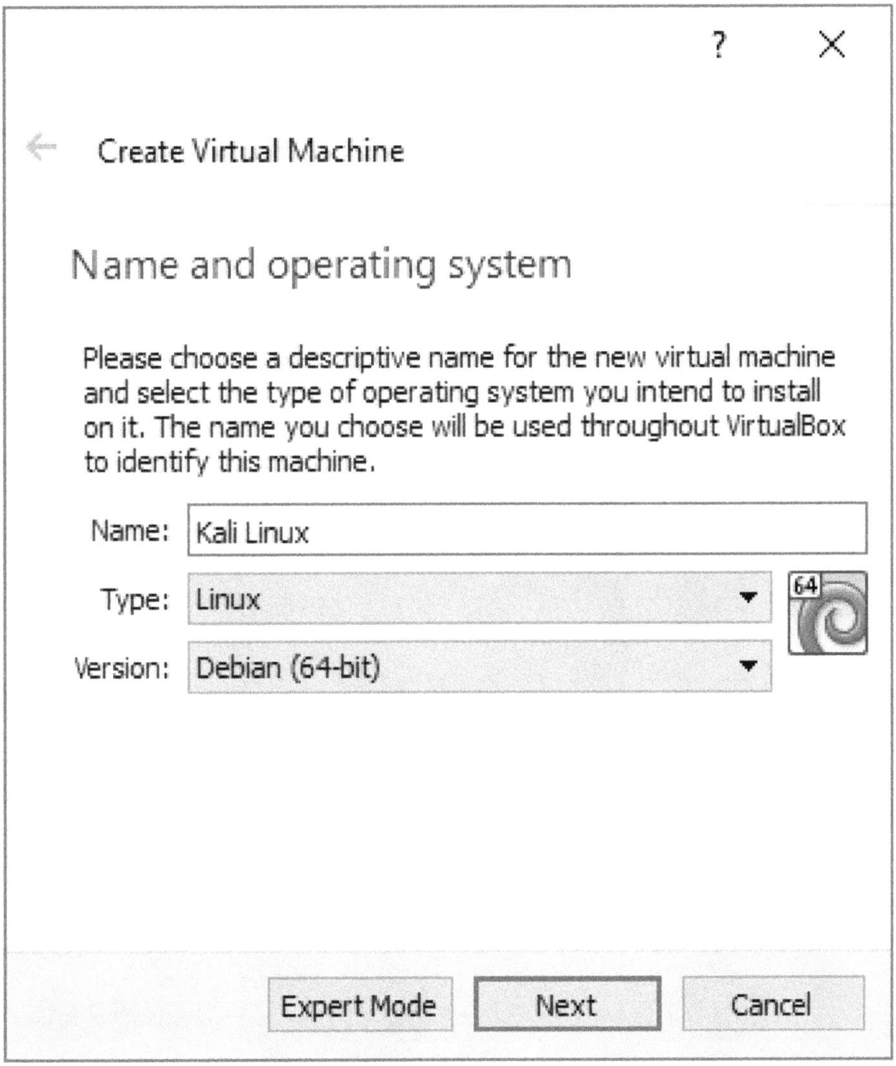

Figure 2.7 *Name and Operating System*

In the first step, shown in Figure 2.7, "Name and Operating System" [page 27], you must assign a name to your new virtual machine. Use "Kali Linux." You must also indicate what kind of operating system will be used. Since Kali Linux is based on Debian GNU/Linux, select Linux for the type and Debian (32-bit) or Debian (64-bit) for the version. Although any other Linux version will most likely work, this will help distinguish between the various virtual machines that you might have installed.

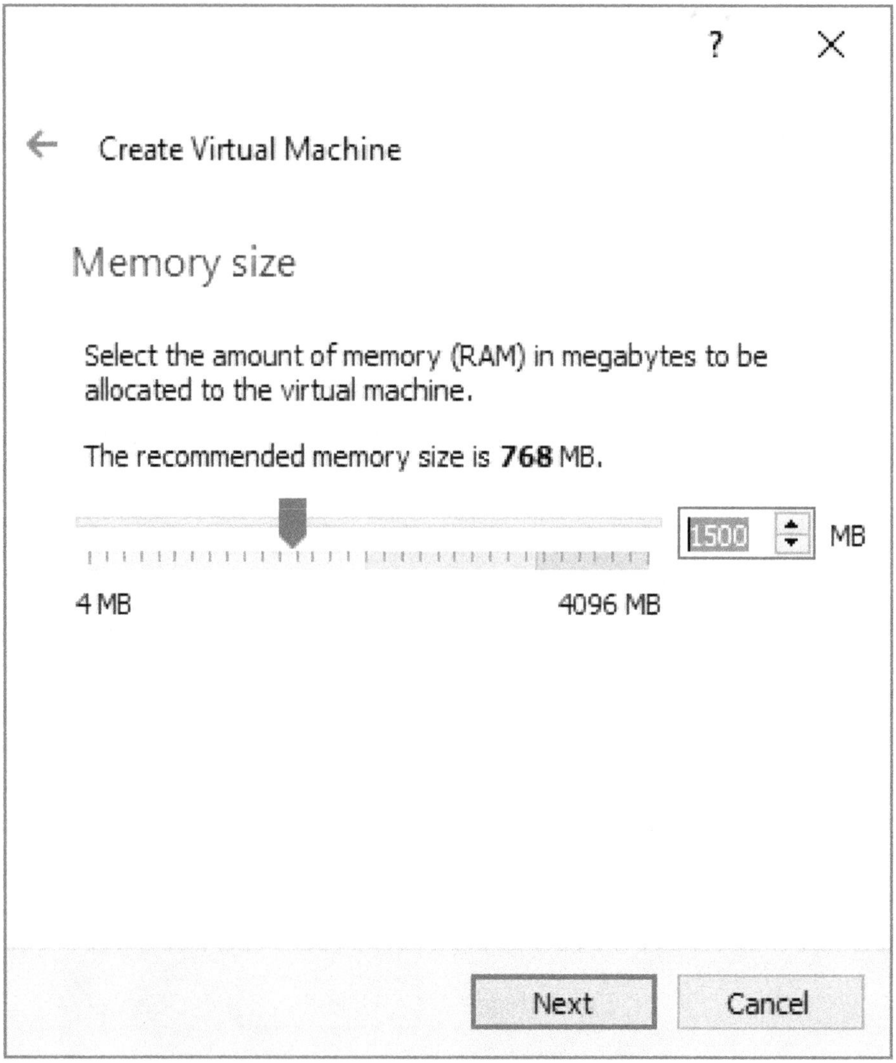

Figure 2.8 *Memory Size*

In the second step, you must decide how much memory to allocate to the virtual machine. While the recommended size of 768 MB is acceptable for a Debian virtual machine acting as a server, it is definitely not enough to run a Kali desktop system, especially not for a Kali Linux live system since the live system uses memory to store changes made to the file system. We recommend increasing the value to 1500 MB (Figure 2.8, "Memory Size" [page 28]) and highly recommend that you allocate no less than 2048 MB of RAM.

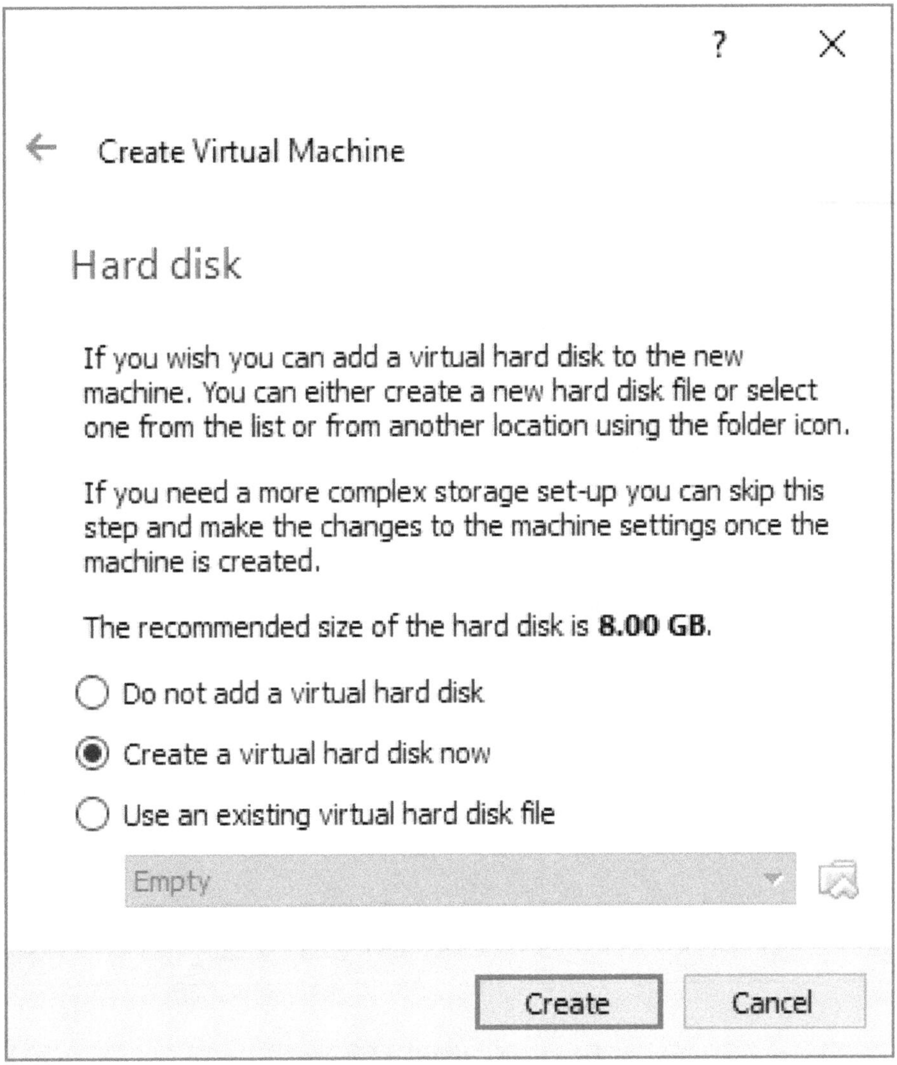

Figure 2.9 *Hard disk*

In the third step (shown in Figure 2.9, "Hard disk" [page 29]), you are prompted to choose a physical or virtual hard disk for your new virtual machine. Although a hard disk is not required to run Kali Linux as a live system, add one for when we demonstrate the installation procedure later, in chapter 4, "Installing Kali Linux" [page 66].

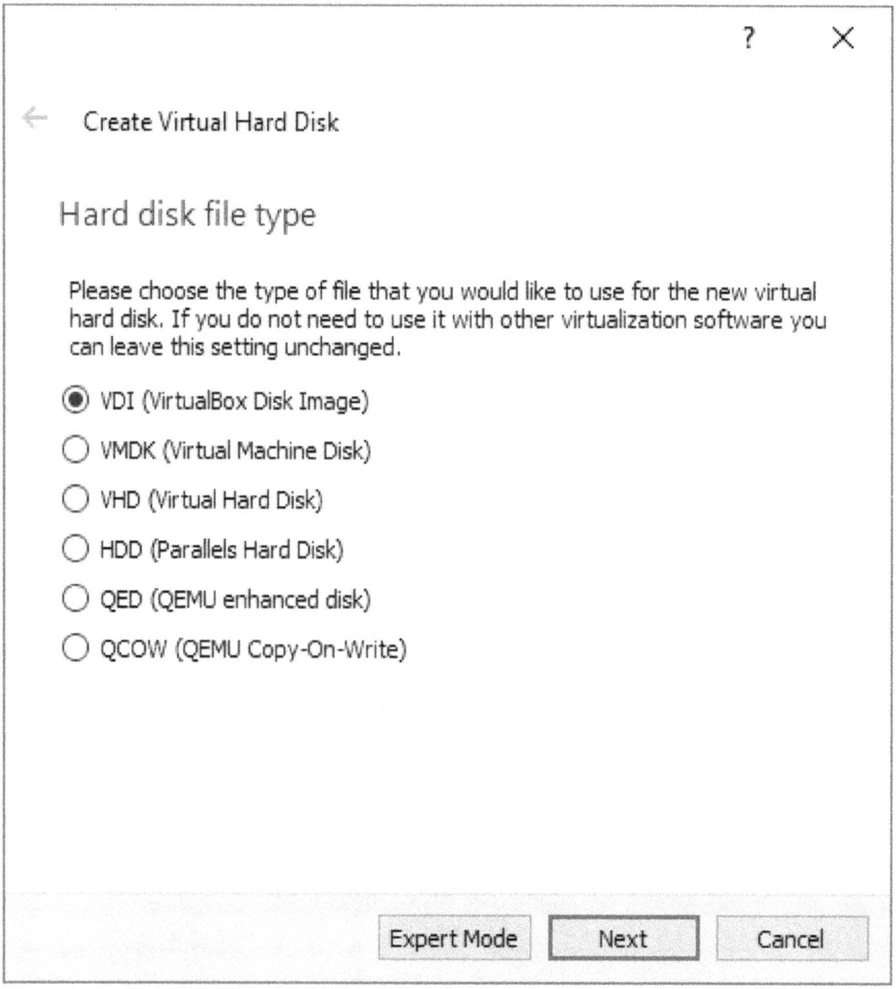

Figure 2.10   *Hard Disk File Type*

The content of the hard disk of the virtual machine is stored on the host machine as a file. VirtualBox is able to store the contents of the hard disk using multiple formats (shown in Figure 2.10, "Hard Disk File Type" [page 30]): the default (VDI) corresponds to VirtualBox's native format; VMDK is the format used by VMware; QCOW is the format used by QEMU. Keep the default value, because you don't have any reason to change it. The ability to use multiple formats is interesting mainly when you want to move a virtual machine from one virtualization tool to another.

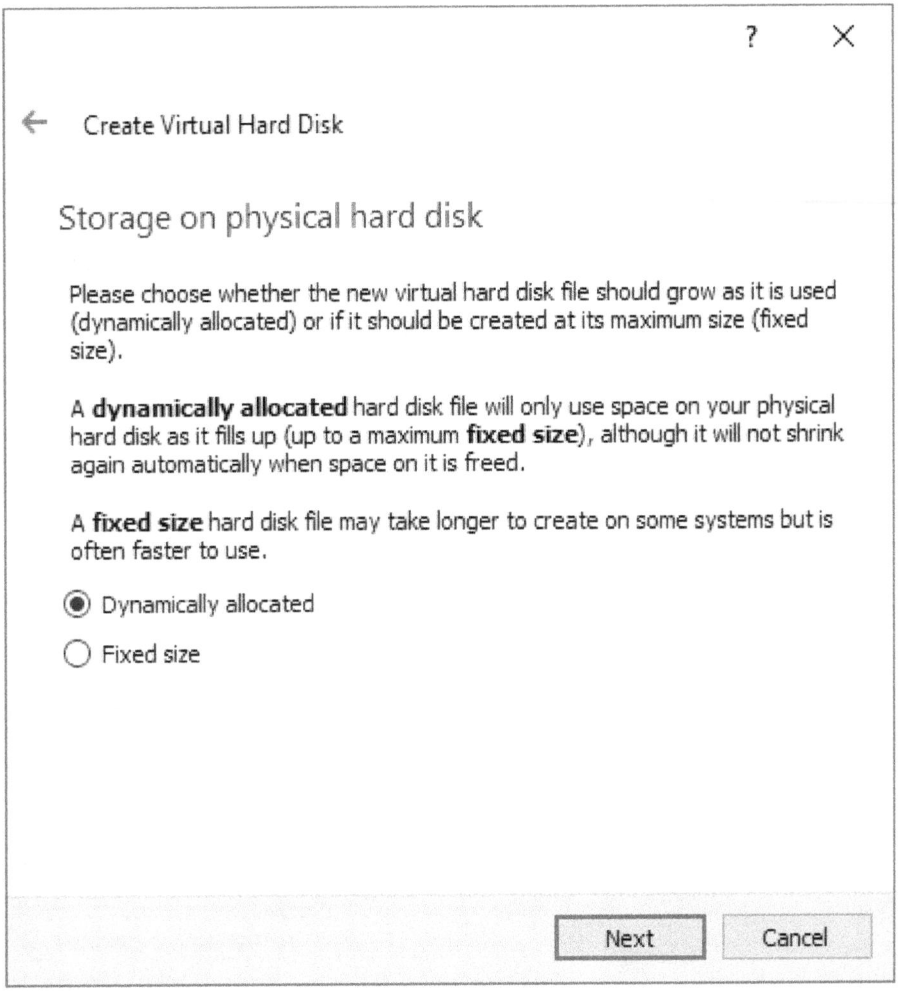

Figure 2.11 *Storage on Physical Hard Disk*

The explanation text in Figure 2.11, "Storage on Physical Hard Disk" [page 31] clearly describes the advantages and drawbacks of dynamic and fixed disk allocation. In this example, we accept the default selection (Dynamically allocated), since we are using a laptop with SSD disks. We don't want to waste space and won't need the extra bit of performance as the machine is already quite fast to begin with.

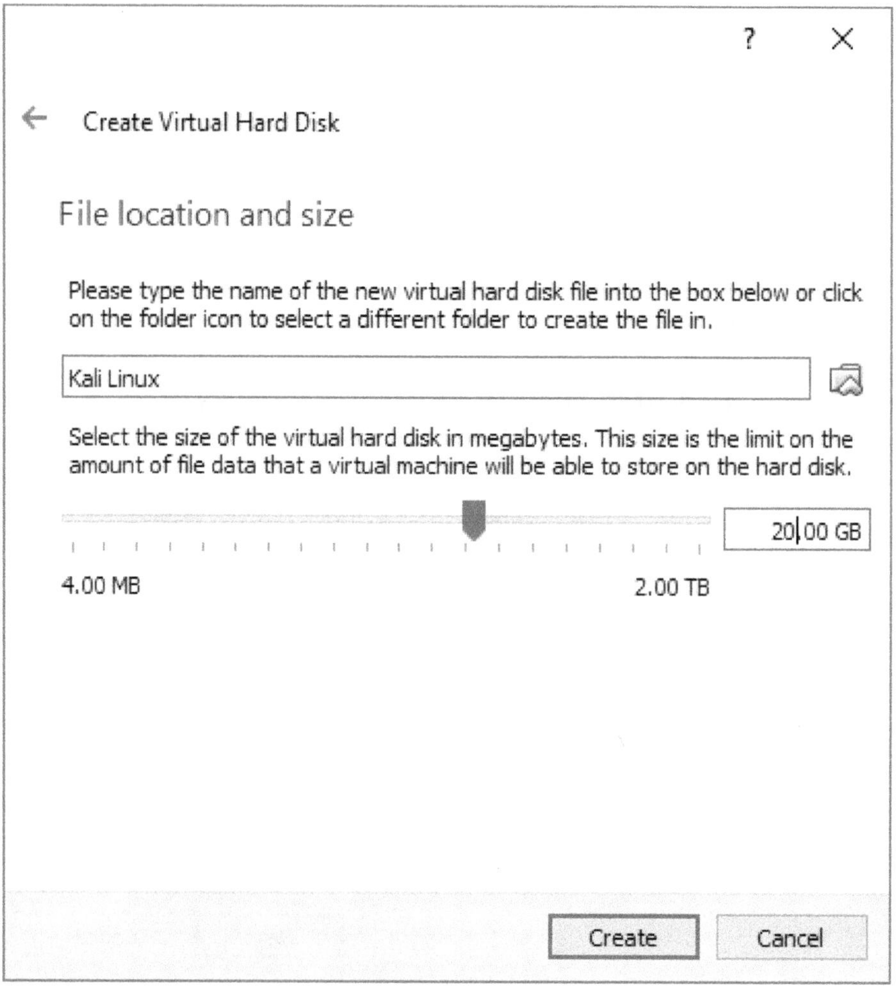

Figure 2.12 *File Location and Size*

The default hard disk size of 8 GB shown in Figure 2.12, "File Location and Size" [page 32] is not enough for a standard installation of Kali Linux, so increase the size to 20 GB. You can also tweak the name and the location of the disk image. This can be handy when you don't have enough space on your hard disk, allowing you to store the disk image on an external drive.

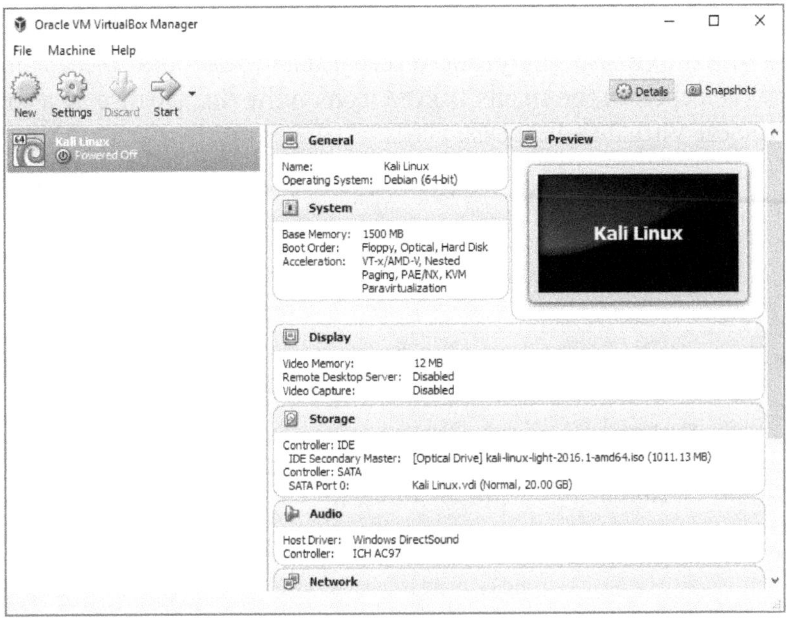

Figure 2.13 *The New Virtual Machine Appears in the List*

The virtual machine has been created but you can't really run it yet, because there is no operating system installed. You also have some settings to tweak. Click on Settings on the VM Manager screen and let's review some of the most useful settings.

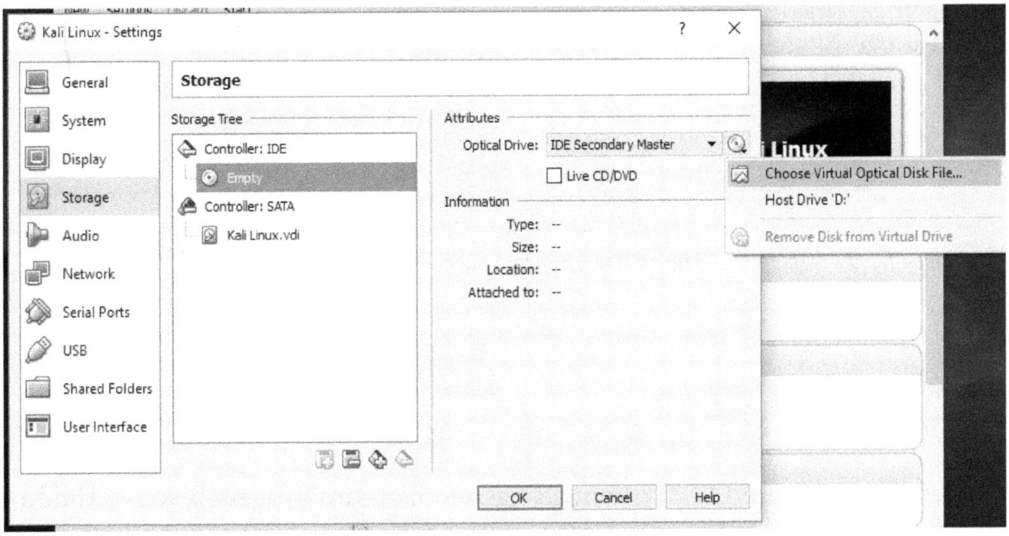

Figure 2.14 *Storage Settings*

In the Storage screen (Figure 2.14, "Storage Settings" [page 33]), you should associate the Kali Linux ISO image with the virtual CD/DVD-ROM reader. First, select the CD-ROM drive in the Storage Tree list and then click on the small CD-ROM icon on the right to display a contextual menu where you can Choose Virtual Optical Disk File....

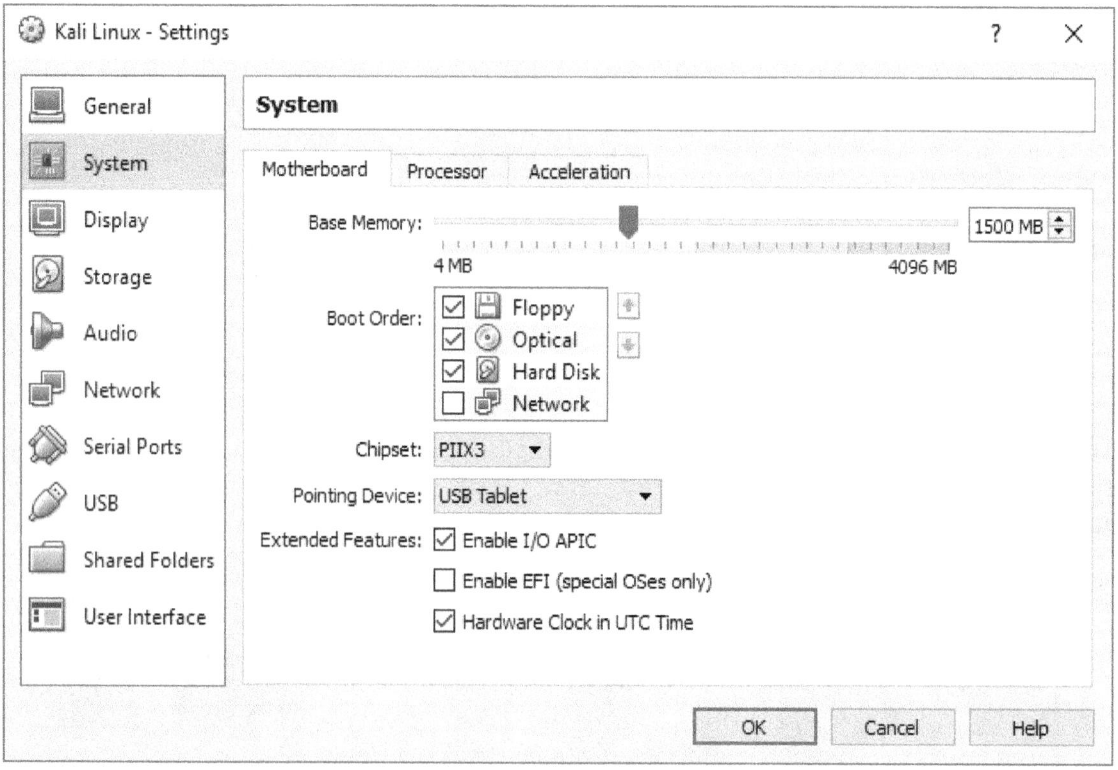

Figure 2.15 *System Settings: Motherboard*

In the System screen (Figure 2.15, "System Settings: Motherboard" [page 34]), you will find a Motherboard tab. Make sure that the boot order indicates that the system will first try to boot from any optical device before trying a hard disk. This is also the tab where you can alter the amount of memory allocated to the virtual machine, should the need arise.

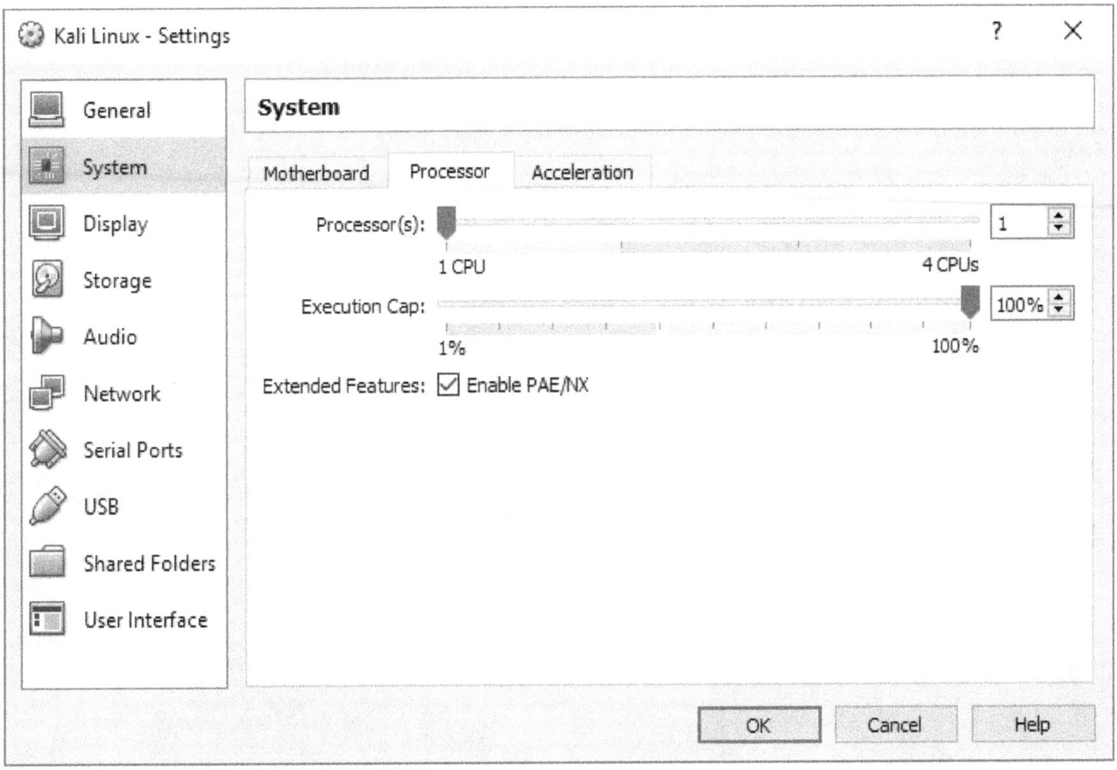

Figure 2.16   *System Settings: Processor*

In the same screen but on the "Processor" tab (Figure 2.16, "System Settings: Processor" [page 35]), you can adjust the number of processors assigned to the virtual machine. Most importantly, if you use a 32-bit image, enable PAE/NX or the Kali image will not boot since the default kernel variant used by Kali for i386 (aptly named "686-pae") is compiled in a way that requires Physical Address Extension (PAE) support in the CPU.

There are many other parameters that can be configured, like the network setup (defining how the traffic on the network card is handled), but the above changes are sufficient to be able to boot a working Kali Linux live system. Finally, click Boot and the VM should boot properly, as shown in Figure 2.17, "Kali Linux Boot Screen in VirtualBox" [page 36]. If not, carefully review all settings and try again.

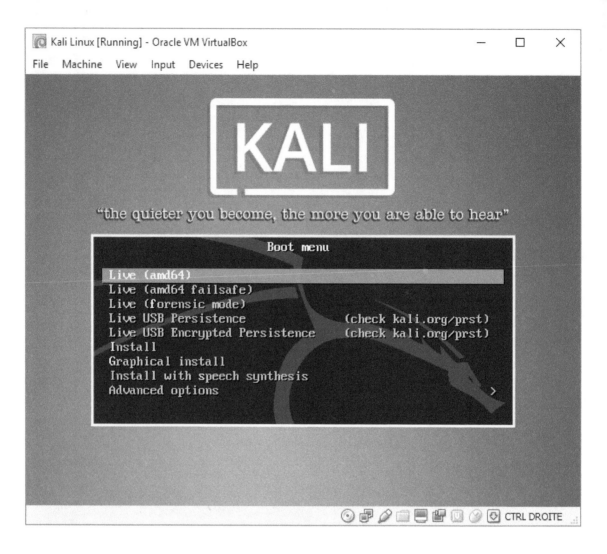

Figure 2.17 *Kali Linux Boot Screen in VirtualBox*

VMware

VMware Workstation Pro is very similar to *VirtualBox* in terms of features and user interface, because they are both designed primarily for desktop usage, but the setup process for a new virtual machine is a bit different.

Figure 2.18 *VMware Start Screen*

The initial screen, shown in Figure 2.18, "VMware Start Screen" [page 37], displays a big Create a New Virtual Machine button that starts a wizard to guide you through the creation of your virtual machine.

Figure 2.19 *New virtual Machine Wizard*

In the first step, you must decide whether you want to be presented with advanced settings during the setup process. In this example, there are no special requirements so choose the typical installation, as shown in Figure 2.19, "New virtual Machine Wizard" [page 37].

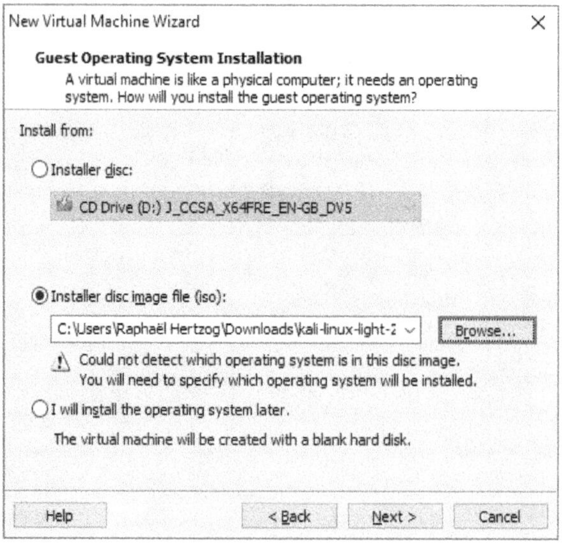

Figure 2.20 *Guest Operating System Installation*

The wizard assumes that you want to install the operating system immediately and asks you to select the ISO image containing the installation program (Figure 2.20, "Guest Operating System Installation" [page 38]). Select "Installer disc image file (iso)" and click on Browse to select the image file.

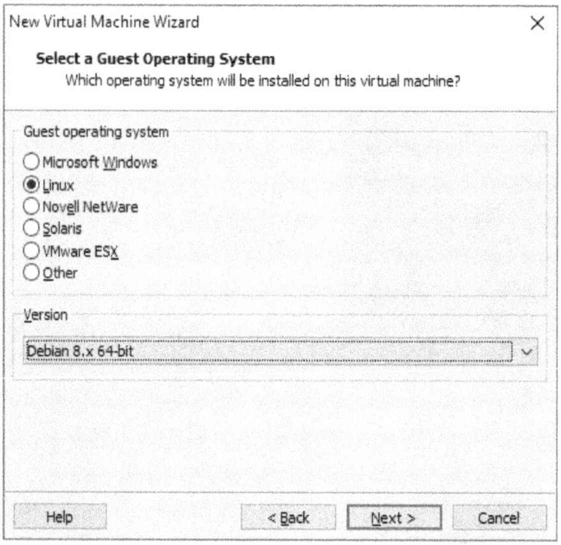

Figure 2.21 *Select a Guest Operating System*

When the operating system (OS) cannot be detected from the selected ISO image, the wizard asks you which guest OS type you intend to run. You should select "Linux" for the OS and "Debian 8.x" for the version, as shown in Figure 2.21, "Select a Guest Operating System" [page 38].

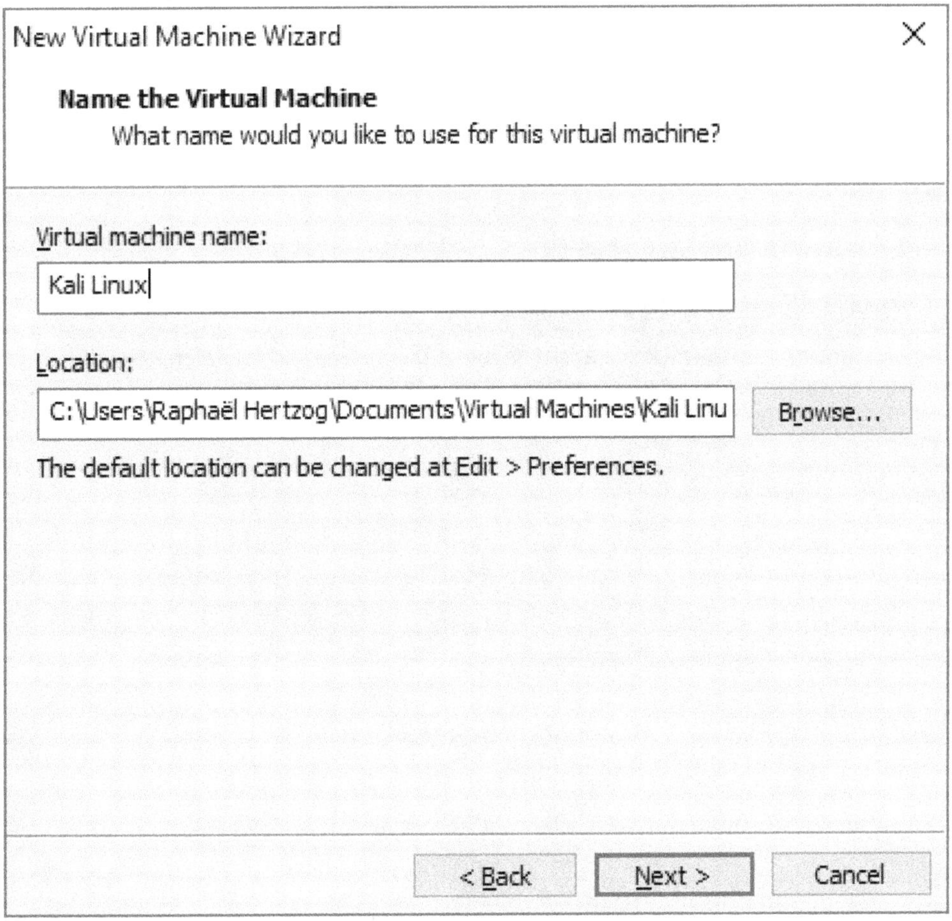

Figure 2.22 *Name the Virtual Machine*

Choose "Kali Linux" as the name of the new virtual machine (Figure 2.22, "Name the Virtual Machine" [page 39]). As with VirtualBox, you also have the option to store the VM files in an alternate location.

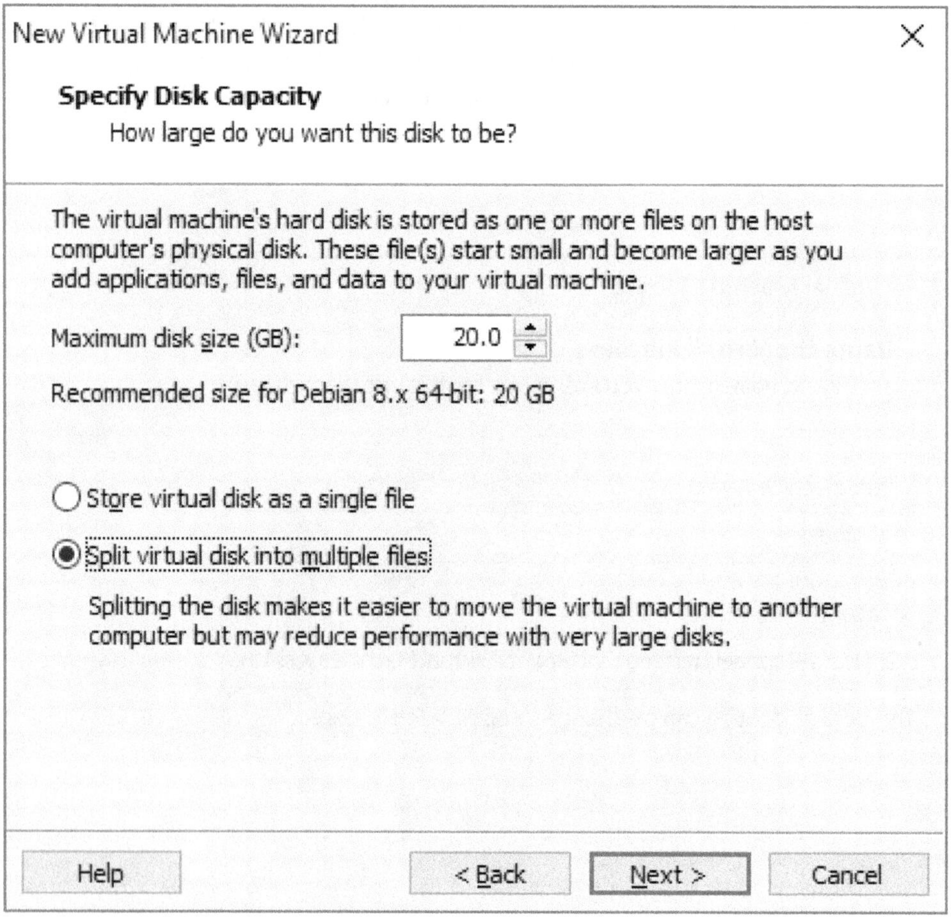

Figure 2.23 *Specify Disk Capacity*

The default hard disk size of 20 GB (Figure 2.23, "Specify Disk Capacity" [page 40]) is usually sufficient but you can adjust it here depending on your expected needs. As opposed to VirtualBox, which can use a single file of varying size, VMware has the ability to store the disk's content over multiple files. In both cases, the goal is to conserve the host's disk space.

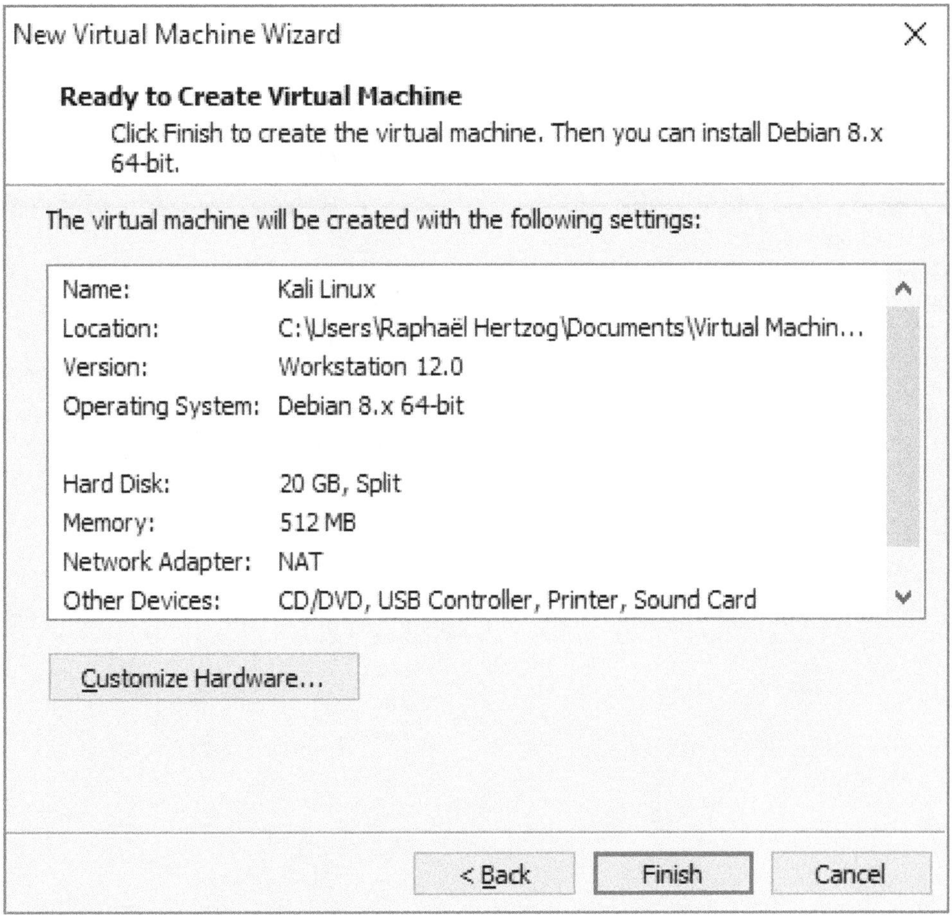

Figure 2.24 *Ready to Create Virtual Machine*

VMware Workstation is now configured to create the new virtual machine. It displays a summary of the choices made so that you can double-check everything before creating the machine. Notice that the wizard opted to allocate only 512 MB of RAM to the virtual machine, which is not enough so click on Customize Hardware... (Figure 2.24, "Ready to Create Virtual Machine" [page 41]) and tweak the Memory setting, as shown in Figure 2.25, "Configure Hardware Window" [page 42].

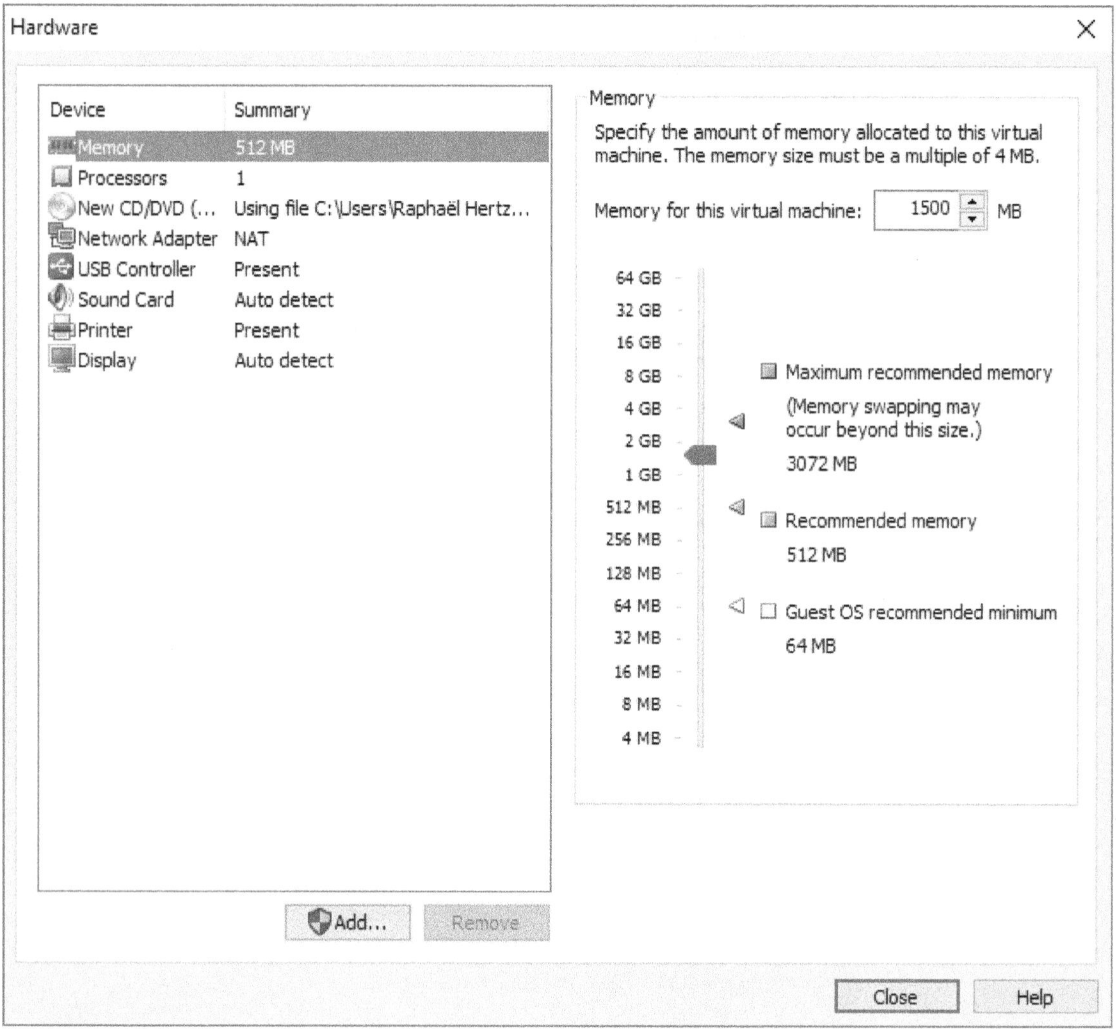

Figure 2.25 *Configure Hardware Window*

After a last click on Finish (Figure 2.24, "Ready to Create Virtual Machine" [page 41]), the virtual machine is now configured and can be started by clicking "Power on this virtual machine" as shown in Figure 2.26, "Kali Linux Virtual Machine Ready" [page 43].

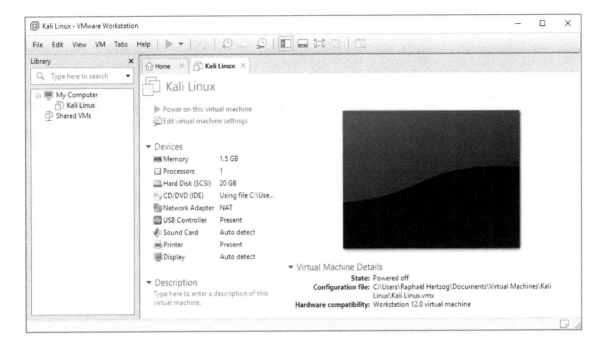

Figure 2.26 *Kali Linux Virtual Machine Ready*

2.3. Summary

In this chapter, you learned about the various Kali Linux ISO images, learned how to verify and download them, and learned how to create bootable USB disks from them on various operating systems. We also discussed how to boot the USB disks and reviewed how to configure the BIOS and startup settings on various hardware platforms so that the USB disks will boot.

Summary Tips:

- www.kali.org is the only official download site for Kali ISOs. Do not download them from any other site, because those downloads could contain malware.

- Always validate the sha256sum of your downloads with the `sha256sum` command to ensure the integrity of your ISO download. If it doesn't match, try the download again or use a different source.

- You must write the Kali Linux ISO image to a bootable media if you want to boot it on a physical machine. Use *Win32 Disk Imager* on Windows, the Disks utility on Linux, or the `dd` command on Mac OS X/macOS. Be *very careful* when writing the image. Selecting the wrong disk could permanently damage data on your machine.

- Configure the BIOS/UEFI setup screens on a PC or hold the Option key on OS X/macOS to allow the machine to boot from the USB drive.

- Virtual machine programs like *VirtualBox* and *VMware Workstation Pro* are especially useful if you want to try out Kali Linux but aren't ready to commit to installing it permanently on your machine or if you have a powerful system and want to run multiple operating systems simultaneously.

Now that you have a working installation of Kali Linux, it is time to delve into some Linux fundamentals that are required for basic and advanced operation of Kali. If you are a moderate to advanced Linux user, consider skimming the next chapter.

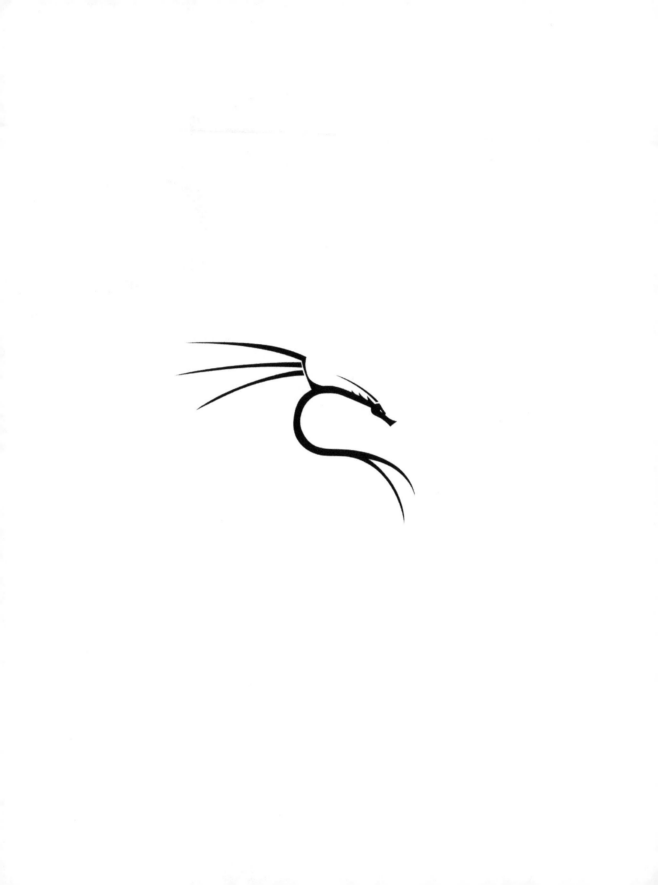

Keywords

Linux kernel
User space
Command line
bash
Filesystem Hierarchy
Unix commands

KALI LINUX
REVEALED

Linux Fundamentals

Contents

Before you can master Kali Linux, you must be at ease with a generic Linux system. Linux proficiency will serve you well, because a large percentage of web, email, and other Internet services run on Linux servers.

In this section, we strive to cover the basics of Linux, but we assume that you already know about computer systems in general, including components such as the CPU, RAM, motherboard, and hard disk, as well as device controllers and their associated connectors.

3.1. What Is Linux and What Is It Doing?

The term "Linux" is often used to refer to the entire operating system, but in reality, Linux is the operating system kernel, which is started by the boot loader, which is itself started by the BIOS/UEFI. The kernel assumes a role similar to that of a conductor in an orchestra—it ensures coordination between hardware and software. This role includes managing hardware, processes, users, permissions, and the file system. The kernel provides a common base to all other programs on the system and typically runs in *ring zero*, also known as *kernel space.*

The User Space	We use the term *user space* to lump together everything that happens outside of the kernel.
	Among the programs running in user space are many core utilities from the GNU project[1], most of which are meant to be run from the command line. You can use them in scripts to automate many tasks. Refer to section 3.4, "Useful Commands" [page 56] for more information about the most important commands.

Let's quickly review the various tasks handled by the Linux kernel.

3.1.1. Driving Hardware

The kernel is tasked, first and foremost, with controlling the computer's hardware components. It detects and configures them when the computer powers on, or when a device is inserted or removed (for example, a USB device). It also makes them available to higher-level software, through a simplified programming interface, so applications can take advantage of devices without having to address details such as which extension slot an option board is plugged into. The programming interface also provides an abstraction layer; this allows video-conferencing software, for example, to use a webcam regardless of its maker and model. The software can use the *Video for Linux* (V4L) interface and the kernel will translate function calls of the interface into actual hardware commands needed by the specific webcam in use.

The kernel exports data about detected hardware through the /proc/ and /sys/ virtual file systems. Applications often access devices by way of files created within /dev/. Specific files rep-

---

[1] http://www.gnu.org

resent disk drives (for instance, /dev/sda), partitions (/dev/sda1), mice (/dev/input/mouse0), keyboards (/dev/input/event0), sound cards (/dev/snd/*), serial ports (/dev/ttyS*), and other components.

There are two types of device files: *block* and *character*. The former has characteristics of a block of data: It has a finite size, and you can access bytes at any position in the block. The latter behaves like a flow of characters. You can read and write characters, but you cannot seek to a given position and change arbitrary bytes. To find out the type of a given device file, inspect the first letter in the output of ls -l. It is either b, for block devices, or c, for character devices:

```
$ ls -l /dev/sda /dev/ttyS0
brw-rw---- 1 root disk     8,  0 Mar 21 08:44 /dev/sda
crw-rw---- 1 root dialout 4, 64 Mar 30 08:59 /dev/ttyS0
```

As you might expect, disk drives and partitions use block devices, whereas mouse, keyboard, and serial ports use character devices. In both cases, the programming interface includes device-specific commands that can be invoked through the *ioctl* system call.

3.1.2. Unifying File Systems

File systems are a prominent aspect of the kernel. Unix-like systems merge all the file stores into a single hierarchy, which allows users and applications to access data by knowing its location within that hierarchy.

The starting point of this hierarchical tree is called the root, represented by the "/" character. This directory can contain named subdirectories. For instance, the home subdirectory of / is called /home/. This subdirectory can, in turn, contain other subdirectories, and so on. Each directory can also contain files, where the data will be stored. Thus, /home/buxy/Desktop/hello.txt refers to a file named hello.txt stored in the Desktop subdirectory of the buxy subdirectory of the home directory, present in the root. The kernel translates between this naming system and the storage location on a disk.

Unlike other systems, Linux possesses only one such hierarchy, and it can integrate data from several disks. One of these disks becomes the root, and the others are *mounted* on directories in the hierarchy (the Linux command is called mount). These other disks are then available under the *mount points*. This allows storing users' home directories (traditionally stored within /home/) on a separate hard disk, which will contain the buxy directory (along with home directories of other users). Once you mount the disk on /home/, these directories become accessible at their usual locations, and paths such as /home/buxy/Desktop/hello.txt keep working.

There are many file system formats, corresponding to many ways of physically storing data on disks. The most widely known are *ext2*, *ext3*, and *ext4*, but others exist. For instance, *VFAT* is the filesystem that was historically used by DOS and Windows operating systems. Linux's support for VFAT allows hard disks to be accessible under Kali as well as under Windows. In any case, you must prepare a file system on a disk before you can mount it and this operation is known as *formatting*.

Commands such as `mkfs.ext3` (where `mkfs` stands for *MaKe FileSystem*) handle formatting. These commands require, as a parameter, a device file representing the partition to be formatted (for instance, `/dev/sda1`, the first partition on the first drive). This operation is destructive and should be run only once, unless you want to wipe a filesystem and start fresh.

There are also network filesystems such as NFS, which do not store data on a local disk. Instead, data are transmitted through the network to a server that stores and retrieves them on demand. Thanks to the file system abstraction, you don't have to worry about how this disk is connected, since the files remain accessible in their usual hierarchical way.

3.1.3. Managing Processes

A process is a running instance of a program, which requires memory to store both the program itself and its operating data. The kernel is in charge of creating and tracking processes. When a program runs, the kernel first sets aside some memory, loads the executable code from the file system into it, and then starts the code running. It keeps information about this process, the most visible of which is an identification number known as the *process identifier* (PID).

Like most modern operating systems, those with Unix-like kernels, including Linux, are capable of multi-tasking. In other words, they allow the system to run many processes at the same time. There is actually only one running process at any one time, but the kernel divides CPU time into small slices and runs each process in turn. Since these time slices are very short (in the millisecond range), they create the appearance of processes running in parallel, although they are active only during their time interval and idle the rest of the time. The kernel's job is to adjust its scheduling mechanisms to keep that appearance, while maximizing global system performance. If the time slices are too long, the application may not appear as responsive as desired. Too short, and the system loses time by switching tasks too frequently. These decisions can be refined with process priorities, where high-priority processes will run for longer periods and with more frequent time slices than low-priority processes.

Multi-Processor Systems (and Variants)	The limitation described above, of only one process running at a time, doesn't always apply: the actual restriction is that there can be only one running process *per processor core*. Multi-processor, multi-core, or *hyper-threaded* systems allow several processes to run in parallel. The same time-slicing system is used, though, to handle cases where there are more active processes than available processor cores. This is not unusual: a basic system, even a mostly idle one, almost always has tens of running processes.

The kernel allows several independent instances of the same program to run, but each is allowed to access only its own time slices and memory. Their data thus remain independent.

3.1.4. Rights Management

Unix-like systems support multiple users and groups and allow control of permissions. Most of the time, a process is identified by the user who started it. That process is only permitted to take actions permitted for its owner. For instance, opening a file requires the kernel to check the process identity against access permissions (for more details on this particular example, see section 3.4.4, "Managing Rights" [page 57]).

3.2. The Command Line

By "command line", we mean a text-based interface that allows you to enter commands, execute them, and view the results. You can run a terminal (a textual screen within the graphical desktop, or the text console itself outside of any graphical interface) and a command interpreter inside it (*the shell*).

3.2.1. How To Get a Command Line

When your system is working properly, the easiest way to access the command line is to run a terminal in your graphical desktop session.

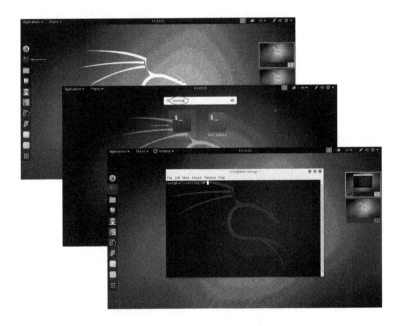

Figure 3.1   *Starting GNOME Terminal*

For instance, on a default Kali Linux system, GNOME Terminal can be started from the list of favorite applications. You can also type "terminal" while in the Activities screen (the one that gets activated when you move the mouse to the top-left corner) and click on the correct application icon that appears (Figure 3.1, "Starting GNOME Terminal" [page 51]).

In the event that your graphical interface is broken, you can still get a command line on virtual consoles (up to six of them can be accessible through the six key combinations of CTRL+ALT+F1 through CTRL+ALT+F6 — the **CTRL** key can be omitted if you are already in text mode, outside of Xorg or Wayland's graphical interface). You get a very basic login screen where you enter your login and password before being granted access to the command line with its shell:

```
Kali GNU/Linux Rolling kali-rolling tty3
kali-rolling login: root
Password:
Last login: Fir Mar 25 12:30:05 EDT 2016 from 192.168.122.1 on pts/2
Linux kali-rolling 4.4.0-kali1-amd4 #1 SMP Debian 4.4.6-1kali1 (2016-03-18) x86_64

The programs included with the Kali GNU/Linux system are free software;
the exact distribution terms for each program are described in the
individual files in /usr/share/doc/*/copyright.

Kali GNU/Linux comes with ABSOLUTELY NO WARRANTY, to the extent
permitted by applicable law.
root@kali-rolling:~#
```

The program handling your input and executing your commands is called a *shell* (or a command-line interpreter). The default shell provided in Kali Linux is *Bash* (it stands for *Bourne Again SHell*). The trailing "$" or "#" character indicates that the shell is awaiting your input. It also indicates whether Bash recognizes you as a normal user (the former case with the dollar) or as a super user (the latter case with the hash).

3.2.2. Command Line Basics: Browsing the Directory Tree and Managing Files

This section only provides a brief overview of the covered commands, all of which have many options not described here, so please refer to the abundant documentation available in their respective manual pages. In penetration tests, you will most often receive shell access to a system after a successful exploit, rather than a graphical user interface. Proficiency with the command line is essential for your success as a security professional.

Once a session is open, the pwd command (which stands for *print working directory*) displays your current location in the filesystem. The current directory is changed with the cd *directory* command (cd is for *change directory*). When you don't specify the target directory, you are taken to your home directory. When you use cd -, you go back to the former working directory (the one in use before the last cd call). The parent directory is always called .. (two dots), whereas the current directory is also known as . (one dot). The ls command allows *listing* the contents of a directory. If you don't provide parameters, ls operates on the current directory.

```
$ pwd
/home/buxy
$ cd Desktop
$ pwd
/home/buxy/Desktop
$ cd .
$ pwd
/home/buxy/Desktop
$ cd ..
$ pwd
/home/buxy
$ ls
Desktop    Downloads  Pictures  Templates
Documents  Music      Public    Videos
```

You can create a new directory with mkdir *directory*, and remove an existing (empty) directory with rmdir *directory*. The mv command allows *moving* and renaming files and directories; *removing* a file is achieved with rm *file*, and copying a file is done with cp *source-file target-file*.

```
$ mkdir test
$ ls
Desktop    Downloads  Pictures  Templates  Videos
Documents  Music      Public    test
$ mv test new
$ ls
Desktop    Downloads  new       Public     Videos
Documents  Music      Pictures  Templates
$ rmdir new
$ ls
Desktop    Downloads  Pictures  Templates  Videos
Documents  Music      Public
```

The shell executes each command by running the first program of the given name that it finds in a directory listed in the PATH environment variable. Most often, these programs are in /bin, /sbin, /usr/bin, or /usr/sbin. For example, the ls command is found in /bin/ls; the which command reports the location of a given executable. Sometimes the command is directly handled by the shell, in which case, it is called a shell built-in command (cd and pwd are among those); the type command lets you query the type of each command.

```
$ echo $PATH
/usr/local/sbin:/usr/local/bin:/usr/sbin:/usr/bin:/sbin:/bin
$ which ls
/bin/ls
```

```
$ type rm
rm is /bin/rm
$ type cd
cd is a shell builtin
```

Note the usage of the echo command, which simply displays a string on the terminal. In this case, it is used to print the contents of an environment variable since the shell automatically substitutes variables with their values before executing the command line.

Environment Variables	Environment variables allow storage of global settings for the shell or various other programs. They are contextual but inheritable. For example, each process has its own set of environment variables (they are contextual). Shells, like login shells, can declare variables, which will be passed down to other programs they execute (they are inheritable).
	These variables can be defined system-wide in /etc/profile or per-user in ~/.profile but variables that are not specific to command line interpreters are better put in /etc/environment, since those variables will be injected into all user sessions thanks to a Pluggable Authentication Module (PAM) – even when no shell is executed.

3.3. The File System

3.3.1. The Filesystem Hierarchy Standard

As with other Linux distributions, Kali Linux is organized to be consistent with the *Filesystem Hierarchy Standard* (FHS), allowing users of other Linux distributions to easily find their way around Kali. The FHS defines the purpose of each directory. The top-level directories are described as follows.

- /bin/: basic programs
- /boot/: Kali Linux kernel and other files required for its early boot process
- /dev/: device files
- /etc/: configuration files
- /home/: user's personal files
- /lib/: basic libraries
- /media/*: mount points for removable devices (CD-ROM, USB keys, and so on)
- /mnt/: temporary mount point
- /opt/: extra applications provided by third parties
- /root/: administrator's (root's) personal files

- /run/: volatile runtime data that does not persist across reboots (not yet included in the FHS)
- /sbin/: system programs
- /srv/: data used by servers hosted on this system
- /tmp/: temporary files (this directory is often emptied at boot)
- /usr/: applications (this directory is further subdivided into bin, sbin, lib according to the same logic as in the root directory) Furthermore, /usr/share/ contains architecture-independent data. The /usr/local/ directory is meant to be used by the administrator for installing applications manually without overwriting files handled by the packaging system (dpkg).
- /var/: variable data handled by daemons. This includes log files, queues, spools, and caches.
- /proc/ and /sys/ are specific to the Linux kernel (and not part of the FHS). They are used by the kernel for exporting data to user space.

3.3.2. The User's Home Directory

The contents of a user's home directory are not standardized but there are still a few noteworthy conventions. One is that a user's home directory is often referred to by a tilde ("~"). That is useful to know because command interpreters automatically replace a tilde with the correct directory (which is stored in the HOME environment variable, and whose usual value is /home/user/).

Traditionally, application configuration files are often stored directly under your home directory, but the filenames usually start with a dot (for instance, the mutt email client stores its configuration in ~/.muttrc). Note that filenames that start with a dot are hidden by default; the ls command only lists them when the -a option is used and graphical file managers need to be explicitly configured to display hidden files.

Some programs also use multiple configuration files organized in one directory (for instance, ~/.ssh/). Some applications (such as the Firefox web browser) also use their directory to store a cache of downloaded data. This means that those directories can end up consuming a lot of disk space.

These configuration files stored directly in your home directory, often collectively referred to as *dotfiles*, have long proliferated to the point that these directories can be quite cluttered with them. Fortunately, an effort led collectively under the FreeDesktop.org umbrella has resulted in the XDG Base Directory Specification, a convention that aims at cleaning up these files and directories. This specification states that configuration files should be stored under ~/.config, cache files under ~/.cache, and application data files under ~/.local (or subdirectories thereof). This convention is slowly gaining traction.

Graphical desktops usually have shortcuts to display the contents of the ~/Desktop/ directory (or whatever the appropriate translation is for systems not configured in English).

Finally, the email system sometimes stores incoming emails into a ~/Mail/ directory.

3.4. Useful Commands

3.4.1. Displaying and Modifying Text Files

The cat *file* command (intended to *concatenate* files to the standard output device) reads a file and displays its contents on the terminal. If the file is too big to fit on a screen, you can use a pager such as less (or more) to display it page by page.

The editor command starts a text editor (such as Vi or Nano) and allows creating, modifying, and reading text files. The simplest files can sometimes be created directly from the command interpreter thanks to redirection: *command >file* creates a file named *file* containing the output of the given command. *command >>file* is similar except that it appends the output of the command to the file rather than overwriting it.

```
$ echo "Kali rules!" > kali-rules.txt
$ cat kali-rules.txt
Kali rules!
$ echo "Kali is the best!" >> kali-rules.txt
$ cat kali-rules.txt
Kali rules!
Kali is the best!
```

3.4.2. Searching for Files and within Files

The find *directory criteria* command searches for files in the hierarchy under *directory* according to several criteria. The most commonly used criterion is -name *filename*, which allows searching for a file by name. You can also use common wildcards such as "*" in the filename search.

```
$ find /etc -name hosts
/etc/hosts
/etc/avahi/hosts
$ find /etc -name "hosts*"
/etc/hosts
/etc/hosts.allow
/etc/hosts.deny
/etc/avahi/hosts
```

The grep *expression files* command searches the contents of the files and extracts lines matching the regular expression. Adding the -r option enables a recursive search on all files contained in the directory. This allows you to look for a file when you only know a part of its contents.

3.4.3. Managing Processes

The `ps aux` command lists the processes currently running and helps to identify them by showing their PID. Once you know the *PID* of a process, the `kill -signal pid` command allows you to send it a signal (if you own the process). Several signals exist; most commonly used are TERM (a request to terminate gracefully) and KILL (a forced kill).

The command interpreter can also run programs in the background if the command is followed by "&". By using the ampersand, you resume control of the shell immediately even though the command is still running (hidden from view as a background process). The `jobs` command lists the processes running in the background; running `fg %job-number` (for *foreground*) restores a job to the foreground. When a command is running in the foreground (either because it was started normally, or brought back to the foreground with `fg`), the Control+Z key combination pauses the process and resumes control of the command line. The process can then be restarted in the background with `bg %job-number` (for *background*).

3.4.4. Managing Rights

Linux is a multi-user system so it is necessary to provide a permissions system to control the set of authorized operations on files and directories, which includes all the system resources and devices (on a Unix system, any device is represented by a file or directory). This principle is common to all Unix-like systems.

Each file or directory has specific permissions for three categories of users:

- Its owner (symbolized by u, as in user)

- Its owner group (symbolized by g, as in group), representing all the members of the group

- The others (symbolized by o, as in other)

Three types of rights can be combined:

- reading (symbolized by r, as in read);

- writing (or modifying, symbolized by w, as in write);

- executing (symbolized by x, as in eXecute).

In the case of a file, these rights are easily understood: read access allows reading the content (including copying), write access allows changing it, and execute access allows running it (which will only work if it is a program).

Two particular rights are relevant to executable files: setuid and setgid (symbolized with the letter "s"). Note that we frequently speak of bit, since each of these boolean values can be represented by a 0 or a 1. These two rights allow any user to execute the program with the rights of the owner or the group, respectively. This mechanism grants access to features requiring higher level permissions than those you would usually have.

Since a setuid root program is systematically run under the super-user identity, it is very important to ensure it is secure and reliable. Any user who manages to subvert a setuid root program to call a command of their choice could then impersonate the root user and have all rights on the system. Penetration testers regularly search for these types of files when they gain access to a system as a way of escalating their privileges.

A directory is handled differently from a file. Read access gives the right to consult the list of its contents (files and directories); write access allows creating or deleting files; and execute access allows crossing through the directory to access its contents (for example, with the cd command). Being able to cross through a directory without being able to read it gives the user permission to access the entries therein that are known by name, but not to find them without knowing their exact name.

The setgid bit also applies to directories. Any newly-created item in such directories is automatically assigned the owner group of the parent directory, instead of inheriting the creator's main group as usual. Because of this, you don't have to change your main group (with the newgrp command) when working in a file tree shared between several users of the same dedicated group.

The *sticky bit* (symbolized by the letter "t") is a permission that is only useful in directories. It is especially used for temporary directories where everybody has write access (such as /tmp/): it restricts deletion of files so that only their owner or the owner of the parent directory can delete them. Lacking this, everyone could delete other users' files in /tmp/.

Three commands control the permissions associated with a file:

- chown *user file* changes the owner of the file

Frequently you want to change the group of a file at the same time that you change the owner. The chown command has a special syntax for that: chown *user:group file*

- chgrp *group file* alters the owner group
- chmod *rights file* changes the permissions for the file

There are two ways of representing rights. Among them, the symbolic representation is probably the easiest to understand and remember. It involves the letter symbols mentioned above. You can define rights for each category of users (u/g/o), by setting them explicitly (with =), by adding

(+), or subtracting (-). Thus the u=rwx,g+rw,o-r formula gives the owner read, write, and execute rights, adds read and write rights for the owner group, and removes read rights for other users. Rights not altered by the addition or subtraction in such a command remain unmodified. The letter a, for all, covers all three categories of users, so that a=rx grants all three categories the same rights (read and execute, but not write).

The (octal) numeric representation associates each right with a value: 4 for read, 2 for write, and 1 for execute. We associate each combination of rights with the sum of the three figures, and a value is assigned to each category of users, in the usual order (owner, group, others).

For instance, the chmod 754 *file* command will set the following rights: read, write and execute for the owner (since 7 = 4 + 2 + 1); read and execute for the group (since 5 = 4 + 1); read-only for others. The 0 means no rights; thus chmod 600 *file* allows for read and write permissions for the owner, and no rights for anyone else. The most frequent right combinations are 755 for executable files and directories, and 644 for data files.

To represent special rights, you can prefix a fourth digit to this number according to the same principle, where the setuid, setgid, and sticky bits are 4, 2, and 1, respectively. The command chmod 4754 will associate the setuid bit with the previously described rights.

Note that the use of octal notation only allows you to set all the rights at once on a file; you cannot use it to add a new right, such as read access for the group owner, since you must take into account the existing rights and compute the new corresponding numerical value.

The octal representation is also used with the umask command, which is used to restrict permissions on newly created files. When an application creates a file, it assigns indicative permissions, knowing that the system automatically removes the rights defined with umask. Enter umask in a shell; you will see a mask such as 0022. This is simply an octal representation of the rights to be systematically removed (in this case, the write rights for the group and other users).

If you give it a new octal value, the umask command modifies the mask. Used in a shell initialization file (for example, ~/.bash_profile), it will effectively change the default mask for your work sessions.

TIP

Recursive operation

Sometimes we have to change rights for an entire file tree. All the commands above have a -R option to operate recursively in sub-directories.

The distinction between directories and files sometimes causes problems with recursive operations. That is why the "X" letter has been introduced in the symbolic representation of rights. It represents a right to execute which applies only to directories (and not to files lacking this right). Thus, chmod -R a+X *directory* will only add execute rights for all categories of users (a) for all of the sub-directories and files for which at least one category of user (even if their sole owner) already has execute rights.

3.4.5. Getting System Information and Logs

The free command displays information on memory; *disk free* (df) reports on the available disk space on each of the disks mounted in the file system. Its -h option (for *human readable*) converts the sizes into a more legible unit (usually mebibytes or gibibytes). In a similar fashion, the free command supports the -m and -g options, and displays its data either in mebibytes or in gibibytes, respectively.

```
$ free
              total        used        free      shared  buff/cache   available
Mem:        2052944      661232      621208       10520      770504     1359916
Swap:             0           0           0
$ df
Filesystem     1K-blocks     Used Available Use% Mounted on
udev             1014584        0   1014584   0% /dev
tmpfs             205296     8940    196356   5% /run
/dev/vda1       30830588 11168116  18073328  39% /
tmpfs            1026472      456   1026016   1% /dev/shm
tmpfs               5120        0      5120   0% /run/lock
tmpfs            1026472        0   1026472   0% /sys/fs/cgroup
tmpfs             205296       36    205260   1% /run/user/132
tmpfs             205296       24    205272   1% /run/user/0
```

The id command displays the identity of the user running the session along with the list of groups they belong to. Since access to some files or devices may be limited to group members, checking available group membership may be useful.

```
$ id
uid=1000(buxy) gid=1000(buxy) groups=1000(buxy),27(sudo)
```

The uname -a command returns a single line documenting the kernel name (Linux), the hostname, the kernel release, the kernel version, the machine type (an architecture string such as x86_64), and the name of the operating system (GNU/Linux). The output of this command should usually be included in bug reports as it clearly defines the kernel in use and the hardware platform you are running on.

```
$ uname -a
Linux kali 4.9.0-kali3-amd64 #1 SMP Debian 4.9.18-1kali1 (2017-04-04) x86_64 GNU/Linux
```

All these commands provide run-time information, but often you need to consult logs to understand what happened on your computer. In particular, the kernel emits messages that it stores in a ring buffer whenever something interesting happens (such as a new USB device being inserted, a failing hard disk operation, or initial hardware detection on boot). You can retrieve the kernel logs with the dmesg command.

Systemd's journal also stores multiple logs (stdout/stderr output of daemons, syslog messages, kernel logs) and makes it easy to query them with `journalctl`. Without any arguments, it just dumps all the available logs in a chronological way. With the -r option, it will reverse the order so that newer messages are shown first. With the -f option, it will continuously print new log entries as they are appended to its database. The -u option can limit the messages to those emitted by a specific systemd unit (ex: `journalctl -u ssh.service`).

3.4.6. Discovering the Hardware

The kernel exports many details about detected hardware through the /proc/ and /sys/ virtual filesystems. Several tools summarize those details. Among them, `lspci` (in the *pciutils* package) lists PCI devices, `lsusb` (in the *usbutils* package) lists USB devices, and `lspcmcia` (in the *pcmciautils* package) lists PCMCIA cards. These tools are very useful for identifying the exact model of a device. This identification also allows more precise searches on the web, which in turn, lead to more relevant documents. Note that the *pciutils* and *usbutils* packages are already installed on the base Kali system but *pcmciautils* must be installed with `apt install pcmciautils`. We will discuss more about package installation and management in a later chapter.

Example 3.1 *Example of information provided by `lspci` and `lsusb`*

```
$ lspci
[...]
00:02.1 Display controller: Intel Corporation Mobile 915GM/GMS/910GML Express Graphics Controller (rev 03)
00:1c.0 PCI bridge: Intel Corporation 82801FB/FBM/FR/FW/FRW (ICH6 Family) PCI Express Port 1 (rev 03)
00:1d.0 USB Controller: Intel Corporation 82801FB/FBM/FR/FW/FRW (ICH6 Family) USB UHCI #1 (rev 03)
[...]
01:00.0 Ethernet controller: Broadcom Corporation NetXtreme BCM5751 Gigabit Ethernet PCI Express (rev 01)
02:03.0 Network controller: Intel Corporation PRO/Wireless 2200BG Network Connection (rev 05)
$ lsusb
Bus 005 Device 004: ID 413c:a005 Dell Computer Corp.
Bus 005 Device 008: ID 413c:9001 Dell Computer Corp.
Bus 005 Device 007: ID 045e:00dd Microsoft Corp.
Bus 005 Device 006: ID 046d:c03d Logitech, Inc.
[...]
Bus 002 Device 004: ID 413c:8103 Dell Computer Corp. Wireless 350 Bluetooth
```

These programs have a -v option that lists much more detailed (but usually unnecessary) information. Finally, the `lsdev` command (in the *procinfo* package) lists communication resources used by devices.

The `lshw` program is a combination of the above programs and displays a long description of the hardware discovered in a hierarchical manner. You should attach its full output to any report about hardware support problems.

3.5. Summary

In this section, we took a whirlwind tour of the Linux landscape. We discussed the kernel and user space, reviewed many common Linux shell commands, discussed processes and how to manage them, reviewed user and group security concepts, discussed the FHS, and toured some of the most common directories and files found on Kali Linux.

Summary Tips:

- Linux is often used to refer to the entire operating system but in reality Linux itself is the operating system kernel that is started by the boot loader, which is itself started by the BIOS/UEFI.

- User space refers to everything that happens outside of the kernel. Among the programs running in user space, there are many core utilities from the GNU project[2], most of which are meant to be run from the command line (a text-based interface that allows you to enter commands, execute them, and view the results). A shell executes your commands within that interface.

- Common commands include: `pwd` (print working directory), `cd` (change directory), `ls` (list file or directory contents), `mkdir` (make directory), `rmdir` (remove directory), `mv`, `rm`, and `cp` (move, remove, or copy file or directory respectively), `cat` (concatenate or show file), `less/more` (show files a page at a time), `editor` (start a text editor), `find` (locate a file or directory), `free` (display memory information), `df` (show disk free space), `id` display the identity of the user along with the list of groups they belong to), `dmesg` (review kernel logs), and `journalctl` (show all available logs).

- You can inspect the hardware on a Kali system with several commands: `lspci` (list PCI devices), `lsusb` (list USB devices), and `lspcmcia` lists PCMCIA cards.

- A process is a running instance of a program, which requires memory to store both the program itself and its operating data. You can manage processes with commands like: `ps` (show processes), `kill` (kill processes), `bg` (send process to background), `fg` (bring background process to foreground), and `jobs` (show background processes).

- Unix-like systems are multi-user. They support multiple users and groups and allow control over actions, based on permissions. You can manage file and directory rights with several commands, including: `chmod` (change permissions), `chown` (change owner), and `chgrp` (change group).

- As with other professional Linux distributions, Kali Linux is organized to be consistent with the *Filesystem Hierarchy Standard* (FHS), allowing users coming from other Linux distributions to easily find their way around Kali.

- Traditionally, application configuration files are stored under your home directory, in hidden files or directories starting with a period (or dot).

---

[2]`http://www.gnu.org`

Now that you have a handle on Linux fundamentals, let's get Kali Linux set up and running.

Keywords

Installation
Unattended
installation
ARM devices
Troubleshooting

KALI LINUX
REVEALED

Installing Kali Linux

Contents

In this chapter, we will focus on the Kali Linux installation process. First, we will discuss the minimum installation requirements (section 4.1, "Minimal Installation Requirements" [page 66]) to ensure that your real or virtual system is well-configured to handle the type of installation that you will pursue. Then we will go through each step of the installation process (section 4.2, "Step by Step Installation on a Hard Drive" [page 66]) for a plain installation, as well as for a more secure installation involving a fully encrypted file system. We will also discuss *preseeding*, which allows unattended installations (section 4.3, "Unattended Installations" [page 91]) by providing predetermined answers to installation questions. We will also show you how to install Kali Linux on various ARM devices (section 4.4, "ARM Installations" [page 94]), which expands Kali's capabilities far beyond the desktop. Finally, we will show you what to do in the rare case of an installation failure (section 4.5, "Troubleshooting Installations" [page 95]), so you can work through the issue and successfully finish a tough install.

4.1. Minimal Installation Requirements

The installation requirements for Kali Linux vary depending on what you would like to install. On the low end, you can set up Kali as a basic Secure Shell (SSH) server with no desktop, using as little as 128 MB of RAM (512 MB recommended) and 2 GB of disk space. On the higher end, if you opt to install the default GNOME desktop and the *kali-linux-full* meta-package, you should really aim for at least 2048 MB of RAM and 20 GB of disk space.

Besides the RAM and hard disk requirements, your computer needs to have a CPU supported by at least one of the amd64, i386, armel, armhf, or arm64 architectures.

4.2. Step by Step Installation on a Hard Drive

In this section, we assume that you have a bootable USB drive or DVD (see section 2.1.4, "Copying the Image on a DVD-ROM or USB Key" [page 19] for details on how to prepare such a drive) and that you booted from it to start the installation process.

4.2.1. Plain Installation

First, we will take a look at a standard Kali installation, with an unencrypted file system.

Booting and Starting the Installer

Once the BIOS has begun booting from the USB drive or DVD-ROM, the Isolinux boot loader menu appears, as shown in Figure 4.1, "Boot Screen" [page 67]. At this stage, the Linux kernel is not yet loaded; this menu allows you to choose the kernel to boot and enter optional parameters to be transferred to it in the process.

For a standard installation, you only need to choose Install or Graphical Install (with the arrow keys), then press the Enter key to initiate the remainder of the installation process.

Each menu entry hides a specific boot command line, which can be configured as needed by pressing the Tab key before validating the entry and booting.

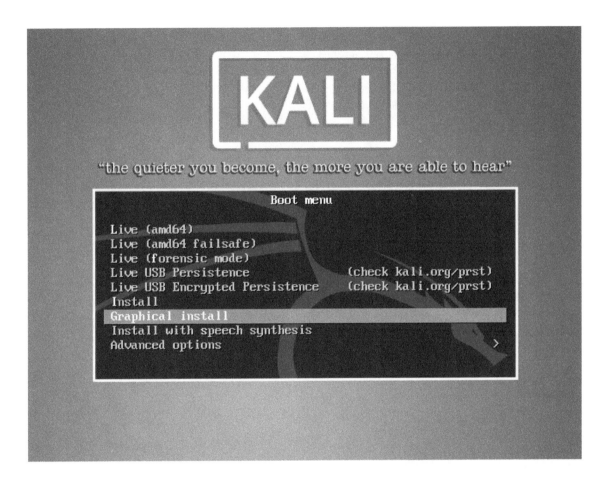

Figure 4.1 *Boot Screen*

Once booted, the installation program guides you step-by-step through the process. We will take a look at each of these steps in detail. We will cover installation from a standard Kali Linux DVD-ROM; installations from a mini.iso may look slightly different. We will also address graphical mode installation, but the only difference from classic text-mode installation is the appearance. The versions pose identical questions and present identical options.

Selecting the Language

As shown in Figure 4.2, "Selecting the Language" [page 68], the installation program begins in English but the first step allows you to choose the language that will be used for the rest of the installation process. This language choice is also used to define more relevant default choices in subsequent stages (notably the keyboard layout).

Navigating with the Keyboard Some steps in the installation process require you to enter information. These screens have several areas that may gain focus (text entry area, checkboxes, list of choices, OK and Cancel buttons), and the Tab key allows you to move from one to another.

In graphical installation mode, you can use the mouse as you would normally on an installed graphical desktop.

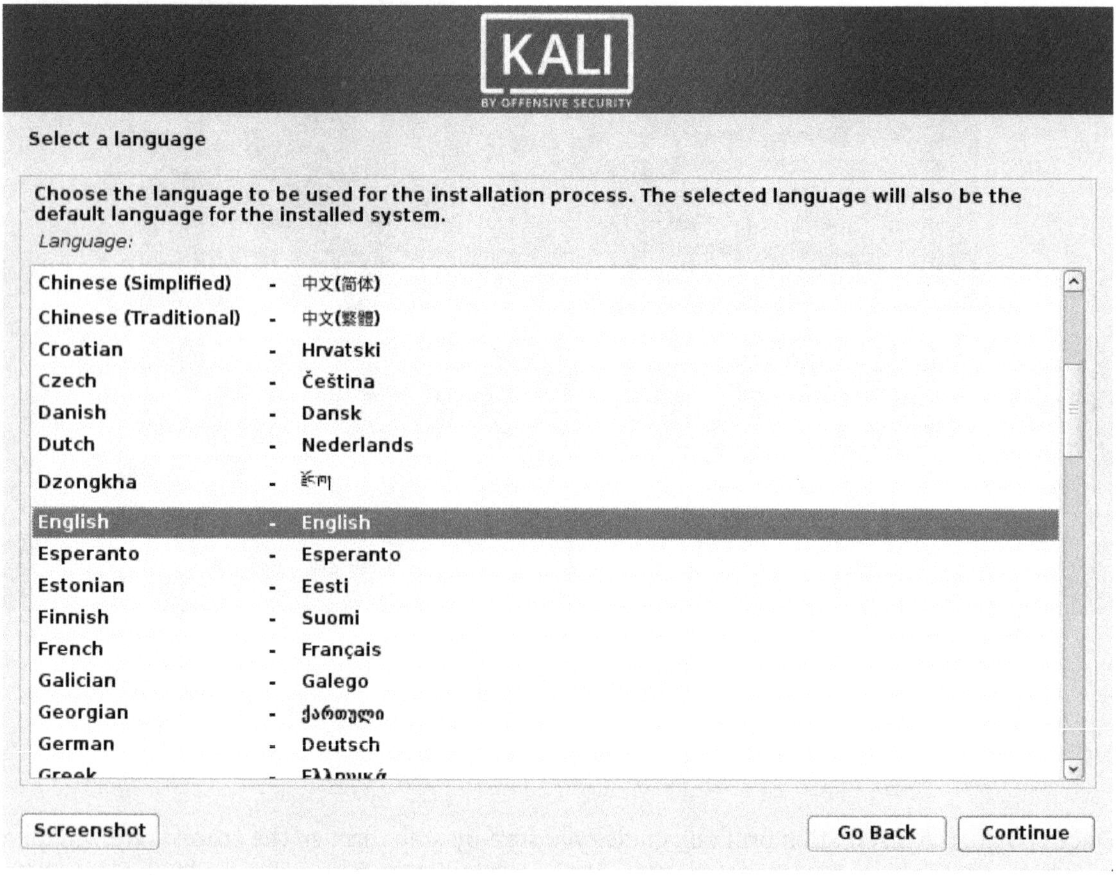

Figure 4.2 *Selecting the Language*

Selecting the Country

The second step (Figure 4.3, "Selecting the Country" [page 69]) consists in choosing your country. Combined with the language, this information enables the installation program to offer the most appropriate keyboard layout. This will also influence the configuration of the time zone. In the United States, a standard QWERTY keyboard is suggested and the installer presents a choice of appropriate time zones.

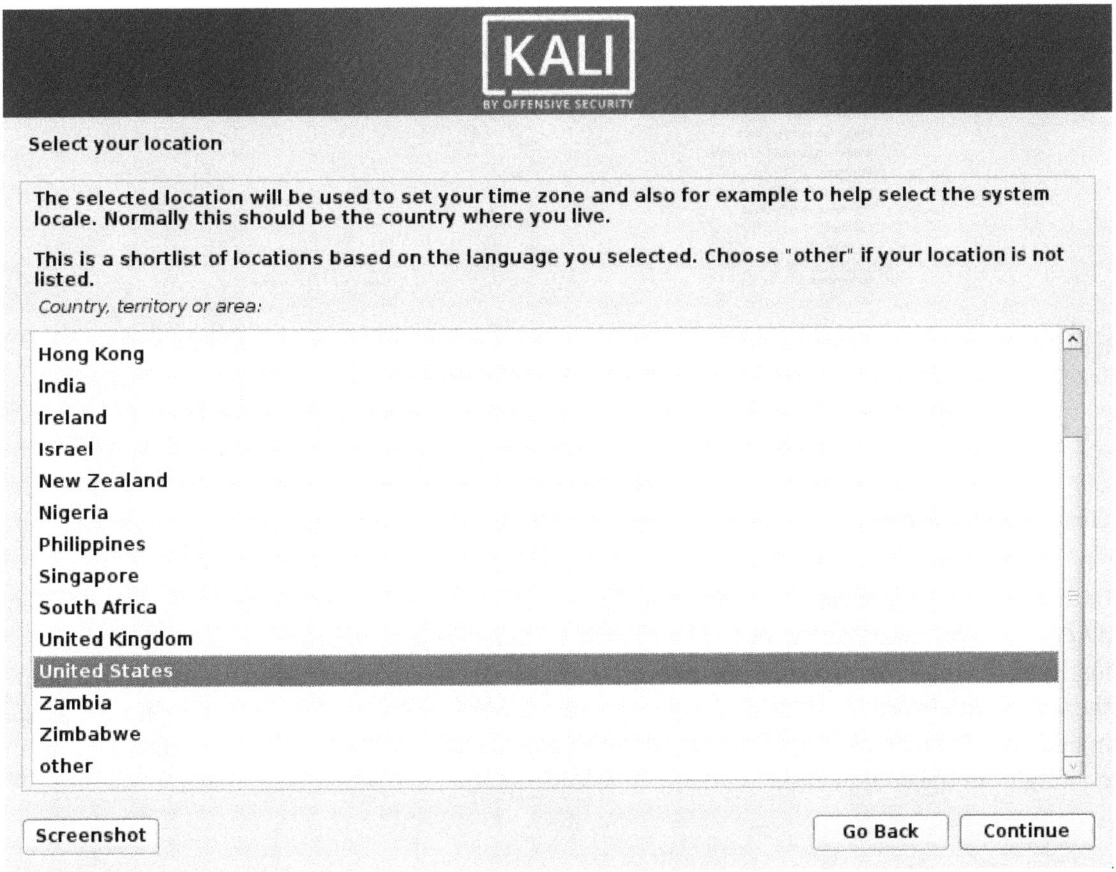

Figure 4.3 *Selecting the Country*

Selecting the Keyboard Layout

The proposed American English keyboard corresponds to the usual QWERTY layout as shown in Figure 4.4, "Choice of Keyboard" [page 70].

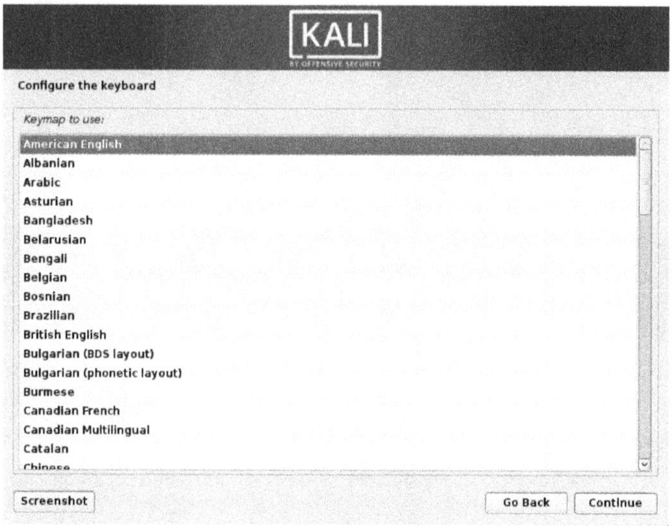

Figure 4.4   *Choice of Keyboard*

Detecting Hardware

In the vast majority of cases, the hardware detection step is completely automatic. The installer detects your hardware and tries to identify the boot device used in order to access its content. It loads the modules corresponding to the various hardware components detected and then mounts the boot device in order to read it. The previous steps were completely contained in the boot image included on the boot device, a file of limited size and loaded into memory by the bootloader when booting from the boot device.

Loading Components

With the contents of the boot device now available, the installer loads all the files necessary to continue with its work. This includes additional drivers for the remaining hardware (especially the network card), as well as all the components of the installation program.

Detecting Network Hardware

In this step, the installer will try to automatically identify the network card and load the corresponding module. If automatic detection fails, you can manually select the module to load. If all else fails, you can load a specific module from a removable device. This last solution is usually only needed if the appropriate driver is not included in the standard Linux kernel, but available elsewhere, such as the manufacturer's website.

This step must absolutely be successful for network installations (such as those done when booting from a mini.iso), since the Debian packages must be loaded from the network.

Configuring the Network

In order to automate the process as much as possible, the installer attempts an automatic network configuration using dynamic host configuration protocol (DHCP) (for IPv4 and IPv6) and ICMPv6's Neighbor Discovery Protocol (for IPv6), as shown in Figure 4.5, "Network Autoconfiguration" [page 71].

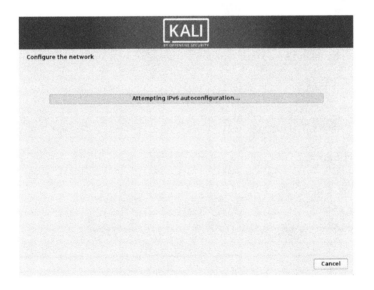

Figure 4.5   *Network Autoconfiguration*

If the automatic configuration fails, the installer offers more choices: try again with a normal DHCP configuration, attempt DHCP configuration by declaring the name of the machine, or set up a static network configuration.

This last option requires an IP address, a subnet mask, an IP address for a potential gateway, a machine name, and a domain name.

Configuration without DHCP If the local network is equipped with a DHCP server that you do not wish to use because you prefer to define a static IP address for the machine during installation, you can add the **netcfg/use_dhcp=false** option when booting. You just need to edit the desired menu entry by pressing the Tab key and adding the desired option before pressing the Enter key.

Root Password

The installer prompts for a password (Figure 4.6, "Root Password" [page 72]) since it automatically creates a super-user root account. The installer also asks for a confirmation of the password to prevent any input error which would later be difficult to adjust.

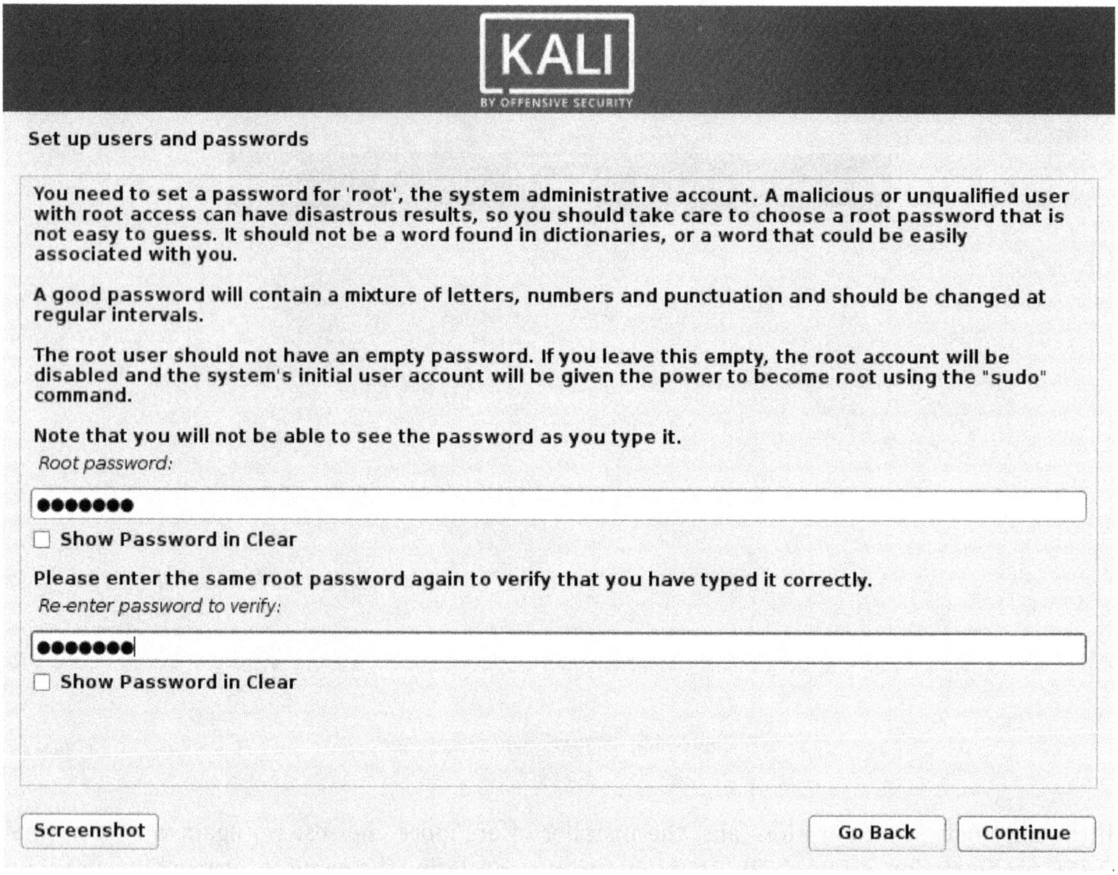

Figure 4.6 *Root Password*

The Administrator Password	The root user's password should be long (eight characters or more) and impossible to guess, since attackers target Internet-connected computers and servers with automated tools, attempting to log in with obvious passwords. Sometimes attackers leverage dictionary attacks, using many combinations of words and numbers as passwords. Avoid using the names of children or parents and dates of birth, because these are easily guessed.
	These remarks are equally applicable to other user passwords but the consequences of a compromised account are less drastic for users without administrative rights.
	If you are lacking inspiration, don't hesitate to use a password generator, such as pwgen (found in the package of the same name, which is already included in the base Kali installation).

Configuring the Clock

If the network is available, the system's internal clock will be updated from a network time protocol (NTP) server. This is beneficial because it ensures timestamps on logs will be correct from the first boot.

If your country spans multiple timezones, you will be asked to select the timezone that you want to use, as shown in Figure 4.7, "Timezone Selection" [page 73].

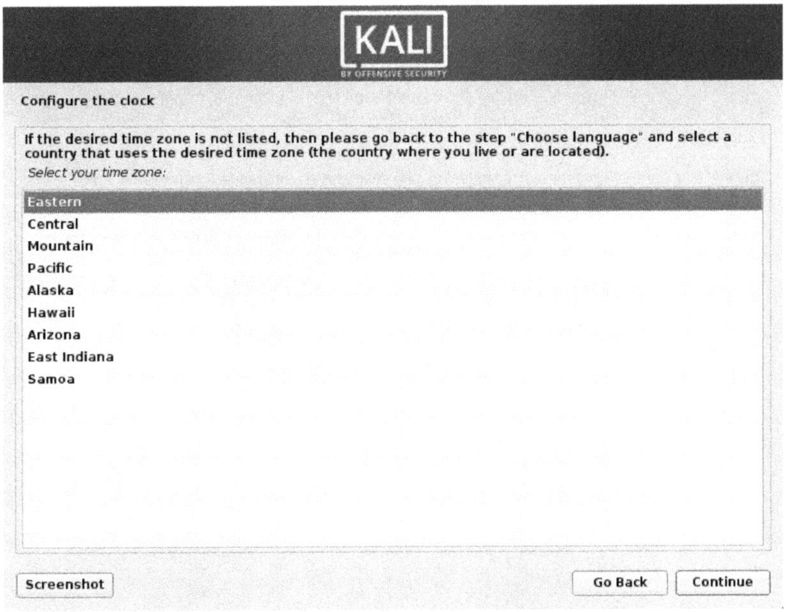

Figure 4.7 *Timezone Selection*

Detecting Disks and Other Devices

This step automatically detects the hard drives on which Kali may be installed, each of which will be presented in the next step: partitioning.

Partitioning

Partitioning is an indispensable step in installation, which consists of dividing the available space on the hard drives into discrete sections (*partitions*) according to the intended function of the computer and those partitions. Partitioning also involves choosing the file systems to be used. All of these decisions will have an influence on performance, data security, and server administration.

The partitioning step is traditionally difficult for new users. However, the Linux file systems and partitions, including virtual memory (or *swap* partitions) must be defined as they form the foundation of the system. This task can become complicated if you have already installed another operating system on the machine and you want the two to coexist. In this case, you must make sure not to alter its partitions, or if need be, resize them without causing damage.

To accommodate more common (and simpler) partition schemes, most users will prefer the *Guided* mode that recommends partition configurations and provides suggestions each step of the way. More advanced users will appreciate the *Manual* mode, which allows for more advanced configurations. Each mode shares certain capabilities.

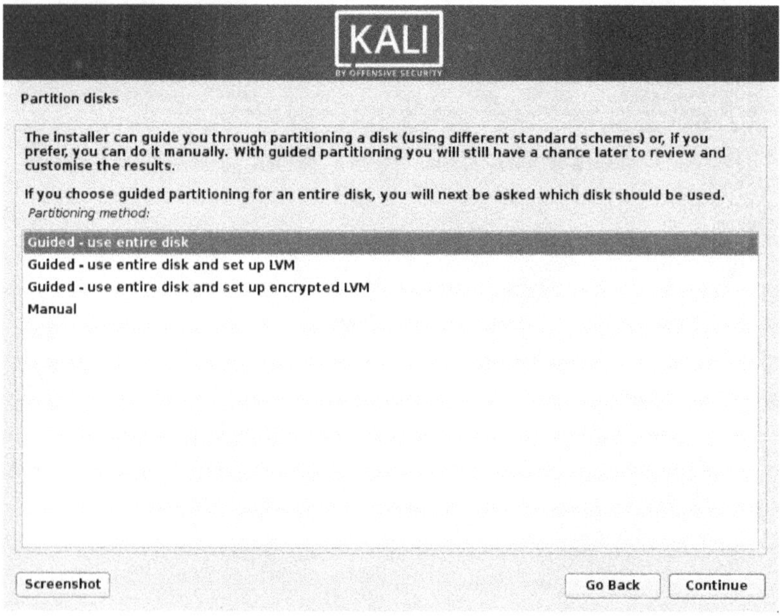

Figure 4.8 *Choice of Partitioning Mode*

Guided Partitioning The first screen in the partitioning tool (Figure 4.8, "Choice of Partitioning Mode" [page 74]) presents entry points for the guided and manual partitioning modes. "Guided - use entire disk" is the simplest and most common partition scheme, which will allocate an entire disk to Kali Linux.

The next two selections use Logical Volume Manager (LVM) to set up logical (instead of physical), optionally encrypted, partitions. We will discuss LVM and encryption later in this chapter.

Finally, the last choice initiates manual partitioning, which allows for more advanced partitioning schemes, such as installing Kali Linux alongside other operating systems. We will discuss manual mode in the next section.

In this example, we will allocate an entire hard disk to Kali, so we select "Guided - use entire disk" to proceed to the next step.

The next screen (shown in Figure 4.9, "Disk to Use for Guided Partitioning" [page 75]) allows you to choose the disk where Kali will be installed by selecting the corresponding entry (for example, "Virtual disk 1 (vda) - 32.2 GB Virtio Block Device"). Once selected, guided partitioning will continue. This option will erase all of the data on this disk, so choose wisely.

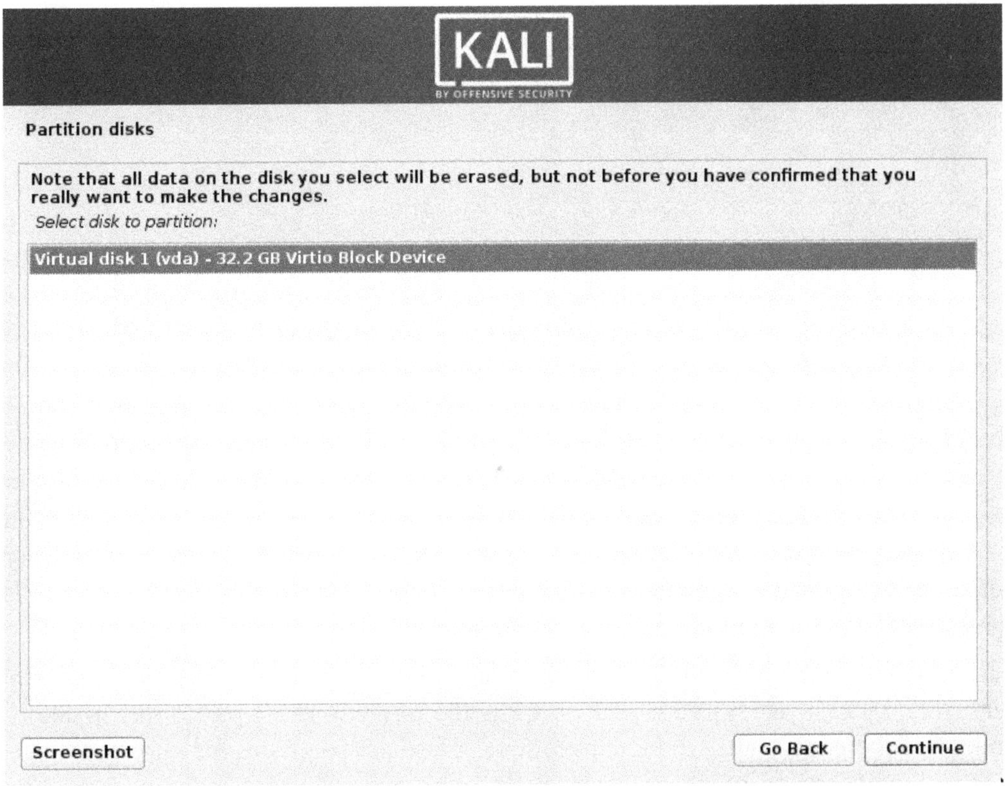

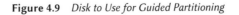

Figure 4.9 *Disk to Use for Guided Partitioning*

Next, the guided partitioning tool offers three partitioning methods, which correspond to different usages, as shown in Figure 4.10, "Guided Partition Allocation" [page 76].

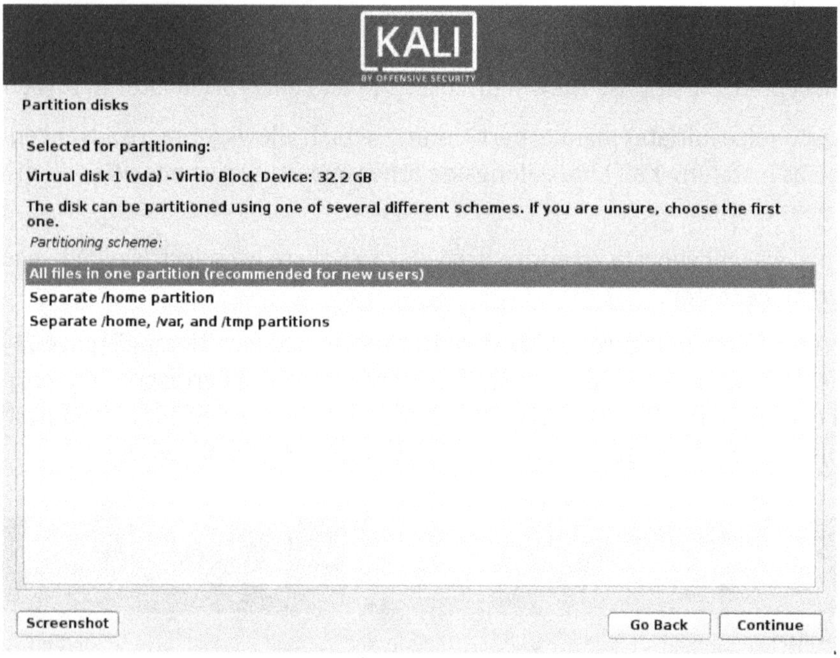

Figure 4.10 *Guided Partition Allocation*

The first method is called "All files in one partition." The entire Linux system tree is stored in a single file system, corresponding to the root ("/") directory. This simple and robust partitioning scheme works perfectly well for personal or single-user systems. Despite the name, two partitions will actually be created: the first will house the complete system, the second the virtual memory (or "swap").

The second method, "Separate /home/ partition," is similar, but splits the file hierarchy in two: one partition contains the Linux system (/), and the second contains "home directories" (meaning user data, in files and subdirectories available under /home/). One benefit to this method is that it is easy to preserve the users' data if you have to reinstall the system.

The last partitioning method, called "Separate /home, /var, and /tmp partitions," is appropriate for servers and multi-user systems. It divides the file tree into many partitions: in addition to the root (/) and user accounts (/home/) partitions, it also has partitions for server software data (/var/), and temporary files (/tmp/). One benefit to this method is that end users cannot lock up the server by consuming all available hard drive space (they can only fill up /tmp/ and /home/). At the same time, daemon data (especially logs) can no longer clog up the rest of the system.

After choosing the type of partition, the installer presents a summary of your selections on the screen as a partition map (Figure 4.11, "Validating Partitioning" [page 77]). You can modify each partition individually by selecting a partition. For example, you could choose another file system if the standard (*ext4*) isn't appropriate. In most cases, however, the proposed partitioning is reasonable and you can accept it by selecting "Finish partitioning and write changes to disk." It may go without saying, but choose wisely as this will erase the contents of the selected disk.

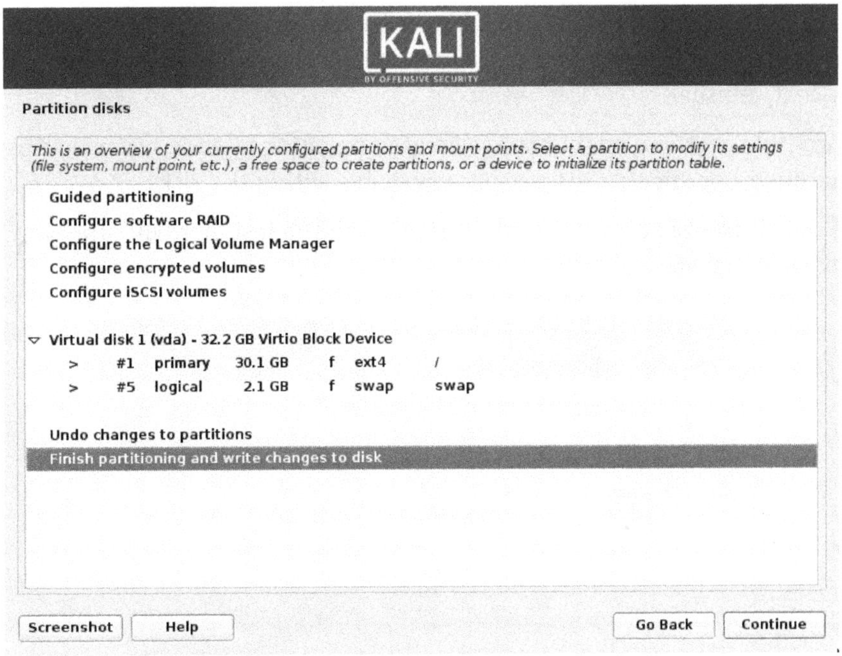

Figure 4.11   *Validating Partitioning*

Manual Partitioning   Selecting Manual at the main "Partition disks" screen (Figure 4.8, "Choice of Partitioning Mode" [page 74]) permits greater flexibility, allowing you to choose more advanced configurations and specifically dictate the purpose and size of each partition. For example, this mode allows you to install Kali alongside other operating systems, enable a software-based redundant array of independent disks (RAID) to protect data from hard disk failures, and safely resize existing partitions without losing data, among other things.

Shrinking a Windows Partition   To install Kali Linux alongside an existing operating system (Windows or other), you will need available, unused hard drive space for the partitions dedicated to Kali. In most cases, this means shrinking an existing partition and reusing the freed space.

If you are using the manual partitioning mode, the installer can shrink a Windows partition quite easily. You only need to choose the Windows partition and enter its new size (this works the same with both FAT and NTFS partitions).

If you are a less experienced user working on a system with existing data, please be very careful with this setup method as it is very easy to make mistakes that could lead to data loss.

The first screen in the manual installer is actually the same as the one shown in Figure 4.11, "Validating Partitioning" [page 77], except that it doesn't include any new partitions to create. It is up to you to add those.

First, you will see an option to enter "Guided partitioning" followed by several configuration options. Next, the installer will show the available disks, their partitions, and any possible free space that has not yet been partitioned. You can select each displayed element and press the Enter key to interact with it, as usual.

If the disk is entirely new, you might have to create a partition table. You can do this by selecting the disk. Once done, you should see free space available within the disk.

To make use of this free space, you should select it and the installer will offer you two ways to create partitions in that space.

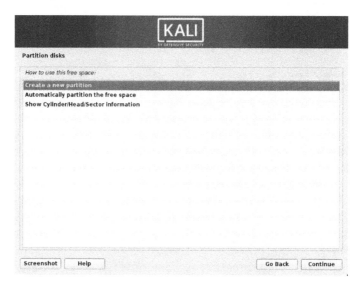

Figure 4.12   *Creating Partitions in the Free Space*

The first entry will create a single partition with the characteristics (including the size) of your choice. The second entry will use all the free space and will create multiple partitions in it with the help of the guided partitioning wizard (see section 4.2.1.12.1, "Guided Partitioning" [page 75]). This option is particularly interesting when you want to install Kali alongside another operating system but when you don't want to micro-manage the partition layout. The last entry will show the cylinder/head/sector numbers of the start and of the end of the free space.

When you select to "Create a new partition," you will enter into the meat of the manual partitioning sequence. After selecting this option, you will be prompted for a partition size. If the disk uses an MSDOS partition table, you will be given the option to create a primary or logical partition. (Things to know: You can only have four primary partitions but many more logical partitions. The partition containing /boot, and thus the kernel, must be a primary one, logical partitions reside in an extended partition, which consumes one of the four primary partitions.) Then you should see the generic partition configuration screen:

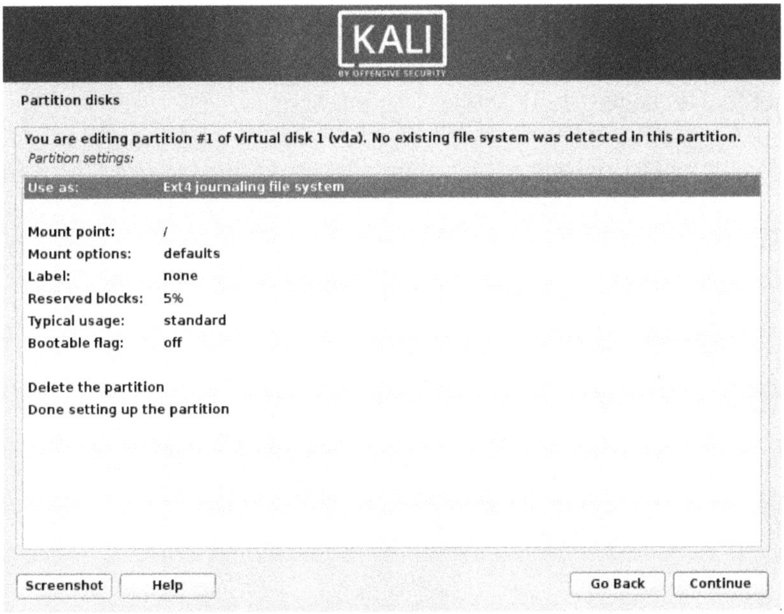

Figure 4.13 *Partition Configuration Screen*

To summarize this step of manual partitioning, let's take a look at what you can do with the new partition. You can:

- Format it and include it in the file tree by choosing a mount point. The mount point is the directory that will house the contents of the file system on the selected partition. Thus, a partition mounted at /home/ is traditionally intended to contain user data, while "/" is known as the *root* of the file tree, and therefore the root of the partition that will actually host the Kali system.

- Use it as a *swap partition*. When the Linux kernel lacks sufficient free memory, it will store inactive parts of RAM in a special swap partition on the hard disk. The virtual memory subsystem makes this transparent to applications. To simulate the additional memory, Windows uses a swap (paging) file that is directly contained in a file system. Conversely, Linux uses a partition dedicated to this purpose, hence the term swap partition.

- Make it into a "physical volume for encryption" to protect the confidentiality of data on certain partitions. This case is automated in the guided partitioning. See section 4.2.2, "Installation on a Fully Encrypted File System" [page 85] for more information.

- Make it a "physical volume for LVM" (not covered in this book). Note that this feature is used by the guided partitioning when you set up encrypted partitions.

- Use it as a RAID device (not covered in this book).

- Choose not to use the partition, and leave it unchanged.

When finished, you can either back out of manual partitioning by selecting "Undo changes to partitions" or write your changes to the disk by selecting "Finish partitioning and write changes to disk" from the manual installer screen (Figure 4.11, "Validating Partitioning" [page 77]).

Copying the Live Image

This next step, which doesn't require any user interaction, copies the contents of the live image to the target file system, as shown in Figure 4.14, "Copying the Data from the Live Image" [page 80].

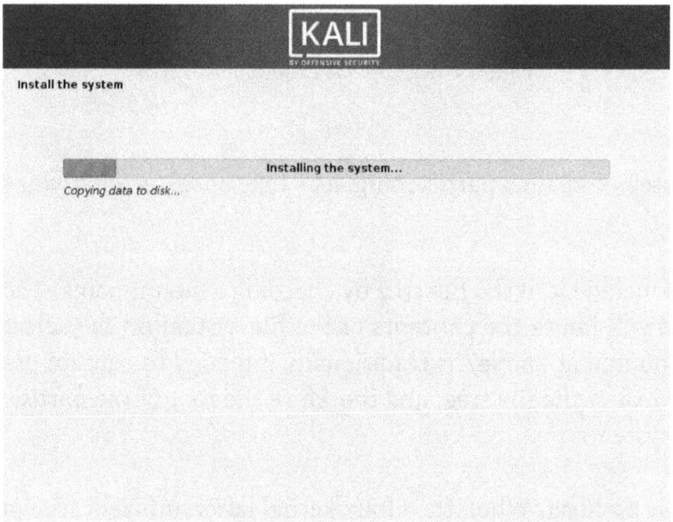

Figure 4.14 *Copying the Data from the Live Image*

Configuring the Package Manager (apt)

In order to be able to install additional software, APT needs to be configured and told where to find Debian packages. In Kali, this step is mostly non-interactive as we force the mirror to be http.kali.org. You just have to confirm whether you want to use this mirror (Figure 4.15, "Use a Network Mirror?" [page 81]). If you don't use it, you won't be able to install supplementary packages with apt unless you configure a package repository later.

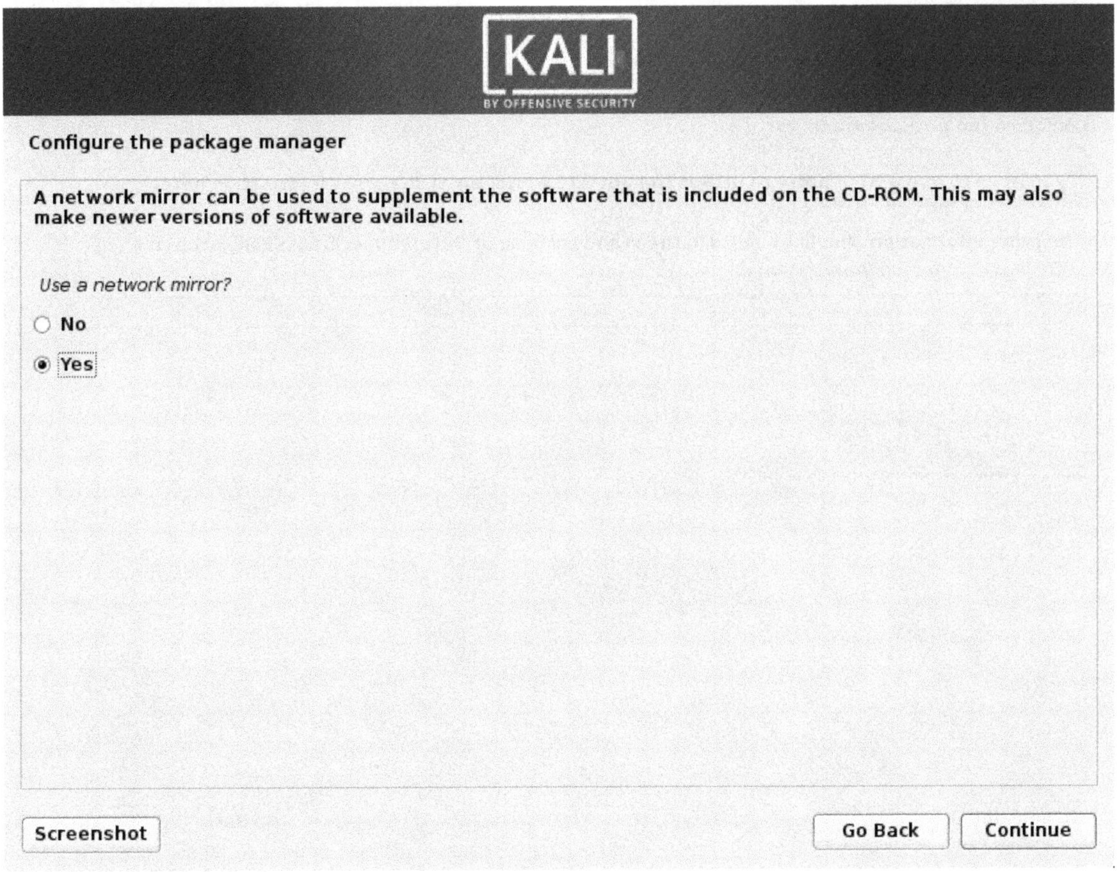

Figure 4.15 *Use a Network Mirror?*

If you want to use a local mirror instead of http.kali.org, you can pass its name on the kernel command line (at boot-time) with a syntax like this: mirror/http/hostname=*my.own.mirror*.

Finally, the program proposes to use an *HTTP proxy* as shown in Figure 4.16, "Use an HTTP Proxy" [page 82]. An HTTP proxy is a server that forwards HTTP requests for network users. It sometimes helps to speed up downloads by keeping a copy of files that have been transferred through it (we then speak of a caching proxy). In some cases, it is the only means of accessing an external web server; in such cases the installer will only be able to download the Debian packages if you properly fill in this field during installation. If you do not provide a proxy address, the installer will attempt to connect directly to the Internet.

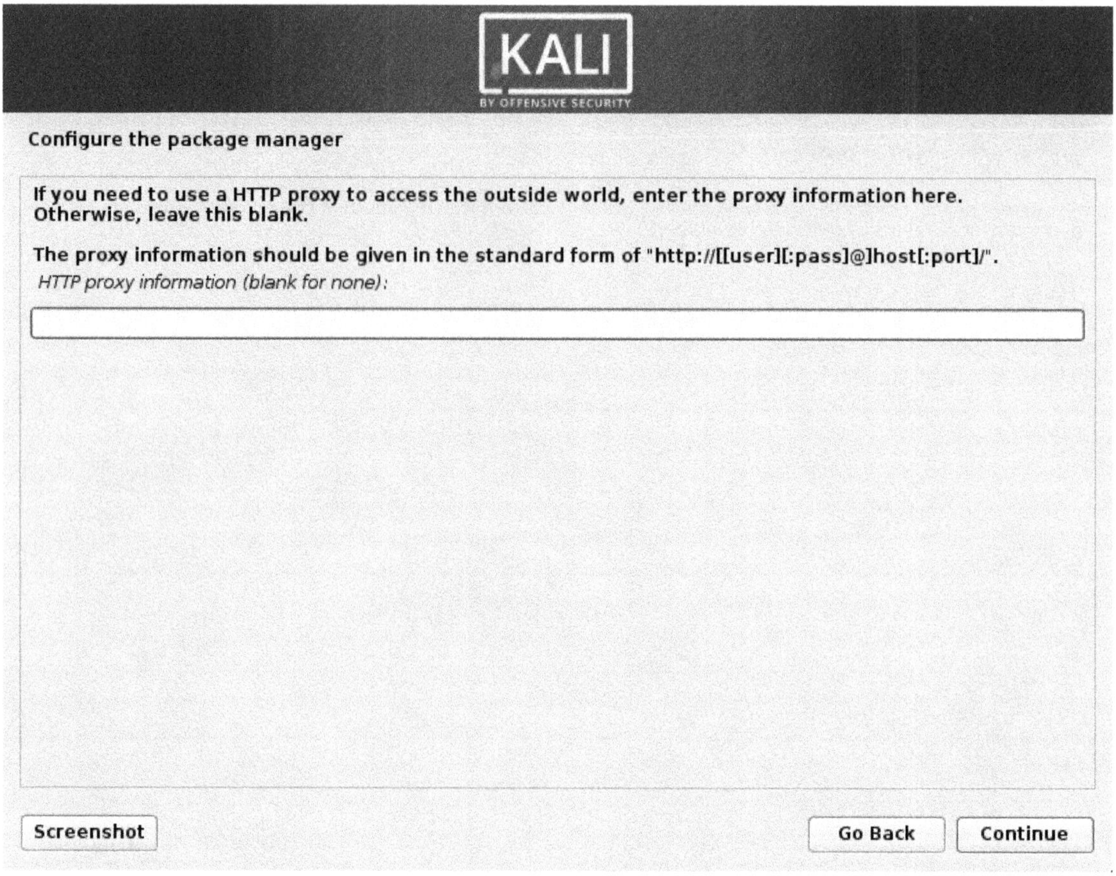

Figure 4.16 *Use an HTTP Proxy*

Next, the Packages.xz and Sources.xz files will be automatically downloaded to update the list of packages recognized by APT.

Installing the GRUB Boot Loader

The boot loader is the first program started by the BIOS. This program loads the Linux kernel into memory and then executes it. The boot loader often offers a menu that allows you to choose the kernel to load or the operating system to boot.

Due to its technical superiority, GRUB is the default boot loader installed by Debian: it works with most file systems and therefore doesn't require an update after each installation of a new kernel, since it reads its configuration during boot and finds the exact position of the new kernel.

You should install GRUB to the Master Boot Record (MBR) unless you already have another Linux system installed that knows how to boot Kali Linux. As noted in Figure 4.17, "Install the GRUB Boot Loader on a Hard Disk" [page 83], modifying the MBR will make unrecognized operating systems that depend on it unbootable until you fix GRUB's configuration.

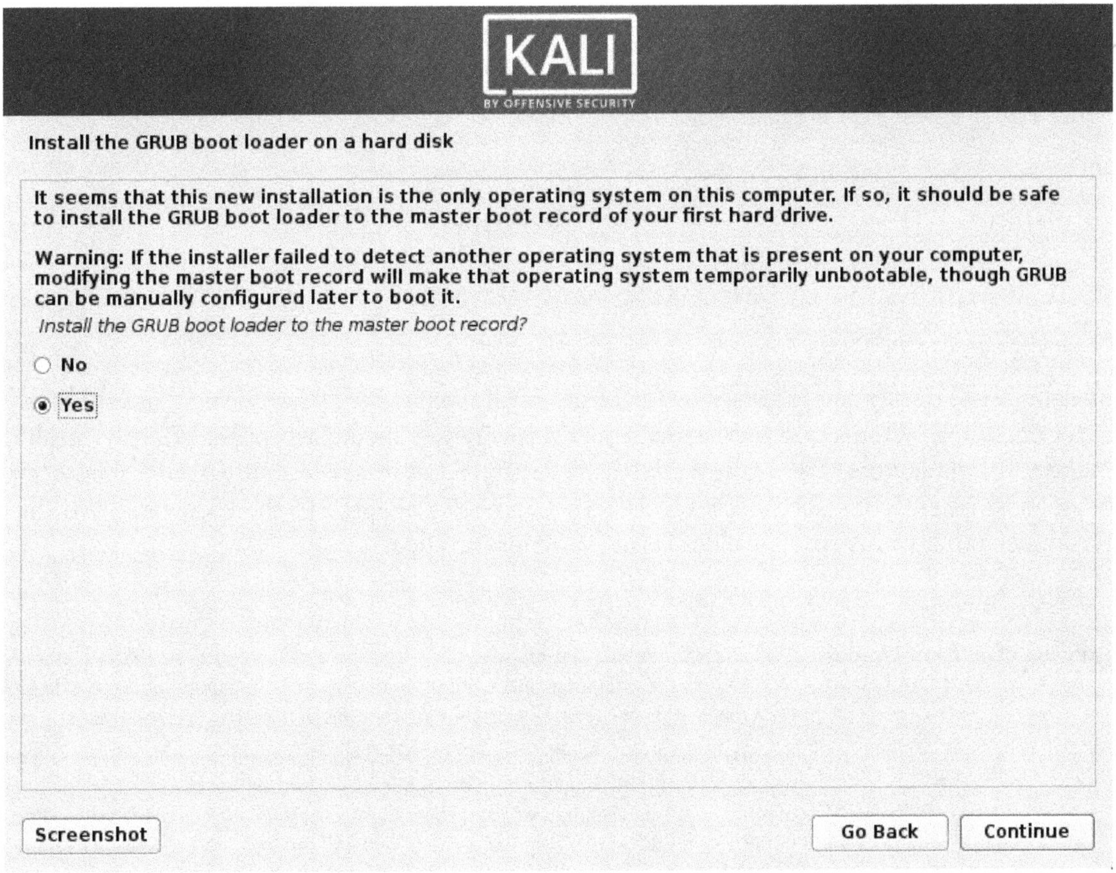

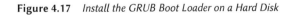

Figure 4.17 *Install the GRUB Boot Loader on a Hard Disk*

In this step (Figure 4.18, "Device for Boot Loader Installation" [page 84]), you must select which device GRUB will be installed on. This should be your current boot drive.

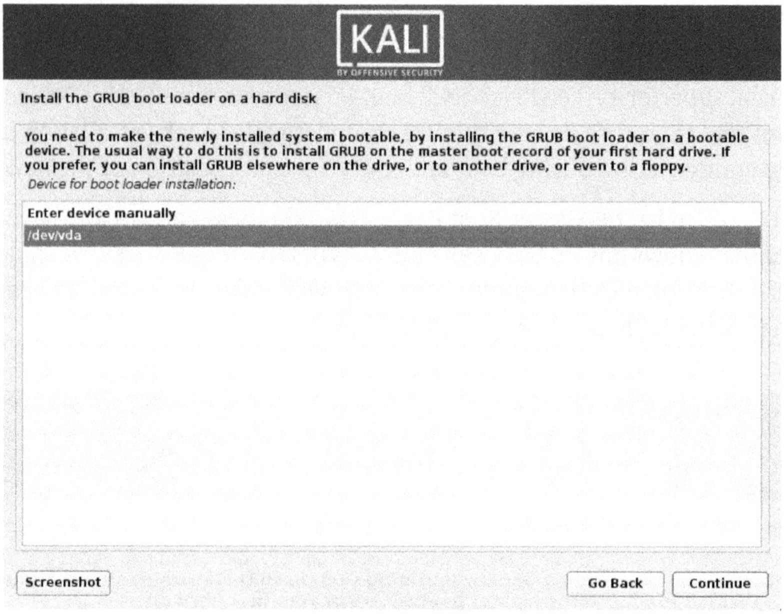

Figure 4.18 *Device for Boot Loader Installation*

By default, the boot menu proposed by GRUB shows all the installed Linux kernels, as well as any other operating systems that were detected. This is why you should accept the offer to install it in the Master Boot Record. Keeping older kernel versions preserves the ability to boot the system if the most recently installed kernel is defective or poorly adapted to the hardware. We thus recommend that you keep a few older kernel versions installed.

Beware: The Boot Loader and Dual Boot	This phase in the installation process detects the operating systems that are already installed on the computer and will automatically add corresponding entries in the boot menu. However, not all installation programs do this.
	In particular, if you install (or reinstall) Windows thereafter, the boot loader will be erased. Kali will still be on the hard drive, but will no longer be accessible from the boot menu. You would then have to start the Kali installer with the **rescue/enable=true** parameter on the kernel command line to reinstall the boot loader. This operation is described in detail in the Debian installation manual.
	➡ http://www.debian.org/releases/stable/amd64/ch08s07.html

Finishing the Installation and Rebooting

Now that installation is complete, the program asks you to remove the DVD-ROM from the reader (or unplug your USB drive) so that your computer can boot into your new Kali system after the installer restarts the system (Figure 4.19, "Installation Complete" [page 85]).

Finally, the installer will do some cleanup work, like removing packages that are specific to creating the live environment.

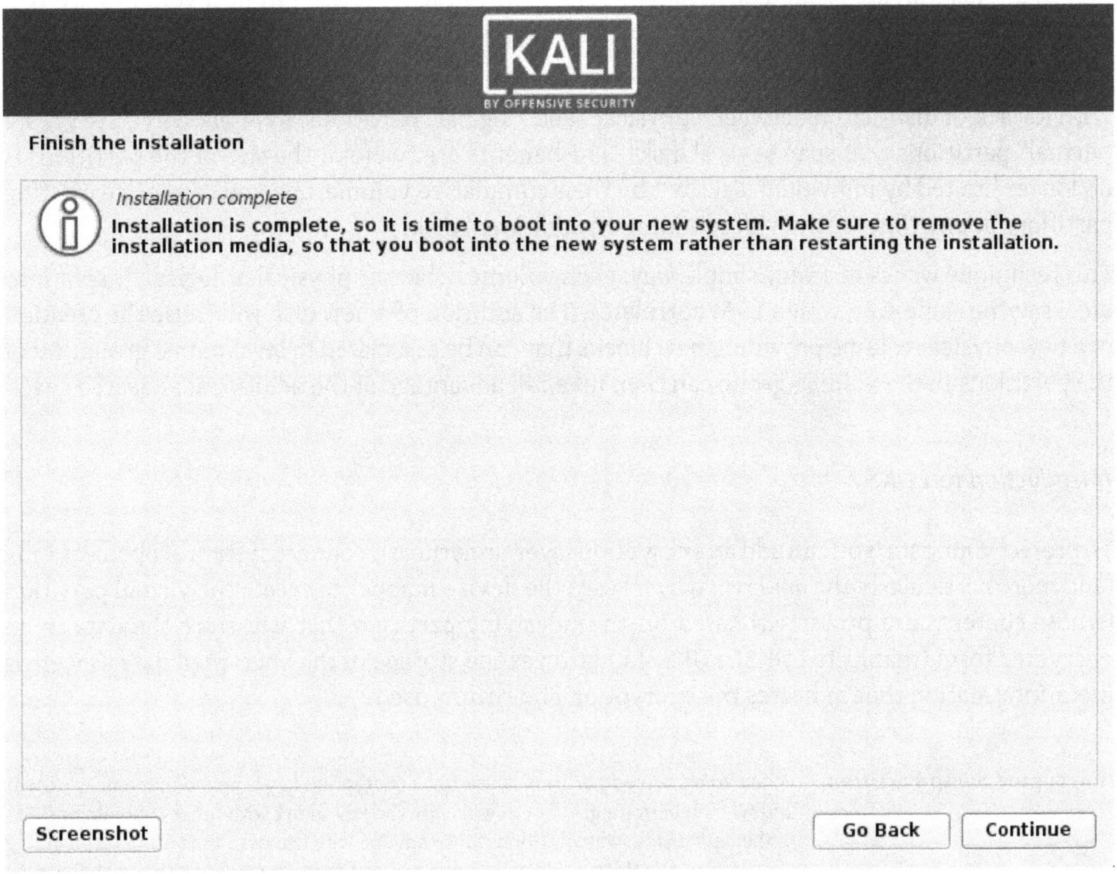

Figure 4.19 *Installation Complete*

4.2.2. Installation on a Fully Encrypted File System

To guarantee the confidentiality of your data, you can set up encrypted partitions. This will protect your data if your laptop or hard drive is lost or stolen. The partitioning tool can help you in this process, both in guided and manual mode.

The guided partitioning mode will combine the use of two technologies: Linux Unified Key Setup (LUKS) for encrypting partitions and Logical Volume Management (LVM) for managing storage dynamically. Both features can also be set up and configured through manual partitioning mode.

Introduction to LVM

Let's discuss LVM first. Using LVM terminology, a *virtual partition* is a logical volume, which is part of a *volume group*, or an association of several physical volumes. Physical volumes are real partitions (or virtual partitions exported by other abstractions, such as a software RAID device or an encrypted partition).

With its lack of distinction between "physical" and "logical" partitions, LVM allows you to create "virtual" partitions that span several disks. The benefits are twofold: the size of the partitions is no longer limited by individual disks but by their cumulative volume, and you can resize existing partitions at any time, such as after adding an additional disk.

This technique works in a very simple way: each volume, whether physical or logical, is split into blocks of the same size, which LVM correlates. The addition of a new disk will cause the creation of a new physical volume providing new blocks that can be associated to any volume group. All of the partitions in the volume group can then take full advantage of the additional allocated space.

Introduction to LUKS

To protect your data, you can add an encryption layer underneath your file system of choice. Linux (and more particularly the *dm-crypt* driver) uses the device mapper to create the virtual partition (whose contents are protected) based on an underlying partition that will store the data in an encrypted form (thanks to LUKS). LUKS standardizes the storage of the encrypted data as well as meta-information that indicates the encryption algorithms used.

Encrypted Swap Partition When an encrypted partition is used, the encryption key is stored in memory (RAM), and when hibernating, a laptop will copy the key, along with other contents of RAM, to the hard disk's swap partition. Since anyone with access to the swap file (including a technician or a thief) could extract the key and decrypt your data, the swap file must be protected with encryption.

Because of this, the installer will warn you if you try to use an encrypted partition alongside an unencrypted swap partition.

Setting Up Encrypted Partitions

The installation process for encrypted LVM is the same as a standard installation except for the partitioning step (Figure 4.20, "Guided Partitioning with Encrypted LVM" [page 87]) where you will instead select "Guided - use entire disk and set up encrypted LVM." The net result will be a system that cannot be booted or accessed until the encryption passphrase is provided. This will encrypt and protect the data on your disk.

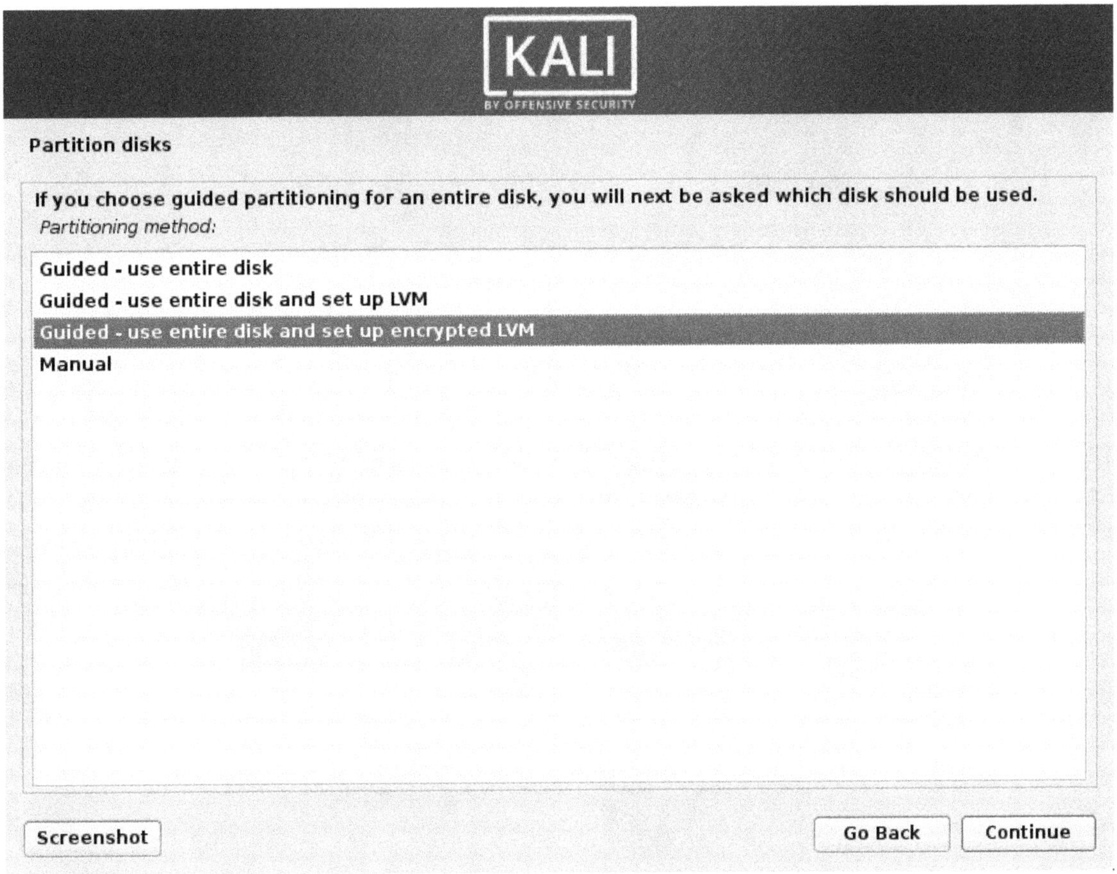

Figure 4.20 *Guided Partitioning with Encrypted LVM*

The guided partitioning installer will automatically assign a physical partition for the storage of encrypted data, as shown in Figure 4.21, "Confirm Changes to the Partition Table" [page 88]. At this point, the installer will confirm the changes before they are written on the disk.

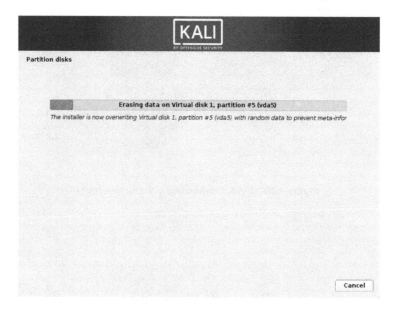

Figure 4.21 *Confirm Changes to the Partition Table*

This new partition is then initialized with random data, as shown in Figure 4.22, "Erasing Data on Encrypted Partition" [page 88]. This makes the areas that contain data indistinguishable from the unused areas, making it more difficult to detect, and subsequently attack, the encrypted data.

Figure 4.22 *Erasing Data on Encrypted Partition*

Next, the installer asks you to enter an encryption passphrase (Figure 4.23, "Enter Your Encryption Passphrase" [page 89]). In order to view the contents of the encrypted partition, you will need to enter this passphrase every time you reboot the system. Note the warning in the installer: your encrypted system will only be as strong as this passphrase.

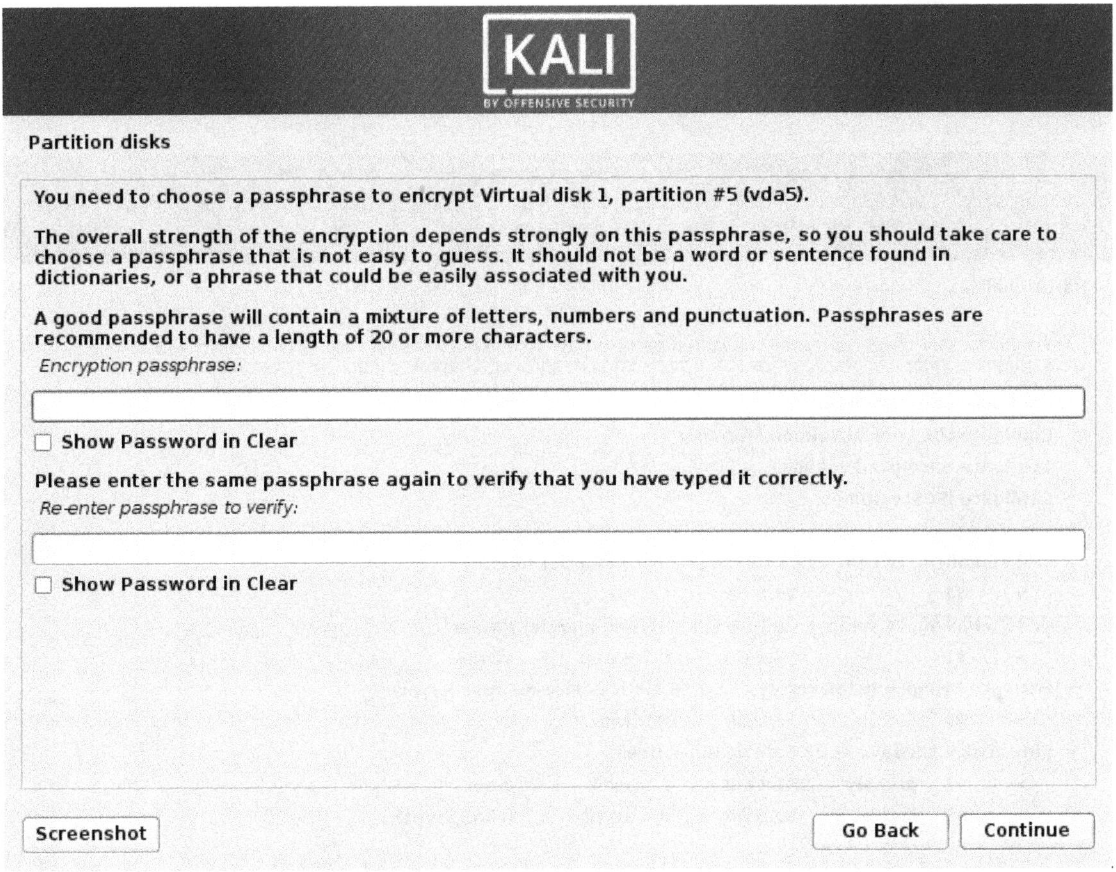

KALI
BY OFFENSIVE SECURITY

Partition disks

You need to choose a passphrase to encrypt Virtual disk 1, partition #5 (vda5).

The overall strength of the encryption depends strongly on this passphrase, so you should take care to choose a passphrase that is not easy to guess. It should not be a word or sentence found in dictionaries, or a phrase that could be easily associated with you.

A good passphrase will contain a mixture of letters, numbers and punctuation. Passphrases are recommended to have a length of 20 or more characters.

Encryption passphrase:

☐ Show Password in Clear

Please enter the same passphrase again to verify that you have typed it correctly.

Re-enter passphrase to verify:

☐ Show Password in Clear

Screenshot   Go Back   Continue

Figure 4.23 *Enter Your Encryption Passphrase*

The partitioning tool now has access to a new virtual partition whose contents are stored encrypted in the underlying physical partition. Since LVM uses this new partition as a physical volume, it can protect several partitions (or LVM logical volumes) with the same encryption key, including the swap partition (see sidebar "Encrypted Swap Partition" [page 86]). Here, LVM is not used to make it easy to extend the storage size, but just for the convenience of the indirection allowing to split a single encrypted partition into multiple logical volumes.

End of the Guided Partitioning with Encrypted LVM

Next, the resulting partitioning scheme is displayed (Figure 4.24, "Validating Partitioning for Encrypted LVM Installation" [page 90]) so you can tweak settings as needed.

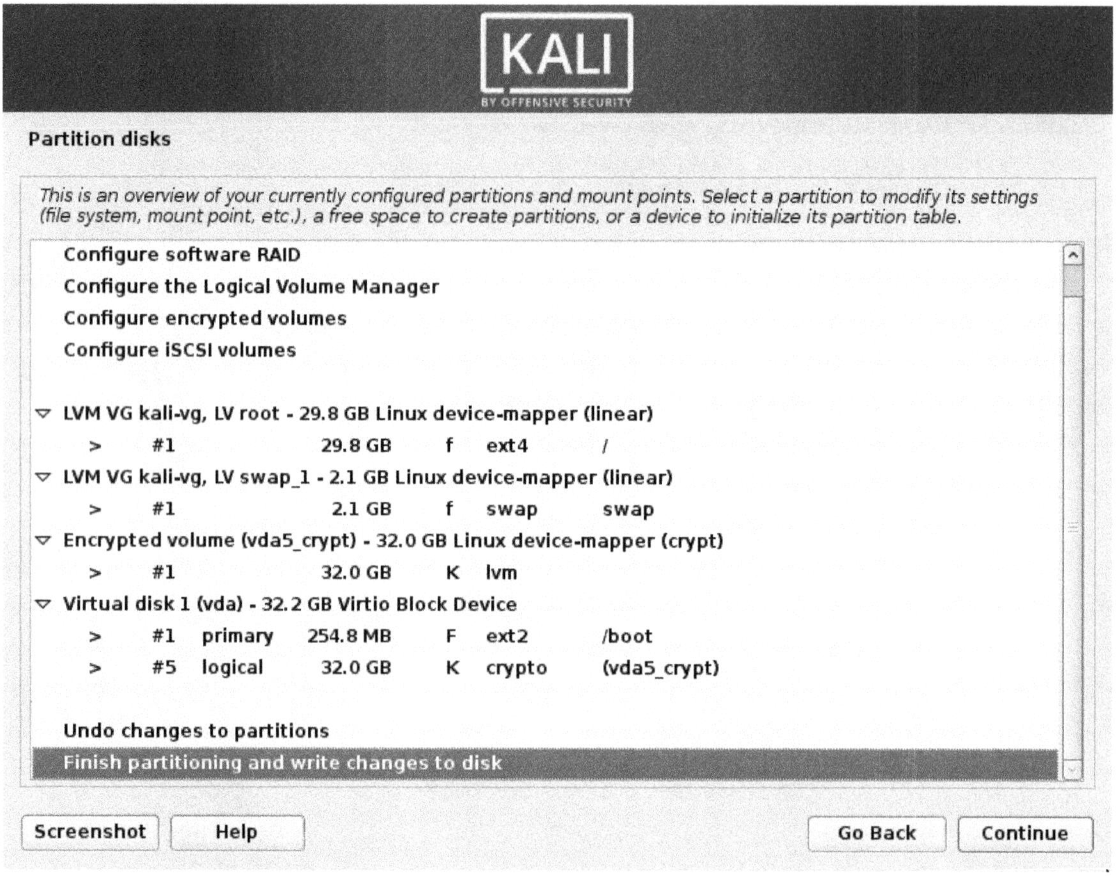

Figure 4.24 *Validating Partitioning for Encrypted LVM Installation*

Finally, after validating the partition setup, the tool asks for confirmation to write the changes on the disks, as shown in Figure 4.25, "Confirm Partitions to be Formatted" [page 91].

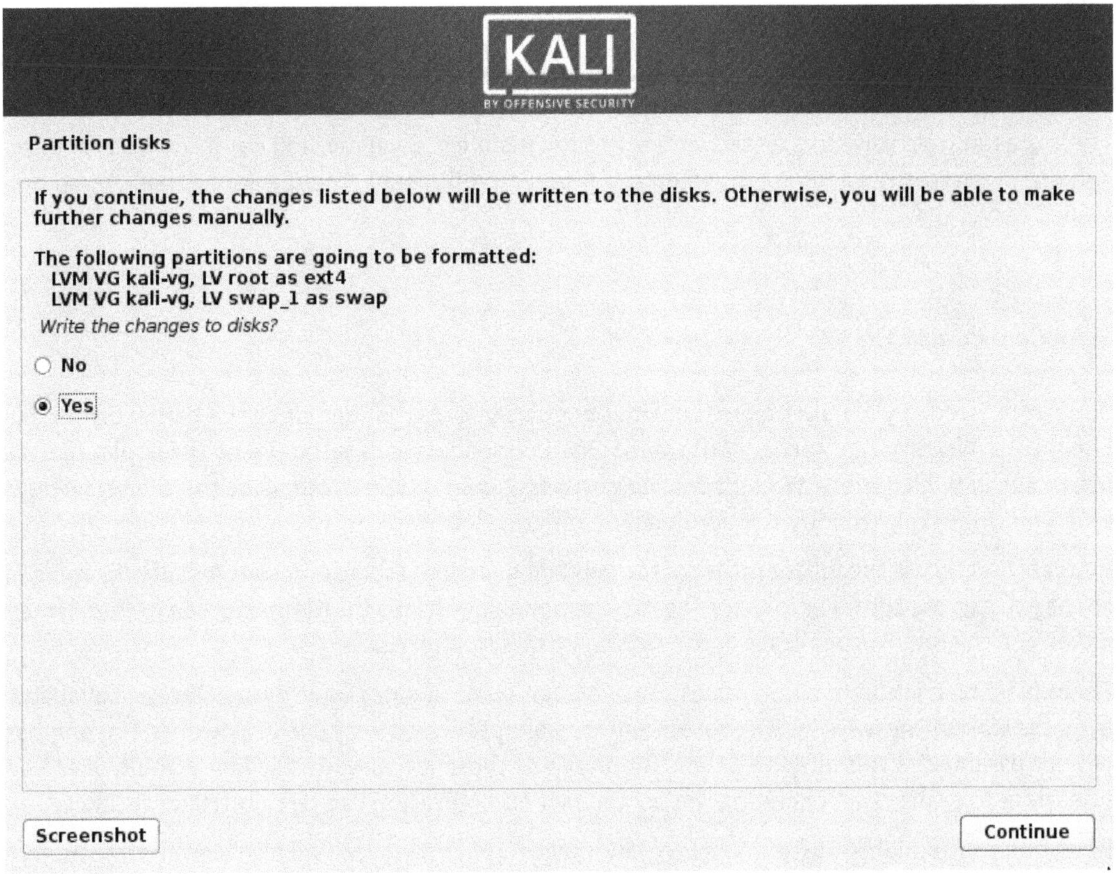

Figure 4.25 *Confirm Partitions to be Formatted*

Finally, the installation process continues as usual as documented in section 4.2.1.14, "Configuring the Package Manager (apt)" [page 81].

4.3. Unattended Installations

The Debian and Kali installers are very modular: at the basic level, they are just executing many scripts (packaged in tiny packages called udeb—for µdeb or micro-deb) one after another. Each script relies on debconf (see "The debconf Tool" [page 214]), which interacts with you, the user, and stores installation parameters. Because of this, the installer can also be automated through debconf preseeding, a function that allows you to provide unattended answers to installation questions.

4.3.1. Preseeding Answers

There are multiple ways to preseed answers to the installer. Each method has its own advantages and disadvantages. Depending on when the preseeding happens, the questions that can be preseeded vary.

With Boot Parameters

You can preseed any installer question with boot parameters that end up in the kernel command-line, accessible through /proc/cmdline. Some bootloaders will let you edit these parameters interactively (which is practical for testing purposes), but if you want to make the changes persistent, you will have to modify the bootloader configuration.

You can directly use the full identifier of the debconf questions (such as debian-installer/language= en) or you can use abbreviations for the most common questions (like language=en or hostname= duke). See the full list[1] of aliases in the Debian installation manual.

There is no restriction on which questions you can preseed since boot parameters are available from the start of the installation process and they are processed very early. However, the number of boot parameters is limited to 32 and a number of those are already used by default. It is also important to realize that changing the boot loader configuration can be non-trivial at times.

In section 9.3, "Building Custom Kali Live ISO Images" [page 236] you will also learn how to modify the Isolinux configuration when you generate your own Kali ISO image.

With a Preseed File in the Initrd

You can add a file named preseed.cfg at the root of the installer's initrd (this is the initrd which is used to start the installer). Usually, this requires rebuilding the debian-installer source package to generate new versions of the initrd. However, live-build offers a convenient way to do this, which is detailed in section 9.3, "Building Custom Kali Live ISO Images" [page 236].

This method also does not have any restrictions on the questions that you can preseed as the preseed file is available immediately after boot. In Kali, we already make use of this feature to customize the behavior of the official Debian installer.

---

[1] https://www.debian.org/releases/stable/amd64/apbs02#preseed-aliases

With a Preseed File in the Boot Media

You can add a preseed file on the boot media (CD or USB key); preseeding then happens as soon as the media is mounted, which means right after the questions about language and keyboard layout. The preseed/file boot parameter can be used to indicate the location of the preseeding file (for instance, /cdrom/preseed.cfg when installing from a CD-ROM, or /hd-media/preseed.cfg when installing from a USB-key).

You may not preseed answers to language and country options as the preseeding file is loaded later in the process, once the hardware drivers have been loaded. On the positive side, live-build makes it easy to put a supplementary file in the generated ISO images (see section 9.3, "Building Custom Kali Live ISO Images" [page 236]).

With a Preseed File Loaded from the Network

You can make a preseed file available on the network through a web server and tell the installer to download that preseed file by adding the boot parameter preseed/url=http://*server*/preseed.cfg (or by using the url alias).

However, when using this method, remember that the network must first be configured. This means that network-related debconf questions (in particular hostname and domain name) and all the preceding questions (like language and country) cannot be preseeded with this method. This method is most often used in combination with boot parameters preseeding those specific questions.

This preseeding method is the most flexible one as you can change the installation configuration without changing the installation media.

Delaying the Language, Country, Keyboard Questions	To overcome the limitation of not being able to preseed the language, country, and keyboard questions, you can add the boot parameter auto-install/enable=true (or auto=true). With this option the questions will be asked later in the process, after the network has been configured and thus after download of the preseed file.
	The downside is that the first steps (notably network configuration) will always happen in English and if there are errors the user will have to work through English screens (with a keyboard configured in QWERTY).

4.3.2. Creating a Preseed File

A preseed file is a plain text file in which each line contains the answer to one Debconf question. A line is split across four fields separated by white space (spaces or tabs). For instance, d-i mirror/ suite string kali-rolling:

- The first field indicates the owner of the question. For example, "d-i" is used for questions relevant to the installer. You may also see a package name, for questions coming from Debian packages (as in this example: atftpd atftpd/use_inetd boolean false).

- The second field is an identifier for the question.

- The third field lists the type of question.

- The fourth and final field contains the value for the expected answer. Note that it must be separated from the third field with a single space; additional space characters are considered part of the value.

The simplest way to write a preseed file is to install a system by hand. Then the `debconf-get-selections --installer` command will provide the answers you provided to the installer. You can obtain answers directed to other packages with `debconf-get-selections`. However, a cleaner solution is to write the preseed file by hand, starting from an example and then going through the documentation. With this approach, only questions where the default answer needs to be overridden can be preseeded. Provide the priority=critical boot parameter to instruct Debconf to only ask critical questions, and to use the default answer for others.

Installation Guide Appendix	The Debian installation guide, available online, includes detailed documentation on the use of a preseed file in an appendix. It also includes a detailed and commented sample file, which can serve as a base for local customizations.
	➡ https://www.debian.org/releases/stable/amd64/apb.html
	➡ https://www.debian.org/releases/stable/example-preseed.txt
	Note however that the above links document the stable version of Debian and that Kali uses the testing version so you may encounter slight differences. You can also consult the installation manual hosted on the Debian-installer project's website. It may be more up-to-date.
	➡ http://d-i.alioth.debian.org/manual/en.amd64/apb.html

4.4. ARM Installations

Kali Linux runs on a wide variety of ARM-based devices (laptops, embedded computers, and developer boards, for example) but you cannot use the traditional Kali installer on these devices since they often have specific requirements in terms of kernel or boot loader configuration.

To make those devices more accessible to Kali users, Offensive Security developed scripts to build disk images[2] that are ready for use with various ARM devices. They provide those images for download on their website:

➡ https://www.offensive-security.com/kali-linux-arm-images/

---

[2]https://github.com/offensive-security/kali-arm-build-scripts

Since these images are available, your task of installing Kali on an ARM device is greatly simplified. Here are the basic steps:

1. Download the image for your ARM device and ensure that the checksum matches the one provided on the website (see section 2.1.3, "Verifying Integrity and Authenticity" [page 16] for explanations on how to do that). Note that the images are usually xz-compressed; make sure to uncompress them with unxz.

2. Depending on the storage expansion slot available on your specific ARM device, acquire an SD card, micro SD card, or eMMC module that has a capacity of at least 8 GB.

3. Copy the downloaded image to the storage device with dd. This is similar to the process of copying an ISO image onto a USB key (see section 2.1.4, "Copying the Image on a DVD-ROM or USB Key" [page 19]).

    ```
    # dd if=kali-image.img of=/dev/something bs=512k
    ```

4. Plug the SD-card/eMMC into your ARM device.

5. Boot your ARM device and log into it (*user "root", password "toor"*). If you don't have a screen connected, then you will have to figure out the IP address that has been assigned via DHCP and connect to that address over SSH. Some DHCP servers have tools or web interfaces to show the current leases. If you don't have anything like that, use a sniffer to look for DHCP lease traffic.

6. Change the root password and generate new SSH host keys, especially if the device will be permanently running on a public network! The steps are relatively straightforward, see "Generating New SSH Host Keys " [page 111].

7. Enjoy your new ARM device running Kali Linux!

Special Cases and More Detailed Documentation	These instructions are generic and while they work for most devices, there are always exceptions. For example, Chromebooks require *developer mode* and other devices require a special keypress in order to boot from external media.
	Since ARM devices are added relatively frequently and their specifications are so dynamic, we won't cover specific installation instructions for various ARM devices here. Instead, refer to the dedicated "Kali on ARM" section of the Kali documentation website for information about each ARM device supported by Offensive Security:
	➡ http://docs.kali.org/category/kali-on-arm

4.5. Troubleshooting Installations

The installer is quite reliable, but you may encounter bugs or face external problems such as: network problems, bad mirrors, and insufficient disk space. Because of this, it is quite useful to be able to troubleshoot problems that appear in the installation process.

When the installer fails, it will show you a rather unhelpful screen such as the one shown in Figure 4.26, "Installation Step Failed" [page 96].

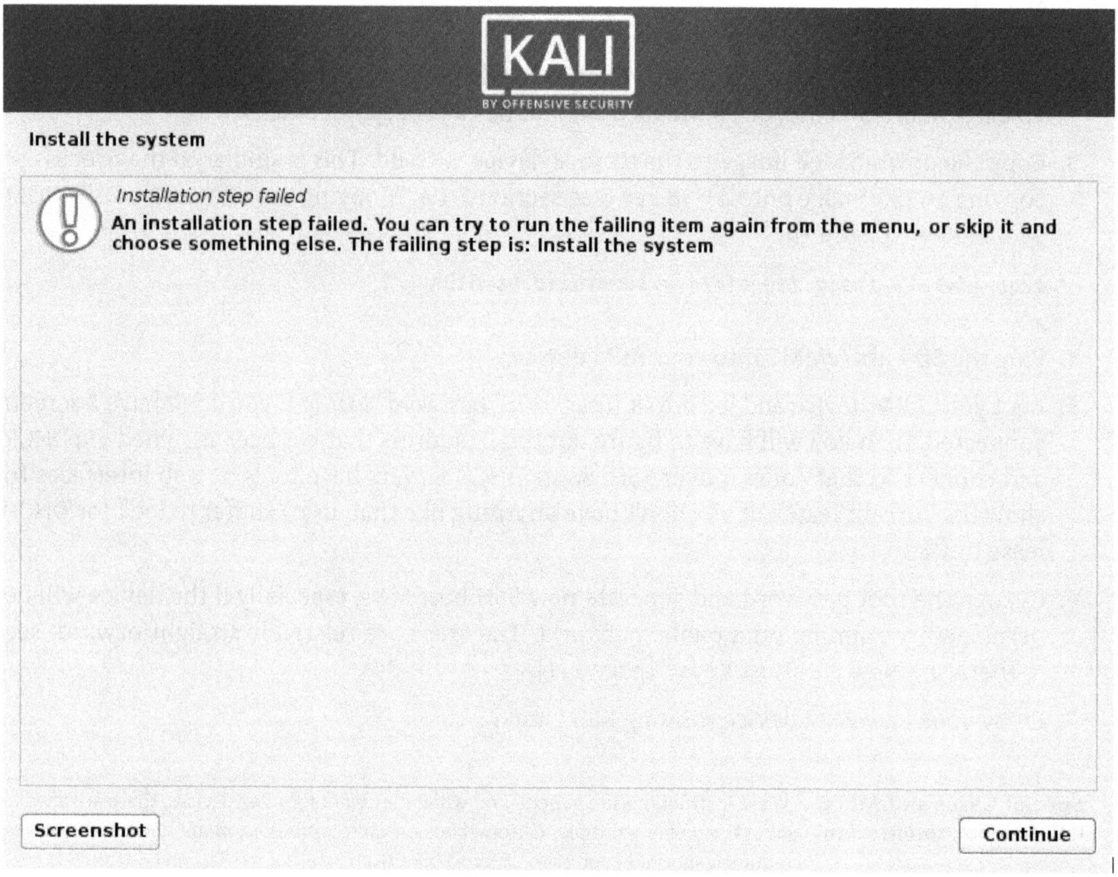

Figure 4.26 *Installation Step Failed*

At this point, it is good to know that the installer makes use of multiple virtual consoles: the main screen that you see is running either on the fifth console (for the graphical installer, CTRL+Shift+F5) or on the first console (for the textual installer, CTRL+Shift+F1). In both cases, the fourth console (CTRL+Shift+F4) displays logs of what is happening and you can usually see a more useful error message there, such as the one in Figure 4.27, "The Log Screen of the Installer" [page 97], which reveals that the installer has run out of disk space.

```
tion:
Apr 15 19:04:24 main-menu[833]: (process:5559): line 88:
Apr 15 19:04:24 main-menu[833]: (process:5559): /lib/partman/active_partition/copy/choices: not foun
d
Apr 15 19:04:24 main-menu[833]: (process:5559):
Apr 15 19:04:24 main-menu[833]: (process:5559): /lib/partman/choose_partition/60partition_tree/do_op
tion:
Apr 15 19:04:24 main-menu[833]: (process:5559): line 88:
Apr 15 19:04:24 main-menu[833]: (process:5559): /lib/partman/active_partition/copy/choices: not foun
d
Apr 15 19:04:24 main-menu[833]: (process:5559):
Apr 15 19:04:24 main-menu[833]: (process:5559): /lib/partman/free_space/50new/do_option:
Apr 15 19:04:24 main-menu[833]: (process:5559): line 226:
Apr 15 19:04:24 main-menu[833]: (process:5559): /lib/partman/active_partition/copy/choices: not foun
d
Apr 15 19:04:24 main-menu[833]: (process:5559):
Apr 15 19:04:24 main-menu[833]: (process:5559): /lib/partman/free_space/50new/do_option:
Apr 15 19:04:24 main-menu[833]: (process:5559): line 226:
Apr 15 19:04:24 main-menu[833]: (process:5559): /lib/partman/active_partition/copy/choices: not foun
d
Apr 15 19:04:24 main-menu[833]: (process:5559):
Apr 15 19:04:24 main-menu[833]: DEBUG: resolver (libgcc1): package doesn't exist (ignored)
Apr 15 19:04:24 main-menu[833]: INFO: Menu item 'live-installer' selected
Apr 15 19:04:24 base-installer: info: Using squashfs support for /cdrom/live/filesystem.squashfs
Apr 15 19:04:24 anna-install: Installing squashfs-modules
Apr 15 19:04:24 anna[8545]: DEBUG: resolver (kernel-image-4.3.0-kali1-amd64-di): package doesn't exi
st (ignored)
Apr 15 19:04:24 anna[8545]: DEBUG: retrieving squashfs-modules-4.3.0-kali1-amd64-di 4.3.3-5kali4
Apr 15 19:04:24 kernel: [  165.758382] squashfs: version 4.0 (2009/01/31) Phillip Lougher
Apr 15 19:04:24 kernel: [  165.764051] loop: module loaded
Apr 15 19:04:45 base-installer: error: The tar process copying the live system failed (only 9238 out
 of 119223 files have been copied, last file was ).
Apr 15 19:04:45 main-menu[833]: (process:849  ): tar: write error: No space left on device
Apr 15 19:04:45 main-menu[833]: (process:8491): tar: write error: Broken pipe
Apr 15 19:04:45 main-menu[833]: WARNING **: Configuring 'live-installer' failed with error code 1
Apr 15 19:04:45 main-menu[833]: WARNING **: Menu item 'live-installer' failed.
```

Figure 4.27   *The Log Screen of the Installer*

The second and third consoles (CTRL+Shift+F2 and CTRL+Shift+F3, respectively) host shells that you can use to investigate the current situation in more detail. Most of the command line tools are provided by BusyBox so the feature set is rather limited, but it is enough to figure out most of the problems that you are likely to encounter.

What Can be Done in the Installer Shell

You can inspect and modify the debconf database with debconf-get and debconf-set. These commands are especially convenient for testing preseeding values.

You can inspect any file (such as the full installation log available in /var/log/syslog) with cat or more. You can edit any file with nano, including all files being installed onto the system. The root file system will be mounted on /target once the partitioning step of the installation process has completed.

Once network access has been configured, you can use wget and nc (netcat) to retrieve and export data over the network.

Once you click Continue from the main installer failure screen (Figure 4.26, "Installation Step Failed" [page 96]), you will be returned to a screen that you will normally never see (the Main Menu shown in Figure 4.28, "Main Menu of the Installer" [page 98]), which allows you to launch one installation step after another. If you managed to fix the problem through the shell access (congratulations!) then you can retry the step that failed.

Figure 4.28 *Main Menu of the Installer*

If you are unable to resolve the problem, you might want to file a bug report. The report must then include the installer logs, which you can retrieve with the main menu's "Save debug logs" function. It offers multiple ways to export the logs, as shown in Figure 4.29, "Save Debug Logs (1/2)" [page 99].

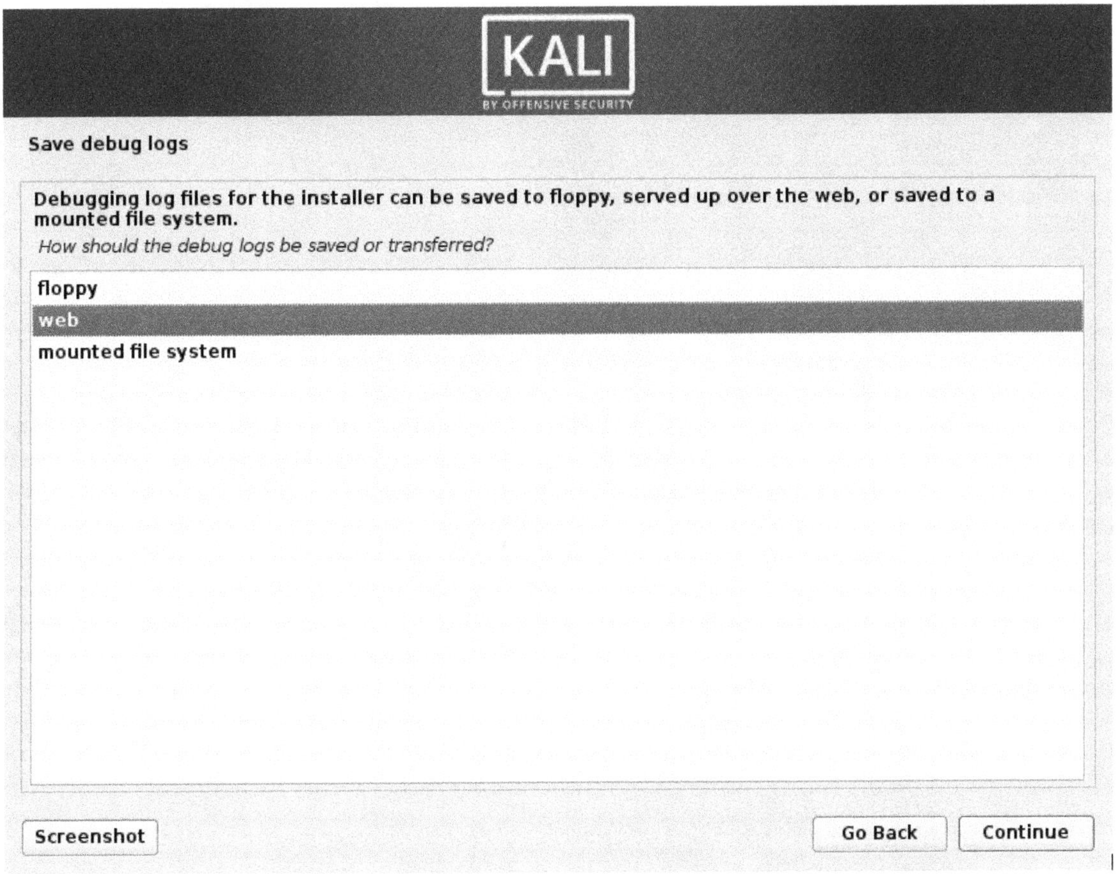

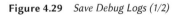

Figure 4.29 *Save Debug Logs (1/2)*

The most convenient method, and the one that we recommend, is to let the installer start a web server hosting the log files (Figure 4.30, "Save Debug Logs (2/2)" [page 100]). You can then launch a browser from another computer on the same network and download all the log files and screenshots that you have taken with the Screenshot button available on each screen.

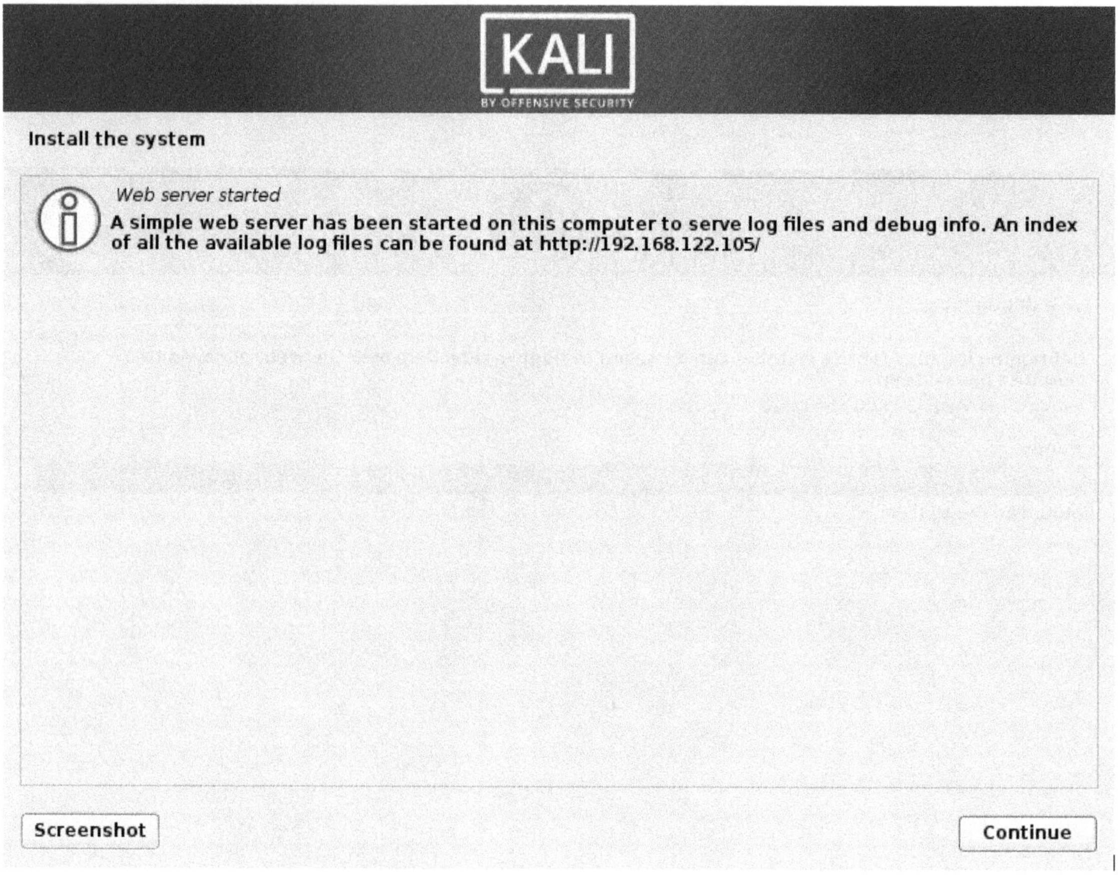

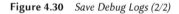

Figure 4.30 *Save Debug Logs (2/2)*

4.6. Summary

In this chapter, we focused on the Kali Linux installation process. We discussed Kali Linux's minimum installation requirements, the installation process for standard and fully encrypted file systems, preseeding, which allows unattended installations, how to install Kali Linux on various ARM devices, and what to do in the rare case of an installation failure.

Summary Tips:

- The installation requirements for Kali Linux vary from a basic SSH server with no desktop, as little as 128 MB RAM (512 MB recommended) and 2 GB disk space, to the higher-end *kali-linux-full* meta-package, with at least 2048 MB of RAM and 20 GB of disk space. In addition, your machine must have a CPU supported by at least one of the amd64, i386, armel, armhf, or arm64 architectures.

- Kali can easily be installed as the primary operating system, alongside other operating systems through partitioning and boot loader modification, or as a virtual machine.

- To guarantee the confidentiality of your data, you can set up encrypted partitions. This will protect your data if your laptop or hard drive is lost or stolen.

- The installer can also be automated through debconf preseeding, a function that allows you to provide unattended answers to installation questions.

- A preseed file is a plain text file in which each line contains the answer to one Debconf question. A line is split across four fields separated by white space (spaces or tabs). You can preseed answers to the installer with boot parameters, with a preseed file in initrd, with a preseed file on the boot media, or with a preseed file from the network.

- Kali Linux runs on a wide variety of ARM-based devices such as laptops, embedded computers, and developer boards. ARM installation is fairly straightforward. Download the proper image, burn it to an SD card, USB drive, or embedded multi-media controller (eMMC) module, plug it in, boot the ARM device, find your device on the network, log in, and change the SSH password and SSH host keys.

- You can debug failed installations with virtual consoles (accessible with the CTRL+Shift and function keys), `debconf-get` and `debconf-set` commands, reading the `/var/log/syslog` log file, or by submitting a bug report with log files retrieved with the installer's "Save debug logs" function.

Now that we have discussed Linux fundamentals and Kali Linux installation, let's discuss configuration so you can begin to tailor Kali to suit your needs.

Keywords

Network
Users and groups
Services
Apache
PostgreSQL
SSH

KALI LINUX
REVEALED

Configuring Kali Linux

Contents

In this chapter, we will take a look at various ways you can configure Kali Linux. First, in section 5.1, "Configuring the Network" [page 104], we will show you how to configure your network settings using a graphical environment and the command line. In section 5.2, "Managing Unix Users and Unix Groups" [page 107], we will talk about users and groups, showing you how to create and modify user accounts, set passwords, disable accounts, and manage groups. Finally, we will discuss services in section 5.3, "Configuring Services" [page 109] and explain how to set up and maintain generic services and also focus on three very important and specific services: SSH, PostgreSQL, and Apache.

5.1. Configuring the Network

5.1.1. On the Desktop with *NetworkManager*

In a typical desktop installation, you'll have *NetworkManager* already installed and it can be controlled and configured through GNOME's control center and through the top-right menu as shown in Figure 5.1, "Network Configuration Screen" [page 104].

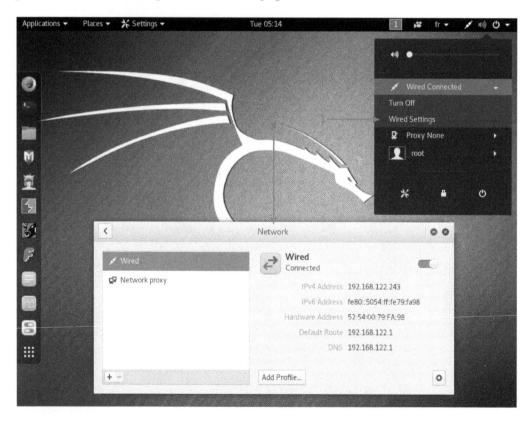

Figure 5.1 *Network Configuration Screen*

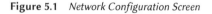

The default network configuration relies on DHCP to obtain an IP address, DNS server, and gateway, but you can use the gear icon in the lower-right corner to alter the configuration in many ways (for example: set the MAC address, switch to a static setup, enable or disable IPv6, and add additional routes). You can create profiles to save multiple wired network configurations and easily switch between them. For wireless networks, their settings are automatically tied to their public identifier (SSID).

NetworkManager also handles connections by mobile broadband (Wireless Wide Area Network WWAN) and by modems using point-to-point protocol over ethernet (PPPoE). Last but not least, it provides integration with many types of virtual private networks (VPN) through dedicated plugins: SSH, OpenVPN, Cisco's VPNC, PPTP, Strongswan. Check out the *network-manager-** packages; most of them are not installed by default. Note that you need the packages suffixed with -gnome to be able to configure them through the graphical user interface.

5.1.2. On the Command Line with Ifupdown

Alternatively, when you prefer not to use (or don't have access to) a graphical desktop, you can configure the network with the already-installed *ifupdown* package, which includes the `ifup` and `ifdown` tools. These tools read definitions from the `/etc/network/interfaces` configuration file and are at the heart of the `/etc/init.d/networking` init script that configures the network at boot time.

Each network device managed by *ifupdown* can be deconfigured at any time with `ifdown network-device`. You can then modify `/etc/network/interfaces` and bring the network back up (with the new configuration) with `ifup network-device`.

Let's take a look at what we can put in ifupdown's configuration file. There are two main directives: auto *network-device*, which tells *ifupdown* to automatically configure the network interface once it is available, and iface *network-device inet/inet6 type* to configure a given interface. For example, a plain DHCP configuration looks like this:

```
auto lo
iface lo inet loopback

auto eth0
iface eth0 inet dhcp
```

Note that the special configuration for the loopback device should always be present in this file. For a fixed IP address configuration, you have to provide more details such as the IP address, the network, and the IP of the gateway:

```
auto eth0
iface eth0 inet static
  address 192.168.0.3
  netmask 255.255.255.0
  broadcast 192.168.0.255
  network 192.168.0.0
  gateway 192.168.0.1
```

For wireless interfaces, you must have the *wpasupplicant* package (included in Kali by default), which provides many wpa-* options that can be used in /etc/network/interfaces. Have a look at /usr/share/doc/wpasupplicant/README.Debian.gz for examples and explanations. The most common options are wpa-ssid (which defines the name of the wireless network to join) and wpa-psk (which defines the passphrase or the key protecting the network).

```
iface wlan0 inet dhcp
  wpa-ssid MyNetWork
  wpa-psk plaintextsecret
```

5.1.3. On the Command Line with *systemd-networkd*

While *ifupdown* is the historical tool used by Debian, and while it is still the default for server or other minimal installations, there is a newer tool worth considering: *systemd-networkd*. Its integration with the *systemd* init system makes it a very attractive choice. It is not specific to Debian-based distributions (contrary to *ifupdown*) and has been designed to be very small, efficient, and relatively easy to configure if you understand the syntax of systemd unit files. This is an especially attractive choice if you consider *NetworkManager* bloated and hard to configure.

You configure systemd-networkd by placing .network files into the /etc/systemd/network/ directory. Alternatively, you can use /lib/systemd/network/ for packaged files or /run/systemd/network/ for files generated at run-time. The format of those files is documented in systemd.network(5). The Match section indicates the network interfaces the configuration applies to. You can specify the interface in many ways, including by media access control (MAC) address or device type. The Network section defines the network configuration.

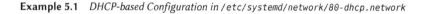

Example 5.1 *DHCP-based Configuration in /etc/systemd/network/80-dhcp.network*

```
[Match]
Name=en*

[Network]
DHCP=yes
```

Example 5.2 *Static Configuration in /etc/systemd/network/50-static.network*

```
[Match]
Name=enp2s0

[Network]
Address=192.168.0.15/24
Gateway=192.168.0.1
DNS=8.8.8.8
```

Note that system-networkd is disabled by default, so if you want to use it, you should enable it. It also depends on systemd-resolved for proper integration of DNS resolution, which in turn requires you to replace /etc/resolv.conf with a symlink to /run/system/resolve/resolv.conf, which is managed by systemd-resolved.

```
# systemctl enable systemd-networkd
# systemctl enable systemd-resolved
# systemctl start systemd-networkd
# systemctl start systemd-resolved
# ln -sf /run/system/resolve/resolv.conf /etc/resolv.conf
```

Although systemd-networkd suffers from some limitations, like the lack of integrated support for wireless networks, you can rely on a pre-existing external wpa_supplicant configuration for wireless support. However, it is particularly useful in containers and virtual machines and was originally developed for environments in which a container's network configuration depended on its host's network configuration. In this scenario, systemd-networkd makes it easier to manage both sides in a consistent manner while still supporting all sorts of virtual network devices that you might need in this type of scenario (see systemd.netdev(5)).

5.2. Managing Unix Users and Unix Groups

The database of Unix users and groups consists of the textual files /etc/passwd (list of users), /etc/shadow (encrypted passwords of users), /etc/group (list of groups), and /etc/gshadow (encrypted passwords of groups). Their formats are documented in passwd(5), shadow(5), group(5), and gshadow(5) respectively. While these files can be manually edited with tools like vipw and vigr, there are higher level tools to perform the most common operations.

5.2.1. Creating User Accounts

Although Kali is most often run while authenticated as the root user, you may often need to create non-privileged user accounts for various reasons, particularly if you are using Kali as a primary operating system. The most typical way to add a user is with the `adduser` command, which takes a required argument: the username for the new user that you would like to create.

The `adduser` command asks a few questions before creating the account but its usage is fairly straightforward. Its configuration file, `/etc/adduser.conf`, includes many interesting settings. You can, for example, define the range of user identifiers (UIDs) that can be used, dictate whether or not users share a common group or not, define default shells, and more.

The creation of an account triggers the population of the user's home directory with the contents of the `/etc/skel/` template. This provides the user with a set of standard directories and configuration files.

In some cases, it will be useful to add a user to a group (other than their default main group) in order to grant additional permissions. For example, a user who is included in the *sudo* group has full administrative privileges through the `sudo` command. This can be achieved with a command such as `adduser` *user group.*

Using getent to Consult the User Database   The getent (get entries) command checks the system databases (including those of users and groups) using the appropriate library functions, which in turn call the name service switch (NSS) modules configured in the `/etc/nsswitch.conf` file. The command takes one or two arguments: the name of the database to check, and a possible search key. Thus, the command `getent passwd kaliuser1` will return the information from the user database regarding the user `kaliuser1`.

```
root@kali:~# getent passwd kaliuser1
kaliuser1:x:1001:1001:Kali User
    ➥ ,4444,123-867-5309,321-867-5309:/home/kaliuser1:/bin/
    ➥ bash
```

5.2.2. Modifying an Existing Account or Password

The following commands allow modification of the information stored in specific fields of the user databases:

- `passwd`—permits a regular user to change their password, which in turn, updates the `/etc/shadow` file.

- `chfn`—(CHange Full Name), reserved for the super-user (root), modifies the GECOS, or "general information" field.

- `chsh`—(CHange SHell) changes the user's login shell. However, available choices will be limited to those listed in `/etc/shells`; the administrator, on the other hand, is not bound by this restriction and can set the shell to any program chosen.

- `chage`—(CHange AGE) allows the administrator to change the password expiration settings by passing the user name as an argument or list current settings using the -l *user* option.

Alternatively, you can also force the expiration of a password using the `passwd -e user` command, which forces the user to change their password the next time they log in.

5.2.3. Disabling an Account

You may find yourself needing to disable an account (lock out a user) as a disciplinary measure, for the purposes of an investigation, or simply in the event of a prolonged or definitive absence of a user. A disabled account means the user cannot login or gain access to the machine. The account remains intact on the machine and no files or data are deleted; it is simply inaccessible. This is accomplished by using the command `passwd -l user` (lock). Re-enabling the account is done in similar fashion, with the -u option (unlock).

5.2.4. Managing Unix Groups

The `addgroup` and `delgroup` commands add or delete a group, respectively. The `groupmod` command modifies a group's information (its gid or identifier). The command `gpasswd group` changes the password for the group, while the `gpasswd -r group` command deletes it.

Working with Several Groups

Each user may be a member of many groups. A user's main group is, by default, created during initial user configuration. By default, each file that a user creates belongs to the user, as well as to the user's main group. This is not always desirable; for example, when the user needs to work in a directory shared by a group other than their main group. In this case, the user needs to change groups using one of the following commands: newgrp, which starts a new shell, or sg, which simply executes a command using the supplied alternate group. These commands also allow the user to join a group to which they do not currently belong. If the group is password protected, they will need to supply the appropriate password before the command is executed.

Alternatively, the user can set the setgid bit on the directory, which causes files created in that directory to automatically belong to the correct group. For more details, see sidebar " setgid directory and *sticky bit*" [page 58].

The id command displays the current state of a user, with their personal identifier (uid variable), current main group (gid variable), and the list of groups to which they belong (groups variable).

5.3. Configuring Services

In this section we will take a look at services (sometimes called daemons), or programs that run as a background process and perform various functions for the system. We will start by discussing configuration files and will proceed to explain how some important services (such as SSH, PostgreSQL, and Apache) function and how they can be configured.

5.3.1. Configuring a Specific Program

When you want to configure an unknown package, you must proceed in stages. First, you should read what the package maintainer has documented. The /usr/share/doc/*package*/README. Debian file is a good place to start. This file will often contain information about the package, including pointers that may refer you to other documentation. You will often save yourself a lot of time, and avoid a lot of frustration, by reading this file first since it often details the most common errors and solutions to most common problems.

Next, you should look at the software's official documentation. Refer to section 6.1, "Documentation Sources" [page 124] for tips on how to find various documentation sources. The dpkg -L *package* command gives a list of files included in the package; you can therefore quickly identify the available documentation (as well as the configuration files, located in /etc/). Also, dpkg -s *package* displays the package meta-data and shows any possible recommended or suggested packages; in there, you can find documentation or perhaps a utility that will ease the configuration of the software.

Finally, the configuration files are often self-documented by many explanatory comments detailing the various possible values for each configuration setting. In some cases, you can get software up and running by uncommenting a single line in the configuration file. In other cases, examples of configuration files are provided in the /usr/share/doc/*package*/examples/ directory. They may serve as a basis for your own configuration file.

5.3.2. Configuring SSH for Remote Logins

SSH allows you to remotely log into a machine, transfer files, or execute commands. It is an industry standard tool (ssh) and service (sshd) for connecting to machines remotely.

While the *openssh-server* package is installed by default, the *SSH* service is disabled by default and thus is not started at boot time. You can manually start the SSH service with systemctl start ssh or configure it to start at boot time with systemctl enable ssh.

The SSH service has a relatively sane default configuration, but given its powerful capabilities and sensitive nature, it is good to know what you can do with its configuration file, /etc/ssh/sshd_config. All the options are documented in sshd_config(5).

The default configuration disables password-based logins for the root user, which means you must first set up SSH keys with ssh-keygen. You can extend this to all users by setting PasswordAuthentication to no, or you can lift this restriction by changing PermitRootLogin to yes (instead of the default prohibit-password). The SSH service listens by default on port 22 but you can change this with the Port directive.

To apply the new settings, you should run systemctl reload ssh.

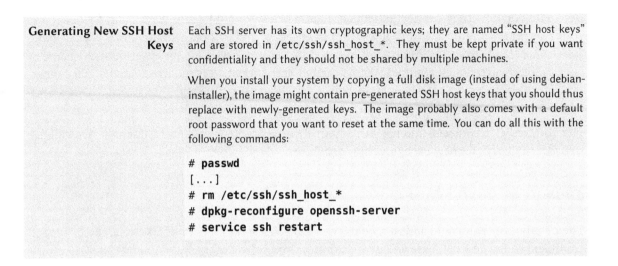

Generating New SSH Host Keys

Each SSH server has its own cryptographic keys; they are named "SSH host keys" and are stored in /etc/ssh/ssh_host_*. They must be kept private if you want confidentiality and they should not be shared by multiple machines.

When you install your system by copying a full disk image (instead of using debian-installer), the image might contain pre-generated SSH host keys that you should thus replace with newly-generated keys. The image probably also comes with a default root password that you want to reset at the same time. You can do all this with the following commands:

```
# passwd
[...]
# rm /etc/ssh/ssh_host_*
# dpkg-reconfigure openssh-server
# service ssh restart
```

5.3.3. Configuring PostgreSQL Databases

PostgreSQL is a database server. It is rarely useful on its own but is used by many other services to store data. Those services will generally access the database server over the network and usually require authentication credentials to be able to connect. Setting up those services thus requires creating PostgreSQL databases and user accounts with appropriate privileges on the database. To be able to do that, we need the service to be running, so let's start it with systemctl start postgresql.

Multiple PostgreSQL versions supported

The PostgreSQL packaging allows for multiple versions of the database server to be co-installed. It is also possible to handle multiple *clusters* (a cluster is a collection of databases served by the same postmaster). To achieve this, the configuration files are stored in /etc/postgresql/*version/cluster-name/*.

In order for clusters to run side-by-side, each new cluster gets assigned the next available port number (usually 5433 for the second cluster). The postgresql.service file is an empty shell, making it easy to act on all clusters together as each cluster has its own unit (postgresql@*version-cluster*.service).

Connection Type and Client Authentication

By default, PostgreSQL listens for incoming connections in two ways: on TCP port 5432 of the local-host interface and on file-based socket /var/run/postgresql/.s.PGSQL.5432. This can be configured in postgresql.conf with various directives: listen_addresses for the addresses to listen to, port for the TCP port, and unix_socket_directories to define the directory where the file-based sockets are created.

Depending on how they connect, clients are authenticated in different ways. The `pg_hba.conf` configuration file defines who is allowed to connect on each socket and how they are authenticated. By default, connections on the file-based socket use the Unix user account as the name of the PostgreSQL user, and it assumes that no further authentication is required. On the TCP connection, PostgreSQL requires the user to authenticate with a username and a password (though not a Unix username/password but rather one managed by PostgreSQL itself).

The postgres user is special and has full administrative privileges over all databases. We will use this identity to create new users and new databases.

Creating Users and Databases

The `createuser` command adds a new user and `dropuser` removes one. Likewise, the `createdb` command adds a new database and `dropdb` removes one. Each of these commands have their own manual pages but we will discuss some of the options here. Each command acts on the default cluster (running on port 5432) but you can pass --port=*port* to modify users and databases of an alternate cluster.

These commands must connect to the PostgreSQL server to do their job and they must be authenticated as a user with sufficient privileges to be able to execute the specified operation. The easiest way to achieve this is to use the postgres Unix account and connect over the file-based socket:

```
# su - postgres
$ createuser -P king_phisher
Enter password for new role:
Enter it again:
$ createdb -T template0 -E UTF-8 -O king_phisher king_phisher
$ exit
```

In the example above, the -P option asks `createuser` to query for a password once it creates the new king_phisher user. Looking at the `createdb` command, the -O defines the user owning the new database (which will thus have full rights to create tables and grant permissions and so on). We also want to be able to use Unicode strings, so we add the -E UTF-8 option to set the encoding, which in turn requires us to use the -T option to pick another database template.

We can now test that we can connect to the database over the socket listening on localhost (-h localhost) as the king_phisher user (-U king_phisher):

```
# psql -h localhost -U king_phisher king_phisher
Password for user king_phisher:
psql (9.5.2)
SSL connection (protocol: TLSv1.2, cipher: ECDHE-RSA-AES256-GCM-SHA384, bits: 256,
    ➥ compression: off)
Type "help" for help.

king_phisher=>
```

As you can see, the connection was successful.

Managing PostgreSQL Clusters

First, it is worth noting that the concept of "PostgreSQL cluster" is a Debian-specific addition and that you will not find any reference to this term in the official PostgreSQL documentation. From the point of view of the PostgreSQL tools, such a cluster is just an instance of a database server running on a specific port.

That said, Debian's *postgresql-common* package provides multiple tools to manage such clusters: pg_createcluster, pg_dropcluster, pg_ctlcluster, pg_upgradecluster, pg_renamecluster, and pg_lsclusters. We won't cover all those tools here, but you can refer to their respective manual pages for more information.

What you must know is that when a new major version of PostgreSQL gets installed on your system, it will create a new cluster that will run on the next port (usually 5433) and you will keep using the old version until you migrate your databases from the old cluster to the new one.

You can retrieve a list of all the clusters and their status with pg_lsclusters. More importantly, you can automate the migration of your cluster to the latest PostgreSQL version with pg_upgradecluster *old-version cluster-name*. For this to succeed, you might have to first remove the (empty) cluster created for the new version (with pg_dropcluster *new-version cluster-name*). The old cluster is not dropped in the process, but it also won't be started automatically. You can drop it once you have checked that the upgraded cluster works fine.

5.3.4. Configuring Apache

A typical Kali Linux installation includes the Apache web server, provided by the *apache2* package. Being a network service, it is disabled by default. You can manually start it with systemctl start apache2.

With more and more applications being distributed as web applications, it is important to have some knowledge of Apache in order to host those applications, whether for local usage or for making them available over the network.

Apache is a modular server and many features are implemented by external modules that the main program loads during its initialization. The default configuration only enables the most common modules, but enabling new modules is easily done by running a2enmod *module*. Use a2dismod *module* to disable a module. These programs actually only create (or delete) symbolic links in /etc/apache2/mods-enabled/, pointing at the actual files (stored in /etc/apache2/mods-available/).

There are many modules available, but two are worth initial consideration: PHP and SSL. Web applications written with PHP are executed by the Apache web server with the help of the dedicated module provided by the *libapache-mod-php* package, and its installation automatically enables the module.

Apache 2.4 includes the SSL module required for secure HTTP (HTTPS) out of the box. It first needs to be enabled with `a2enmod ssl`, then the required directives must be added to the configuration files. A configuration example is provided in `/etc/apache2/sites-available/default-ssl.conf`. See `http://httpd.apache.org/docs/2.4/mod/mod_ssl.html` for more information.

The full list of standard Apache modules can be found online at `http://httpd.apache.org/docs/2.4/mod/index.html`.

With its default configuration, the web server listens on port 80 (as configured in `/etc/apache2/ports.conf`), and serves pages from the `/var/www/html/` directory by default (as configured in `/etc/apache2/sites-enabled/000-default.conf`).

Configuring Virtual Hosts

A virtual host is an extra identity for the web server. The same Apache process can serve multiple websites (say www.kali.org and www.offensive-security.com) because the HTTP requests embed both the name of the website requested and the URL localpart (this feature is known as *name-based virtual hosts*).

The default configuration for Apache 2 enables name-based virtual hosts. In addition, a default virtual host is defined in the /etc/apache2/sites-enabled/000-default.conf file; this virtual host will be used if no host matching the request sent by the client is found.

> **Important**
>
> ⚠ Requests concerning unknown virtual hosts will always be served by the first defined virtual host, which is why the package ships a `000-default.conf` configuration file, which sorts first among all other files that you might create.

Each extra virtual host is then described by a file stored in `/etc/apache2/sites-available/`. The file is usually named after the hostname of the website followed by a .conf suffix (for example: `www.example.com.conf`). You can then enable the new virtual host with `a2ensite www.example.com`. Here is a minimal virtualhost configuration for a website whose files are stored in `/srv/www.example.com/www/` (defined with the DocumentRoot option):

```
<VirtualHost *:80>
ServerName www.example.com
ServerAlias example.com
```

```
DocumentRoot /srv/www.example.com/www
</VirtualHost>
```

You might also consider adding CustomLog and ErrorLog directives to configure Apache to output logs in files dedicated to the virtual host.

Common Directives

This section briefly reviews some of the commonly-used Apache configuration directives.

The main configuration file usually includes several Directory blocks; they allow specifying different behaviors for the server depending on the location of the file being served. Such a block commonly includes Options and AllowOverride directives:

```
<Directory /var/www>
Options Includes FollowSymLinks
AllowOverride All
DirectoryIndex index.php index.html index.htm
</Directory>
```

The DirectoryIndex directive contains a list of files to try when the client request matches a directory. The first existing file in the list is used and sent as a response.

The Options directive is followed by a list of options to enable. The None value disables all options; correspondingly, All enables them all except MultiViews. Available options include:

- ExecCGI—indicates that CGI scripts can be executed.
- FollowSymLinks—tells the server that symbolic links can be followed, and that the response should contain the contents of the target of such links.
- SymLinksIfOwnerMatch—also tells the server to follow symbolic links, but only when the link and its target have the same owner.
- Includes—enables *Server Side Includes* (SSI). These are directives embedded in HTML pages and executed on the fly for each request.
- Indexes—tells the server to list the contents of a directory if the HTTP request sent by the client points to a directory without an index file (that is, when no files mentioned by the DirectoryIndex directive exist in this directory).
- MultiViews—enables content negotiation; this can be used by the server to return a web page matching the preferred language as configured in the browser.

Requiring Authentication   In some circumstances, access to part of a website needs to be restricted, so only legitimate users who provide a username and a password are granted access to the contents.

The .htaccess file contains Apache configuration directives enforced each time a request concerns an element from the directory where the .htaccess file is stored. These directives are recursive, expanding the scope to all subdirectories.

Most of the directives that can occur in a Directory block are also legal in an .htaccess file. The AllowOverride directive lists all the options that can be enabled or disabled by way of .htaccess. A common use of this option is to restrict ExecCGI, so that the administrator chooses which users are allowed to run programs under the web server's identity (the www-data user).

Example 5.3   *.htaccess File Requiring Authentication*

```
Require valid-user
AuthName "Private directory"
AuthType Basic
AuthUserFile /etc/apache2/authfiles/htpasswd-private
```

Basic Authentication Offers No Security	The authentication system used in the above example (Basic) has minimal security as the password is sent in clear text (it is only encoded as *base64*, which is a simple encoding rather than an encryption method). It should also be noted that the documents protected by this mechanism also go over the network in the clear. If security is important, the entire HTTP session should be encrypted with Transport Layer Security (TLS).

The /etc/apache2/authfiles/htpasswd-private file contains a list of users and passwords; it is commonly manipulated with the htpasswd command. For example, the following command is used to add a user or change their password:

```
# htpasswd /etc/apache2/authfiles/htpasswd-private user
New password:
Re-type new password:
Adding password for user user
```

Restricting Access   The Require directive controls access restrictions for a directory (and its subdirectories, recursively).

It can be used to restrict access based on many criteria; we will stop at describing access restriction based on the IP address of the client but it can be made much more powerful than that, especially when several Require directives are combined within a RequireAll block.

For instance, you could restrict access to the local network with the following directive:

```
Require ip 192.168.0.0/16
```

5.4. Managing Services

Kali uses systemd as its init system, which is not only responsible for the boot sequence, but also permanently acts as a full featured service manager, starting and monitoring services.

systemd can be queried and controlled with systemctl. Without any argument, it runs the systemctl list-units command, which outputs a list of the active *units*. If you run systemctl status, the output shows a hierarchical overview of the running services. Comparing both outputs, you immediately see that there are multiple kinds of units and that services are only one among them.

Each service is represented by a *service unit*, which is described by a service file usually shipped in /lib/systemd/system/ (or /run/systemd/system/, or /etc/systemd/system/; they are listed by increasing order of importance, and the last one wins). Each is possibly modified by other *service-name*.service.d/*.conf files in the same set of directories. Those unit files are plain text files whose format is inspired by the well-known "*.ini" files of Microsoft Windows, with *key = value* pairs grouped between [*section*] headers. Here we see a sample service file for /lib/systemd/system/ssh.service:

```
[Unit]
Description=OpenBSD Secure Shell server
After=network.target auditd.service
ConditionPathExists=!/etc/ssh/sshd_not_to_be_run

[Service]
EnvironmentFile=-/etc/default/ssh
ExecStart=/usr/sbin/sshd -D $SSHD_OPTS
ExecReload=/bin/kill -HUP $MAINPID
KillMode=process
Restart=on-failure
RestartPreventExitStatus=255
Type=notify

[Install]
WantedBy=multi-user.target
Alias=sshd.service
```

Target units are another part of systemd's design. They represent a desired state that you want to attain in terms of activated units (which means a running service in the case of service units). They exist mainly as a way to group dependencies on other units. When the system starts, it enables the units required to reach the default.target (which is a symlink to graphical.target, and which in turn depends on multi-user.target). So all the dependencies of those targets get activated during boot.

Such dependencies are expressed with the Wants directive on the target unit. But you don't have to edit the target unit to add new dependencies, you can also create a symlink pointing to the dependent unit in the /etc/systemd/system/*target-name*.target.wants/ directory. And this is exactly what systemctl enable *foo.service* does. When you enable a service, you tell systemd to add a dependency on the targets listed in the WantedBy entry of the [Install] section of the service unit file. Conversely, systemctl disable *foo.service* drops the same symlink and thus the dependency.

The enable and disable commands do not change anything regarding the current status of the services. They only influence what will happen at next boot. If you want to run the service immediately, you should execute systemctl start *foo.service*. Conversely, you can stop it with systemctl stop *foo.service*. You can also inspect the current status of a service with systemctl status *foo.service*, which usefully includes the latest lines of the associated log. After having changed the configuration of a service, you may wish to reload it or restart it: those operations are done with systemctl reload *foo.service* and systemctl restart *foo. service* respectively.

```
# systemctl status postgresql
● postgresql.service - PostgreSQL RDBMS
   Loaded: loaded (/lib/systemd/system/postgresql.service; disabled; vendor preset:
      ➥ disabled)
   Active: inactive (dead)
# ls -al /etc/systemd/system/multi-user.target.wants/postgresql.service
ls: cannot access '/etc/systemd/system/multi-user.target.wants/postgresql.service': No
   ➥ such file or directory
# systemctl enable postgresql
[...]
# ls -al /etc/systemd/system/multi-user.target.wants/postgresql.service
lrwxrwxrwx 1 root root 38 Apr 21 16:21 /etc/systemd/system/multi-user.target.wants/
   ➥ postgresql.service -> /lib/systemd/system/postgresql.service
# systemctl status postgresql
● postgresql.service - PostgreSQL RDBMS
   Loaded: loaded (/lib/systemd/system/postgresql.service; enabled; vendor preset:
      ➥ disabled)
   Active: inactive (dead)
# systemctl start postgresql
# systemctl status postgresql
● postgresql.service - PostgreSQL RDBMS
   Loaded: loaded (/lib/systemd/system/postgresql.service; enabled; vendor preset:
      ➥ disabled)
   Active: active (exited) since Thu 2016-04-21 16:22:29 EDT; 2s ago
  Process: 6355 ExecStart=/bin/true (code=exited, status=0/SUCCESS)
 Main PID: 6355 (code=exited, status=0/SUCCESS)

Apr 21 16:22:29 kali-rolling systemd[1]: Starting PostgreSQL RDBMS...
Apr 21 16:22:29 kali-rolling systemd[1]: Started PostgreSQL RDBMS.
```

5.5. Summary

In this chapter, we learned how to configure Kali Linux. We configured network settings, talked about users and groups, and discussed how to create and modify user accounts, set passwords, disable accounts, and manage groups. Finally, we discussed services and explained how to set up and maintain generic services, specifically SSH, PostgreSQL, and Apache.

Summary Tips:

- In a typical desktop installation, you will have *NetworkManager* already installed and it can be controlled and configured through GNOME's control center and through the top-right menu.

- You can configure the network from the command line with the `ifup` and `ifdown` tools, which read their instructions from the `/etc/network/interfaces` configuration file. An even newer tool, *systemd-networkd* works with the *systemd* init system.

- By default, the database of Unix users and groups consists of the textual files `/etc/passwd` (list of users), `/etc/shadow` (encrypted passwords of users), `/etc/group` (list of groups), and `/etc/gshadow` (encrypted passwords of groups).

- You can use the `getent` command to consult the user database and other system databases.

- The `adduser` command asks a few questions before creating the account, but is a straight-forward way to create a new user account.

- Several commands can be used to modify specific fields in the user database including: `passwd` (change password), `chfn` (change full name and the GECOS, or general information field), `chsh` (change login shell), `chage` (change password age), and `passwd -e` *user* (forces the user to change their password the next time they log in).

- Each user can be a member of one or multiple groups. Several commands can be used to modify group identity: `newgrp` changes the current group ID, `sg` executes a command using the supplied alternate group, the setgid bit can be placed on a directory, causing files created in that directory to automatically belong to the correct group. In addition, the `id` command displays the current state of a user including a list of their group membership.

- You can manually start SSH with `systemctl start ssh` or permanently enable it with `systemctl enable ssh`. The default configuration disables password-based logins for the root user, which means you must first setup SSH keys with `ssh-keygen`.

- PostgreSQL is a database server. It is rarely useful on its own but is used by many other services to store data.

- A typical Kali Linux installation includes the Apache web server, provided by the *apache2* package. Being a network service, it is disabled by default. You can manually start it with `systemctl start apache2`.

- With its default configuration, Apache listens on port 80 (as configured in `/etc/apache2/ports.conf`), and serves pages from the `/var/www/html/` directory by default (as configured in `/etc/apache2/sites-enabled/000-default.conf`).

Now that we have tackled Linux fundamentals and Kali Linux installation and configuration, let's discuss how to troubleshoot Kali and teach you some tools and tricks to get you back up and running when you run into problems.

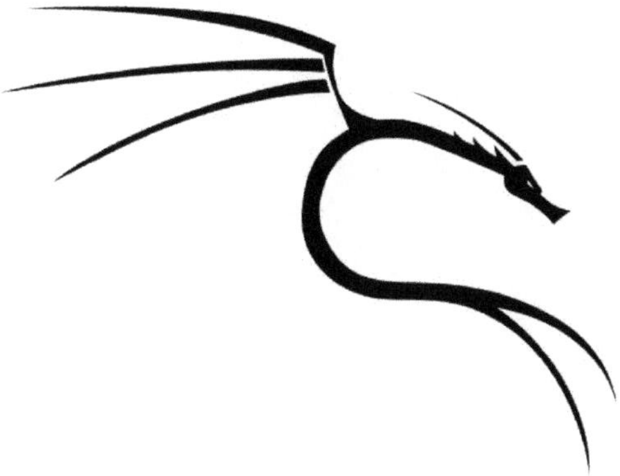

Keywords

Documentation
Forums
IRC channel
Bug report

KALI LINUX
REVEALED

Helping Yourself and Getting Help

Contents

No matter how many years of experience you have, there is no doubt that—sooner or later—you will encounter a problem. Solving that problem is then often a matter of understanding it and then taking advantage of various resources to find a solution or work-around.

In this chapter, we will discuss the various information sources available and discuss the best strategies for finding the help you need or the solution to a problem you might be facing. We will also take you on a tour of some of the Kali Linux community resources available, including the web forums and Internet Relay Chat (IRC) channel. Lastly, we will introduce bug reporting and show you how to take advantage of bug filing systems to troubleshoot problems and lay out strategies to help you file your own bug report so that undocumented issues can be handled quickly and effectively.

6.1. Documentation Sources

Before you can understand what is really going on when there is a problem, you need to know the theoretical role played by each program involved in the problem. One of the best ways to do this is to review the program's documentation. Let's begin by discussing where, exactly, you can find documentation since it is often scattered.

How to Avoid RTFM Answers	This acronym stands for "read the f***ing manual," but can also be expanded in a friendlier variant, "read the fine manual." This phrase is sometimes used in (terse) responses to questions from newbies. It is rather abrupt, and betrays a certain annoyance at a question asked by someone who has not even bothered to read the documentation. Some say that this classic response is better than no response at all since this at least hints that the answer lies within the documentation.
	When you are posting questions, don't necessarily be offended by the occasional RTFM response, but do what you can to at least show that you have taken the time to do some research before posting the question; mention the sources that you have consulted and describe the various steps that you have personally taken to find information. This will go a long way to show that you are not lazy and are truly seeking knowledge. Following Eric Raymond's guidelines is a good way to avoid the most common mistakes and get useful answers.
	➡ http://catb.org/~esr/faqs/smart-questions.html

6.1.1. Manual Pages

Manual pages, while relatively terse in style, contain a great deal of essential information. To view a manual page, simply type man *manual-page*. The manual page usually coincides with the command name. For example, to learn about the possible options for the cp command, you would type man cp at the command prompt.

Man pages not only document programs accessible from the command line, but also configuration files, system calls, C library functions, and so forth. Sometimes names can collide. For example, the shell's read command has the same name as the read system call. This is why manual pages are organized in the following numbered sections:

1. Commands that can be executed from the command line
2. System calls (functions provided by the kernel)
3. Library functions (provided by system libraries)
4. Devices (on Unix-like systems, these are special files, usually placed in the /dev/ directory)
5. Configuration files (formats and conventions)
6. Games
7. Sets of macros and standards
8. System administration commands
9. Kernel routines

You can specify the section of the manual page that you are looking for: to view the documentation for the read system call, you would type man 2 read. When no section is explicitly specified, the first section that has a manual page with the requested name will be shown. Thus, man shadow returns shadow(5) because there are no manual pages for *shadow* in sections 1–4.

Of course, if you do not know the names of the commands, the manual is not going to be of much use to you. Enter the apropos command, which searches manual pages (or more specifically their short descriptions) for any keywords that you provide. The apropos command then returns a list of manual pages whose summary mentions the requested keywords along with the one-line summary from the manual page. If you choose your keywords well, you will find the name of the command that you need.

Example 6.1 *Finding cp with apropos*

```
$ apropos "copy file"
cp (1)              - copy files and directories
cpio (1)            - copy files to and from archives
gvfs-copy (1)       - Copy files
gvfs-move (1)       - Copy files
hcopy (1)           - copy files from or to an HFS volume
install (1)         - copy files and set attributes
ntfscp (8)          - copy file to an NTFS volume.
```

Browsing Documentation by Following Links   Many manual pages have a "See Also" section, usually near the end of the document, which refers to other manual pages relevant to similar commands, or to external documentation. You can use this section to find relevant documentation even when the first choice is not optimal.

In addition to man, you can use konqueror (in KDE) and yelp (in GNOME) to search man pages as well.

6.1.2. Info Documents

The GNU project has written manuals for most of its programs in the *info* format; this is why many manual pages refer to the corresponding *info* documentation. This format offers some advantages but the default program to view these documents (also called info) is slightly more complex. You would be well advised to use pinfo instead (from the *pinfo* package). To install it, simply run apt update followed by apt install pinfo (see section 8.2.2.2, "Installing Packages with APT" [page 177]).

The *info* documentation has a hierarchical structure and if you invoke pinfo without parameters, it will display a list of the nodes available at the first level. Usually, nodes bear the name of the corresponding commands.

You can use the arrow keys to navigate between nodes. Alternatively, you could also use a graphical browser (which is a lot more user-friendly) such as konqueror or yelp.

As far as language translations are concerned, the *info* system is always in English and is not suitable for translation, unlike the man page system. However, when you ask the pinfo program to display a non-existing *info* page, it will fall back on the *man* page by the same name (if it exists), which might be translated.

6.1.3. Package-Specific Documentation

Each package includes its own documentation and even the least documented programs generally have a README file containing some interesting and/or important information. This documentation is installed in the /usr/share/doc/*package*/ directory (where *package* represents the name of the package). If the documentation is particularly large, it may not be included in the program's main package, but might be offloaded to a dedicated package which is usually named *package*-doc. The main package generally recommends the documentation package so that you can easily find it.

The /usr/share/doc/*package*/ directory also contains some files provided by Debian, which complete the documentation by specifying the package's particularities or improvements compared to a traditional installation of the software. The README.Debian file also indicates all of the adaptations that were made to comply with the Debian Policy. The changelog.Debian.gz file allows the user to follow the modifications made to the package over time; it is very useful to try to understand what has changed between two installed versions that do not have the same behavior. Finally, there is sometimes a NEWS.Debian.gz file that documents the major changes in the program that may directly concern the administrator.

6.1.4. Websites

In many cases, you can find websites that are used to distribute free software programs and to bring together the community of its developers and users. These sites are loaded with relevant information in various forms such as official documentation, frequently asked questions (FAQ), and mailing list archives. In most cases, the FAQ or mailing list archives address problems that you have encountered. As you search for information online, it is immensely valuable to master search syntax. One quick tip: try restricting a search to a specific domain, like the one dedicated to the program that is giving you trouble. If the search returns too many pages or if the results do not match what you seek, you can add the keyword **kali** or **debian** to limit results and target relevant information.

From the Error to a Solution	If the software returns a very specific error message, enter it into a search engine (between double quotes, ", in order to search for the complete phrase, rather than the individual keywords). In most cases, the first links returned will contain the answer that you need.
	In other cases, you will get very general errors, such as "Permission denied". In this case, it is best to check the permissions of the elements involved (files, user ID, groups, etc.). In short, don't get in the habit of always using a search engine to find a solution to your problem. You will find it is much too easy to forget to use common sense.

If you do not know the address of the software's website, there are various means of locating it. First, look for a Homepage field in the package's meta-information (`apt show` *package*). Alternatively, the package description may contain a link to the program's official website. If no URL is indicated, the package maintainer may have included a URL in the `/usr/share/doc/`*package*`/copyright` file. Finally, you may be able to use a search engine (such as Google, DuckDuckGo, Yahoo, etc.) to find the software's website.

6.1.5. Kali Documentation at docs.kali.org

The Kali project maintains a collection of useful documentation at `http://docs.kali.org`. While this book covers a large part of what you should know about Kali Linux, the documentation there might still be useful as it contains step-by-step instructions (much like how-tos) on many topics.

➡ `http://docs.kali.org/`

Let's review the various topics covered there:

- Getting started: a series of instructions, including download instructions, for those new to Kali
- Kali Linux Live: documentation describing how to use Kali Linux as a live system
- Installing Kali Linux: various documents describing Kali Linux installation, including how to install it side-by-side with other operating systems

- Kali Linux on ARM: many recipes about running Kali Linux on various ARM-based devices
- Using Kali Linux: multiple how-tos covering many common requests
- Customizing Kali Linux: instructions for the tinkerers who like to rebuild Kali based on their own requirements
- Kali Community Support: pointers to the various communities where you can get support and explanations on how to submit bug reports
- Kali Linux Policies: explanations about what makes Kali Linux special when compared to other Linux distributions
- The Kali Linux Dojo: videos of Black Hat and DEF CON workshops

6.2. Kali Linux Communities

There are many Kali Linux communities around the world using many different tools to communicate (forums and social networks, for example). In this section, we will only present two official Kali Linux communities.

6.2.1. Web Forums on forums.kali.org

The official community forums for the Kali Linux project are located at forums.kali.org[1]. Like every web-based forum, you must create an account to be able to post and the system remembers what posts you have already seen, making it easy to follow conversations on a regular basis.

Before posting, you should read the forum rules:

➡ `http://docs.kali.org/community/kali-linux-community-forums`

We won't copy them here but it is worth noting that you are not allowed to speak about illegal activities such as breaking into other people's networks. You must be respectful of other community members so as to create a welcoming community. Advertising is banned and off-topic discussions are to be avoided. There are enough categories to cover everything that you would like to discuss about Kali Linux.

6.2.2. #kali-linux IRC Channel on Freenode

IRC is a real-time chat system. Discussions happen in chat rooms that are called *channels* and are usually centered around a particular topic or community. The Kali Linux project uses the #kali-linux channel on the Freenode[2] network (you can use chat.freenode.net as IRC server, on port 6667 for a TLS-encrypted connection or port 6666 for a clear-text connection).

---

[1]`http://forums.kali.org`
[2]`http://www.freenode.net`

To join the discussions on IRC, you have to use an IRC client such as `hexchat` (in graphical mode) or `irssi` (in console mode). There is also a web-based client available on webchat.freenode.net[3].

While it is really easy to join the conversation, you should be aware that IRC channels have their own rules and that there are channel operators (their nickname is prefixed with @) who can enforce the rules: they can kick you out of the channel (or even ban you if you continue to disobey the rules). The #kali-linux channel is no exception. The rules have been documented here:

➡ `http://docs.kali.org/community/kali-linux-irc-channel`

To summarize the rules: you have to be friendly, tolerant, and reasonable. You should avoid off-topic discussions. In particular, discussions about illegal activities, warez/cracks/pirated software, politics, and religions are forbidden. Keep in mind that your IP address will be available to others.

If you want to ask for help, follow the recommendations listed in "How to Avoid RTFM Answers" [page 124]: do your research first and share the results. When you are asked for supplementary information, please provide it accurately (if you must provide some verbose output, don't paste it in the channel directly, instead use a service like Pastebin[4] and post only the Pastebin URL).

Do not expect an immediate answer. Even though IRC is a real-time communication platform, participants log in from all over the world, so time zones and work schedules vary. It may take a few minutes or hours for someone to respond to your question. However, when others include your nickname in a reply, your nick will be highlighted and most IRC clients will notify you, so leave your client connected and be patient.

6.3. Filing a Good Bug Report

If all of your efforts to resolve a problem fail, it is possible that the problem is due to a bug in the program. In this case, the problem may have resulted in a bug report. You can search for bug reports to find a solution to your problem but let's take a look at the procedure of reporting a bug to Kali, Debian, or directly to the upstream developers so you understand the process should you need to submit your own report.

The goal of a bug report is to provide enough information so that the developers or maintainers of the (supposedly) faulty program can reproduce the problem, debug its behavior, and develop a fix. This means that your bug report must contain appropriate information and must be directed to the correct person or project team. The report must also be well-written and thorough, ensuring a faster response.

The exact procedure for the bug report will vary depending on where you will submit the report (Kali, Debian, upstream developers) but there are some generic recommendations that apply to all cases. In this chapter we will discuss those recommendations.

---

[3]`http://webchat.freenode.net`
[4]`http://pastebin.com`

6.3.1. Generic Recommendations

Let's discuss some general recommendations and guidelines that will help you submit a bug report that is clear, comprehensive, and improves the chances that the bug will be addressed by the developers in a timely fashion.

How to Communicate

Write Your Report in English The Free Software community is international and unless you know your interlocutor, you should be using plain English. If you are a native speaker of English, use simple sentences and avoid constructions that might be hard to understand for people with limited English skills. Even though most developers are highly intelligent, not all of them have strong English language skills. It is best never to assume.

Be Respectful of the Developers' Work Remember that most Free Software developers (including those behind Kali Linux) are benevolent and are spending their limited free time to work on the software that you are freely using. Many are doing this out of altruism. Thus, when you file a bug report, be respectful (even if the bug looks like an obvious mistake by the developer) and don't assume that they owe you a fix. Thank them for their contribution instead.

If you know how to modify and recompile the software, offer to assist the developers in testing any patches that they submit to you. This will show them that you are willing to invest your own time as well.

Be Reactive and Ready to Provide More Information In some cases, the developer will come back to you with requests for more information or requests for you to try to re-create the problem perhaps by using different options or using an updated package. You should try to respond to those queries as quickly as possible. The quicker you submit your response, the higher the chance that they will be able to solve it quickly while the initial analysis is still fresh in their mind.

While you should aim to respond quickly, you should also not go too fast: the data submitted must be correct and it must contain everything that the developers requested. They will be annoyed if they have to request something a second time.

What to Put in the Bug Report

Instructions to Reproduce the Problem To be able to reproduce the issue, the developers need to know what you are using, where you got it from, and how you installed it.

You should provide precise, step-by-step instructions describing how to reproduce the problem. If you need to use some data to reproduce the problem, attach the corresponding file to the bug report. Try to come up with the minimal set of instructions needed to reproduce the bug.

Give Some Context and Set Your Expectations Explain what you were trying to do and how you expected the program to behave.

In some cases, the bug is only triggered because you were using the program in a way that it was not designed to operate by the developers. By explaining what you were trying to achieve, you will allow the developers to clearly see when this is the case.

In some other cases, the behavior that you describe as a bug might actually be the normal behavior. Be explicit about what you expected the program to do. This will clarify the situation for the developers. They may either improve the behavior or improve the documentation, but at least they know that the behavior of their program is confusing some users!

Be Specific Include the versions numbers of the software that you use, possibly with the version numbers of their dependencies. When you refer to something that you downloaded, include its complete URL.

When you get an error message, quote it exactly as you saw it. If possible, include a copy of your screen output or a screenshot. Include a copy of any relevant log file, ensuring that you remove any sensitive data first.

Mention Possible Fixes or Workarounds Before filing the bug report, you probably tried to resolve the problem. Explain what you tried and what results you received. Be very clear about what is a fact and what was just a hypothesis on your part.

If you did an Internet search and found some explanations about a similar problem, you can mention them, in particular when you found other similar bug reports in the Debian bug tracker or in the upstream bug tracker.

If you found a way of achieving the desired result without triggering the bug, please document that as well. This will help other users who are hit by the same issue.

Long Bug Reports Are Fine A two-line bug report is insufficient; providing all the information needed usually requires several paragraphs (or sometimes pages) of text.

Supply all the information you can. Try to stick to what is relevant, but if you are uncertain, too much is better than too little.

If your bug report is really long, take some time to structure the content and provide a short summary at the start.

Miscellaneous Tips

Avoid Filing Duplicate Bug Reports In the Free Software world, all bug trackers are public. Open issues can be browsed and they even have a search feature. Thus, before filing a new bug report, try to determine if your problem has already been reported by someone else.

If you find an existing bug report, subscribe to it and possibly add supplementary information. Do not post comments such as "Me too" or "+1"; they serve no purpose. But you can indicate that you are available for further tests if the original submitter did not offer this.

If you have not found any report of your problem, go ahead and file it. If you have found related tickets, be sure to mention them.

Ensure You Use the Latest Version It is very frustrating for developers to receive bug reports for problems that they have already solved or problems that they can't reproduce with the version that they are using (developers almost always use the latest version of their product). Even when older versions are maintained by the developers, the support is often limited to security fixes and major problems. Are you sure that your bug is one of those?

That is why, before filing a bug report, you should make sure that you are using the latest version of the problematic system and application and that you can reproduce the problem in that situation.

If Kali Linux does not offer the latest version of the application (neither in kali-rolling nor in kali-bleeding-edge, see section 8.1.3.3, "The Kali-Bleeding-Edge Repository" [page 174]), you have alternative solutions: you can try a manual installation of the latest version in a throw-away virtual machine, or you can review the upstream ChangeLog (or Git commit history) to see that there hasn't been any change that could fix the problem that you are seeing (and then file the bug even though you did not try the latest version).

Do Not Mix Multiple Issues in a Single Bug Report File one bug report per issue. That way, the subsequent discussions do not get too messy and each bug can be fixed according to its own schedule. If you don't do that, either the single bug needs to be repurposed multiple times and can only be closed when all issues have been fixed, or the developers must file the supplementary reports that you should have created in the first place.

6.3.2. Where to File a Bug Report

To be able to decide where to file the bug report, you must have a good understanding of the problem and you must have identified in which piece of software the problem lies.

Ideally, you track the problem down to a file on your system and then you can use dpkg to find out which package owns that file and where that package comes from. Let's assume that you found a bug in a graphical application. After looking at the list of running processes (the output of ps auxf), you discovered that the application was started with the /usr/bin/sparta executable:

```
$ dpkg -S /usr/bin/sparta
sparta: /usr/bin/sparta
$ dpkg -s sparta | grep ^Version:
Version: 1.0.1+git20150729-0kali1
```

You learn that /usr/bin/sparta is provided by the sparta package, which is in version 1.0.1+git 20150729-0kali1. The fact that the version string contains kali indicates to you that the package comes from Kali Linux (or is modified by Kali Linux). Any package that does not have kali in its version string (or in its package name) comes straight from Debian (Debian Testing in general).

Double Check Before Filing Bugs against Debian	If you find a bug in a package imported straight from Debian, it should ideally be reported and fixed on the Debian side. However, before doing this, ensure that the problem is reproducible on a plain Debian system since Kali may have caused the problem by modifying other packages or dependencies.
	The easiest way to accomplish this is to setup a virtual machine running Debian Testing. You can find an installation ISO for Debian Testing on the Debian Installer website:
	➡ `https://www.debian.org/devel/debian-installer/`
	If you can confirm the problem in the virtual machine, then you can submit the bug to Debian by running `reportbug` within the virtual machine and following the instructions provided.

Most bug reports about the behavior of applications should be directed to their upstream projects except when facing an integration problem: in that case, the bug is a mistake in the way the software gets packaged and integrated into Debian or Kali. For example, if an application offers compile-time options that the package does not enable or the application does not work because of a missing library (thus putting into light a missing dependency in the package meta-information), you may be facing an integration problem. When you don't know what kind of problem you face, it is usually best to file the issue on both sides and to cross-reference them.

Identifying the upstream project and finding where to file the bug report is usually easy. You just have to browse the upstream website, which is referenced in the Homepage field of the packaging meta-data:

```
$ dpkg -s sparta | grep ^Homepage:
Homepage: https://github.com/SECFORCE/sparta
```

6.3.3. How to File a Bug Report

Filing a Bug Report in Kali

Kali uses a web-based bug tracker at `http://bugs.kali.org` where you can consult all the bug reports anonymously, but if you would like to comment or file a new bug report, you will need to register an account.

Signing Up for a Bug Tracker Account   To begin, simply click *Signup for new account* on the bug tracker website, as shown in Figure 6.1, "Kali Bug Tracker Start Page" [page 134].

Figure 6.1 *Kali Bug Tracker Start Page*

Next, provide a username, e-mail address, and response to the CAPTCHA challenge. Then click the Signup button to proceed (Figure 6.2, "Signup Page" [page 134]).

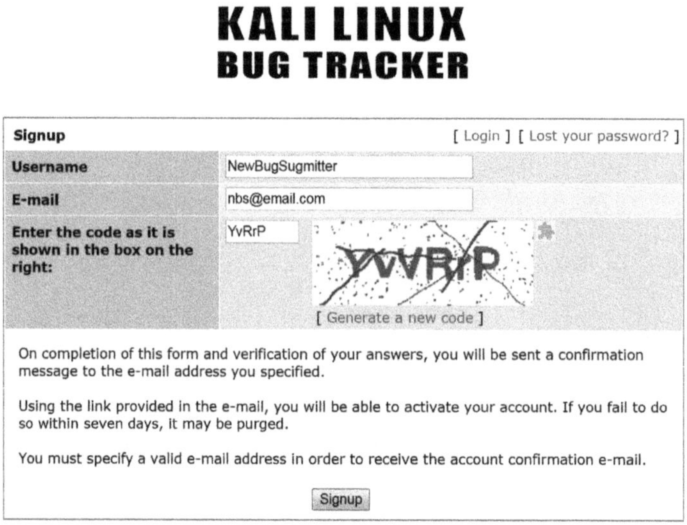

Figure 6.2 *Signup Page*

If successful, the next page (Figure 6.3, "Signup Confirmation Page" [page 135]) will notify you that the account registration has been processed, and the bug tracker system will send a confirmation email to the address you provided. You will need to click the link in the email in order to activate your account.

Once your account has been activated, click Proceed to continue to the bug tracker login page.

KALI LINUX
BUG TRACKER

**Account registration
processed.**

Congratulations, you have registered successfully ! You are now being sent a confirmation e-mail to verify your e-mail address. Visiting the link sent to you in this e-mail will activate your account.

You have seven days to complete the account confirmation process; if you fail to do so within this period, the newly-registered account may be purged.

[Proceed]

Figure 6.3   *Signup Confirmation Page*

Creating the Report   To begin your report, log into your account and click the Report Issue link on the landing page. You will be presented a form with many fields to fill, as shown in Figure 6.4, "Form to report a bug" [page 136].

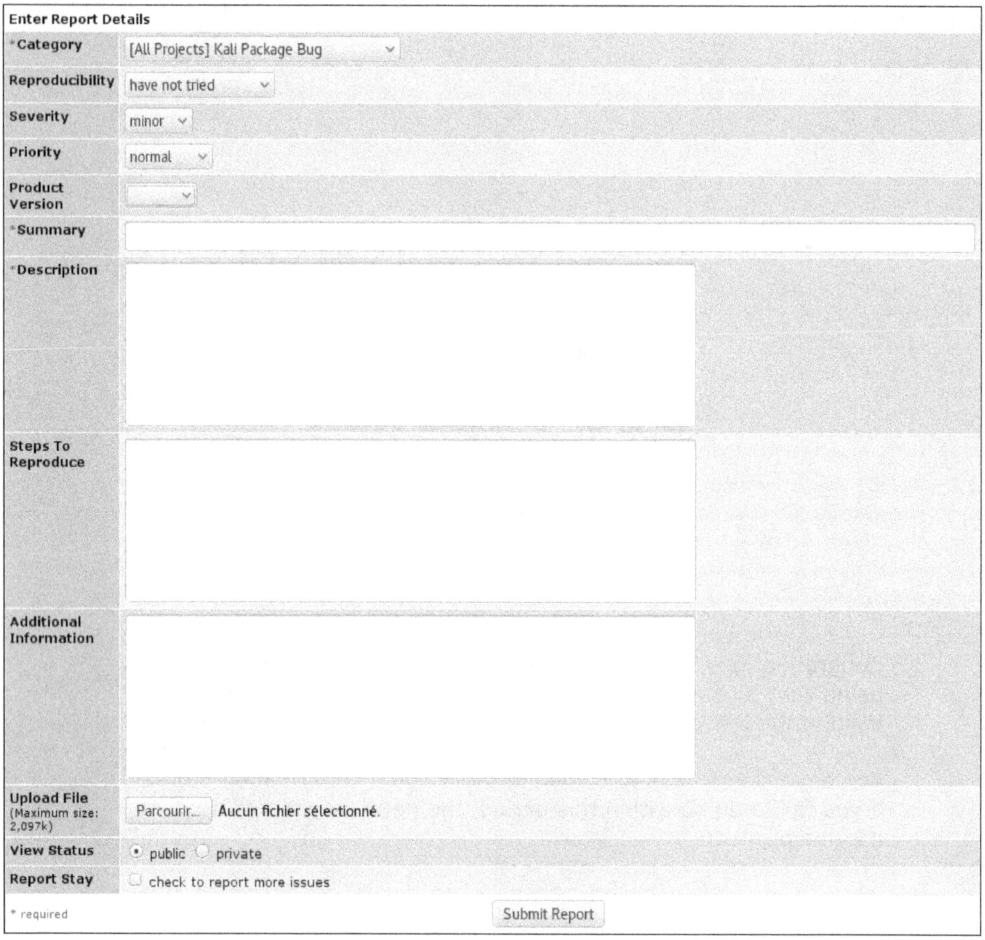

Figure 6.4 *Form to report a bug*

Here is a rundown of all the fields on the form:

Category (mandatory)   This field describes the category of the bug you are submitting. Reports that can be attributed to a specific package should be filed in the Kali Package Bug or Kali Package Improvement categories. Other reports should use the General Bug or Feature Requests categories. The remaining categories are for specific use cases: Tool Upgrade can be used to notify the Kali developers of the availability of a new version of a software packaged in Kali. New Tool Requests can be used to suggest new tools to package and integrate in the Kali distribution.

Reproducibility This field documents whether the problem is reproducible in a predictable way or if it happens only somewhat randomly.

Severity and Priority Those fields are best left unmodified as they are mainly for the developers. They can use them to sort the list of issues according to the severity of the problem and to the priority at which it must be handled.

Product Version This field should indicate what version of Kali Linux you are running (or the one which is the closest to what you are running). Think twice before reporting an issue on an old release that is no longer supported.

Summary (mandatory) This is essentially the title of your bug report and it is the first thing that people will see. Make sure that it conveys the reason why you are filing the report. Avoid generic descriptions like "X doesn't work" and opt instead for "X fails with error Y under condition Z."

Description (mandatory) This is the body of your report. Here you should enter all of the information you collected about the problem that you are experiencing. Don't forget all the recommendations given in the former section.

Steps to Reproduce In this field, list all the detailed instructions explaining how to trigger the problem.

Additional Information In this section, you can provide any additional information you believe is relevant to the issue. If you have a fix or workaround for the issue, please provide it in this section.

Upload File Not everything can be explained with plain text. This field lets you attach arbitrary files to your reports: screenshots to show the error, sample documents triggering the problem, log files, etc.

View Status Leave that field set to "public" so that everybody can see your bug report. Use "private" only for security-related reports containing information about undisclosed security vulnerabilities.

Filing a Bug Report in Debian

Debian uses a (mostly) email-based bug tracking system known as Debbugs. To open a new bug report, you will send an email (with a special syntax) to submit@bugs.debian.org. This will allocate a bug number *XXXXXX* and inform you that you can send additional information by mailing *XXX XXX*@bugs.debian.org. Each bug is associated to a Debian package. You can browse all the bugs of a given package (including the bug that you are thinking of reporting) at https://bugs.debian.org/ *package.* You can check the history of a given bug at https://bugs.debian.org/*XXXXXX*.

Setting Up Reportbug   While you can open a new bug with a simple e-mail, we recommend using `reportbug` because it will help you draft a solid bug report with all the required information. Ideally, you should run it from a Debian system (for example, in the virtual machine where you reproduced the problem).

The first run of `reportbug` starts a configuration script. First, select a skill level. You should choose Novice or Standard; we use the latter because it offers more fine-grained control. Next, select an interface and enter your personal details. Finally, select a user interface. The configuration script will allow you to use a local mail transport agent, an SMTP server, or as a last resort, a Debian SMTP server.

```
Welcome to reportbug! Since it looks like this is the first time you have
used reportbug, we are configuring its behavior. These settings will be
saved to the file "/root/.reportbugrc", which you will be free to edit
further.
Please choose the default operating mode for reportbug.

1 novice    Offer simple prompts, bypassing technical questions.

2 standard  Offer more extensive prompts, including asking about things
            that a moderately sophisticated user would be expected to
            know about Debian.

3 advanced  Like standard, but assumes you know a bit more about Debian,
    ➡ including "incoming".

4 expert    Bypass most handholding measures and preliminary triage
            routines. This mode should not be used by people unfamiliar
            with Debian's policies and operating procedures.

Select mode: [novice] standard
Please choose the default interface for reportbug.

1 text    A text-oriented console user interface

2 gtk2    A graphical (GTK+) user interface.

3 urwid   A menu-based console user interface

Select interface: text
Will reportbug often have direct Internet access? (You should answer
yes to this question unless you know what you are doing and plan to
check whether duplicate reports have been filed via some other channel.)
```

```
[Y|n|q|?]? Y
What real name should be used for sending bug reports?
[root]> Raphaël Hertzog
Which of your email addresses should be used when sending bug reports?
(Note that this address will be visible in the bug tracking system, so you
may want to use a webmail address or another address with good spam
filtering capabilities.)
[root@localhost.localdomain]> buxy@kali.org
Do you have a "mail transport agent" (MTA) like Exim, Postfix or SSMTP
configured on this computer to send mail to the Internet? [y|N|q|?]? N
Please enter the name of your SMTP host. Usually it's called something
like "mail.example.org" or "smtp.example.org". If you need to use a
different port than default, use the <host>:<port> alternative
format. Just press ENTER if you don't have one or don't know, and so a
Debian SMTP host will be used.
>
Please enter the name of your proxy server. It should only use this
parameter if you are behind a firewall. The PROXY argument should be
formatted as a valid HTTP URL, including (if necessary) a port number; for
example, http://192.168.1.1:3128/. Just press ENTER if you don't have one
or don't know.
>
Default preferences file written. To reconfigure, re-run reportbug with
the "--configure" option.
```

Using Reportbug   With the setup phase completed, the actual bug report can begin. You will be prompted for a package name, although you can also provide the package name directly on the command line with reportbug *package*).

```
Running 'reportbug' as root is probably insecure! Continue [y|N|q|?]? y
Please enter the name of the package in which you have found a problem, or
type 'other' to report a more general problem. If you don't know what
package the bug is in, please contact debian-user@lists.debian.org for
assistance.
> wireshark
```

Contrary to the advice given above, if you don't know against which package to file the bug, you should get in touch with a Kali support forum (described in section 6.2, "Kali Linux Communities" [page 128]). In the next step, reportbug downloads the list of bugs filed against the given package and lets you browse them to see if you can find yours.

```
*** Welcome to reportbug.  Use ? for help at prompts. ***
Note: bug reports are publicly archived (including the email address of
the submitter).
Detected character set: UTF-8
```

```
Please change your locale if this is incorrect.

Using '"Raphaël Hertzog" <buxy@kali.org>' as your from address.
Getting status for wireshark...
Verifying package integrity...
Checking for newer versions at madison...
Will send report to Debian (per lsb_release).
Querying Debian BTS for reports on wireshark (source)...
35 bug reports found:

Bugs with severity important
    1) #478200  tshark: seems to ignore read filters when writing to…
    2) #776206  mergecap: Fails to create output file > 2GB
    3) #780089  wireshark: "On gnome wireshark has not title bar. Does…
Bugs with severity normal
    4) #151017  ethereal: "Protocol Hierarchy Statistics" give misleading…
    5) #275839  doesn't correctly dissect ESMTP pipelining
[...]
   35) #815122  wireshark: add OID 1.3.6.1.4.1.11129.2.4.2
(24-35/35) Is the bug you found listed above [y|N|b|m|r|q|s|f|e|?]? ?
y - Problem already reported; optionally add extra information.
N - (default) Problem not listed above; possibly check more.
b - Open the complete bugs list in a web browser.
m - Get more information about a bug (you can also enter a number
    without selecting "m" first).
r - Redisplay the last bugs shown.
q - I'm bored; quit please.
s - Skip remaining problems; file a new report immediately.
f - Filter bug list using a pattern.
e - Open the report using an e-mail client.
? - Display this help.
(24-35/35) Is the bug you found listed above [y|N|b|m|r|q|s|f|e|?]? n
Maintainer for wireshark is 'Balint Reczey <balint@balintreczey.hu>'.
Looking up dependencies of wireshark...
```

If you find your bug already filed, you can choose to send supplementary information, otherwise, you are invited to file a new bug report:

```
Briefly describe the problem (max. 100 characters allowed). This will be
the bug email subject, so keep the summary as concise as possible, for
example: "fails to send email" or "does not start with -q option
specified" (enter Ctrl+c to exit reportbug without reporting a bug).
> does not dissect protocol foobar
Rewriting subject to 'wireshark: does not dissect protocol foobar'
```

After providing a one-line summary of your problem, you must rate its severity along an extended scale:

```
How would you rate the severity of this problem or report?

1 critical           makes unrelated software on the system (or the whole
                     system) break, or causes serious data loss, or
                     introduces a security hole on systems where you install
                     the package.
2 grave              makes the package in question unusable by most or all
                     users, or causes data loss, or introduces a security
                     hole allowing access to the accounts of users who use
                     the package.
3 serious            is a severe violation of Debian policy (that is, the
                     problem is a violation of a 'must' or 'required'
                     directive); may or may not affect the usability of the
                     package. Note that non-severe policy violations may be
                     'normal,' 'minor,' or 'wishlist' bugs. (Package
                     maintainers may also designate other bugs as 'serious' and
                     thus release-critical; however, end users should not do
                     so.). For the canonical list of issues worthing a serious
                     severity you can refer to this webpage:
                     http://release.debian.org/testing/rc_policy.txt
4 important          a bug which has a major effect on the usability of a
                     package, without rendering it completely unusable to
                     everyone.
5 does-not-build     a bug that stops the package from being built from source.
                     (This is a 'virtual severity'.)
6 normal             a bug that does not undermine the usability of the whole
                     package; for example, a problem with a particular option
                     or menu item.
7 minor              things like spelling mistakes and other minor cosmetic
                     errors that do not affect the core functionality of the
                     package.
8 wishlist           suggestions and requests for new features.

Please select a severity level: [normal]
```

If you are unsure, just keep the default severity of normal.

You can also tag your report with a few keywords:

```
Do any of the following apply to this report?

1 d-i       This bug is relevant to the development of debian-installer.
2 ipv6      This bug affects support for Internet Protocol version 6.
3 l10n      This bug reports a localization/internationalization issue.
4 lfs       This bug affects support for large files (over 2 gigabytes).
5 newcomer  This bug has a known solution but the maintainer requests someone
            else implement it.
```

```
6 patch     You are including a patch to fix this problem.
7 upstream  This bug applies to the upstream part of the package.
8 none

Please select tags: (one at a time) [none]
```

Most tags are rather esoteric, but if your report includes a fix, you should select the patch tag.

Once this is completed, reportbug opens a text editor with a template that you should edit (Example 6.2, "Template generated by reportbug" [page 142]). It contains a few questions that you should delete and answer, as well as some information about your system that has been automatically collected. Notice how the first few lines are structured. They should not be modified as they will be parsed by the bug tracker to assign the report to the correct package.

Example 6.2 *Template generated by reportbug*

```
Subject: wireshark: does not dissect protocol foobar

Package: wireshark
Version: 2.0.2+ga16e22e-1
Severity: normal

Dear Maintainer,

*** Reporter, please consider answering these questions, where appropriate ***

   * What led up to the situation?
   * What exactly did you do (or not do) that was effective (or
     ineffective)?
   * What was the outcome of this action?
   * What outcome did you expect instead?

*** End of the template - remove these template lines ***


-- System Information:
Debian Release: stretch/sid
  APT prefers testing
  APT policy: (500, 'testing')
Architecture: amd64 (x86_64)
Foreign Architectures: i386

Kernel: Linux 4.4.0-1-amd64 (SMP w/4 CPU cores)
Locale: LANG=fr_FR.utf8, LC_CTYPE=fr_FR.utf8 (charmap=UTF-8)
Shell: /bin/sh linked to /bin/dash
Init: systemd (via /run/systemd/system)
```

```
Versions of packages wireshark depends on:
ii  wireshark-qt  2.0.2+ga16e22e-1

wireshark recommends no packages.

wireshark suggests no packages.

-- no debconf information
```

Once you save the report and close the text editor, you return to reportbug, which provides many other options and offers to send the resulting report.

```
Spawning sensible-editor...
Report will be sent to "Debian Bug Tracking System" <submit@bugs.debian.org>
Submit this report on wireshark (e to edit) [Y|n|a|c|e|i|l|m|p|q|d|t|s|?]? ?
Y - (default) Submit the bug report via email.
n - Don't submit the bug report; instead, save it in a temporary file (exits reportbug).
a - Attach a file.
c - Change editor and re-edit.
e - Re-edit the bug report.
i - Include a text file.
l - Pipe the message through the pager.
m - Choose a mailer to edit the report.
p - print message to stdout.
q - Save it in a temporary file and quit.
d - Detach an attachment file.
t - Add tags.
s - Add a X-Debbugs-CC recipient (a CC but after BTS processing).
? - Display this help.
Submit this report on wireshark (e to edit) [Y|n|a|c|e|i|l|m|p|q|d|t|s|?]? Y
Saving a backup of the report at /tmp/reportbug-wireshark-backup-20160328-19073-87oJWJ
Connecting to reportbug.debian.org via SMTP...

Bug report submitted to: "Debian Bug Tracking System" <submit@bugs.debian.org>
Copies will be sent after processing to:
  buxy@kali.org

If you want to provide additional information, please wait to receive the
bug tracking number via email; you may then send any extra information to
n@bugs.debian.org (e.g. 999999@bugs.debian.org), where n is the bug
number. Normally you will receive an acknowledgement via email including
the bug report number within an hour; if you haven't received a
confirmation, then the bug reporting process failed at some point
(reportbug or MTA failure, BTS maintenance, etc.).
```

Filing a Bug Report in another Free Software Project

There is a large diversity of free software projects, using different workflows and tools. This diversity also applies to the bug trackers in use. While many projects are hosted on GitHub and use GitHub Issues to track their bugs, there are also many others hosting their own trackers, based on Bugzilla, Trac, Redmine, Flyspray, and others. Most of them are web-based and require you to register an account to submit a new ticket.

We will not cover all the trackers here. It is up to you to learn the specifics of various trackers for other free software projects, but since GitHub is relatively popular, we will take a brief look at it here. As with other trackers, you must first create an account and sign in. Next, click the Issues tab, as shown in Figure 6.5, "Main page of a GitHub project" [page 144].

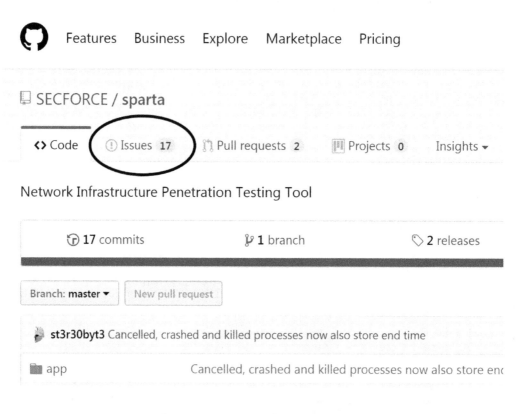

Figure 6.5 *Main page of a GitHub project*

You can then browse (and search) the list of open issues. Once you are confident that your bug is not yet filed, you can click on the New issue button (Figure 6.6, "Issues page of a GitHub project" [page 145]).

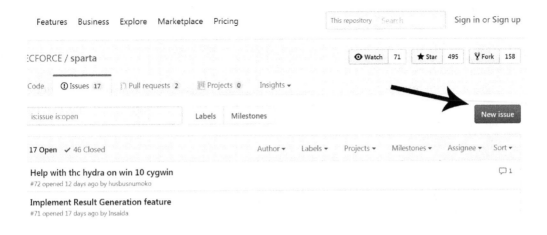

Figure 6.6   *Issues page of a GitHub project*

You are now on a page where you must describe your problem (Figure 6.7, "GitHub form to file a new issue" [page 145]). Although there is no template like the one found in `reportbug`, the bug reporting mechanism is fairly straight-forward, allowing you to attach files, apply formatting to text, and much more. Of course, for best results, be sure to follow our guidelines for creating a detailed and well-described report.

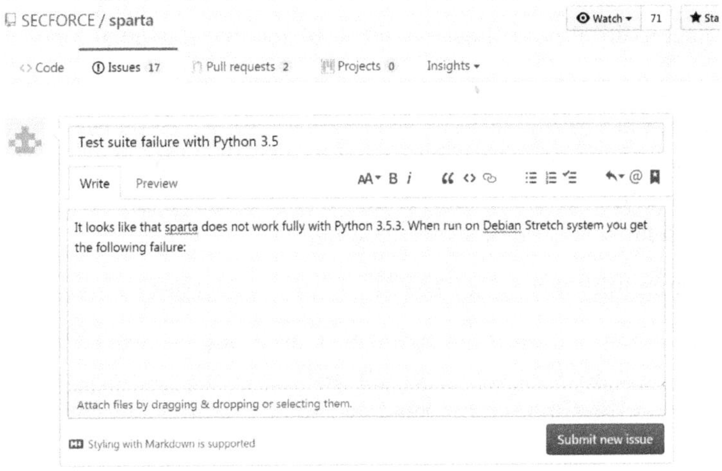

Figure 6.7   *GitHub form to file a new issue*

6.4. Summary

In this section, we discussed various methods to help you find documentation and information about programs and how to find help with problems you may encounter. We took a look at man and info pages and the `apropos` and `info` commands. We discussed bug trackers, provided some tips on how to search for and submit good bug reports, and provided some tips to help you figure out who owns the program or project in question.

Summary Tips:

- Before you can understand what is really going on when there is a problem, you need to know the theoretical role played by each program involved in the problem. One of the best ways to do this is to review the program's documentation.

- To view a manual page, simply type man *manual-page*, filling in the name of the command after an optional section number.

- The `apropos` command returns a list of manual pages whose summary mentions the requested keywords, along with the one-line summary from the manual page.

- The GNU project has written manuals for most of its programs in the *info* format. This is why many manual pages refer to corresponding *info* documentation.

- Each package includes its own documentation and even the least documented programs generally have a `README` file containing some interesting and/or important information. This documentation is installed in the `/usr/share/doc/`*package*`/` directory.

- In most cases, the FAQ or mailing list archives of a program's official website may address problems that you have encountered.

- The Kali project maintains a collection of useful documentation at `http://docs.kali.org`.

- The Kali Linux project uses the #kali-linux channel on the Freenode[5] IRC network. You can use chat.freenode.net as IRC server, on port 6667 for a TLS-encrypted connection or port 6666 for a clear-text connection. To join the discussions on IRC, you have to use an IRC client such as `hexchat` (in graphical mode) or `irssi` (in console mode). There is also a web-based client available on webchat.freenode.net[6].

- The official community forums for the Kali Linux project are located at forums.kali.org[7].

- If you uncover a bug in a program, you can search bug reports or file your own. Be sure to follow the guidelines that we have outlined to ensure your report is clear, comprehensive, and improves the chances that the bug will be addressed by the developers in a timely fashion.

---

[5]`https://www.freenode.net`
[6]`https://webchat.freenode.net`
[7]`https://forums.kali.org`

- Some bug reports should be filed to Kali, while others may be filed on the Debian side. A command like **dpkg -s *package-name* | grep ^Version:** will reveal the version number and will be tagged as "kali" if it is a Kali-modified package.

- Identifying an upstream project and finding where to file the bug report is usually easy. Simply browse the upstream website that is referenced in the Homepage field of the packaging meta-data.

- Kali uses a web-based bug tracker at `https://bugs.kali.org` where you can consult all the bug reports anonymously, but if you would like to comment or file a new bug report, you will need to register an account.

- Debian uses a (mostly) email-based bug tracking system known as Debbugs. To open a new bug report, you can send an email (with a special syntax) to submit@bugs.debian.org or you can use the `reportbug` command, which will guide you through the process.

- While many projects are hosted on GitHub and use GitHub Issues to track their bugs, there are also many others hosting their own trackers. You may have to research the basics of third-party bug trackers if you need to post to them.

Now that you have the basic tools for navigating Linux, installing and configuring Kali, and troubleshooting your system and getting help, it is time to look at locking down Kali so that you can protect your installation as well as your client's data.

Keywords

Security policy
Firewall
iptables
Monitoring
Logging

KALI LINUX
REVEALED

Securing and Monitoring Kali Linux

Contents

As you begin to use Kali Linux for increasingly sensitive and higher-profile work, you will likely need to take the security of your installation more seriously. In this chapter, we will first discuss security policies, highlighting various points to consider when defining such a policy, and outlining some of the threats to your system and to you as a security professional. We will also discuss security measures for laptop and desktop systems and focus on firewalls and packet filtering. Finally, we will discuss monitoring tools and strategies and show you how to best implement them to detect potential threats to your system.

7.1. Defining a Security Policy

It is impractical to discuss security in broad strokes since the idea represents a vast range of concepts, tools, and procedures, none of which apply universally. Choosing among them requires a precise idea of what your goals are. Securing a system starts with answering a few questions. Rushing headlong into implementing an arbitrary set of tools runs the risk of focusing on the wrong aspects of security.

It is usually best to determine a specific goal. A good approach to help with that determination starts with the following questions:

- *What* are you trying to protect? The security policy will be different depending on whether you want to protect computers or data. In the latter case, you also need to know which data.

- What are you trying to protect *against*? Is it leakage of confidential data? Accidental data loss? Revenue loss caused by disruption of service?

- Also, *who* are you trying to protect against? Security measures will be quite different for guarding against a typo by a regular user of the system versus protecting against a determined external attacker group.

The term "risk" is customarily used to refer collectively to these three factors: what to protect, what should be prevented, and who might make this happen. Modeling the risk requires answers to these three questions. From this risk model, a security policy can be constructed and the policy can be implemented with concrete actions.

Permanent Questioning Bruce Schneier, a world expert in security matters (not only computer security), tries to counter one of security's most important myths with a motto: "Security is a process, not a product." Assets to be protected change over time and so do threats and the means available to potential attackers. Even if a security policy has initially been perfectly designed and implemented, you should never rest on your laurels. The risk components evolve and the response to that risk must evolve accordingly.

Extra constraints are also worth taking into account as they can restrict the range of available policies. How far are you willing to go to secure a system? This question has a major impact on which policy to implement. Too often, the answer is only defined in terms of monetary costs, but other elements should also be considered, such as the amount of inconvenience imposed on system users or performance degradation.

Once the risk has been modeled, you can start thinking about designing an actual security policy.

There are extremes that can come into play when deciding the level of security protections to adopt. On one hand, it can be extremely simple to provide basic system security.

For instance, if the system to be protected only comprises a second-hand computer, the sole use of which is to add a few numbers at the end of the day, deciding not to do anything special to protect it would be quite reasonable. The intrinsic value of the system is low and the value of the data are zero since they are not stored on the computer. A potential attacker infiltrating this system would only gain a calculator. The cost of securing such a system would probably be greater than the cost of a breach.

At the other end of the spectrum, you might want to protect the confidentiality of secret data in the most comprehensive way possible, trumping any other consideration. In this case, an appropriate response would be the total destruction of the data (securely erasing the files, shredding of the hard disks to bits, then dissolving these bits in acid, and so on). If there is an additional requirement that data must be kept in store for future use (although not necessarily readily available), and if cost still isn't a factor, then a starting point would be storing the data on iridium–platinum alloy plates stored in bomb-proof bunkers under various mountains in the world, each of which being (of course) both entirely secret and guarded by entire armies.

Extreme though these examples may seem, they would nevertheless be an adequate response to certain defined risks, insofar as they are the outcome of a thought process that takes into account the goals to reach and the constraints to fulfill. When coming from a reasoned decision, no security policy is more, or less, respectable than any other.

Coming back to a more typical case, an information system can be segmented into consistent and mostly independent subsystems. Each subsystem will have its own requirements and constraints, and so the risk assessment and the design of the security policy should be undertaken separately for each. A good principle to keep in mind is that a small attack surface is easier to defend than a large one. The network organization should also be designed accordingly: the sensitive services should be concentrated on a small number of machines, and these machines should only be accessible via a minimal number of routes or check-points. The logic is straightforward: it is easier to secure these checkpoints than to secure all the sensitive machines against the entirety of the outside world. It is at this point that the usefulness of network filtering (including by firewalls) becomes apparent. This filtering can be implemented with dedicated hardware but a simpler and more flexible solution is to use a software firewall such as the one integrated in the Linux kernel.

7.2. Possible Security Measures

As the previous section explained, there is no single response to the question of how to secure Kali Linux. It all depends on how you use it and what you are trying to protect.

7.2.1. On a Server

If you run Kali Linux on a publicly accessible server, you most likely want to secure network services by changing any default passwords that might be configured (see section 7.3, "Securing Network Services" [page 153]) and possibly also by restricting their access with a firewall (see section 7.4, "Firewall or Packet Filtering" [page 153]).

If you hand out user accounts either directly on the server or on one of the services, you want to ensure that you set strong passwords (they should resist brute-force attacks). At the same time, you might want to setup *fail2ban*, which will make it much harder to brute-force passwords over the network (by filtering away IP addresses that exceed a limit of failed login attempts). Install *fail2ban* with `apt update` followed by `apt install fail2ban`.

If you run web services, you probably want to host them over HTTPS to prevent network intermediaries from sniffing your traffic (which might include authentication cookies).

7.2.2. On a Laptop

The laptop of a penetration tester is not subject to the same risks as a public server: for instance, you are less likely to be subject to random scans from script kiddies and even when you are, you probably won't have any network services enabled.

Real risk often arises when you travel from one customer to the next. For example, your laptop could be stolen while traveling or seized by customs. That is why you most likely want to use full disk encryption (see section 4.2.2, "Installation on a Fully Encrypted File System" [page 85]) and possibly also setup the "nuke" feature (see "Adding a Nuke Password for Extra Safety" [page 245]): the data that you have collected during your engagements are confidential and require the utmost protection.

You may also need firewall rules (see section 7.4, "Firewall or Packet Filtering" [page 153]) but not for the same purpose as on the server. You might want to forbid all outbound traffic except the traffic generated by your VPN access. This is meant as a safety net, so that when the VPN is down, you immediately notice it (instead of falling back to the local network access). That way, you do not divulge the IP addresses of your customers when you browse the web or do other online activities. In addition, if you are performing a local internal engagement, it is best to remain in control of all of your activity to reduce the noise you create on the network, which can alert the customer and their defense systems.

7.3. Securing Network Services

In general, it is a good idea to disable services that you do not use. Kali makes it easy to do this since most network services are disabled by default.

As long as services remain disabled, they do not pose any security threat. However, you must be careful when you enable them because:

- there is no firewall by default, so if they listen on all network interfaces, they are effectively publicly available.

- some services have no authentication credentials and let you set them on first use; others have default (and thus widely known) credentials preset. Make sure to (re)set any password to something that only you know.

- many services run as root with full administrator privileges, so the consequences of unauthorized access or a security breach are therefore usually severe.

Default Credentials We won't list here all tools that come with default credentials, instead you should check the README.Debian file of the respective packages, as well as docs.kali.org[1] and tools.kali.org[2] to see if the service needs some special care to be secured.

If you run in live mode, the password of the root account is "*toor*." Thus you should not enable SSH before changing the password of the root account, or before having tweaked its configuration to disallow password-based logins.

Also note that the BeEF project (from the already-installed package *beef-xss*) is also known to have default credentials user "beef", password "beef") hardcoded in its default configuration file.

7.4. Firewall or Packet Filtering

A *firewall* is a piece of computer equipment with hardware, software, or both that parses the incoming or outgoing network packets (coming to or leaving from a local network) and only lets through those matching certain predefined conditions.

A filtering network gateway is a type of firewall that protects an entire network. It is usually installed on a dedicated machine configured as a gateway for the network so that it can parse all packets that pass in and out of the network. Alternatively, a local firewall is a software service that runs on one particular machine in order to filter or limit access to some services on that machine, or possibly to prevent outgoing connections by rogue software that a user could, willingly or not, have installed.

---

[1]https://docs.kali.org
[2]https://tools.kali.org

The Linux kernel embeds the *netfilter* firewall. There is no turn-key solution for configuring any firewall since network and user requirements differ. However, you can control *netfilter* from user space with the `iptables` and `ip6tables` commands. The difference between these two commands is that the former works for IPv4 networks, whereas the latter works on IPv6. Since both network protocol stacks will probably be around for many years, both tools will need to be used in parallel. You can also use the excellent GUI-based `fwbuilder` tool, which provides a graphical representation of the filtering rules.

However you decide to configure it, *netfilter* is Linux's firewall implementation, so let's take a closer look at how it works.

7.4.1. Netfilter Behavior

Netfilter uses four distinct tables, which store rules regulating three kinds of operations on packets:

- filter concerns filtering rules (accepting, refusing, or ignoring a packet);
- nat (Network Address Translation) concerns translation of source or destination addresses and ports of packets;
- mangle concerns other changes to the IP packets (including the ToS—*Type of Service*—field and options);
- raw allows other manual modifications on packets before they reach the connection tracking system.

Each table contains lists of rules called *chains*. The firewall uses standard chains to handle packets based on predefined circumstances. The administrator can create other chains, which will only be used when referred by one of the standard chains (either directly or indirectly).

The filter table has three standard chains:

- INPUT: concerns packets whose destination is the firewall itself;
- OUTPUT: concerns packets emitted by the firewall;
- FORWARD: concerns packets passing through the firewall (which is neither their source nor their destination).

The nat table also has three standard chains:

- PREROUTING: to modify packets as soon as they arrive;
- POSTROUTING: to modify packets when they are ready to go on their way;
- OUTPUT: to modify packets generated by the firewall itself.

These chains are illustrated in Figure 7.1, "How *Netfilter* Chains are Called" [page 155].

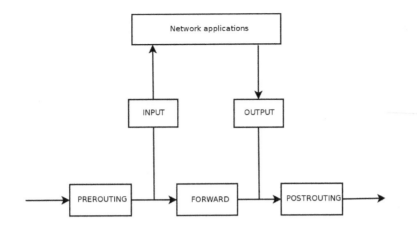

Figure 7.1 *How Netfilter Chains are Called*

Each chain is a list of rules; each rule is a set of conditions and an action to perform when the conditions are met. When processing a packet, the firewall scans the appropriate chain, one rule after another, and when the conditions for one rule are met, it jumps (hence the -j option in the commands) to the specified action to continue processing. The most common behaviors are standardized and dedicated actions exist for them. Taking one of these standard actions interrupts the processing of the chain, since the packets fate is already sealed (barring an exception mentioned below). Listed below are the *Netfilter* actions.

- ACCEPT: allow the packet to go on its way.
- REJECT: reject the packet with an Internet control message protocol (ICMP) error packet (the --reject-with *type* option of `iptables` determines the type of error to send).
- DROP: delete (ignore) the packet.
- LOG: log (via `syslogd`) a message with a description of the packet. Note that this action does not interrupt processing, and the execution of the chain continues at the next rule, which is why logging refused packets requires both a LOG and a REJECT/DROP rule. Common parameters associated with logging include:
    - --log-level, with default value warning, indicates the `syslog` severity level.
    - --log-prefix allows specifying a text prefix to differentiate between logged messages.
    - --log-tcp-sequence, --log-tcp-options, and --log-ip-options indicate extra data to be integrated into the message: respectively, the TCP sequence number, TCP options, and IP options.
- ULOG: log a message via `ulogd`, which can be better adapted and more efficient than `syslogd` for handling large numbers of messages; note that this action, like LOG, also returns processing to the next rule in the calling chain.
- *chain_name*: jump to the given chain and evaluate its rules.

- RETURN: interrupt processing of the current chain and return to the calling chain; in case the current chain is a standard one, there's no calling chain, so the default action (defined with the -P option to `iptables`) is executed instead.

- SNAT (only in the nat table): apply *Source Network Address Translation* (SNAT). Extra options describe the exact changes to apply, including the --to-source *address:port* option, which defines the new source IP address and/or port.

- DNAT (only in the nat table): apply *Destination Network Address Translation* (DNAT). Extra options describe the exact changes to apply, including the --to-destination *address:port* option, which defines the new destination IP address and/or port.

- MASQUERADE (only in the nat table): apply *masquerading* (a special case of *Source NAT*).

- REDIRECT (only in the nat table): transparently redirect a packet to a given port of the firewall itself; this can be used to set up a transparent web proxy that works with no configuration on the client side, since the client thinks it connects to the recipient whereas the communications actually go through the proxy. The --to-ports *port(s)* option indicates the port, or port range, where the packets should be redirected.

Other actions, particularly those concerning the mangle table, are outside the scope of this text. The `iptables(8)` and `ip6tables(8)` man pages have a comprehensive list.

What is ICMP? *Internet Control Message Protocol* (ICMP) is the protocol used to transmit ancillary information on communications. It tests network connectivity with the `ping` command, which sends an ICMP *echo request* message, which the recipient is meant to answer with an ICMP *echo reply* message. It signals a firewall rejecting a packet, indicates an overflow in a receive buffer, proposes a better route for the next packets in the connection, and so on. This protocol is defined by several RFC documents. RFC777 and RFC792 were the first, but many others extended and/or revised the protocol.

➡ http://www.faqs.org/rfcs/rfc777.html

➡ http://www.faqs.org/rfcs/rfc792.html

For reference, a receive buffer is a small memory zone storing data between the time it arrives from the network and the time the kernel handles it. If this zone is full, new data cannot be received and ICMP signals the problem so that the emitter can slow down its transfer rate (which should ideally reach an equilibrium after some time).

Note that although an IPv4 network can work without ICMP, ICMPv6 is strictly required for an IPv6 network, since it combines several functions that were, in the IPv4 world, spread across ICMPv4, *Internet Group Membership Protocol* (IGMP), and *Address Resolution Protocol* (ARP). ICMPv6 is defined in RFC4443.

➡ http://www.faqs.org/rfcs/rfc4443.html

7.4.2. Syntax of `iptables` and `ip6tables`

The `iptables` and `ip6tables` commands are used to manipulate tables, chains, and rules. Their -t *table* option indicates which table to operate on (by default, filter).

Commands

The major options for interacting with chains are listed below:

- -L *chain* lists the rules in the chain. This is commonly used with the -n option to disable name resolution (for example, `iptables -n -L INPUT` will display the rules related to incoming packets).

- -N *chain* creates a new chain. You can create new chains for a number of purposes, including testing a new network service or fending off a network attack.

- -X *chain* deletes an empty and unused chain (for example, `iptables -X ddos-attack`).

- -A *chain rule* adds a rule at the end of the given chain. Remember that rules are processed from top to bottom so be sure to keep this in mind when adding rules.

- -I *chain rule_num rule* inserts a rule before the rule number *rule_num*. As with the -A option, keep the processing order in mind when inserting new rules into a chain.

- -D *chain rule_num* (or -D *chain rule*) deletes a rule in a chain; the first syntax identifies the rule to be deleted by its number (`iptables -L --line-numbers` will display these numbers), while the latter identifies it by its contents.

- -F *chain* flushes a chain (deletes all its rules). For example, to delete all of the rules related to outgoing packets, you would run `iptables -F OUTPUT`. If no chain is mentioned, all the rules in the table are deleted.

- -P *chain action* defines the default action, or "policy" for a given chain; note that only standard chains can have such a policy. To drop all incoming traffic by default, you would run `iptables -P INPUT DROP`.

Rules

Each rule is expressed as *conditions* -j *action action_options*. If several conditions are described in the same rule, then the criterion is the conjunction (logical *AND*) of the conditions, which is at least as restrictive as each individual condition.

The -p *protocol* condition matches the protocol field of the IP packet. The most common values are tcp, udp, icmp, and icmpv6. This condition can be complemented with conditions on the TCP ports, with clauses such as --source-port *port* and --destination-port*port*.

Prefixing a condition with an exclamation mark negates the condition. For example, negating a condition on the -p option matches "any packet with a different protocol than the one specified." This negation mechanism can be applied to all other conditions as well.

The -s *address* or -s *network/mask* condition matches the source address of the packet. Correspondingly, -d *address* or -d *network/mask* matches the destination address.

The -i *interface* condition selects packets coming from the given network interface. -o *interface* selects packets going out on a specific interface.

The --state *state* condition matches the state of a packet in a connection (this requires the ipt_conntrack kernel module, for connection tracking). The NEW state describes a packet starting a new connection, ESTABLISHED matches packets belonging to an already existing connection, and RELATED matches packets initiating a new connection related to an existing one (which is useful for the ftp-data connections in the "active" mode of the FTP protocol).

There are many available options for iptables and ip6tables and mastering them all requires a great deal of study and experience. However, one of the options you will use most often is the one to block malicious network traffic from a host or range of hosts. For example, to silently block incoming traffic from the IP address 10.0.1.5 and the 31.13.74.0/24 class C subnet:

```
# iptables -A INPUT -s 10.0.1.5 -j DROP
# iptables -A INPUT -s 31.13.74.0/24 -j DROP
# iptables -n -L INPUT
Chain INPUT (policy ACCEPT)
target     prot opt source               destination
DROP       all  --  10.0.1.5             0.0.0.0/0
DROP       all  --  31.13.74.0/24        0.0.0.0/0
```

Another commonly-used iptables command is to permit network traffic for a specific service or port. To allow users to connect to SSH, HTTP, and IMAP, you could run the following commands:

```
# iptables -A INPUT -m state --state NEW -p tcp --dport 22 -j ACCEPT
# iptables -A INPUT -m state --state NEW -p tcp --dport 80 -j ACCEPT
# iptables -A INPUT -m state --state NEW -p tcp --dport 143 -j ACCEPT
# iptables -n -L INPUT
Chain INPUT (policy ACCEPT)
target     prot opt source               destination
DROP       all  --  10.0.1.5             0.0.0.0/0
DROP       all  --  31.13.74.0/24        0.0.0.0/0
ACCEPT     tcp  --  0.0.0.0/0            0.0.0.0/0            state NEW tcp dpt:22
ACCEPT     tcp  --  0.0.0.0/0            0.0.0.0/0            state NEW tcp dpt:80
ACCEPT     tcp  --  0.0.0.0/0            0.0.0.0/0            state NEW tcp dpt:143
```

It is considered to be good computer *hygiene* to clean up old and unnecessary rules. The easiest way to delete iptables rules is to reference the rules by line number, which you can retrieve with the --line-numbers option. Be wary though: dropping a rule will renumber all the rules appearing further down in the chain.

```
# iptables -n -L INPUT --line-numbers
Chain INPUT (policy ACCEPT)
num  target      prot opt source            destination
1    DROP        all  --  10.0.1.5          0.0.0.0/0
2    DROP        all  --  31.13.74.0/24     0.0.0.0/0
3    ACCEPT      tcp  --  0.0.0.0/0         0.0.0.0/0          state NEW tcp dpt:22
4    ACCEPT      tcp  --  0.0.0.0/0         0.0.0.0/0          state NEW tcp dpt:80
5    ACCEPT      tcp  --  0.0.0.0/0         0.0.0.0/0          state NEW tcp dpt:143
# iptables -D INPUT 2
# iptables -D INPUT 1
# iptables -n -L INPUT --line-numbers
Chain INPUT (policy ACCEPT)
num  target      prot opt source            destination
1    ACCEPT      tcp  --  0.0.0.0/0         0.0.0.0/0          state NEW tcp dpt:22
2    ACCEPT      tcp  --  0.0.0.0/0         0.0.0.0/0          state NEW tcp dpt:80
3    ACCEPT      tcp  --  0.0.0.0/0         0.0.0.0/0          state NEW tcp dpt:143
```

There are more specific conditions, depending on the generic conditions described above. For more information refer to iptables(8) and ip6tables(8)

7.4.3. Creating Rules

Each rule creation requires one invocation of iptables or ip6tables. Typing these commands manually can be tedious, so the calls are usually stored in a script so that the system is automatically configured the same way every time the machine boots. This script can be written by hand but it can also be interesting to prepare it with a high-level tool such as fwbuilder.

```
# apt install fwbuilder
```

The principle is simple. In the first step, describe all the elements that will be involved in the actual rules:

- The firewall itself, with its network interfaces
- The networks, with their corresponding IP ranges
- The servers
- The ports belonging to the services hosted on the servers

Next, create the rules with simple drag-and-drop actions on the objects as shown in Figure 7.2, "Fwbuilder's Main Window" [page 160]. A few contextual menus can change the condition (negating it, for instance). Then the action needs to be chosen and configured.

As far as IPv6 is concerned, you can either create two distinct rulesets for IPv4 and IPv6, or create only one and let fwbuilder translate the rules according to the addresses assigned to the objects.

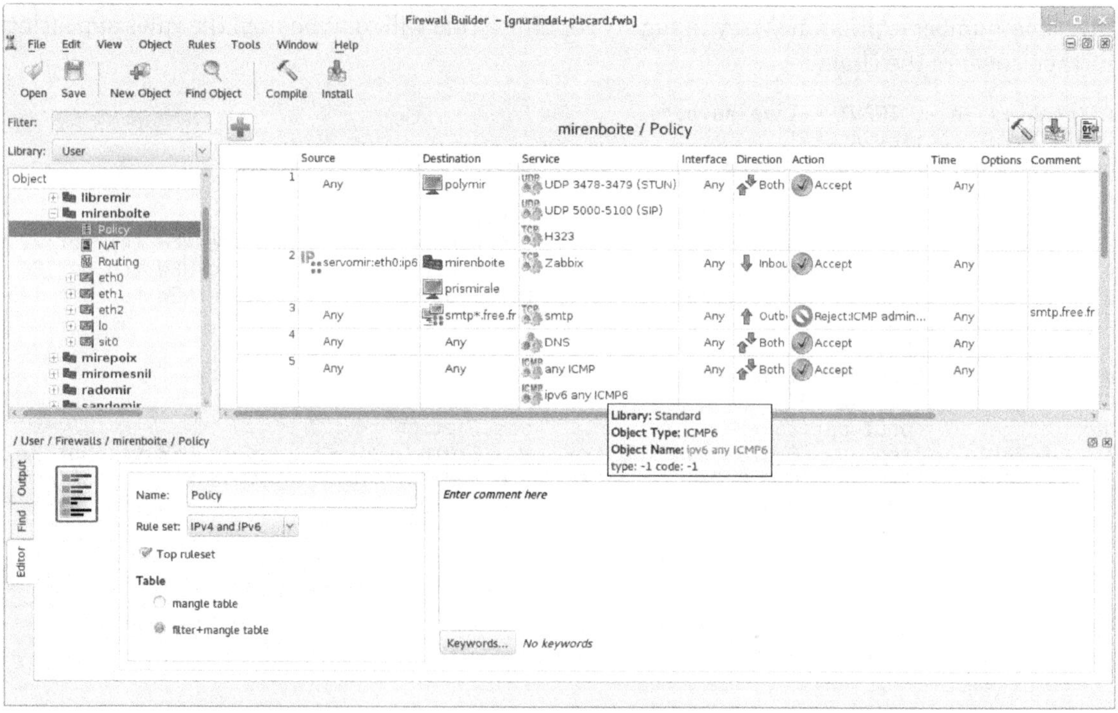

Figure 7.2 *Fwbuilder's Main Window*

`fwbuilder` will generate a script configuring the firewall according to the rules that you have defined. Its modular architecture gives it the ability to generate scripts targeting different systems including `iptables` for Linux, `ipf` for FreeBSD, and `pf` for OpenBSD.

7.4.4. Installing the Rules at Each Boot

In order to implement the firewall rules each time the machine is booted, you will need to register the configuration script in an up directive of the `/etc/network/interfaces` file. In the following example, the script is stored under `/usr/local/etc/arrakis.fw`.

```
auto eth0
iface eth0 inet static
    address 192.168.0.1
    network 192.168.0.0
    netmask 255.255.255.0
    broadcast 192.168.0.255
    up /usr/local/etc/arrakis.fw
```

This example assumes that you are using *ifupdown* to configure the network interfaces. If you are using something else (like *NetworkManager* or *systemd-networkd*), then refer to their respective documentation to find out ways to execute a script after the interface has been brought up.

7.5. Monitoring and Logging

Data confidentiality and protection is an important aspect of security but it is equally important to ensure availability of services. As an administrator and security practitioner, you must ensure that everything works as expected, and it is your responsibility to detect anomalous behavior and service degradation in a timely manner. Monitoring and logging software plays a key role in this aspect of security, providing insight into what is happening on the system and the network.

In this section, we will review some tools that can be used to monitor several aspects of a Kali system.

7.5.1. Monitoring Logs with `logcheck`

The `logcheck` program monitors log files every hour by default and sends unusual log messages in emails to the administrator for further analysis.

The list of monitored files is stored in `/etc/logcheck/logcheck.logfiles`. The default values work fine if the `/etc/rsyslog.conf` file has not been completely overhauled.

`logcheck` can report in various levels of detail: *paranoid*, *server*, and *workstation*. *paranoid* is *very* verbose and should probably be restricted to specific servers such as firewalls. *server* is the default mode and is recommended for most servers. *workstation* is obviously designed for workstations and is extremely terse, filtering out more messages than the other options.

In all three cases, `logcheck` should probably be customized to exclude some extra messages (depending on installed services), unless you really want to receive hourly batches of long uninteresting emails. Since the message selection mechanism is rather complex, `/usr/share/doc/logcheck-database/README.logcheck-database.gz` is a required—if challenging—read.

The applied rules can be split into several types:

- those that qualify a message as a cracking attempt (stored in a file in the `/etc/logcheck/cracking.d/` directory);
- ignored cracking attempts (`/etc/logcheck/cracking.ignore.d/`);
- those classifying a message as a security alert (`/etc/logcheck/violations.d/`);
- ignored security alerts (`/etc/logcheck/violations.ignore.d/`);
- finally, those applying to the remaining messages (considered as *system events*).

ignore.d files are used to (obviously) ignore messages. For example, a message tagged as a cracking attempt or a security alert (following a rule stored in a `/etc/logcheck/violations.d/myfile` file) can only be ignored by a rule in a `/etc/logcheck/violations.ignore.d/myfile` or `/etc/logcheck/violations.ignore.d/myfile-`*extension* file.

A system event is always signaled unless a rule in one of the `/etc/logcheck/ignore.d.`{`paranoid,server,workstation`}`/` directories states the event should be ignored. Of course, the only directories taken into account are those corresponding to verbosity levels equal or greater than the selected operation mode.

7.5.2. Monitoring Activity in Real Time

`top` is an interactive tool that displays a list of currently running processes. The default sorting is based on the current amount of processor use and can be obtained with the P key. Other sort orders include a sort by occupied memory (M key), by total processor time (T key), and by process identifier (N key). The k key kills a process by entering its process identifier. The r key changes the priority of a process.

When the system seems to be overloaded, `top` is a great tool to see which processes are competing for processor time or consuming too much memory. In particular, it is often interesting to check if the processes consuming resources match the real services that the machine is known to host. An unknown process running as the "www-data" user should really stand out and be investigated since it's probably an instance of software installed and executed on the system through a vulnerability in a web application.

`top` is a very flexible tool and its manual page gives details on how to customize its display and adapt it to your personal needs and habits.

The `gnome-system-monitor` graphical tool is similar to `top` and it provides roughly the same features.

7.5.3. Detecting Changes

Once a system is installed and configured, most system files should stay relatively static until the system is upgraded. Therefore, it is a good idea to monitor changes in system files since any unexpected change could be cause for alarm and should be investigated. This section presents a few of the most common tools used to monitor system files, detect changes, and optionally notify you as the administrator of the system.

Auditing Packages with dpkg --verify

`dpkg --verify` (or `dpkg -V`) is an interesting tool since it displays the system files that have been modified (potentially by an attacker), but this output should be taken with a grain of salt. To do its job, dpkg relies on checksums stored in its own database which is stored on the hard disk (found in /var/lib/dpkg/info/*package*.md5sums). A thorough attacker will therefore modify these files so they contain the new checksums for the subverted files, or an advanced attacker will compromise the package on your Debian mirror. To protect against this class of attack, use APT's digital signature verification system (see section 8.3.6, "Validating Package Authenticity" [page 202]) to properly verify the packages.

What Is a File Fingerprint?	As a reminder: a fingerprint is a value, often a number (although in hexadecimal notation), that contains a kind of signature for the contents of a file. This signature is calculated with an algorithm (MD5 or SHA1 being well-known examples) that more or less guarantees that even the tiniest change in the file contents will result in a change of the fingerprint; this is known as the "avalanche effect". A simple numerical fingerprint then serves as a litmus test to check whether the contents of a file have been altered. These algorithms are not reversible; in other words, for most of them, knowing a fingerprint doesn't allow finding the corresponding contents. Recent mathematical advances seem to weaken the absoluteness of these principles but their use is not called into question so far, since creating different contents yielding the same fingerprint still seems to be quite a difficult task.

Running dpkg -V will verify all installed packages and will print out a line for each file that fails verification. Each character denotes a test on some specific meta-data. Unfortunately, dpkg does not store the meta-data needed for most tests and will thus output question marks for them. Currently only the checksum test can yield a 5 on the third character (when it fails).

```
# dpkg -V
??5??????   /lib/systemd/system/ssh.service
??5?????? c /etc/libvirt/qemu/networks/default.xml
??5?????? c /etc/lvm/lvm.conf
??5?????? c /etc/salt/roster
```

In the example above, dpkg reports a change to SSH's service file that the administrator made to the packaged file instead of using an appropriate /etc/systemd/system/ssh.service override (which would be stored below /etc like any configuration change should be). It also lists multiple configuration files (identified by the "c" letter on the second field) that had been legitimately modified.

Monitoring Files: AIDE

The Advanced Intrusion Detection Environment (AIDE) tool checks file integrity and detects any change against a previously-recorded image of the valid system. The image is stored as a database (/var/lib/aide/aide.db) containing the relevant information on all files of the system (fingerprints, permissions, timestamps, and so on).

You can install AIDE by running apt update followed by apt install aide. You will first initialize the database with aideinit; it will then run daily (via the /etc/cron.daily/aide script) to check that nothing relevant changed. When changes are detected, AIDE records them in log files (`/var/log/aide/*.log`) and sends its findings to the administrator by email.

> **Protecting the Database** Since AIDE uses a local database to compare the states of the files, the validity of its results is directly linked to the validity of the database. If an attacker gets root permissions on a compromised system, they will be able to replace the database and cover their tracks. One way to prevent this subversion is to store the reference data on read-only storage media.

You can use options in `/etc/default/aide` to tweak the behavior of the *aide* package. The AIDE configuration proper is stored in `/etc/aide/aide.conf` and `/etc/aide/aide.conf.d/` (actually, these files are only used by `update-aide.conf` to generate `/var/lib/aide/aide.conf.autogenerated`). The configuration indicates which properties of which files need to be checked. For instance, the contents of log files changes routinely, and such changes can be ignored as long as the permissions of these files stay the same, but both contents and permissions of executable programs must be constant. Although not very complex, the configuration syntax is not fully intuitive and we recommend reading the `aide.conf(5)` manual page for more details.

A new version of the database is generated daily in `/var/lib/aide/aide.db.new`; if all recorded changes were legitimate, it can be used to replace the reference database.

Tripwire is very similar to AIDE; even the configuration file syntax is almost the same. The main addition provided by *tripwire* is a mechanism to sign the configuration file so that an attacker cannot make it point at a different version of the reference database.

Samhain also offers similar features as well as some functions to help detect rootkits (see the sidebar "The *checksecurity* and *chkrootkit/rkhunter* packages" [page 164]). It can also be deployed globally on a network and record its traces on a central server (with a signature).

> **The *checksecurity* and *chkrootkit/rkhunter* packages** *checksecurity* consists of several small scripts that perform basic checks on the system (searching for empty passwords, new setuid files, and so on) and warn you if these conditions are detected. Despite its explicit name, you should not rely solely on it to make sure a Linux system is secure.
>
> The *chkrootkit* and *rkhunter* packages detect certain *rootkits* potentially installed on the system. As a reminder, these are pieces of software designed to hide the compromise of a system while discreetly keeping control of the machine. The tests are not 100 percent reliable but they can usually draw your attention to potential problems.

7.6. Summary

In this chapter, we took a look at the concept of security policies, highlighting various points to consider when defining such a policy and outlining some of the threats to your system and to you personally as a security professional. We discussed laptop and desktop security measures as well as firewalls and packet filtering. Finally, we reviewed monitoring tools and strategies and showed how to best implement them to detect potential threats to your system.

Summary Tips:

- Take time to define a comprehensive security policy.

- If you are running Kali on a publicly accessible server, change any default passwords for services that might be configured (see section 7.3, "Securing Network Services" [page 153]) and restrict their access with a firewall (see section 7.4, "Firewall or Packet Filtering" [page 153]) prior to launching them.

- Use *fail2ban* to detect and block password-guessing attacks and remote brute force password attacks.

- If you run web services, host them over HTTPS to prevent network intermediaries from sniffing your traffic (which might include authentication cookies).

- Real risk often arises when you travel from one customer to the next. For example, your laptop could be stolen while traveling or seized by customs. Prepare for these unfortunate possibilities by using full disk encryption (see section 4.2.2, "Installation on a Fully Encrypted File System" [page 85]) and consider the nuke feature (see "Adding a Nuke Password for Extra Safety" [page 245]) to protect your clients data.

- Implement firewall rules (see section 7.4, "Firewall or Packet Filtering" [page 153]) to forbid all outbound traffic except the traffic generated by your VPN access. This is meant as a safety net, so that when the VPN is down you immediately notice it (instead of falling back to the local network access).

- Disable services that you do not use. Kali makes it easy to do this since all external network services are disabled by default.

- The Linux kernel embeds the *netfilter* firewall. There is no turn-key solution for configuring any firewall, since network and user requirements differ. However, you can control *netfilter* from user space with the `iptables` and `ip6tables` commands.

- The `logcheck` program monitors log files every hour by default and sends unusual log messages in emails to the administrator for further analysis.

- `top` is an interactive tool that displays a list of currently running processes.

- `dpkg --verify` (or `dpkg -V`) displays the system files that have been modified (potentially by an attacker), but relies on checksums, which may be subverted by a clever attacker.

- The Advanced Intrusion Detection Environment (AIDE) tool checks file integrity and detects any changes against a previously-recorded image of the valid system.

- Tripwire is very similar to AIDE but uses a mechanism to sign the configuration file, so that an attacker cannot make it point at a different version of the reference database.

- Consider the use of `rkhunter`, `checksecurity`, and `chkrootkit` to help detect rootkits on your system.

In the next chapter, we are going to dig into Debian fundamentals and package management. You will quickly understand the power behind Kali's Debian roots and learn how the developers have harnessed that power. Be warned, the next chapter is fairly dense, but it is critical that you understand Debian basics and package management if you are going to be a Kali power user.

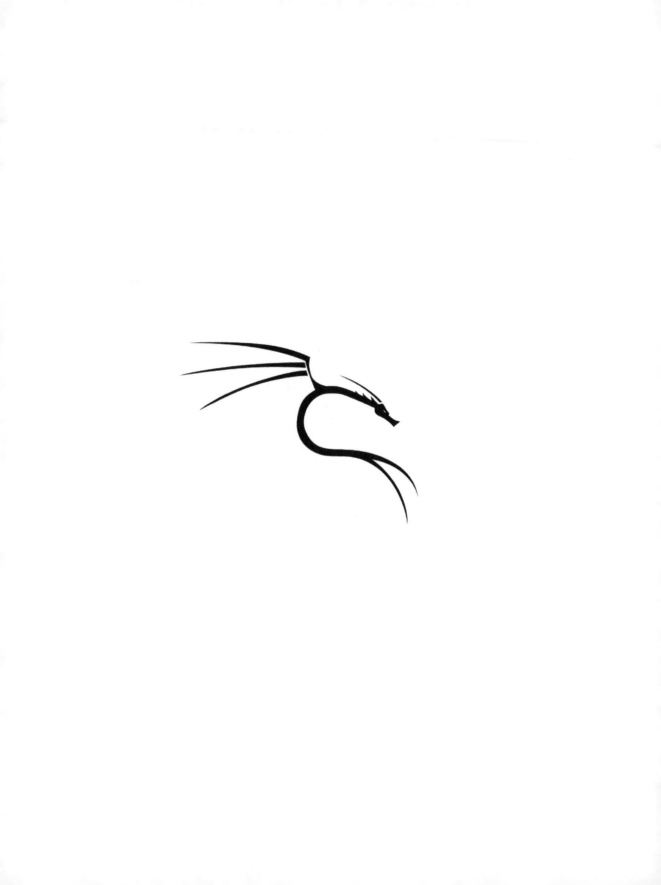

Keywords

dpkg
apt
sources.list
Upgrades
Package repositories

KALI LINUX
REVEALED

Debian Package Management

Contents

After the basics of Linux, it is time to learn the package management system of a Debian-based distribution. In such distributions, including Kali, the Debian package is the canonical way to make software available to end-users. Understanding the package management system will give you a great deal of insight into how Kali is structured, enable you to more effectively troubleshoot issues, and help you quickly locate help and documentation for the wide array of tools and utilities included in Kali Linux.

In this chapter, we will introduce the Debian package management system and introduce dpkg and the APT suite of tools. One of the primary strengths of Kali Linux lies in the flexibility of its package management system, which leverages these tools to provide near-seamless installation, upgrades, removal, and manipulation of application software, and even of the base operating system itself. It is critical that you understand how this system works to get the most out of Kali and streamline your efforts. The days of painful compilations, disastrous upgrades, debugging gcc, make, and configure problems are long gone, however, the number of available applications has exploded and you need to understand the tools designed to take advantage of them. This is also a critical skill because there are a number of security tools that, due to licensing or other issues, cannot be included in Kali but have Debian packages available for download. It is important that you know how to process and install these packages and how they impact the system, especially when things do not go as expected.

We will begin with some basic overviews of APT, describe the structure and contents of binary and source packages, take a look at some basic tools and scenarios, and then dig deeper to help you wring every ounce of utility from this spectacular package system and suite of tools.

8.1. Introduction to APT

Let's begin with some basic definitions, an overview, and some history about Debian packages, starting with dpkg and APT.

8.1.1. Relationship between APT and dpkg

A Debian package is a compressed archive of a software application. A *binary package* (a .deb file) contains files that can be directly used (such as programs or documentation), while a *source package* contains the source code for the software and the instructions required for building a binary package. A Debian package contains the application's files as well as other *metadata* including the names of the dependencies the application needs, as well as scripts that enable the execution of commands at different stages in the package's lifecycle (installation, removal, and upgrades).

The dpkg tool was designed to process and install .deb packages, but if it encountered an unsatisfied dependency (like a missing library) that would prevent the package from installing, dpkg would simply list the missing dependency, because it had no awareness or built-in logic to find or process the packages that might satisfy those dependencies. The Advanced Package Tool (APT), including apt and apt-get, were designed to address these shortcomings and could automatically resolve these issues. We will talk about both dpkg and the APT tools in this chapter.

The base command for handling Debian packages on the system is dpkg, which performs installation or analysis of .deb packages and their contents. However, dpkg has only a partial view of the Debian universe: it knows what is installed on the system and whatever you provide on the command line, but knows nothing of the other available packages. As such, it will fail if a dependency is not met. APT addresses the limitations.

APT is a set of tools that help manage Debian packages, or applications on your Debian system. You can use APT to install and remove applications, update packages, and even upgrade your entire system. The magic of APT lies in the fact that it is a complete package management system that will not only install or remove a package, but will consider the requirements and dependencies of the packaged application (and even their requirements and dependencies) and attempt to satisfy them automatically. APT relies on dpkg but APT differs from dpkg, as the former installs the latest package from an online source and works to resolve dependencies while dpkg installs a package located on your local system and does not automatically resolve dependencies.

If you have been around long enough to remember compiling programs with gcc (even with the help of utilities such as make and configure), you likely remember that it was a painful process, especially if the application had several dependencies. By deciphering the various warnings and error messages, you may be able to determine which part of the code was failing and most often that failure was due to a missing library or other dependency. You would then track down that missing library or dependency, correct it, and try again. Then, if you were lucky, the compile would complete, but often the build would fail again, complaining about another broken dependency.

APT was designed to help alleviate that problem, collate program requirements and dependencies, and resolve them. This functionality works out-of-the-box on Kali Linux, but it isn't foolproof. It is important that you understand how Debian and Kali's packaging system works because you will need to install packages, update software, or troubleshoot problems with packages. You will use APT in your day-to-day work with Kali Linux and in this chapter, we will introduce you to APT and show you how to install, remove, upgrade, and manage packages, and even show you how to move packages between different Linux distributions. We will also talk about graphical tools that leverage APT, show you how to validate the authenticity of packages, and delve into the concept of a rolling distribution, a technique that brings daily updates to your Kali system.

Before we dig in and show you how to use dpkg and APT to install and manage packages, it is important that we delve into some of the inner workings of APT and discuss some terminology surrounding it.

Package Source and Source Package	The word *source* can be ambiguous. A source package—a package containing the source code of a program—should not be confused with a package source—a repository (website, FTP server, CD-ROM, local directory, etc.) that contains packages.

APT retrieves its packages from a repository, a package storage system or simply, "package source". The `/etc/apt/sources.list` file lists the different repositories (or sources) that publish Debian packages.

8.1.2. Understanding the `sources.list` File

The `sources.list` file is the key configuration file for defining package sources, and it is important to understand how it is laid out and how to configure it since APT will not function without a properly defined list of package sources. Let's discuss its syntax, take a look at the various repositories that are used by Kali Linux, and discuss mirrors and mirror redirection, then you will be ready to put APT to use.

Each active line of the `/etc/apt/sources.list` file (and of the `/etc/apt/sources.list.d/*.list` files) contains the description of a source, made of three parts separated by spaces. Commented lines begin with a # character:

```
# deb cdrom:[Debian GNU/Linux 2016.1 _Kali-rolling_ - Official Snapshot amd64 LIVE/
   ➥ INSTALL Binary 20160830-11:29]/ kali-rolling contrib main non-free

deb http://http.kali.org/kali kali-rolling main non-free contrib
```

Let's take a look at the syntax of this file. The first field indicates the source type:

- deb for binary packages,
- deb-src for source packages.

The second field gives the base URL of the source: this can consist of a Debian mirror or any other package archive set up by a third party. The URL can start with file:// to indicate a local source installed in the system's file hierarchy, with http:// to indicate a source accessible from a web server, or with ftp:// for a source available on an FTP server. The URL can also start with cdrom: for CD-ROM/DVD-ROM/Blu-ray disc-based installations, although this is less frequent since network-based installation methods are more and more common.

The cdrom entries describe the CD/DVD-ROMs you have. Contrary to other entries, a CD-ROM is not always available, since it has to be inserted into the drive and usually only one disc can be read at a time. For those reasons, these sources are managed in a slightly different way and need to be added with the apt-cdrom program, usually executed with the add parameter. The latter will then request the disc to be inserted in the drive and will browse its contents looking for Packages files. It will use these files to update its database of available packages (this operation is usually done by the apt update command). After that, APT will request the disc if it needs a package stored on it.

The syntax of the last field depends on the structure of the repository. In the simplest cases, you can simply indicate a subdirectory (with a required trailing slash) of the desired source (this is often a simple ". /", which refers to the absence of a subdirectory—the packages are then directly at the specified URL). But in the most common case, the repositories will be structured like a Debian mirror, with multiple distributions each having multiple components. In those cases, name the chosen distribution, then the components (or sections) to enable. Let's take a moment to introduce these sections.

Debian and Kali use three sections to differentiate packages according to the licenses chosen by the authors of each work.

Main contains all packages that fully comply with the Debian Free Software Guidelines[1].

The non-free archive is different because it contains software that does not (entirely) conform to these principles but which can nevertheless be distributed without restrictions.

Contrib (contributions) is a set of open source software that cannot function without some non-free elements. These elements may include software from the non-free section or non-free files such as game ROMs, BIOS of consoles, etc. Contrib also includes free software whose compilation requires proprietary elements, such as VirtualBox, which requires a non-free compiler to build some of its files.

Now, let's take a look at the standard Kali Linux package sources, or repositories.

8.1.3. Kali Repositories

A standard sources.list file for a system running Kali Linux refers to one repository (kali-rolling) and the three previously mentioned components: main, contrib, and non-free:

```
# Main Kali repository
deb http://http.kali.org/kali kali-rolling main contrib non-free
```

Let's take a look at the various Kali repositories.

The Kali-Rolling Repository

This is the main repository for end-users. It should always contain installable and recent packages. It is managed by a tool that merges Debian Testing and the Kali-specific packages in a way that ensures that each package's dependencies can be satisfied within kali-rolling. In other words, barring any bug in maintainer scripts, all packages should be installable.

Since Debian Testing evolves daily, so does Kali Rolling. The Kali-specific packages are also regularly updated as we monitor the upstream releases of the most important packages.

---

[1]https://www.debian.org/social_contract#guidelines

The Kali-Dev Repository

This repository is not for public use. It is a space where Kali developers resolve dependency problems arising from the merge of the Kali-specific packages into Debian Testing.

It is also the place where updated packages land first, so if you need an update that was released recently and that has not yet reached kali-rolling, you might be able to grab it from this repository. This is not recommended for regular users.

The Kali-Bleeding-Edge Repository

This repository contains packages automatically built out of the upstream Git (or Subversion) repository. The upside is that you immediately have access to the latest features and bug fixes less than 24 hours after they have been committed. This is an ideal way to verify if a bug that you reported upstream has been fixed.

The downside is that these packages have not been tested or vetted: if the upstream changes impacted the packaging (adding a new dependency), then that package might not work. Because of this, the repository is marked in such a way that APT does not automatically install packages from it, particularly during an upgrade.

You can register the repository either by editing /etc/apt/sources.list or by creating a new file under the /etc/apt/sources.list.d directory, which has the benefit of leaving the original system sources.list file un-altered. In this example, we opt to create a separate /etc/apt/sources.list.d/kali-bleeding-edge.list file like this:

```
# Kali Bleeding Edge repository
deb http://http.kali.org/kali kali-bleeding-edge main contrib non-free
```

The Kali Linux Mirrors

The sources.list extracts above refer to http.kali.org: this is a server running MirrorBrain[2], which will redirect your HTTP requests to an official mirror close to you. MirrorBrain monitors each mirror to ensure that they are working and up-to-date; it will always redirect you to a good mirror.

Debugging a Mirror Redirection	If you have a problem with the mirror (for instance because apt update fails), you can use curl -sI to see where you are being redirected:

	```$ curl -sI http://http.kali.org/README```
	```HTTP/1.1 302 Found```
	```Date: Mon, 11 Apr 2016 09:43:21 GMT```

---

[2]http://mirrorbrain.org

```
Server: Apache/2.4.10 (Debian)
X-MirrorBrain-Mirror: ftp.free.fr
X-MirrorBrain-Realm: country
Link: <http://http.kali.org/README.meta4>; rel=describedby;
    ➥ type="application/metalink4+xml"
Link: <http://ftp.free.fr/pub/kali/README>; rel=duplicate;
    ➥ pri=1; geo=fr
Link: <http://de-rien.fr/kali/README>; rel=duplicate; pri=2;
    ➥ geo=fr
Link: <http://ftp.halifax.rwth-aachen.de/kali/README>; rel=
    ➥ duplicate; pri=3; geo=de
Link: <http://ftp.belnet.be/kali/kali/README>; rel=duplicate;
    ➥  pri=4; geo=be
Link: <http://ftp2.nluug.nl/os/Linux/distr/kali/README>; rel=
    ➥ duplicate; pri=5; geo=nl
Location: http://ftp.free.fr/pub/kali/README
Content-Type: text/html; charset=iso-8859-1
```

If the problem persists, you can edit /etc/apt/sources.list and hardcode the
name of another known working mirror in place of (or before) the http.kali.org
entry.

We also have a second MirrorBrain instance: where http.kali.org hosts the package repositories,
cdimage.kali.org hosts the released ISO images.

➥ http://cdimage.kali.org

If you want to request a list of official Kali Linux Mirrors, you can add .mirrorlist to any valid URL
pointing to http.kali.org or cdimage.kali.org.

➥ http://http.kali.org/README.mirrorlist

➥ http://cdimage.kali.org/README.mirrorlist

These lists are not exhaustive due to some MirrorBrain limitations (most notably mirrors restricted to some countries do not appear in the list unless you are in the given country). But
they contain the best mirrors: they are well maintained and have large amounts of bandwidth
available.

8.2. Basic Package Interaction

Armed with a basic understanding of the APT landscape, let's take a look at some basic package
interactions including the initialization of APT; installation, removal, and purging of packages;
and upgrading of the Kali Linux system. Then let's venture from the command line to take a look
at some graphical APT tools.

8.2.1. Initializing APT

APT is a vast project and tool set, whose original plans included a graphical interface. From a client perspective, it is centered around the command-line tool apt-get as well as apt, which was later developed to overcome design flaws of apt-get.

There are graphical alternatives developed by third parties, including synaptic and aptitude, which we will discuss later. We tend to prefer apt, which we use in the examples that follow. We will, however, detail some of the major syntax differences between tools, as they arise.

When working with APT, you should first download the list of currently available packages with apt update. Depending on the speed of your connection, this can take some time because various packages' list, sources' list and translation files have grown in size alongside Debian development. Of course, CD/DVD installation sets install much more quickly, because they are local to your machine.

8.2.2. Installing Packages

Thanks to the thoughtful design of the Debian package system, you can install packages, with or without their dependencies, fairly easily. Let's take a look at package installation with dpkg and apt.

Installing Packages with dpkg

dpkg is the core tool that you will use (either directly or indirectly through APT) when you need to install a package. It is also a go-to choice if you are operating offline, since it doesn't require an Internet connection. Remember, dpkg will not install any dependencies that the package might require. To install a package with dpkg, simply provide the -i or --install option and the path to the .deb. This implies that you have previously downloaded (or obtained in some other way) the .deb file of the package to install.

```
# dpkg -i man-db_2.7.0.2-5_amd64.deb
(Reading database ... 86425 files and directories currently installed.)
Preparing to unpack man-db_2.7.0.2-5_amd64.deb ...
Unpacking man-db (2.7.0.2-5) over (2.7.0.2-4) ...
Setting up man-db (2.7.0.2-5) ...
Updating database of manual pages ...
Processing triggers for mime-support (3.58) ...
```

We can see the different steps performed by dpkg and can see at what point any error may have occurred. The -i or --install option performs two steps automatically: it unpacks the package and runs the configuration scripts. You can perform these two steps independently (as apt does behind the scenes) with the --unpack and --configure options, respectively:

```
# dpkg --unpack man-db_2.7.0.2-5_amd64.deb
(Reading database ... 86425 files and directories currently installed.)
Preparing to unpack man-db_2.7.0.2-5_amd64.deb ...
Unpacking man-db (2.7.0.2-5) over (2.7.0.2-5) ...
Processing triggers for mime-support (3.58) ...
# dpkg --configure man-db
Setting up man-db (2.7.0.2-5) ...
Updating database of manual pages ...
```

Note that the "Processing triggers" lines refer to code that is automatically executed whenever a package adds, removes, or modifies files in some monitored directories. For instance, the *mime-support* package monitors /usr/lib/mime/packages and executes the update-mime command whenever something changes in that directory (like /usr/lib/mime/packages/man-db in the specific case of man-db).

Sometimes dpkg will fail to install a package and return an error. However, you can order dpkg to ignore this and only issue a warning with various --force-* options. Issuing the dpkg --force-help command will display a complete list of these options. For example, you can use dpkg to forcibly install zsh:

```
$ dpkg -i --force-overwrite zsh_5.2-5+b1_amd64.deb
```

A frequent error, which you are bound to encounter sooner or later, is a file collision. When a package contains a file that is already installed by another package, dpkg will refuse to install it. The following types of messages will then appear:

```
Unpacking libgdm (from .../libgdm_3.8.3-2_amd64.deb) ...
dpkg: error processing /var/cache/apt/archives/libgdm_3.8.3-2_amd64.deb (--unpack):
 ➥ trying to overwrite '/usr/bin/gdmflexiserver', which is also in package gdm3
 ➥ 3.4.1-9
```

In this case, if you think that replacing this file is not a significant risk to the stability of your system (which is usually the case), you can use --force-overwrite to overwrite the file.

While there are many available --force-* options, only --force-overwrite is likely to be used regularly. These options exist for exceptional situations, and it is better to leave them alone as much as possible in order to respect the rules imposed by the packaging mechanism. Do not forget, these rules ensure the consistency and stability of your system.

Installing Packages with APT

Although APT is much more advanced than dpkg and does a lot more behind the scenes, you will find that interacting with packages is quite simple. You can add a package to the system with a simple apt install *package.* APT will automatically install the necessary dependencies:

```
# apt install kali-linux-gpu
Reading package lists... Done
Building dependency tree
Reading state information... Done
The following additional packages will be installed:
  oclgausscrack oclhashcat
The following NEW packages will be installed:
  kali-linux-gpu oclgausscrack oclhashcat
0 upgraded, 3 newly installed, 0 to remove and 416 not upgraded.
Need to get 2,494 kB of archives.
After this operation, 51.5 MB of additional disk space will be used.
Do you want to continue? [Y/n]
Get:1 http://archive-2.kali.org/kali kali-rolling/non-free amd64 oclhashcat amd64 2.01+
    ➡ git20160114-0kali2 [2,451 kB]
Get:2 http://archive-2.kali.org/kali kali-rolling/main amd64 oclgausscrack amd64 1.3-1
    ➡ kali2 [37.2 kB]
Get:3 http://archive-2.kali.org/kali kali-rolling/main amd64 kali-linux-gpu amd64
    ➡ 2016.3.2 [6,412 B]
Fetched 2,494 kB in 0s (3,060 kB/s)
Selecting previously unselected package oclhashcat.
(Reading database ... 317084 files and directories currently installed.)
Preparing to unpack .../0-oclhashcat_2.01+git20160114-0kali2_amd64.deb ...
Unpacking oclhashcat (2.01+git20160114-0kali2) ...
Selecting previously unselected package oclgausscrack.
Preparing to unpack .../1-oclgausscrack_1.3-1kali2_amd64.deb ...
Unpacking oclgausscrack (1.3-1kali2) ...
Selecting previously unselected package kali-linux-gpu.
Preparing to unpack .../2-kali-linux-gpu_2016.3.2_amd64.deb ...
Unpacking kali-linux-gpu (2016.3.2) ...
Setting up oclhashcat (2.01+git20160114-0kali2) ...
Setting up oclgausscrack (1.3-1kali2) ...
Setting up kali-linux-gpu (2016.3.2) ...
```

You can also use apt-get install *package*, or aptitude install *package*. For simple package installation, they do essentially the same thing. As you will see later, the differences are more meaningful for upgrades or when dependencies resolution do not have any perfect solution.

If sources.list lists several distributions, you can specify the package version with apt install *package=version*, but indicating its distribution of origin (kali-rolling, kali-dev, or kali-bleeding-edge) with apt install *package/distribution* is usually preferred.

As with dpkg, you can also instruct apt to forcibly install a package and overwrite files with --force-overwrite, but the syntax is a bit strange since you are passing the argument through to dpkg:

```
# apt -o Dpkg::Options::="--force-overwrite" install zsh
```

8.2.3. Upgrading Kali Linux

As a rolling distribution, Kali Linux has spectacular upgrade capabilities. In this section, we will take a look at how simple it is to upgrade Kali, and we will discuss strategies for planning your updates.

We recommend regular upgrades, because they will install the latest security updates. To upgrade, use apt update followed by either apt upgrade, apt-get upgrade, or aptitude safe-upgrade. These commands look for installed packages that can be upgraded without removing any packages. In other words, the goal is to ensure the least intrusive upgrade possible. The apt-get command line tool is slightly more demanding than aptitude or apt because it will refuse to install packages that were not installed beforehand.

The apt tool will generally select the most recent version number (except for packages from kali-bleeding-edge, which are ignored by default whatever their version number).

To tell apt to use a specific distribution when searching for upgraded packages, you need to use the -t or --target-release option, followed by the name of the distribution you want (for example: apt -t kali-rolling upgrade). To avoid specifying this option every time you use apt, you can add APT::Default-Release "kali-rolling"; in the file /etc/apt/apt.conf.d/local.

For more important upgrades, such as major version upgrades, use apt full-upgrade. With this instruction, apt will complete the upgrade even if it has to remove some obsolete packages or install new dependencies. This is also the command that you should use for regular upgrades of your Kali Rolling system. It is so simple that it hardly needs explanation: APT's reputation is based on this great functionality.

Unlike apt and aptitude, apt-get doesn't know the full-upgrade command. Instead, you should use apt-get dist-upgrade (distribution upgrade), a well-known command that apt and aptitude also accept for backwards compatibility.

Be Aware of Important Changes	To anticipate some of these problems, you can install the *apt-listchanges* package, which displays information about possible problems at the beginning of a package upgrade. This information is compiled by the package maintainers and put in /usr/share/doc/*package*/NEWS.Debian files for your benefit. Reading these files (possibly through *apt-listchanges*) should help you avoid nasty surprises.

Since becoming a rolling distribution, Kali can receive upgrades several times a day. However, that might not be the best strategy. So, how often should you upgrade Kali Linux? There is no hard rule but there are some guidelines that can help you. You should upgrade:

- When you are aware of a security issue that is fixed in an update
- When you suspect that an updated version might fix a bug that you are experiencing
- Before reporting a bug to make sure it is still present in the latest version that you have available

- Often enough to get the security fixes that you have not heard about

There are also cases where it is best to not upgrade. For example, it might not be a good idea to upgrade:

- If you can't afford any breakage (for example, because you go offline, or because you are about to give a presentation with your computer); it is best to do the upgrade later, when you have enough time to troubleshoot any issue introduced in the process.

- If a disruptive change happened recently (or is still ongoing) and you fear that all issues have not yet been discovered. For example, when a new GNOME version is released, not all packages are updated at the same time and you are likely to have a mix of packages with the old version and the new version. Most of the time this is fine and it helps everybody to release those updates progressively, but there are always exceptions and some applications might be broken due to such discrepancies.

- If the `apt full-upgrade` output tells you that it will remove packages that you consider important for your work. In those cases, you want to review the situation and try to understand why `apt` wants to remove them. Maybe the packages are currently broken and in this case you might want to wait until fixed versions are available, or they have been obsoleted and you should identify their replacements and then proceed with the full upgrade anyway.

In general, we recommend that you upgrade Kali at least once a week. You can certainly upgrade daily but it doesn't make sense to do it more often than that. Even if mirrors are synchronized four times a day, the updates coming from Debian usually land only once a day.

8.2.4. Removing and Purging Packages

Removing a package is even simpler than installing one. Let's take a look at how to remove a package with dpkg and apt.

To remove a package with dpkg, supply the -r or --remove option, followed by the name of a package. This removal is not, however, complete: all of the configuration files, maintainer scripts, log files (system logs), data generated by the daemon (such as the content of an LDAP server directory or the content of a database for an SQL server), and most other user data handled by the package remain intact. The remove option makes it easy to uninstall a program and later re-install it with the same configuration. Also remember that dependencies are not removed. Consider this example:

```
# dpkg --remove kali-linux-gpu
(Reading database ... 317681 files and directories currently installed.)
Removing kali-linux-gpu (2016.3.2) ...
```

You can also remove packages from the system with apt remove *package*. APT will automatically delete the packages that depend on the package that is being removed. Like the dpkg example, configuration files and user data will not be removed.

Through the addition of suffixes to package names, you can use apt (or apt-get and aptitude) to install certain packages and remove others on the same command line. With an apt install command, add "-" to the names of the packages you wish to remove. With an apt remove command, add "+" to the names of the packages you wish to install.

The next example shows two different ways to install *package1* and to remove *package2*.

```
# apt install package1 package2-
[...]
# apt remove package1+ package2
[...]
```

This can also be used to exclude packages that would otherwise be installed, for example due to a Recommends (discussed later). In general, the dependency solver will use that information as a hint to look for alternative solutions.

To remove all data associated with a package, you can purge the package with the dpkg -P *package*, or apt purge *package* commands. This will completely remove the package and all user data, and in the case of apt, will delete dependencies as well.

```
# dpkg -r debian-cd
(Reading database ... 97747 files and directories currently installed.)
Removing debian-cd (3.1.17) ...
# dpkg -P debian-cd
(Reading database ... 97401 files and directories currently installed.)
Removing debian-cd (3.1.17) ...
Purging configuration files for debian-cd (3.1.17) ...
```

Warning! Given the definitive nature of purge, do not execute it lightly. You will lose everything associated with that package.

8.2.5. Inspecting Packages

Next, let's take a look at some of the tools that can be used to inspect Debian packages. We will learn of dpkg, apt, and apt-cache commands that can be used to query and visualize the package database.

Querying dpkg's Database and Inspecting .deb Files

We will begin with several dpkg options that query the internal dpkg database. This database resides on the filesystem at /var/lib/dpkg and contains multiple sections including configuration scripts (/var/lib/dpkg/info), a list of files the package installed (/var/lib/dpkg/info/*.list), and the status of each package that has been installed (/var/lib/dpkg/status). You can use dpkg to interact with the files in this database. Note that most options are available in a long version (one or more relevant words, preceded by a double dash) and a short version (a single letter, often the initial of one word from the long version, and preceded by a single dash). This convention is so common that it is a POSIX standard.

First, let's take a look at --listfiles *package* (or -L), which lists the files that were installed by the specified package:

```
$ dpkg -L base-passwd
/.
/usr
/usr/sbin
/usr/sbin/update-passwd
/usr/share
/usr/share/lintian
/usr/share/lintian/overrides
/usr/share/lintian/overrides/base-passwd
/usr/share/doc-base
/usr/share/doc-base/users-and-groups
/usr/share/base-passwd
/usr/share/base-passwd/group.master
/usr/share/base-passwd/passwd.master
/usr/share/man
/usr/share/man/pl
/usr/share/man/pl/man8
/usr/share/man/pl/man8/update-passwd.8.gz
[...]
/usr/share/doc
/usr/share/doc/base-passwd
/usr/share/doc/base-passwd/users-and-groups.txt.gz
/usr/share/doc/base-passwd/changelog.gz
/usr/share/doc/base-passwd/copyright
/usr/share/doc/base-passwd/README
/usr/share/doc/base-passwd/users-and-groups.html
```

Next, dpkg --search *file* (or -S), finds any packages containing the file or path passed in the argument. For example, to find the package containing /bin/date:

```
$ dpkg -S /bin/date
coreutils: /bin/date
```

The dpkg --status *package* (or -s) command displays the headers of an installed package. For example, to search the headers for the coreutils package:

```
$ dpkg -s coreutils
Package: coreutils
Essential: yes
Status: install ok installed
```

```
Priority: required
Section: utils
Installed-Size: 13855
Maintainer: Michael Stone <mstone@debian.org>
Architecture: amd64
Multi-Arch: foreign
Version: 8.23-3
Replaces: mktemp, realpath, timeout
Pre-Depends: libacl1 (>= 2.2.51-8), libattr1 (>= 1:2.4.46-8), libc6 (>= 2.17),
    ➥ libselinux1 (>= 2.1.13)
Conflicts: timeout
Description: GNU core utilities
This package contains the basic file, shell and text manipulation
utilities which are expected to exist on every operating system.
.
Specifically, this package includes:
arch base64 basename cat chcon chgrp chmod chown chroot cksum comm cp
csplit cut date dd df dir dircolors dirname du echo env expand expr
factor false flock fmt fold groups head hostid id install join link ln
logname ls md5sum mkdir mkfifo mknod mktemp mv nice nl nohup nproc numfmt
od paste pathchk pinky pr printenv printf ptx pwd readlink realpath rm
rmdir runcon sha*sum seq shred sleep sort split stat stty sum sync tac
tail tee test timeout touch tr true truncate tsort tty uname unexpand
uniq unlink users vdir wc who whoami yes
Homepage: http://gnu.org/software/coreutils
```

The dpkg --list (or -l) command displays the list of packages known to the system and their installation status. You can also use grep on the output to search for certain fields, or provide wildcards (such as b*) to search for packages that match a particular partial search string. This will show a summary of the packages. For example, to show a summary list of all packages that start with 'b':

```
$ dpkg -l 'b*'
Desired=Unknown/Install/Remove/Purge/Hold
| Status=Not/Inst/Conf-files/Unpacked/halF-conf/Half-inst/trig-aWait/Trig-pend
|/ Err?=(none)/Reinst-required (Status,Err: uppercase=bad)
||/ Name           Version      Architecture Description
+++-==============-============-============-===============================
ii  b43-fwcutter   1:019-3      amd64        utility for extracting Broadcom 4
ii  backdoor-facto 3.4.2-0kali1 all          Patch win32/64 binaries with shel
un  backupninja    <none>       <none>       (no description available)
un  backuppc       <none>       <none>       (no description available)
ii  baobab         3.22.1-1     amd64        GNOME disk usage analyzer
[...]
```

The dpkg --contents *file.deb* (or -c) command lists all the files in a particular .deb file:

```
$ dpkg -c /var/cache/apt/archives/gnupg_1.4.18-6_amd64.deb
drwxr-xr-x root/root          0 2014-12-04 23:03 ./
drwxr-xr-x root/root          0 2014-12-04 23:03 ./lib/
drwxr-xr-x root/root          0 2014-12-04 23:03 ./lib/udev/
drwxr-xr-x root/root          0 2014-12-04 23:03 ./lib/udev/rules.d/
-rw-r--r-- root/root       2711 2014-12-04 23:03 ./lib/udev/rules.d/60-gnupg.rules
drwxr-xr-x root/root          0 2014-12-04 23:03 ./usr/
drwxr-xr-x root/root          0 2014-12-04 23:03 ./usr/lib/
drwxr-xr-x root/root          0 2014-12-04 23:03 ./usr/lib/gnupg/
-rwxr-xr-x root/root      39328 2014-12-04 23:03 ./usr/lib/gnupg/gpgkeys_ldap
-rwxr-xr-x root/root      92872 2014-12-04 23:03 ./usr/lib/gnupg/gpgkeys_hkp
-rwxr-xr-x root/root      47576 2014-12-04 23:03 ./usr/lib/gnupg/gpgkeys_finger
-rwxr-xr-x root/root      84648 2014-12-04 23:03 ./usr/lib/gnupg/gpgkeys_curl
-rwxr-xr-x root/root       3499 2014-12-04 23:03 ./usr/lib/gnupg/gpgkeys_mailto
drwxr-xr-x root/root          0 2014-12-04 23:03 ./usr/bin/
-rwxr-xr-x root/root      60128 2014-12-04 23:03 ./usr/bin/gpgsplit
-rwxr-xr-x root/root    1012688 2014-12-04 23:03 ./usr/bin/gpg
[...]
```

The dpkg --info *file.deb* (or -I) command displays the headers of the specified .deb file:

```
$ dpkg -I /var/cache/apt/archives/gnupg_1.4.18-6_amd64.deb
 new debian package, version 2.0.
 size 1148362 bytes: control archive=3422 bytes.
    1264 bytes,     26 lines      control
    4521 bytes,     65 lines      md5sums
     479 bytes,     13 lines  *   postinst              #!/bin/sh
     473 bytes,     13 lines  *   preinst               #!/bin/sh
 Package: gnupg
 Version: 1.4.18-6
 Architecture: amd64
 Maintainer: Debian GnuPG-Maintainers <pkg-gnupg-maint@lists.alioth.debian.org>
 Installed-Size: 4888
 Depends: gpgv, libbz2-1.0, libc6 (>= 2.15), libreadline6 (>= 6.0), libusb-0.1-4 (>=
 ➥ 2:0.1.12), zlib1g (>= 1:1.1.4)
 Recommends: gnupg-curl, libldap-2.4-2 (>= 2.4.7)
 Suggests: gnupg-doc, libpcsclite1, parcimonie, xloadimage | imagemagick | eog
 Section: utils
 Priority: important
 Multi-Arch: foreign
 Homepage: http://www.gnupg.org
 Description: GNU privacy guard - a free PGP replacement
  GnuPG is GNU's tool for secure communication and data storage.
  It can be used to encrypt data and to create digital signatures.
  It includes an advanced key management facility and is compliant
```

```
  with the proposed OpenPGP Internet standard as described in RFC 4880.
[...]
```

You can also use dpkg to compare package version numbers with the --compare-versions option, which is often called by external programs, including configuration scripts executed by dpkg itself. This option requires three parameters: a version number, a comparison operator, and a second version number. The different possible operators are: lt (strictly less than), le (less than or equal to), eq (equal), ne (not equal), ge (greater than or equal to), and gt (strictly greater than). If the comparison is correct, dpkg returns 0 (success); if not, it gives a non-zero return value (indicating failure). Consider these comparisons:

```
$ dpkg --compare-versions 1.2-3 gt 1.1-4
$ echo $?
0
$ dpkg --compare-versions 1.2-3 lt 1.1-4
$ echo $?
1
$ dpkg --compare-versions 2.6.0pre3-1 lt 2.6.0-1
$ echo $?
1
```

Note the unexpected failure of the last comparison: for dpkg, the string "pre" (usually denoting a pre-release) has no particular meaning, and dpkg simply interprets it as a string, in which case "2.6.0pre3-1" is alphabetically greater than "2.6.0-1". When we want a package's version number to indicate that it is a pre-release, we use the tilde character, "~":

```
$ dpkg --compare-versions 2.6.0~pre3-1 lt 2.6.0-1
$ echo $?
0
```

Querying the Database of Available Packages with apt-cache and apt

The apt-cache command can display much of the information stored in APT's internal database. This information is a sort of cache since it is gathered from the different sources listed in the sources.list file. This happens during the apt update operation.

VOCABULARY

Cache

A cache is a temporary storage system used to speed up frequent data access when the usual access method is expensive (performance-wise). This concept can be applied in numerous situations and at different scales, from the core of microprocessors up to high-end storage systems.

In the case of APT, the reference `Packages` files are those located on Debian mirrors. That said, it would be very ineffective to push every search through the online package databases. That is why APT stores a copy of those files (in `/var/lib/apt/lists/`) and searches are done within those local files. Similarly, `/var/cache/apt/archives/` contains a cached copy of already downloaded packages to avoid downloading them again if you need to reinstall them.

To avoid excessive disk usage when you upgrade frequently, you should regularly sort through the `/var/cache/apt/archives/` directory. Two commands can be used for this: `apt clean` (or `apt-get clean`) entirely empties the directory; `apt autoclean` (`apt-get autoclean`) only removes packages that can no longer be downloaded because they have disappeared from the mirror and are therefore useless. Note that the configuration parameter `APT::Clean-Installed` can be used to prevent the removal of `.deb` files that are currently installed. Also, note that apt drops the downloaded files once they have been installed, so this matters mainly when you use other tools.

The `apt-cache` command can do keyword-based package searches with `apt-cache search key word`. It can also display the headers of the package's available versions with `apt-cache show package`. This command provides the package's description, its dependencies, and the name of its maintainer. This feature is particularly useful in determining the packages that are installed via meta-packages, such as *kali-linux-wireless*, *kali-linux-web*, and *kali-linux-gpu*. Note that `apt search`, `apt show`, `aptitude search`, and `aptitude show` work in the same way.

An Alternative: axi-cache

`apt-cache search` is a very rudimentary tool, basically implementing grep on package's descriptions. It often returns too many results or none at all, when too many keywords are included.

`axi-cache search` *term*, on the other hand, provides better results, sorted by relevancy. It uses the *Xapian* search engine and is part of the *apt-xapian-index* package, which indexes all package information (and more, like the `.desktop` files from all Debian packages). It knows about tags and returns results in a matter of milliseconds.

```
$ axi-cache search forensics graphical
5 results found.
Results 1-5:
100% autopsy - graphical interface to SleuthKit
82% forensics-colorize - show differences between files using
    ➡ color graphics
73% dff - Powerful, efficient and modular digital forensic
    ➡ framework
53% gpart - Guess PC disk partition table, find lost
    ➡ partitions
46% testdisk - Partition scanner and disk recovery tool, and
    ➡ PhotoRec file recovery tool
```

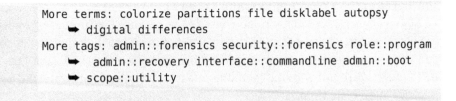
```
More terms: colorize partitions file disklabel autopsy
        ➡ digital differences
More tags: admin::forensics security::forensics role::program
        ➡ admin::recovery interface::commandline admin::boot
        ➡ scope::utility
```

Some features are more rarely used. For instance, apt-cache policy displays the priorities of package sources as well as those of individual packages. Another example is apt-cache dumpavail, which displays the headers of all available versions of all packages. apt-cache pkgnames displays the list of all the packages that appear at least once in the cache.

8.2.6. Troubleshooting

Sooner or later, you will run into a problem when interacting with a package. In this section, we will outline some basic troubleshooting steps that you can take and provide some tools that will lead you closer to a potential solution.

Handling Problems after an Upgrade

In spite of the Kali/Debian maintainers' best efforts, a system upgrade isn't always as smooth as we would hope. New software versions may be incompatible with previous ones (for instance, their default behavior or their data format may have changed), or bugs may slip through the cracks despite the testing performed by package maintainers and Debian Unstable users.

Leveraging Bug Reports   You might sometimes find that a new version of software doesn't work at all. This generally happens if the application isn't particularly popular and hasn't been tested enough. The first thing to do is to have a look at the Kali bug tracker[3] and at the Debian bug tracking system[4] at https://bugs.debian.org/*package* , and check whether the problem has already been reported. If it hasn't, you should report it yourself (see section 6.3, "Filing a Good Bug Report" [page 129] for detailed instructions). If it is already known, the bug report and the associated messages are usually an excellent source of information related to the bug. In some cases, a patch already exists and has been made available in the bug report itself; you can then recompile a fixed version of the broken package locally (see section 9.1, "Modifying Kali Packages" [page 222]). In other cases, users may have found a workaround for the problem and shared their insights about it in their replies to the report; those instructions may help you work around the problem until a fix or patch is released. In a best-case scenario, the package may have already been fixed and you may find details in the bug report.

---

[3]http://bugs.kali.org
[4]https://bugs.debian.org

Downgrading to a Working Version   When the problem is a clear regression (where the former version worked), you can try to downgrade the package. In this case, you will need a copy of the old version. If you have access to the old version in one of the repositories configured in APT, you can use a simple one-liner command to downgrade (see section 8.2.2.2, "Installing Packages with APT" [page 177]). But with Kali's rolling release, you will usually only find a single version of each package at any one time.

You can still try to find the old .deb file and install it manually with dpkg. Old .deb files can be found in multiple places:

- in APT's cache in /var/cache/apt/archives/
- in the pool directory on your usual Kali mirror (removed and obsolete packages are kept for three to four days to avoid problems with users not having the latest package indices)
- in http://snapshot.debian.org if the affected package was provided by Debian and not by Kali; this service keeps historical versions of all Debian packages

Dealing with Broken Maintainer Scripts   Sometimes the upgrade gets interrupted because one of the package maintainer scripts fails (usually, it is the postinst). In those cases, you can try to diagnose the problem, and possibly work around it, by editing the problematic script.

Here we rely on the fact that maintainer scripts are stored in /var/lib/dpkg/info/ and that we can review and modify them.

Since maintainer scripts are usually simple shell scripts, it is possible to add a set -x line just after the shebang line and arrange them to be rerun (with dpkg --configure -a for postinst) to see precisely what is happening and where it is failing. This output can also nicely complement any bug report that you might file.

With this newly gained knowledge, you can either fix the underlying problem or transform the failing command into a working one (for example by adding || true at the end of the line).

Note that this tip does not work for a failing preinst since that script is executed even before the package gets installed so it is not yet in its final location. It does work for postrm and prerm although you will need to execute a package removal (respectively upgrade) to trigger them.

The dpkg Log File

The dpkg tool keeps a log of all of its actions in /var/log/dpkg.log. This log is extremely verbose, since it details all the stages of each package. In addition to offering a way to track dpkg's behavior, it helps to keep a history of the development of the system: you can find the exact moment when each package has been installed or updated, and this information can be extremely useful in understanding a recent change in behavior. Additionally, with all versions being recorded, it is easy to cross-check the information with the changelog.Debian.gz for packages in question, or even with online bug reports.

```
# tail /var/log/dpkg.log
2016-12-22 09:04:05 status installed kali-linux-gpu:amd64 2016.3.2
2016-12-22 09:20:07 startup packages remove
2016-12-22 09:20:07 status installed kali-linux-gpu:amd64 2016.3.2
2016-12-22 09:20:07 remove kali-linux-gpu:amd64 2016.3.2 <none>
2016-12-22 09:20:07 status half-configured kali-linux-gpu:amd64 2016.3.2
2016-12-22 09:20:07 status half-installed kali-linux-gpu:amd64 2016.3.2
2016-12-22 09:20:07 status config-files kali-linux-gpu:amd64 2016.3.2
2016-12-22 09:20:07 status config-files kali-linux-gpu:amd64 2016.3.2
2016-12-22 09:20:07 status config-files kali-linux-gpu:amd64 2016.3.2
2016-12-22 09:20:07 status not-installed kali-linux-gpu:amd64 <none>
```

Reinstalling Packages with apt --reinstall and aptitude reinstall

When you mistakenly damage your system by removing or modifying certain files, the easiest way to restore them is to reinstall the affected package. Unfortunately, the packaging system finds that the package is already installed and politely refuses to reinstall it. To avoid this, use the --reinstall option of the apt and apt-get commands. The following command reinstalls *postfix* even if it is already present:

```
# apt --reinstall install postfix
```

The aptitude command line is slightly different but achieves the same result with aptitude reinstall postfix. The dpkg command does not prevent re-installation, but it is rarely called directly.

Do Not Use apt --reinstall to Recover from an Attack	Using apt --reinstall to restore packages modified during an attack will certainly not recover the system as it was.
	After an attack, you can't rely on anything: dpkg and apt might have been replaced by malicious programs, not reinstalling the files as you would like them to. The attacker might also have altered or created files outside the control of dpkg.

Remember that you can specify a specific distribution with apt as well, which means you can roll back to an older version of a package (if for instance you know that it works well), provided that it is still available in one of the sources referenced by the sources.list file:

```
# apt install w3af/kali-rolling
```

Leveraging --force-* to Repair Broken Dependencies

If you are not careful, the use of a --force-* option or some other malfunction can lead to a system where the APT family of commands will refuse to function. In effect, some of these options allow installation of a package when a dependency is not met, or when there is a conflict. The result is an inconsistent system from the point of view of dependencies, and the APT commands will refuse to execute any action except those that will bring the system back to a consistent state (this often consists of installing the missing dependency or removing a problematic package). This usually results in a message like this one, obtained after installing a new version of *rdesktop* while ignoring its dependency on a newer version of *libc6*:

```
# apt full-upgrade
[...]
You might want to run 'apt-get -f install' to correct these.
The following packages have unmet dependencies:
rdesktop: Depends: libc6 (>= 2.5) but 2.3.6.ds1-13etch7 is installed
E: Unmet dependencies. Try using -f.
```

If you are a courageous administrator who is certain of the correctness of your analysis, you may choose to ignore a dependency or conflict and use the corresponding --force-* option. In this case, if you want to be able to continue to use apt or aptitude, you must edit /var/lib/dpkg/status to delete or modify the dependency, or conflict, that you have chosen to override.

This manipulation is an ugly hack and should never be used, except in the most extreme case of necessity. Quite frequently, a more fitting solution is to recompile the package that is causing the problem or use a new version (potentially corrected) from a repository providing backports (backports are newer versions especially recompiled to work in an older environment).

8.2.7. Frontends: aptitude and synaptic

APT is a C++ program whose code mainly resides in the libapt-pkg shared library. Thanks to this shared library, it opened the door for the creation of user interfaces (front-ends), since the shared library code can easily be reused. Historically, apt-get was only designed as a test front-end for libapt-pkg but its success tends to obscure this fact.

Over time, despite the popularity of command line interfaces like apt and apt-get, various graphical interfaces were developed. We will take a look at two of those interfaces in this section: aptitude and synaptic.

Aptitude

Aptitude, shown in Figure 8.1, "The aptitude package manager" [page 191], is an interactive program that can be used in semi-graphical mode on the console. You can browse the list of installed and available packages, look up all the information, and select packages to install or remove. The program is designed specifically to be used by administrators so its default behavior is much more intelligent than APT's, and its interface much easier to understand.

```
 Actions   Undo   Package   Resolver   Search   Options   Views   Help
C-T: Menu   ?: Help   q: Quit   u: Update   g: Download/Install/Remove Pkgs
aptitude 0.6.11               Will use 6,202 kB of disk spac DL Size: 2,765 kB
--\ Installed Packages (270)
  --\ admin - Administrative utilities (install software, manage users, etc) (43
    --\ main - The main Debian archive (43)
i A   acpi-support-base                      0.142-6          0.142-6
i     acpid                                  1:2.0.23-2       1:2.0.23-2
i A   adduser                                3.113+nmu3       3.113+nmu3
i A   apt                                    1.0.9.6          1.0.9.6
i A   apt-utils                              1.0.9.6          1.0.9.6
i     aptitude                               0.6.11-1+b1      0.6.11-1+b1
i A   aptitude-common                        0.6.11-1         0.6.11-1
terminal-based package manager
aptitude is a package manager with a number of useful features, including: a    #
mutt-like syntax for matching packages in a flexible manner, dselect-like
persistence of user actions, the ability to retrieve and display the Debian
changelog of most packages, and a command-line mode similar to that of apt-get.

aptitude is also Y2K-compliant, non-fattening, naturally cleansing, and
housebroken.
Homepage: http://aptitude.alioth.debian.org/


Tags: admin::configuring, admin::package-management, implemented-in::c++,
```

Figure 8.1   *The aptitude package manager*

When you run `aptitude`, you are shown a list of packages sorted by state (installed, not-installed, or installed but not available on the mirrors), while other sections display tasks, virtual packages, and new packages that appeared recently on mirrors. To facilitate thematic browsing, other views are available.

In all cases, `aptitude` displays a list combining categories and packages on the screen. Categories are organized through a tree structure, whose branches can respectively be unfolded or folded with the Enter, [, and] keys. The + key should be used to mark a package for installation, - to mark it for removal, and _ to purge it. Note that these keys can also be used for categories, in which case the corresponding actions will be applied to all the packages of the category. The u key updates the lists of available packages and Shift+u prepares a global system upgrade. The g key switches to a summary view of the requested changes (and typing g again will apply the changes), and q quits the current view. If you are in the initial view, this will close `aptitude`.

aptitude's Documentation   This section does not cover the finer details of using `aptitude`, it rather focuses on giving you a user survival kit. `aptitude` is rather well documented and we advise you to use its complete manual available in the *aptitude-doc-en* package.

➡ `file:///usr/share/doc/aptitude/html/en/index.html`

To search for a package, you can type / followed by a search pattern. This pattern matches the name of the package but can also be applied to the description (if preceded by ~d), to the section (with ~s), or to other characteristics detailed in the documentation. The same patterns can filter the list of displayed packages: type the l key (as in *limit*) and enter the pattern.

Managing the *automatic flag* of Debian packages (see section 8.3.4, "Tracking Automatically Installed Packages" [page 199]) is a breeze with `aptitude`. It is possible to browse the list of installed packages and mark packages as automatic with Shift+m or you can remove the mark with the m key. Automatic packages are displayed with an "A" in the list of packages. This feature also offers a simple way to visualize the packages in use on a machine, without all the libraries and dependencies that you don't really care about. The related pattern that can be used with l (to activate the filter mode) is ~i!~M. It specifies that you only want to see installed packages (~i) not marked as automatic (!~M).

Using aptitude on the Command-Line Interface   Most of Aptitude's features are accessible via the interactive interface as well as via the command-line. These command-lines will seem familiar to regular users of `apt-get` and `apt-cache`.

The advanced features of `aptitude` are also available on the command-line. You can use the same package search patterns as in the interactive version. For example, if you want to clean up the list of manually installed packages, and if you know that none of the locally installed programs require any particular libraries or Perl modules, you can mark the corresponding packages as automatic with a single command:

```
# aptitude markauto '~slibs|~sperl'
```

Here, you can clearly see the power of the search pattern system of `aptitude`, which enables the instant selection of all the packages in the `libs` and `perl` sections.

Beware, if some packages are marked as automatic and if no other package depends on them, they will be removed immediately (after a confirmation request).

Managing Recommendations, Suggestions, and Tasks   Another interesting feature of `aptitude` is the fact that it respects recommendations between packages while still giving users the choice not to install them on a case-by-case basis. For example, the *gnome* package recommends *gdebi* (among others). When you select the former for installation, the latter will also be selected (and marked as automatic if not already installed on the system). Typing g will make it obvious: *gdebi* appears on the summary screen of pending actions in the list of packages installed automatically to satisfy dependencies. However, you can decide not to install it by deselecting it before confirming the operations.

Note that this recommendation tracking feature does not apply to upgrades. For instance, if a new version of *gnome* recommends a package that it did not recommend formerly, the package won't be marked for installation. However, it will be listed on the upgrade screen so that the administrator can still select it for installation.

Suggestions between packages are also taken into account, but in a manner adapted to their specific status. For example, since *gnome* suggests *dia-gnome*, the latter will be displayed on the summary screen of pending actions (in the section of packages suggested by other packages). This way, it is visible and the administrator can decide whether to take the suggestion into account or not. Since it is only a suggestion and not a dependency or a recommendation, the package will not be selected automatically—its selection requires manual intervention (thus, the package will not be marked as automatic).

In the same spirit, remember that `aptitude` makes intelligent use of the concept of tasks. Since tasks are displayed as categories in the screens of packages lists, you can either select a full task for installation or removal or browse the list of packages included in the task to select a smaller subset.

Better Solver Algorithms To conclude this section, let's note that `aptitude` has more elaborate algorithms compared to `apt` when it comes to resolving difficult situations. When a set of actions is requested and when these combined actions would lead to an incoherent system, `aptitude` evaluates several possible scenarios and presents them in order of decreasing relevance. However, these algorithms are not foolproof. Fortunately, there is always the possibility to manually select the actions to perform. When the currently selected actions lead to contradictions, the upper part of the screen indicates a number of broken packages (you can directly navigate to those packages by pressing b). Then you can manually build a solution. In particular, you can get access to the different available versions by selecting the package with Enter. If the selection of one of these versions solves the problem, you should not hesitate to use the function. When the number of broken packages gets down to zero, you can safely go to the summary screen of pending actions for a last check before you apply them.

Aptitude's Log   Like dpkg, aptitude keeps a trace of executed actions in its logfile (/var/log/aptitude). However, since both commands work at a very different level, you cannot find the same information in their respective logfiles. While dpkg logs all the operations executed on individual packages step by step, aptitude gives a broader view of high-level operations like a system-wide upgrade.

Beware, this logfile only contains a summary of operations performed by aptitude. If other front-ends (or even dpkg itself) are occasionally used, then aptitude's log will only contain a partial view of the operations, so you can't rely on it to build a trustworthy history of the system.

Synaptic

Synaptic is a graphical package manager that features a clean and efficient graphical interface (shown in Figure 8.2, "`synaptic` Package Manager" [page 194]) based on GTK+ and GNOME. Its many ready-to-use filters give fast access to newly available packages, installed packages, upgradable packages, obsolete packages, and so on. If you browse through these lists, you can select the operations to be done on the packages (install, upgrade, remove, purge); these operations are not performed immediately, but put into a task list. A single click on a button then validates the operations and they are performed in one go.

Figure 8.2 *synaptic Package Manager*

8.3. Advanced APT Configuration and Usage

Now it is time to dive into some more advanced topics. First, we will take a look at advanced configuration of APT, which will allow you to set more permanent options that will apply to APT tools. We will then show how package priorities can be manipulated, which opens the door for advanced fine-tuned, customized updates and upgrades. We will also show how to handle multiple distributions so that you can start experimenting with packages coming from other distributions. Next, we will take a look at how to track automatically installed packages, a capability that enables you to manage packages that are installed through dependencies. We will also explain how multi-arch support opens the door for running packages built for various hardware architectures. Last but not least, we will discuss the cryptographic protocols and utilities in place that will let you validate each package's authenticity.

8.3.1. Configuring APT

Before we dive into the configuration of APT, let's take a moment to discuss the configuration mechanism of the Debian system. Historically, configuration was handled by dedicated configuration files. However, in modern Linux systems like Debian and Kali, configuration directories with the .d suffix are becoming more commonly used. Each directory represents a configuration file that is split into multiple files. In this sense, all of the files in /etc/apt/apt.conf.d/ are instructions for the configuration of APT. APT processes the files in alphabetical order, so that the later files can modify configuration elements defined in the earlier files.

This structure brings some flexibility to administrators and package maintainers, allowing them to make software configuration changes through file additions without having to change an existing file. This is especially helpful for package maintainers because they can use this approach to adapt the configuration of other software to ensure that it perfectly co-exists with theirs, without breaking the Debian policy that explicitly forbids modifying configuration files of other packages. Because of the .d configuration mechanism, you don't have to manually follow multiple package configuration instructions typically found in the package's /usr/share/doc/*package* /README.Debian file, since the installer can drop in configuration files.

Beware of Configuration Files Generated from .d Directories	While APT has native support of its /etc/apt/apt.conf.d directory, this is not always the case. For some applications (like exim, for example), the .d directory is a Debian-specific addition used as input to dynamically generate the canonical configuration file used by the application. In those cases, the packages provide an "update-*" command (for example: update-exim4.conf) that will concatenate the files from the .d directory and overwrite the main configuration file.

In those cases, you must not manually edit the main configuration file as your changes will be lost on the next execution of the update-* command, and you must also not forget to run the former command after having edited a file out of the .d directory (or your changes will not be used). |

Armed with an understanding of the .d configuration mechanism, let's talk about how you can leverage it to configure APT. As we have discussed, you can alter APT's behavior through command-line arguments to dpkg like this example, which performs a forced overwrite install of zsh:

```
# apt -o Dpkg::Options::="--force-overwrite" install zsh
```

Obviously this is very cumbersome, especially if you use options frequently, but you can also use the .d directory configuration structure to configure certain aspects of APT by adding directives to a file in the /etc/apt/apt.conf.d/ directory. For example, this (and any other) directive can easily be added to a file in /etc/apt/apt.conf.d/. The name of this file is somewhat arbitrary, but a common convention is to use either local or 99local:

```
$ cat /etc/apt/apt.conf.d/99local
Dpkg::Options {
    "--force-overwrite";
}
```

There are many other helpful configuration options and we certainly can't cover them all, but one we will touch on involves network connectivity. For example, if you can only access the web through a proxy, add a line like Acquire::http::proxy "http://*yourproxy*:3128". For an FTP proxy, use Acquire::ftp::proxy "ftp://*yourproxy*".

To discover more configuration options, read the apt.conf(5) manual page with the man apt.conf command (for details on manual pages, see section 6.1.1, "Manual Pages" [page 124]).

8.3.2. Managing Package Priorities

One of the most important aspects in the configuration of APT is the management of the priorities associated with each package source. For instance, you might want to extend your Kali Rolling system with one or two newer packages from Debian Unstable or Debian Experimental. It is possible to assign a priority to each available package (the same package can have several priorities depending on its version or the distribution providing it). These priorities will influence APT's behavior: for each package, it will always select the version with the highest priority (except if this version is older than the installed one and its priority is less than 1000).

APT defines several default priorities. Each installed package version has a priority of 100. A non-installed version has a priority of 500 by default but it can jump to 990 if it is part of the target release (defined with the -t command-line option or the APT::Default-Release configuration directive).

You can modify the priorities by adding entries in the /etc/apt/preferences file with the names of the affected packages, their version, their origin and their new priority.

APT will never install an older version of a package (that is, a package whose version number is lower than the one of the currently installed package) except when its priority is higher than 1000. APT will always install the highest priority package that follows this constraint. If two packages have the same priority, APT installs the newest one (whose version number is the highest). If two packages of same version have the same priority but differ in their content, APT installs the version that is not installed (this rule has been created to cover the case of a package update without the increment of the revision number, which is usually required).

In more concrete terms, a package whose priority is less than 0 will never be installed. A package with a priority ranging between 0 and 100 will only be installed if no other version of the package is already installed. With a priority between 100 and 500, the package will only be installed if there is no other newer version installed or available in another distribution. A package of priority between 501 and 990 will only be installed if there is no newer version installed or available in the target distribution. With a priority between 990 and 1000, the package will be installed except if the installed version is newer. A priority greater than 1000 will always lead to the installation of the package even if it forces APT to downgrade to an older version.

When APT checks `/etc/apt/preferences`, it first takes into account the most specific entries (often those specifying the concerned package), then the more generic ones (including for example all the packages of a distribution). If several generic entries exist, the first match is used. The available selection criteria include the package's name and the source providing it. Every package source is identified by the information contained in a `Release` file that APT downloads together with the `Packages` files. These files specify the origin, usually "Kali" for the packages from Kali's official mirrors and "Debian" for the packages from Debian's official mirrors, but the origin can also be a person's or an organization's name for third-party repositories. The `Release` file also provides the name of the distribution together with its version. Let's have a look at its syntax through some realistic case studies of this mechanism.

Priority of Kali-Bleeding-Edge and Debian Experimental	If you listed kali-bleeding-edge or Debian experimental in your `sources.list` file, the corresponding packages will almost never be installed because their default APT priority is 1. This is of course a specific case, designed to keep users from installing bleeding edge packages by mistake. The packages can only be installed by typing `apt install` *package*`/kali-bleeding-edge`, assuming of course that you are aware of the risks and potential headaches of life on the edge. It is still possible (though *not* recommended) to treat packages of kali-bleeding-edge/experimental like those of other distributions by giving them a priority of 500. This is done with a specific entry in `/etc/apt/preferences`:

```
Package: *
Pin: release a=kali-bleeding-edge
Pin-Priority: 500
```

Let's suppose that you only want to use packages from Kali and that you only want Debian packages installed when explicitly requested. You could write the following entries in the `/etc/apt/preferences` file (or in any file in `/etc/apt/preferences.d/`):

```
Package: *
Pin: release o=Kali
Pin-Priority: 900

Package: *
Pin: release o=Debian
Pin-Priority: -10
```

In the last two examples, you have seen a=kali-bleeding-edge, which defines the name of the selected distribution and o=Kali and o=Debian, which limit the scope to packages whose origin are Kali and Debian, respectively.

Let's now assume that you have a server with several local programs depending on the version 5.22 of Perl and that you want to ensure that upgrades will not install another version of it. You could use this entry:

```
Package: perl
Pin: version 5.22*
Pin-Priority: 1001
```

The reference documentation for this configuration file is available in the manual page apt_pref erences(5), which you can display with man apt_preferences.

Adding Comments in **/etc/apt/preferences**	There is no official syntax for comments in /etc/apt/preferences, but some textual descriptions can be provided by prepending one or more Explanation fields into each entry:
	Explanation: The package xserver-xorg-video-intel provided Explanation: in experimental can be used safely Package: xserver-xorg-video-intel Pin: release a=experimental Pin-Priority: 500

8.3.3. Working with Several Distributions

Given that apt is such a marvelous tool, you will likely want to dive in and start experimenting with packages coming from other distributions. For example, after installing a Kali Rolling system, you might want to try out a software package available in Kali Dev, Debian Unstable, or Debian Experimental without diverging too much from the system's initial state.

Even if you will occasionally encounter problems while mixing packages from different distributions, apt manages such coexistence very well and limits risks very effectively (provided that the package dependencies are accurate). First, list all distributions used in /etc/apt/sources.list and define your reference distribution with the APT::Default-Release parameter (see section 8.2.3, "Upgrading Kali Linux" [page 179]).

Let's suppose that Kali Rolling is your reference distribution but that Kali Dev and Debian Unstable are also listed in your sources.list file. In this case, you can use apt install *package/* unstable to install a package from Debian Unstable. If the installation fails due to some unsatisfiable dependencies, let it solve those dependencies within Unstable by adding the -t unstable parameter.

In this situation, upgrades (`upgrade` and `full-upgrade`) are done within Kali Rolling except for packages already upgraded to another distribution: those will follow updates available in the other distributions. We will explain this behavior with the help of the default priorities set by APT below. Do not hesitate to use `apt-cache policy` (see sidebar "Using `apt-cache policy`" [page 199]) to verify the given priorities.

Everything relies on the fact that APT only considers packages of higher or equal version than the installed package (assuming that `/etc/apt/preferences` has not been used to force priorities higher than 1000 for some packages).

> **Using `apt-cache policy`** To gain a better understanding of the mechanism of priority, do not hesitate to execute `apt-cache policy` to display the default priority associated with each package source. You can also use `apt-cache policy` *package* to display the priorities of all available versions of a given package.

Let's assume that you have installed version 1 of a first package from *Kali Rolling* and that version 2 and 3 are available respectively in *Kali Dev* and *Debian Unstable*. The installed version has a priority of 100 but the version available in *Kali Rolling* (the very same) has a priority of 990 (because it is part of the target release). Packages in *Kali Dev* and *Debian Unstable* have a priority of 500 (the default priority of a non-installed version). The winner is thus version 1 with a priority of 990. The package stays in *Kali Rolling*.

Let's take the example of another package whose version 2 has been installed from *Kali Dev*. Version 1 is available in *Kali Rolling* and version 3 in *Debian Unstable*. Version 1 (of priority 990—thus lower than 1000) is discarded because it is lower than the installed version. This only leaves version 2 and 3, both of priority 500. Faced with this alternative, APT selects the newest version, the one from *Debian Unstable*. If you don't want a package installed from *Kali Dev* to migrate to *Debian Unstable*, you have to assign a priority lower than 500 (490 for example) to packages coming from *Debian Unstable*. You can modify `/etc/apt/preferences` to this effect:

```
Package: *
Pin: release a=unstable
Pin-Priority: 490
```

8.3.4. Tracking Automatically Installed Packages

One of the essential functionalities of `apt` is the tracking of packages installed only through dependencies. These packages are called *automatic* and often include libraries.

With this information, when packages are removed, the package managers can compute a list of automatic packages that are no longer needed (because there are no manually installed packages depending on them). The command `apt autoremove` will get rid of those packages. Aptitude does not have this command because it removes them automatically as soon as they are identified. In all cases, the tools display a clear message listing the affected packages.

It is a good habit to mark as automatic any package that you don't need directly so that they are automatically removed when they aren't necessary anymore. You can use `apt-mark auto` *package* to mark the given package as automatic, whereas `apt-mark manual` *package* does the opposite. `aptitude markauto` and `aptitude unmarkauto` work in the same way, although they offer more features for marking many packages at once (see section 8.2.7.1, "Aptitude" [page 190]). The console-based interactive interface of `aptitude` also makes it easy to review the automatic flag on many packages.

You might want to know why an automatically installed package is present on the system. To get this information from the command line, you can use `aptitude why` *package* (apt and apt-get have no similar feature):

```
$ aptitude why python-debian
i   aptitude             Recommends apt-xapian-index
i A apt-xapian-index Depends     python-debian (>= 0.1.15)
```

8.3.5. Leveraging Multi-Arch Support

All Debian packages have an Architecture field in their control information. This field can contain either "all" (for packages that are architecture-independent) or the name of the architecture that it targets (like amd64, or armhf). In the latter case, by default, dpkg will only install the package if its architecture matches the host's architecture as returned by `dpkg --print-architecture`.

This restriction ensures that you do not end up with binaries compiled for an incorrect architecture. Everything would be perfect except that (some) computers can run binaries for multiple architectures, either natively (an amd64 system can run i386 binaries) or through emulators.

Enabling Multi-Arch

Multi-arch support for dpkg allows users to define foreign architectures that can be installed on the current system. This is easily done with `dpkg --add-architecture`, as in the example below where the i386 architecture needs to be added to the amd64 system in order to run Windows applications using Wine[5]. There is a corresponding `dpkg --remove-architecture` to drop support of a foreign architecture, but it can only be used when no packages of this architecture remain installed.

```
# dpkg --print-architecture
amd64
```

---

[5] https://www.winehq.org/

```
# wine
it looks like wine32 is missing, you should install it.
multiarch needs to be enabled first.  as root, please
execute "dpkg --add-architecture i386 & apt-get update &
apt-get install wine32"
Usage: wine PROGRAM [ARGUMENTS...]   Run the specified program
       wine --help                   Display this help and exit
       wine --version                Output version information and exit
# dpkg --add-architecture i386
# dpkg --print-foreign-architectures
i386
# apt update
[...]
# apt install wine32
[...]
Setting up libwine:i386 (1.8.6-5) ...
Setting up vdpau-driver-all:i386 (1.1.1-6) ...
Setting up wine32:i386 (1.8.6-5) ...
Setting up libasound2-plugins:i386 (1.1.1-1) ...
Processing triggers for libc-bin (2.24-9)
# wine
Usage: wine PROGRAM [ARGUMENTS...]   Run the specified program
    wine --help                   Display this help and exit
    wine --version                Output version information and exit
# dpkg --remove-architecture i386
dpkg: error: cannot remove architecture 'i386' currently in use by the database
# dpkg --print-foreign-architectures
i386
```

APT will automatically detect when dpkg has been configured to support foreign architectures and will start downloading the corresponding Packages files during its update process.

Foreign packages can then be installed with apt install *package*:*architecture*.

> **Using Proprietary i386 Binaries on amd64** There are multiple use cases for multi-arch, but the most popular one is the possibility to execute 32 bit binaries (i386) on 64 bit systems (amd64), in particular since several popular proprietary applications (like Skype) are only provided in 32 bit versions.

Multi-Arch Related Changes

To make multi-arch actually useful and usable, libraries had to be repackaged and moved to an architecture-specific directory so that multiple copies (targeting different architectures) can be installed alongside one another. Such updated packages contain the Multi-Arch: same header field to tell the packaging system that the various architectures of the package can be safely co-installed (and that those packages can only satisfy dependencies of packages of the same architecture).

```
$ dpkg -s libwine
dpkg-query: error: --status needs a valid package name but 'libwine' is not: ambiguous
    ➥ package name 'libwine' with more than one installed instance

Use --help for help about querying packages.
$ dpkg -s libwine:amd64 libwine:i386 | grep ^Multi
Multi-Arch: same
Multi-Arch: same
$ dpkg -L libgcc1:amd64 |grep .so
[...]
/usr/lib/x86_64-linux-gnu/wine/libwine.so.1
$ dpkg -S /usr/share/doc/libwine/copyright
libwine:amd64, libwine:i386: /usr/share/doc/libwine/copyright
```

It is worth noting that Multi-Arch: same packages must have their names qualified with their architecture to be unambiguously identifiable. These packages may also share files with other instances of the same package; dpkg ensures that all packages have bit-for-bit identical files when they are shared. Also, all instances of a package must have the same version, therefore they must be upgraded together.

Multi-Arch support also brings some interesting challenges in the way dependencies are handled. Satisfying a dependency requires either a package marked Multi-Arch: foreign or a package whose architecture matches the one of the package declaring the dependency (in this dependency resolution process, architecture-independent packages are assumed to be of the same architecture as the host). A dependency can also be weakened to allow any architecture to fulfill it, with the *package*:any syntax, but foreign packages can only satisfy such a dependency if they are marked Multi-Arch: allowed.

8.3.6. Validating Package Authenticity

System upgrades are very sensitive operations and you really want to ensure that you only install official packages from the Kali repositories. If the Kali mirror you are using has been compromised, a computer cracker could try to add malicious code to an otherwise legitimate package. Such a package, if installed, could do anything the cracker designed it to do including disclose passwords or confidential information. To circumvent this risk, Kali provides a tamper-proof seal to guarantee—at install time—that a package really comes from its official maintainer and hasn't been modified by a third party.

The seal works with a chain of cryptographic hashes and a signature. The signed file is the Release file, provided by the Kali mirrors. It contains a list of the Packages files (including their compressed forms, Packages.gz and Packages.xz, and the incremental versions), along with their MD5, SHA1, and SHA256 hashes, which ensures that the files haven't been tampered with. These

`Packages` files contain a list of the Debian packages available on the mirror along with their hashes, which ensures in turn that the contents of the packages themselves haven't been altered either.

The trusted keys are managed with the `apt-key` command found in the *apt* package. This program maintains a keyring of GnuPG public keys, which are used to verify signatures in the `Release.gpg` files available on the mirrors. It can be used to add new keys manually (when non-official mirrors are needed). Generally however, only the official Kali keys are needed. These keys are automatically kept up-to-date by the *kali-archive-keyring* package (which puts the corresponding keyrings in `/etc/apt/trusted.gpg.d`). However, the first installation of this particular package requires caution: even if the package is signed like any other, the signature cannot be verified externally. Cautious administrators should therefore check the fingerprints of imported keys before trusting them to install new packages:

```
# apt-key fingerprint
/etc/apt/trusted.gpg.d/debian-archive-jessie-automatic.gpg
-------------------------------------------------------------
pub   4096R/2B90D010 2014-11-21 [expires: 2022-11-19]
      Key fingerprint = 126C 0D24 BD8A 2942 CC7D  F8AC 7638 D044 2B90 D010
uid                   Debian Archive Automatic Signing Key (8/jessie) <ftpmaster@debian.org>

/etc/apt/trusted.gpg.d/debian-archive-jessie-security-automatic.gpg
-------------------------------------------------------------
pub   4096R/C857C906 2014-11-21 [expires: 2022-11-19]
      Key fingerprint = D211 6914 1CEC D440 F2EB  8DDA 9D6D 8F6B C857 C906
uid                   Debian Security Archive Automatic Signing Key (8/jessie) <ftpmaster@debian.org>

/etc/apt/trusted.gpg.d/debian-archive-jessie-stable.gpg
-------------------------------------------------------------
pub   4096R/518E17E1 2013-08-17 [expires: 2021-08-15]
      Key fingerprint = 75DD C3C4 A499 F1A1 8CB5  F3C8 CBF8 D6FD 518E 17E1
uid                   Jessie Stable Release Key <debian-release@lists.debian.org>

/etc/apt/trusted.gpg.d/debian-archive-squeeze-automatic.gpg
-------------------------------------------------------------
pub   4096R/473041FA 2010-08-27 [expires: 2018-03-05]
      Key fingerprint = 9FED 2BCB DCD2 9CDF 7626  78CB AED4 B06F 4730 41FA
uid                   Debian Archive Automatic Signing Key (6.0/squeeze) <ftpmaster@debian.org>

/etc/apt/trusted.gpg.d/debian-archive-squeeze-stable.gpg
-------------------------------------------------------------
pub   4096R/B98321F9 2010-08-07 [expires: 2017-08-05]
      Key fingerprint = 0E4E DE2C 7F3E 1FC0 D033  800E 6448 1591 B983 21F9
uid                   Squeeze Stable Release Key <debian-release@lists.debian.org>

/etc/apt/trusted.gpg.d/debian-archive-wheezy-automatic.gpg
-------------------------------------------------------------
pub   4096R/46925553 2012-04-27 [expires: 2020-04-25]
      Key fingerprint = A1BD 8E9D 78F7 FE5C 3E65  D8AF 8B48 AD62 4692 5553
uid                   Debian Archive Automatic Signing Key (7.0/wheezy) <ftpmaster@debian.org>

/etc/apt/trusted.gpg.d/debian-archive-wheezy-stable.gpg
-------------------------------------------------------------
pub   4096R/65FFB764 2012-05-08 [expires: 2019-05-07]
      Key fingerprint = ED6D 6527 1AAC F0FF 15D1  2303 6FB2 A1C2 65FF B764
uid                   Wheezy Stable Release Key <debian-release@lists.debian.org>
```

```
/etc/apt/trusted.gpg.d/kali-archive-keyring.gpg
-------------------------------------------------
pub   4096R/7D8D0BF6 2012-03-05 [expires: 2018-02-02]
      Key fingerprint = 44C6 513A 8E4F B3D3 0875  F758 ED44 4FF0 7D8D 0BF6
uid                  Kali Linux Repository <devel@kali.org>
sub   4096R/FC0D0DCB 2012-03-05 [expires: 2018-02-02]
```

When a third-party package source is added to the sources.list file, APT needs to be told to trust the corresponding GPG authentication key (otherwise it will keep complaining that it can't ensure the authenticity of the packages coming from that repository). The first step is of course to get the public key. More often than not, the key will be provided as a small text file, which we will call key.asc in the following examples.

To add the key to the trusted keyring, the administrator can run apt-key add < key.asc. Another way is to use the synaptic graphical interface: its Authentication tab in the Settings → Repositories menu provides the ability to import a key from the key.asc file.

For people who prefer a dedicated application and more details on the trusted keys, it is possible to use gui-apt-key (in the package of the same name), a small graphical user interface that manages the trusted keyring.

Once the appropriate keys are in the keyring, APT will check the signatures before any risky operation, so that front-ends will display a warning if asked to install a package whose authenticity can't be ascertained.

8.4. Package Reference: Digging Deeper into the Debian Package System

Now it is time to dive really deep into Debian and Kali's package system. At this point, we are going to move beyond tools and syntax and focus more on the nuts and bolts of the packaging system. This behind-the-scenes view will help you understand how APT works at its foundation and will give you insight into how to seriously streamline and customize your Kali system. You may not necessarily memorize all the material in this section, but the walk-through and reference material will serve you well as you grow in your mastery of the Kali Linux system.

So far, you have interacted with APT's package data through the various tools designed to interface with it. Next, we will dig deeper and take a look inside the packages and look at the internal *meta-information* (or information about other information) used by the package management tools.

This combination of a file archive and of meta-information is directly visible in the structure of a .deb file, which is simply an ar archive, concatenating three files:

```
$ ar t /var/cache/apt/archives/apt_1.4~beta1_amd64.deb
debian-binary
control.tar.gz
data.tar.xz
```

The debian-binary file contains a single version number describing the format of the archive:

```
$ ar p /var/cache/apt/archives/apt_1.4~beta1_amd64.deb debian-binary
2.0
```

The `control.tar.gz` archive contains meta-information:

```
$ ar p /var/cache/apt/archives/apt_1.4~beta1_amd64.deb control.tar.gz | tar -tzf -
./
./conffiles
./control
./md5sums
./postinst
./postrm
./preinst
./prerm
./shlibs
./triggers
```

And finally, the `data.tar.xz` archive (the compression format might vary) contains the actual files to be installed on the file system:

```
$ ar p /var/cache/apt/archives/apt_1.4~beta1_amd64.deb data.tar.xz | tar -tJf -
./
./etc/
./etc/apt/
./etc/apt/apt.conf.d/
./etc/apt/apt.conf.d/01autoremove
./etc/apt/preferences.d/
./etc/apt/sources.list.d/
./etc/apt/trusted.gpg.d/
./etc/cron.daily/
./etc/cron.daily/apt-compat
./etc/kernel/
./etc/kernel/postinst.d/
./etc/kernel/postinst.d/apt-auto-removal
./etc/logrotate.d/
./etc/logrotate.d/apt
./lib/
./lib/systemd/
[...]
```

Note that in this example, you are viewing a `.deb` package in APT's archive cache and that your archive may contain files with different version numbers than what is shown.

In this section, we will introduce this meta-information contained in each package and show you how to leverage it.

8.4.1. The control File

We will begin by looking at the control file, which is contained in the control.tar.gz archive. The control file contains the most vital information about the package. It uses a structure similar to email headers and can be viewed with the dpkg -I command. For example, the control file for *apt* looks like this:

```
$ dpkg -I apt_1.4~beta1_amd64.deb control
Package: apt
Version: 1.4~beta1
Architecture: amd64
Maintainer: APT Development Team <deity@lists.debian.org>
Installed-Size: 3478
Depends: adduser, gpgv | gpgv2 | gpgv1, debian-archive-keyring, init-system-helpers (>=
  ➥ 1.18~), libapt-pkg5.0 (>= 1.3~rc2), libc6 (>= 2.15), libgcc1 (>= 1:3.0),
  ➥ libstdc++6 (>= 5.2)
Recommends: gnupg | gnupg2 | gnupg1
Suggests: apt-doc, aptitude | synaptic | wajig, dpkg-dev (>= 1.17.2), powermgmt-base,
  ➥ python-apt
Breaks: apt-utils (<< 1.3~exp2~)
Replaces: apt-utils (<< 1.3~exp2~)
Section: admin
Priority: important
Description: commandline package manager
 This package provides commandline tools for searching and
 managing as well as querying information about packages
 as a low-level access to all features of the libapt-pkg library.
 .
 These include:
  * apt-get for retrieval of packages and information about them
    from authenticated sources and for installation, upgrade and
    removal of packages together with their dependencies
  * apt-cache for querying available information about installed
    as well as installable packages
  * apt-cdrom to use removable media as a source for packages
  * apt-config as an interface to the configuration settings
  * apt-key as an interface to manage authentication keys
```

In this section, we will walk you through the control file and explain the various fields. Each of these will give you a better understanding of the packaging system, give you more fine-tuned configuration control, and provide you with insight needed to troubleshoot problems that may occur.

Dependencies: the Depends Field

The package dependencies are defined in the Depends field in the package header. This is a list of conditions to be met for the package to work correctly—this information is used by tools such as apt in order to install the required libraries, in appropriate versions fulfilling the dependencies of the package to be installed. For each dependency, you can restrict the range of versions that meet that condition. In other words, it is possible to express the fact that you need the package *libc6* in a version equal to or greater than "2.15" (written "libc6 (>= 2.15)"). Version comparison operators are as follows:

- <<: less than;
- <=: less than or equal to;
- =: equal to (note that "2.6.1" is not equal to "2.6.1-1");
- >=: greater than or equal to;
- >>: greater than.

In a list of conditions to be met, the comma serves as a separator, interpreted as a logical "AND." In conditions, the vertical bar ("|") expresses a logical "OR" (it is an inclusive "OR," not an exclusive "either/or"). Carrying greater priority than "AND," you can use it as many times as necessary. Thus, the dependency "(A OR B) AND C" is written A | B, C. In contrast, the expression "A OR (B AND C)" should be written as "(A OR B) AND (A OR C)", since the Depends field does not tolerate parentheses that change the order of priorities between the logical operators "OR" and "AND". It would thus be written A | B, A | C. See http://www.debian.org/doc/debian-policy/ch-relationships.html for more information.

The dependencies system is a good mechanism for guaranteeing the operation of a program but it has another use with meta-packages. These are empty packages that only describe dependencies. They facilitate the installation of a consistent group of programs preselected by the meta-package maintainer; as such, apt install *meta-package* will automatically install all of these programs using the meta-package's dependencies. The *gnome*, *kde-full*, and *kali-linux-full* packages are examples of meta-packages.

Pre-Depends, a More Demanding Depends

Pre-dependencies, which are listed in the Pre-Depends field in the package headers, complete the normal dependencies; their syntax is identical. A normal dependency indicates that the package in question must be unpacked and configured before configuration of the package declaring the dependency. A pre-dependency stipulates that the package in question must be unpacked and configured before execution of the pre-installation script of the package declaring the pre-dependency, that is before its installation.

A pre-dependency is very demanding for apt because it adds a strict constraint on the ordering of the packages to install. As such, pre-dependencies are discouraged unless absolutely necessary. It is even recommended to consult other developers on debian-devel@lists.debian.org before adding a pre-dependency as it is generally possible to find another solution as a work-around.

Recommends, Suggests, and Enhances Fields

The Recommends and Suggests fields describe dependencies that are not compulsory. The recommended dependencies, the most important, considerably improve the functionality offered by the package but are not indispensable to its operation. The suggested dependencies, of secondary importance, indicate that certain packages may complement and increase their respective utility, but it is perfectly reasonable to install one without the others.

You should always install the recommended packages unless you know exactly why you do not need them. Conversely, it is not necessary to install suggested packages unless you know why you need them.

The Enhances field also describes a suggestion, but in a different context. It is indeed located in the suggested package, and not in the package that benefits from the suggestion. Its interest lies in that it is possible to add a suggestion without having to modify the package that is concerned. Thus, all add-ons, plug-ins, and other extensions of a program can then appear in the list of suggestions related to the software. Although it has existed for several years, this last field is still largely ignored by programs such as apt or synaptic. The original goal was to let a package like *xul-ext-adblock-plus* (a Firefox extension) declare Enhances: firefox, firefox-esr and thus appear in the list of suggested packages associated to *firefox* and *firefox-esr*.

Conflicts: the Conflicts Field

The Conflicts field indicates when a package cannot be installed simultaneously with another. The most common reasons for this are that both packages include a file of the same name, provide the same service on the same transmission control protocol (TCP) port, or would hinder each other's operation.

If it triggers a conflict with an already installed package, dpkg will refuse to install a package, except if the new package specifies that it will replace the installed package, in which case dpkg will choose to replace the old package with the new one. APT always follows your instructions: if you choose to install a new package, it will automatically offer to uninstall the package that poses a problem.

Incompatibilities: the Breaks Field

The Breaks field has an effect similar to that of the Conflicts field, but with a special meaning. It signals that the installation of a package will break another package (or particular versions of it). In general, this incompatibility between two packages is transitory and the Breaks relationship specifically refers to the incompatible versions.

When a package breaks an already installed package, dpkg will refuse to install it, and apt will try to resolve the problem by updating the package that would be broken to a newer version (which is assumed to be fixed and, thus, compatible again).

This type of situation may occur in the case of updates without backwards compatibility: this is the case if the new version no longer functions with the older version and causes a malfunction in another program without making special provisions. The Breaks field helps prevent these types of problems.

Provided Items: the Provides Field

This field introduces the very interesting concept of a *virtual package*. It has many roles, but two are of particular importance. The first role consists in using a virtual package to associate a generic service with it (the package provides the service). The second indicates that a package completely replaces another and that for this purpose, it can also satisfy the dependencies that the other would satisfy. It is thus possible to create a substitution package without having to use the same package name.

Meta-Package and Virtual Package	It is essential to clearly distinguish meta-packages from virtual packages. The former are real packages (including real .deb files), whose only purpose is to express dependencies.
	Virtual packages, however, do not exist physically; they are only a means of identifying real packages based on common, logical criteria (for example, service provided, or compatibility with a standard program or a pre-existing package).

Providing a Service   Let's discuss the first case in greater detail with an example: all mail servers, such as *postfix* or *sendmail* are said to provide the *mail-transport-agent* virtual package. Thus, any package that needs this service to be functional (e.g. a mailing list manager, such as *smartlist* or *sympa*) simply states in its dependencies that it requires a *mail-transport-agent* instead of specifying a large yet incomplete list of possible solutions. Furthermore, it is useless to install two mail servers on the same machine, which is why each of these packages declares a conflict with the *mail-transport-agent* virtual package. A conflict between a package and itself is ignored by the system, but this technique will prohibit the installation of two mail servers side by side.

Interchangeability with Another Package The Provides field is also interesting when the content of a package is included in a larger package. For example, the *libdigest-md5-perl* Perl module was an optional module in Perl 5.6, and has been integrated as standard in Perl 5.8. As such, the package *perl* has since version 5.8 declared Provides: libdigest-md5-perl so that the dependencies on this package are met if the system has Perl 5.8 (or newer). The *libdigest-md5-perl* package itself was deleted, since it no longer had any purpose when old Perl versions were removed.

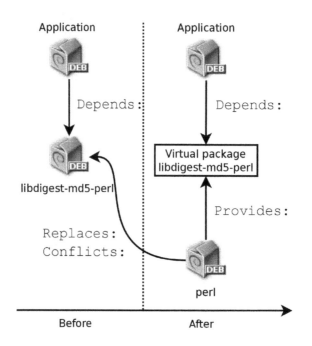

Figure 8.3 *Use of a Provides Field in Order to Not Break Dependencies*

This feature is very useful, since it is never possible to anticipate the vagaries of development and it is necessary to be able to adjust to renaming, and other automatic replacement, of obsolete software.

Replacing Files: The Replaces Field

The Replaces field indicates that the package contains files that are also present in another package, but that the package is legitimately entitled to replace them. Without this specification, dpkg fails, stating that it cannot overwrite the files of another package (technically, it is possible to force it to do so with the --force-overwrite option, but that is not considered standard operation). This allows identification of potential problems and requires the maintainer to study the matter prior to choosing whether to add such a field.

The use of this field is justified when package names change or when a package is included in another. This also happens when the maintainer decides to distribute files differently among various binary packages produced from the same source package: a replaced file no longer belongs to the old package, but only to the new one.

If all of the files in an installed package have been replaced, the package is considered to be removed. Finally, this field also encourages dpkg to remove the replaced package where there is a conflict.

8.4.2. Configuration Scripts

In addition to the control file, the control.tar.gz archive for each Debian package may contain a number of scripts (postinst, postrm, preinst, prerm) called by dpkg at different stages in the processing of a package. We can use dpkg -I to show these files as they reside in a .deb package archive:

```
$ dpkg -I /var/cache/apt/archives/zsh_5.3-1_amd64.deb | head
 new debian package, version 2.0.
 size 814486 bytes: control archive=2557 bytes.
     838 bytes,     20 lines      control
    3327 bytes,     43 lines      md5sums
     969 bytes,     41 lines   *  postinst        #!/bin/sh
     348 bytes,     20 lines   *  postrm          #!/bin/sh
     175 bytes,      5 lines   *  preinst         #!/bin/sh
     175 bytes,      5 lines   *  prerm           #!/bin/sh
 Package: zsh
 Version: 5.3-1
$ dpkg -I zsh_5.3-1_amd64.deb preinst
#!/bin/sh
set -e
# Automatically added by dh_installdeb
dpkg-maintscript-helper symlink_to_dir /usr/share/doc/zsh zsh-common 5.0.7-3 -- "$@"
# End automatically added section
```

The Debian Policy describes each of these files in detail, specifying the scripts called and the arguments they receive. These sequences may be complicated, since if one of the scripts fails, dpkg will try to return to a satisfactory state by canceling the installation or removal in progress (insofar as it is possible).

The dpkg Database   You can traverse the dpkg database on the filesystem at /var/lib/dpkg/. This directory contains a running record of all the packages that have been installed on the system. All of the configuration scripts for installed packages are stored in the /var/lib/dpkg/info/ directory, in the form of a file prefixed with the package's name:

```
$ ls /var/lib/dpkg/info/zsh.*
/var/lib/dpkg/info/zsh.list
/var/lib/dpkg/info/zsh.md5sums
/var/lib/dpkg/info/zsh.postinst
/var/lib/dpkg/info/zsh.postrm
/var/lib/dpkg/info/zsh.preinst
/var/lib/dpkg/info/zsh.prerm
```

This directory also includes a file with the .list extension for each package, containing the list of files that belong to that package:

```
$ head /var/lib/dpkg/info/zsh.list
/.
/bin
/bin/zsh
/bin/zsh5
/usr
/usr/lib
/usr/lib/x86_64-linux-gnu
/usr/lib/x86_64-linux-gnu/zsh
/usr/lib/x86_64-linux-gnu/zsh/5.2
/usr/lib/x86_64-linux-gnu/zsh/5.2/zsh
[...]
```

The /var/lib/dpkg/status file contains a series of data blocks (in the format of the famous mail headers request for comment, RFC 2822) describing the status of each package. The information from the control file of the installed packages is also replicated there.

```
$ more /var/lib/dpkg/status
Package: gnome-characters
Status: install ok installed
Priority: optional
Section: gnome
Installed-Size: 1785
Maintainer: Debian GNOME Maintainers <pkg-gnome-
   ➥ maintainers@lists.alioth.debian.org>
Architecture: amd64
Version: 3.20.1-1
[...]
```

Let's discuss the configuration files and see how they interact. In general, the preinst script is executed prior to installation of the package, while the postinst follows it. Likewise, prerm is invoked before removal of a package and postrm afterwards. An update of a package is equivalent to removal of the previous version and installation of the new one. It is not possible to describe in detail all the possible scenarios here but we will discuss the most common two: an installation/update and a removal.

These sequences can be quite confusing, but a visual representation may help. Manoj Srivastava made these diagrams explaining how the configuration scripts are called by dpkg. Similar diagrams have also been developed by the Debian Women project; they are a bit simpler to understand, but less complete.

➡ https://people.debian.org/~srivasta/MaintainerScripts.html

➡ https://wiki.debian.org/MaintainerScripts

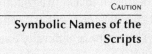

CAUTION

Symbolic Names of the Scripts

The sequences described in this section call configuration scripts by specific names, such as old-prerm or new-postinst. They are, respectively, the prerm script contained in the old version of the package (installed before the update) and the postinst script contained in the new version (installed by the update).

Installation and Upgrade Script Sequence

Here is what happens during an installation (or an update):

1. For an update, dpkg calls the old-prerm upgrade *new-version.*

2. Still for an update, dpkg then executes new-preinst upgrade *old-version*; for a first installation, it executes new-preinst install. It may add the old version in the last parameter if the package has already been installed and removed (but not purged, the configuration files having been retained).

3. The new package files are then unpacked. If a file already exists, it is replaced, but a backup copy is made and temporarily stored.

4. For an update, dpkg executes old-postrm upgrade *new-version.*

5. dpkg updates all of the internal data (file list, configuration scripts, etc.) and removes the backups of the replaced files. This is the point of no return: dpkg no longer has access to all of the elements necessary to return to the previous state.

6. dpkg will update the configuration files, prompting you to decide if it is unable to automatically manage this task. The details of this procedure are discussed in section 8.4.3, "Checksums, Conffiles" [page 214].

7. Finally, dpkg configures the package by executing new-postinst configure *last-version-configured.*

Package Removal

Here is what happens during a package removal.

1. dpkg calls prerm remove.

2. dpkg removes all of the package's files, with the exception of the configuration files and configuration scripts.

3. dpkg executes postrm remove. All of the configuration scripts, except postrm, are removed. If you have not used the purge option, the process stops here.

4. For a complete purge of the package (command issued with dpkg --purge or dpkg -P), the configuration files are also deleted, as well as a certain number of copies (*.dpkg-tmp, *.dpkg-old, *.dpkg-new) and temporary files; dpkg then executes postrm purge.

In some cases, a package might use debconf to require configuration information from you: the four scripts detailed above are then complemented by a config script designed to acquire that information. During installation, this script defines in detail what questions debconf will ask. The responses are recorded in the debconf database for future reference. The script is generally executed by apt prior to installing packages one by one in order to group all the questions together at the beginning of the process. The pre- and post-installation scripts can then use this information to operate according to your wishes.

The debconf Tool	The debconf tool was created to resolve a recurring problem in Debian. All Debian packages unable to function without a minimum of configuration used to ask questions with calls to the echo and read commands in postinst shell scripts (and other similar scripts). This forced the installer to babysit large installations or updates in order to respond to various configuration queries as they arose. These manual interactions have now been almost entirely dispensed with, thanks to debconf.
	The debconf tool has many interesting features: It requires the developer to specify user interaction; it allows localization of all the displayed strings (all translations are stored in the templates file describing the interactions); it provides different frontends for questions (text mode, graphical mode, non-interactive); and it allows creation of a central database of responses to share the same configuration with several computers. The most important feature is that all of the questions can be presented in a row, all at once, prior to starting a long installation or update process. Now, you can go about your business while the system handles the installation on its own, without having to stay there staring at the screen, waiting for questions to pop up.

8.4.3. Checksums, Conffiles

In addition to the maintainer scripts and control data already mentioned in the previous sections, the control.tar.gz archive of a Debian package may contain other interesting files:

```
# ar p /var/cache/apt/archives/bash_4.4-2_amd64.deb control.tar.gz | tar -tzf -
```

```
./
./conffiles
./control
./md5sums
./postinst
./postrm
./preinst
./prerm
```

The first—md5sums—contains the MD5 checksums for all of the package's files. Its main advantage is that it allows dpkg --verify to check if these files have been modified since their installation. Note that when this file doesn't exist, dpkg will generate it dynamically at installation time (and store it in the dpkg database just like other control files).

conffiles lists package files that must be handled as configuration files. Configuration files can be modified by the administrator, and dpkg will try to preserve those changes during a package update.

In effect, in this situation, dpkg behaves as intelligently as possible: if the standard configuration file has not changed between the two versions, it does nothing. If, however, the file has changed, it will try to update this file. Two cases are possible: either the administrator has not touched this configuration file, in which case dpkg automatically installs the new version; or the file has been modified, in which case dpkg asks the administrator which version they wish to use (the old one with modifications, or the new one provided with the package). To assist in making this decision, dpkg offers to display a diff that shows the difference between the two versions. If you choose to retain the old version, the new one will be stored in the same location in a file with the .dpkg-dist suffix. If you choose the new version, the old one is retained in a file with the .dpkg-old suffix. Another available action consists of momentarily interrupting dpkg to edit the file and attempt to reinstate the relevant modifications (previously identified with diff).

dpkg handles configuration file updates, but, while doing so, regularly interrupts its work to ask for input from the administrator. This can be time consuming and inconvenient. Fortunately, you can instruct dpkg to respond to these prompts automatically. The --force-confold option retains the old version of the file, while --force-confnew will use the new version. These choices are respected, even if the file has not been changed by the administrator, which only rarely has the desired effect. Adding the --force-confdef option tells dpkg to decide by itself when possible (in other words, when the original configuration file has not been touched), and only uses --force-confnew or --force-confold for other cases.

These options apply to dpkg, but most of the time the administrator will work directly with the aptitude or apt programs. It is, thus, necessary to know the syntax used to indicate the options to pass to the dpkg command (their command line interfaces are very similar).

```
# apt -o DPkg::options::="--force-confdef" -o DPkg::options::="--force-confold" full-
   ➥ upgrade
```

These options can be stored directly in `apt`'s configuration. To do so, simply write the following line in the `/etc/apt/apt.conf.d/local` file:

```
DPkg::options { "--force-confdef"; "--force-confold"; }
```

Including this option in the configuration file means that it will also be used in a graphical interface such as `aptitude`.

Conversely, you can also force `dpkg` to ask configuration file questions. The `--force-confask` option instructs `dpkg` to display the questions about the configuration files, even in cases where they would not normally be necessary. Thus, when reinstalling a package with this option, `dpkg` will ask the questions again for all of the configuration files modified by the administrator. This is very convenient, especially for reinstalling the original configuration file if it has been deleted and no other copy is available: a normal re-installation won't work, because `dpkg` considers removal as a form of legitimate modification, and, thus, doesn't install the desired configuration file.

8.5. Summary

In this section, we learned more about the Debian package system, discussed the Advanced Package Tool (APT) and `dpkg`, learned about basic package interaction, advanced APT configuration and usage, and dug deeper into the Debian package system with a brief reference of the `.deb` file format. We looked at the `control` file, configuration scripts, checksums, and the `conffiles` file.

Summary Tips:

A Debian package is a compressed archive of a software application. It contains the application's files as well as other metadata including the names of the dependencies that the application needs as well as scripts that enable the execution of commands at different stages in the package's lifecycle (installation, removal, upgrades).

The `dpkg` tool, contrary to `apt` and `apt-get` (of the APT family), has no knowledge of all the available packages that could be used to fulfill package dependencies. Thus, to manage Debian packages, you will likely use the latter tools as they are able to automatically resolve dependency issues.

You can use APT to install and remove applications, update packages, and even upgrade your entire system. Here are the key points that you should know about APT and its configuration:

- The `sources.list` file is the key configuration file for defining package sources (or repositories that contain packages).
- Debian and Kali use three sections to differentiate packages according to the licenses chosen by the authors of each work: main contains all packages that fully comply with the Debian Free Software Guidelines[6]; non-free contains software that does not (entirely) conform to the Free Software Guidelines but can nevertheless be distributed without restrictions; and

---

[6]https://www.debian.org/social_contract#guidelines

contrib (contributions) includes open source software that cannot function without some non-free elements.

- Kali maintains several repositories including: kali-rolling, which is the main repository for end-users and should always contain installable and recent packages; kali-dev, which is used by Kali developers and is not for public use; and kali-bleeding-edge, which often contains untested and un-vetted packages automatically built out of the upstream Git (or Subversion) repository less than twenty-four hours after they have been committed.

- When working with APT, you should first download the list of currently-available packages with `apt update`.

- You can add a package to the system with a simple `apt install package`. APT will automatically install the necessary dependencies.

- To remove a package use `apt remove package`. It will also remove the reverse dependencies of the package (i.e. packages that depend on the package to be removed).

- To remove all data associated with a package, you can "purge" the package with the `apt purge package` command. Unlike a removal, this will not only remove the package but also its configuration files and sometimes the associated user data.

We recommend regular upgrades to install the latest security updates. To upgrade, use `apt update` followed by either `apt upgrade`, `apt-get upgrade`, or `aptitude safe-upgrade`. These commands look for installed packages that can be upgraded without removing any packages.

For more important upgrades, such as major version upgrades, use `apt full-upgrade`. With this instruction, `apt` will complete the upgrade even if it has to remove some obsolete packages or install new dependencies. This is also the command that you should use for regular upgrades of your Kali Rolling system. Review the pros and cons of updates we outlined in this chapter.

Several tools can be used to inspect Debian packages:

- `dpkg --listfiles package` (or -L) lists the files that were installed by the specified package.

- `dpkg --search file` (or -S) finds any packages containing the file or path passed in the argument.

- `dpkg --list` (or -l) displays the list of packages known to the system and their installation status.

- `dpkg --contents file.deb` (or -c) lists all the files in a particular .deb file.

- `dpkg --info file.deb` (or -I) displays the headers of the specified .deb file.

- The various `apt-cache` subcommands display much of the information stored in APT's internal database.

To avoid excessive disk usage, you should regularly sort through `/var/cache/apt/archives/`. Two commands can be used for this: `apt clean` (or `apt-get clean`) entirely empties the directory; `apt autoclean` (`apt-get autoclean`) only removes packages that can no longer be downloaded because they have disappeared from the mirror and are therefore useless.

Aptitude is an interactive program that can be used in semi-graphical mode on the console. It is an extremely robust program that can help you install and troubleshoot packages.

`synaptic` is a graphical package manager that features a clean and efficient graphical interface.

As an advanced user, you can create files in `/etc/apt/apt.conf.d/` to configure certain aspects of APT. You can also manage package priorities, track automatically installed packages, work with several distributions or architectures at once, use cryptographic signatures to validate packages, and upgrade files using the techniques outlined in this chapter.

In spite of the Kali/Debian maintainers' best efforts, a system upgrade isn't always as smooth as we would hope. When this happens, you can look at the Kali bug tracker[7] and at the Debian bug tracking system[8] at https://bugs.debian.org/*package* to check whether the problem has already been reported. You can also try to downgrade the package or to debug and repair a failed package maintainer script.

---

[7]http://bugs.kali.org
[8]https://bugs.debian.org

Keywords

Custom packages
Custom kernel
Custom images
live-build
Persistence

KALI LINUX
REVEALED

Advanced Usage

Contents

Kali has been built as a highly modular and customizable penetration testing framework and allows for some fairly advanced customization and usage. Customizations can happen at multiple levels, beginning at the source code level. The sources of all Kali packages are publicly available. In this chapter, we will show how you can retrieve packages, modify them, and build your own customized packages out of them. The Linux kernel is somewhat of a special case and as such, it is covered in a dedicated section (section 9.2, "Recompiling the Linux Kernel" [page 232]), where we will discuss where to find sources, how to configure the kernel build, and finally how to compile it and how to build the associated kernel packages.

The second level of customization is in the process of building live ISO images. We will show how the `live-build` tool offers plenty of hooks and configuration options to customize the resulting ISO image, including the possibility to use custom Debian packages in place of the packages available on mirrors.

We will also discuss how you can create a persistent live ISO built onto a USB key that will preserve files and operating system changes between reboots.

9.1. Modifying Kali Packages

Modifying Kali packages is usually a task for Kali contributors and developers: they update packages with new upstream versions, they tweak the default configuration for a better integration in the distribution, or they fix bugs reported by users. But you might have specific needs not fulfilled by the official packages and knowing how to build a modified package can thus be very valuable.

You might wonder why you need to bother with the package at all. After all, if you have to modify a piece of software, you can always grab its source code (usually with `git`) and run the modified version directly from the source checkout. This is fine when it is possible and when you use your home directory for this purpose, but if your application requires a system-wide setup (for example, with a `make install` step) then it will pollute your file system with files unknown to `dpkg` and will soon create problems that cannot be caught by package dependencies. Furthermore, with proper packages you will be able to share your changes and deploy them on multiple computers much more easily or revert the changes after having discovered that they were not working as well as you hoped.

So when would you want to modify a package? Let's take a look at a few examples. First, we will assume that you are a heavy user of SET and you noticed a new upstream release but the Kali developers are all busy for a conference and you want to try it out immediately. You want to update the package yourself. In another case, we will assume that you are struggling to get your MIFARE NFC card working and you want to rebuild "libfreefare" to enable debug messages in order to have actionable data to provide in a bug report that you are currently preparing. In a last case, we will assume that the "pyrit" program fails with a cryptic error message. After a web search, you find a commit that you expect to fix your problem in the upstream GitHub repository and you want to rebuild the package with this fix applied.

We will go through all those samples in the following sections. We will try to generalize the explanations so that you can better apply the instructions to other cases but it is impossible to cover all situations that you might encounter. If you hit problems, apply your best judgment to find a solution or go seek help on the most appropriate forums (see chapter 6, "Helping Yourself and Getting Help" [page 124]).

Whatever change you want to make, the general process is always the same: grab the source package, extract it, make your changes, then build the package. But for each step, there are often multiple tools that can handle the task. We picked the most relevant and most popular tools, but our review is not exhaustive.

9.1.1. Getting the Sources

Rebuilding a Kali package starts with getting its source code. A source package is composed of multiple files: the main file is the *.dsc (*Debian Source Control*) file as it lists the other accompanying files, which can be *.tar.*gz, bz2, xz*, sometimes *.diff.gz, or *.debian.tar.*gz, bz2, xz* files.

The source packages are stored on Kali mirrors that are available over HTTP. You could use your web browser to download all the required files but the easiest way to accomplish this is to use the apt source *source_package_name* command. This command requires a deb-src line in the /etc/apt/sources.list file and up-to-date index files (accomplished by running apt update). By default, Kali doesn't add the required line as few Kali users actually need to retrieve source packages but you can easily add it (see sample file in section 8.1.3, "Kali Repositories" [page 173] and the associated explanations in section 8.1.2, "Understanding the sources.list File" [page 172]).

```
$ apt source libfreefare
Reading package lists... Done
NOTICE: 'libfreefare' packaging is maintained in the 'Git' version control system at:
git://anonscm.debian.org/collab-maint/libnfc.git
Please use:
git clone git://anonscm.debian.org/collab-maint/libnfc.git
to retrieve the latest (possibly unreleased) updates to the package.
Need to get 119 kB of source archives.
Get:1 http://archive-2.kali.org/kali kali-rolling/main libfreefare 0.4.0-2 (dsc) [2,090 B]
Get:2 http://archive-2.kali.org/kali kali-rolling/main libfreefare 0.4.0-2 (tar) [113 kB]
Get:3 http://archive-2.kali.org/kali kali-rolling/main libfreefare 0.4.0-2 (diff) [3,640 B]
Fetched 119 kB in 1s (63.4 kB/s)
gpgv: keyblock resource '/home/rhertzog/.gnupg/trustedkeys.gpg': file open error
gpgv: Signature made Tue 04 Mar 2014 06:57:36 PM EST using RSA key ID 40AD1FA6
gpgv: Can't check signature: public key not found
dpkg-source: warning: failed to verify signature on ./libfreefare_0.4.0-2.dsc
dpkg-source: info: extracting libfreefare in libfreefare-0.4.0
dpkg-source: info: unpacking libfreefare_0.4.0.orig.tar.gz
dpkg-source: info: unpacking libfreefare_0.4.0-2.debian.tar.xz
$ cd libfreefare-0.4.0
$ ls
AUTHORS      CMakeLists.txt  COPYING  HACKING       m4           README
ChangeLog    configure.ac    debian   libfreefare   Makefile.am  test
```

```
cmake       contrib         examples  libfreefare.pc.in  NEWS       TODO
$ ls debian
changelog   copyright                 libfreefare-dev.install  rules
compat      libfreefare0.install      libfreefare-doc.install  source
control     libfreefare-bin.install   README.Source            watch
```

In this example, while we received the source package from a Kali mirror, the package is the same as in Debian since the version string doesn't contain "kali." This means that no kali-specific changes have been applied.

If you need a specific version of the source package, which is currently not available in the repositories listed in /etc/apt/sources.list, then the easiest way to download it is to find out the URL of its .dsc file by looking it up on http://pkg.kali.org and then handing that URL over to dget (from the *devscripts* package).

After having looked up the URL of the libreefare source package available in kali-bleeding-edge, you can download it with dget. It will first download the .dsc file, then parse it to know what other files are referenced, and then download those from the same location:

```
$ dget http://http.kali.org/pool/main/libf/libfreefare/libfreefare_0.4.0+0~
    ➥ git1439352548.ffde4d-1.dsc
dget: retrieving http://http.kali.org/pool/main/libf/libfreefare/libfreefare_0.4.0+0~
    ➥ git1439352548.ffde4d-1.dsc
  % Total    % Received % Xferd  Average Speed   Time    Time     Time  Current
                                 Dload  Upload   Total   Spent    Left  Speed
100   364  100   364    0     0    852      0 --:--:-- --:--:-- --:--:--   854
100  1935  100  1935    0     0   2650      0 --:--:-- --:--:-- --:--:-- 19948
dget: retrieving http://http.kali.org/pool/main/libf/libfreefare/libfreefare_0.4.0+0~
    ➥ git1439352548.ffde4d.orig.tar.gz
[...]
dget: retrieving http://http.kali.org/pool/main/libf/libfreefare/libfreefare_0.4.0+0~
    ➥ git1439352548.ffde4d-1.debian.tar.xz
[...]
libfreefare_0.4.0+0~git1439352548.ffde4d-1.dsc:
dscverify: libfreefare_0.4.0+0~git1439352548.ffde4d-1.dsc failed signature check:
gpg: Signature made Wed Aug 12 06:14:03 2015 CEST
gpg:                using RSA key 43EF73F4BD8096DA
gpg: Can't check signature: No public key
Validation FAILED!!
$ dpkg-source -x libfreefare_0.4.0+0~git1439352548.ffde4d-1.dsc
gpgv: Signature made Wed Aug 12 06:14:03 2015 CEST
gpgv:                using RSA key 43EF73F4BD8096DA
gpgv: Can't check signature: No public key
dpkg-source: warning: failed to verify signature on ./libfreefare_0.4.0+0~git1439352548
    ➥ .ffde4d-1.dsc
dpkg-source: info: extracting libfreefare in libfreefare-0.4.0+0~git1439352548.ffde4d
dpkg-source: info: unpacking libfreefare_0.4.0+0~git1439352548.ffde4d.orig.tar.gz
dpkg-source: info: unpacking libfreefare_0.4.0+0~git1439352548.ffde4d-1.debian.tar.xz
```

It is worth noting that `dget` did not automatically extract the source package because it could not verify the PGP signature on the source package. Thus we did that step manually with `dpkg-source -x` *dsc-file.* You can also force the source package extraction by passing the --allow-unauthenticated or -u option. Inversely, you can use --download-only to skip the source package extraction step.

Retrieving Sources from Git

You might have noticed that the `apt source` invocation tells you about a possible Git repository used to maintain the package. It might point to a Debian Git repository or to a Kali Git repository.

All Kali-specific packages are maintained in Git repositories hosted on git.kali.org[1]. You can retrieve the sources from those repositories with `git clone git://git.kali.org/packages/`*source-package.* If the operation doesn't yield the expected sources, try switching to the `kali/master` branch with `git checkout kali/master`.

Contrary to what you get with `apt source`, the obtained tree will not have patches automatically applied. Have a look at `debian/patches/` to learn about the possible changes made by Kali.

```
$ git clone git://git.kali.org/packages/kali-meta
Cloning into 'kali-meta'...
remote: Counting objects: 760, done.
remote: Compressing objects: 100% (614/614), done.
remote: Total 760 (delta 279), reused 0 (delta 0)
Receiving objects: 100% (760/760), 141.01 KiB | 0 bytes/s,
    ➥ done.
Resolving deltas: 100% (279/279), done.
Checking connectivity... done.
$ cd kali-meta
$ ls
debian
$ ls debian
changelog  compat  control  copyright  rules  source
```

You can use the git repositories as another way to retrieve the sources and thus (mostly) follow the other instructions from this section. But when Kali developers work with those repositories, they use another packaging workflow and use tools from the *git-buildpackage* package that we will not cover here. You can learn more about those tools here:

➡ https://honk.sigxcpu.org/piki/projects/git-buildpackage/

---

[1] http://git.kali.org

9.1.2. Installing Build Dependencies

Now that you have the sources, you still need to install build dependencies. They will be necessary to build the desired binary packages but are also likely required for partial builds that you might want to run to test the changes while you make them.

Each source package declares its build dependencies in the Build-Depends field of the debian/ control file. Let's instruct apt to install those (assuming that you are in a directory containing an unpacked source package):

```
$ sudo apt build-dep ./
Note, using directory './' to get the build dependencies
Reading package lists... Done
Building dependency tree
Reading state information... Done
The following NEW packages will be installed:
  autoconf automake autopoint autotools-dev debhelper dh-autoreconf
  dh-strip-nondeterminism gettext intltool-debian libarchive-zip-perl
  libfile-stripnondeterminism-perl libtool po-debconf
0 upgraded, 13 newly installed, 0 to remove and 0 not upgraded.
Need to get 4 456 kB of archives.
After this operation, 14,6 MB of additional disk space will be used.
Do you want to continue? [Y/n]
[…]
```

In this sample, all build dependencies can be satisfied with packages available to APT. This might not always be the case as the tool building kali-rolling does not ensure installability of build dependencies (only dependencies of binary packages are taken into account). In practice, binary dependencies and build dependencies are often tightly coupled and most packages will have their build dependencies satisfiable.

9.1.3. Making Changes

We can't cover all the possible changes that you might want to make to a given package in this section. This would amount to teaching you all the nitty gritty[2] details of Debian packaging. However, we will cover the three common use cases presented earlier and we will explain some of the unavoidable parts (like maintaining the changelog file).

The first thing to do is to change the package version number so that the rebuilt packages can be distinguished from the original packages provided by Kali or Debian. To achieve this, we usually add a suffix identifying the entity (person or company) applying the changes. Since buxy is my IRC nickname, I will use it as a suffix. Such a change is best effected with the dch command (*Debian CHangelog*) from the *devscripts* package, with a command such as dch --local buxy. This invokes

---

[2]https://www.debian.org/doc/manuals/maint-guide/

a text editor (`sensible-editor`, which runs the editor assigned in the VISUAL or EDITOR environment variables, or `/usr/bin/editor` otherwise), which allows you to document the differences introduced by this rebuild. This editor shows that dch really did change the `debian/changelog` file:

```
$ head -n 1 debian/changelog
libfreefare (0.4.0-2) unstable; urgency=low
$ dch --local buxy
[...]
$ head debian/changelog
libfreefare (0.4.0-2buxy1) UNRELEASED; urgency=medium

  * Enable --with-debug configure option.

 -- Raphael Hertzog <buxy@kali.org>  Fri, 22 Apr 2016 10:36:00 -0400

libfreefare (0.4.0-2) unstable; urgency=low

  *  Update debian/copyrtight.
     Fix license to LGPL3+.
```

If you do such changes regularly, you might want to set the DEBFULLNAME and DEBEMAIL environment variables to your full name and your email, respectively. Their values will be used by many packaging tools, including dch, which will embed them on the trailer line shown above (starting with " -- ").

Applying a Patch

In one of our use cases, we have downloaded the *pyrit* source package and we want to apply a patch that we found in the upstream git repository. This is a common operation and it should always be simple. Unfortunately, patches can be handled in different ways depending on the source package format and on the Git packaging workflow in use (when Git is used to maintain the package).

With an Unpacked Source Package   You have run apt source pyrit and you have a pyrit-0.4.0 directory. You can apply your patch directly with patch -p1 < *patch-file*:

```
$ apt source pyrit
[...]
$ cd pyrit-0.4.0
$ wget https://github.com/JPaulMora/Pyrit/commit/14
   ➡ ec997174b8e8fd20d22b6a97c57e19633f12a0.patch -O /tmp/pyrit-patch
[...]
$ patch -p1 </tmp/pyrit-patch
patching file cpyrit/pckttools.py
```

```
Hunk #1 succeeded at 53 (offset -1 lines).
$ dch --local buxy "Apply patch to work with scapy 2.3"
```

At this point, you have manually patched the source code and you can already build binary packages of your modified version (see section 9.1.4, "Starting the Build" [page 230]). But if you try to build an updated source package, it will fail, complaining about "unexpected upstream changes." This is because pyrit (like a majority of the source packages) uses the source format (see debian/source/format file) known as 3.0 (quilt), where changes to the upstream code must be recorded in separate patches stored in debian/patches/ and where the debian/patches/series file indicates the order in which patches must be applied. You can register your changes in a new patch by running dpkg-source --commit:

```
$ dpkg-source --commit
dpkg-source: info: local changes detected, the modified files are:
 pyrit-0.4.0/cpyrit/pckttools.py
Enter the desired patch name: fix-for-scapy-2.3.patch
dpkg-source: info: local changes have been recorded in a new patch: pyrit-0.4.0/debian/
  ➡ patches/fix-for-scapy-2.3.patch
$ tail -n 1 debian/patches/series
fix-for-scapy-2.3.patch
```

> **Quilt Patch Series**   This patch management convention has been popularized by a tool named quilt and the "3.0 (quilt)" source package format is thus compatible with this tool—with the small deviation that it uses debian/patches instead of patches. This tool is available in the package of the same name and you can find a nice tutorial here:
>
> ➡ https://raphaelhertzog.com/2012/08/08/
> how-to-use-quilt-to-manage-patches-in-debian-packages/

If the source package uses the 1.0 or 3.0 (native) source format, then there is no requirement to register your upstream changes in a patch. They are automatically bundled in the resulting source package.

With a Git Repository   If you have used Git to retrieve the source package, the situation is even more complicated. There are multiple Git workflows and associated tools, and obviously not all Debian packages are using the same workflows and tools. The distinction already explained about source format is still relevant but you must also check whether patches are pre-applied in the source tree or whether they are only stored in debian/patches (in this case, they are then applied at build time).

The most popular tool is *git-buildpackage*. It is what we use to manage all repositories on git.kali.org. When you use it, patches are not pre-applied in the source tree but they are stored in debian/patches. You can manually add patches in that directory and list them in debian/patches/

series but users of git-buildpackage tend to use gbp pq to edit the entire patch series as a single branch that you can extend or rebase to your liking. Check gbp-pq(1) to learn how to invoke it.

git-dpm (with associated command of the same name) is another git packaging tool that you can find in use. It records metadata in debian/.git-dpm and keeps patches applied in the source tree by merging a constantly-rebased branch that it builds out of the content of debian/patches.

Tweaking Build Options

You usually have to tweak build options when you want to enable an optional feature or behavior that is not activated in the official package, or when you want to customize parameters that are set at build time through a ./configure option or through variables set in the build environment.

In those cases, the changes are usually limited to debian/rules, which drives the steps in the package build process. In the simplest cases, the lines concerning the initial configuration (./configure ...) or the actual build ($(MAKE) ... or make ...) are easy to spot. If these commands are not explicitly called, they are probably a side effect of another explicit command, in which case, please refer to their documentation to learn more about how to change the default behavior. With packages using dh, you might need to add an override for the dh_auto_configure or dh_auto_build commands (see their respective manual pages for explanations on how to achieve this).

To make those explanations more concrete, let's apply them to our sample use case. You decided to modify libfreefare to pass the --enable-debug option to the ./configure script so that you could get a more verbose output from your near field communication (NFC) tools and file a better bug report about your non-recognized Mifare NFC card. Since the package uses dh to drive the build process, you add (or in this case modify) the override_dh_auto_configure target. Here is the corresponding extract of libfreefare's debian/rules file:

```
override_dh_auto_configure:
        dh_auto_configure -- --without-cutter --disable-silent-rules --enable-debug
```

Packaging a New Upstream Version

Let's take a look at an example at this point, as we discuss packaging upstream versions. Let's say you are a SET power-user and you noticed a new upstream release (7.4.5) that is not yet available in Kali (which only has version 7.4.4). You want to build an updated package and try it out. This is a minor version bump and you thus don't expect the update to require any change at the packaging level.

To update the source package, you extract the new source tarball next to the current source package and you copy the debian directory from the current source package to the new one. Then you bump the version in debian/changelog.

```
$ apt source set
Reading package lists... Done
NOTICE: 'set' packaging is maintained in the 'Git' version control system at:
git://git.kali.org/packages/set.git
Please use:
git clone git://git.kali.org/packages/set.git
to retrieve the latest (possibly unreleased) updates to the package.
Need to get 42.3 MB of source archives.
[...]
dpkg-source: warning: failed to verify signature on ./set_7.4.4-0kali1.dsc
dpkg-source: info: extracting set in set-7.4.4
dpkg-source: info: unpacking set_7.4.4.orig.tar.gz
dpkg-source: info: unpacking set_7.4.4-0kali1.debian.tar.xz
dpkg-source: info: applying edit-config-file
dpkg-source: info: applying fix-path-interpreter.patch
$ wget https://github.com/trustedsec/social-engineer-toolkit/archive/7.4.5.tar.gz -O
   ➡ set_7.4.5.orig.tar.gz
[...]
$ tar xvf set_7.4.5.orig.tar.gz
[...]
social-engineer-toolkit-7.4.5/src/wireless/wifiattack.py
$ cp -a set-7.4.4/debian social-engineer-toolkit-7.4.5/debian
$ cd social-engineer-toolkit-7.4.5
$ dch -v 7.4.5-0buxy1 "New upstream release"
```

That's it. You can now build the updated package.

Depending on the kind of changes that the new upstream version introduces, you may also need to change build dependencies and run-time dependencies, and install new files. Those are much more involved operations that are not covered by this book.

9.1.4. Starting the Build

When all the needed changes have been applied to the sources, you can start generating the actual binary package or .deb file. The whole process is managed by the dpkg-buildpackage command and it looks like this:

```
$ dpkg-buildpackage -us -uc -b
dpkg-buildpackage: source package libfreefare
dpkg-buildpackage: source version 0.4.0-2buxy1
dpkg-buildpackage: source distribution UNRELEASED
dpkg-buildpackage: source changed by Raphael Hertzog <buxy@kali.org>
dpkg-buildpackage: host architecture amd64
[...]
   dh_builddeb
dpkg-deb: building package 'libfreefare0-dbgsym' in '../libfreefare0-dbgsym_0.4.0-2buxy1_amd64.deb'.
dpkg-deb: building package 'libfreefare0' in '../libfreefare0_0.4.0-2buxy1_amd64.deb'.
dpkg-deb: building package 'libfreefare-dev' in '../libfreefare-dev_0.4.0-2buxy1_amd64.deb'.
dpkg-deb: building package 'libfreefare-bin-dbgsym' in '../libfreefare-bin-dbgsym_0.4.0-2buxy1_amd64.deb'.
```

```
dpkg-deb: building package 'libfreefare-bin' in '../libfreefare-bin_0.4.0-2buxy1_amd64.deb'.
dpkg-deb: building package 'libfreefare-doc' in '../libfreefare-doc_0.4.0-2buxy1_all.deb'.
 dpkg-genchanges -b >../libfreefare_0.4.0-2buxy1_amd64.changes
dpkg-genchanges: binary-only upload (no source code included)
 dpkg-source --after-build libfreefare-0.4.0
dpkg-buildpackage: binary-only upload (no source included)
```

The -us -uc options disable signatures on some of the generated files (.dsc, .changes) because this operation will fail if you do not have a GnuPG key associated with the identity you have put in the changelog file. The -b option asks for a "binary-only build." In this case, the source package (.dsc) will not be created, only the binary (.deb) packages will. Use this option to avoid failures during the source package build: if you haven't properly recorded your changes in the patch management system, it might complain and interrupt the build process.

As suggested by dpkg-deb's messages, the generated binary packages are now available in the parent directory (the one that hosts the directory of the source package). You can install them with dpkg -i or apt install.

```
$ sudo apt install ../libfreefare0_0.4.0-2buxy1_amd64.deb \
  ../libfreefare-bin_0.4.0-2buxy1_amd64.deb
Reading package lists... Done
Building dependency tree
Reading state information... Done
Note, selecting 'libfreefare0' instead of '../libfreefare0_0.4.0-2buxy1_amd64.deb'
Note, selecting 'libfreefare-bin' instead of '../libfreefare-bin_0.4.0-2buxy1_amd64.deb'
The following packages will be upgraded:
  libfreefare-bin libfreefare0
2 upgraded, 0 newly installed, 0 to remove and 0 not upgraded.
Need to get 0 B/69,4 kB of archives.
After this operation, 2 048 B of additional disk space will be used.
[...]
```

We prefer apt install over dpkg -i as it will deal with missing dependencies gracefully. But not so long ago, you had to use dpkg as apt was not able to deal with .deb files outside of any repository.

dpkg-buildpackage wrappers More often than not, Debian developers use a higher-level program such as debuild; this runs dpkg-buildpackage as usual, but it also adds an invocation of a program (lintian) that runs many checks to validate the generated package against the Debian policy[3]. This script also cleans up the environment so that local environment variables do not pollute the package build. The debuild command is one of the tools in the *devscripts* suite, which share some consistency and configuration to make the maintainers' task easier.

---

[3]https://www.debian.org/doc/debian-policy/

9.2. Recompiling the Linux Kernel

The kernels provided by Kali include the largest possible number of features, as well as the maximum number of drivers, in order to cover the broadest spectrum of existing hardware configurations. This is why some users prefer to recompile the kernel in order to include only what they specifically need. There are two reasons for this choice. First, it is a way to optimize memory consumption since all kernel code, even if it is never used, occupies physical memory. Because the statically compiled portions of the kernel are never moved to swap space, an overall decrease in system performance will result from having drivers and features built in that are never used. Second, reducing the number of drivers and kernel features reduces the risk of security problems since only a fraction of the available kernel code is being run.

> **Important**
>
> ⚠ If you choose to compile your own kernel, you must accept the consequences: Kali cannot ensure security updates for your custom kernel. By keeping the kernel provided by Kali, you benefit from updates prepared by the Debian Project.

Recompilation of the kernel is also necessary if you want to use certain features that are only available as patches (and not included in the standard kernel version).

The Debian Kernel Handbook The Debian kernel team maintains the *Debian Kernel Handbook* (also available in the *debian-kernel-handbook* package) with comprehensive documentation about most kernel-related tasks and about how official Debian kernel packages are handled. This is the first place you should look into if you need more information than what is provided in this section.

➡ http://kernel-handbook.alioth.debian.org

9.2.1. Introduction and Prerequisites

Unsurprisingly, Debian and Kali manage the kernel in the form of a package, which is not how kernels have traditionally been compiled and installed. Since the kernel remains under the control of the packaging system, it can then be removed cleanly, or deployed on several machines. Furthermore, the scripts associated with these packages automate the interaction with the bootloader and the initrd generator.

The upstream Linux sources contain everything needed to build a Debian package of the kernel but you still need to install the *build-essential* package to ensure that you have the tools required to build a Debian package. Furthermore, the configuration step for the kernel requires the *libncurses5-dev* package. Finally, the *fakeroot* package will enable creation of the Debian package without needing administrative privileges.

```
# apt install build-essential libncurses5-dev fakeroot
```

9.2.2. Getting the Sources

Since the Linux kernel sources are available as a package, you can retrieve them by installing the *linux-source*-version package. The `apt-cache search ^linux-source` command should list the latest kernel version packaged by Kali. Note that the source code contained in these packages does not correspond precisely with that published by Linus Torvalds and the kernel developers[4]; like all distributions, Debian and Kali apply a number of patches, which might (or might not) find their way into the upstream version of Linux. These modifications include backports of fixes/features/drivers from newer kernel versions, new features not yet (entirely) merged in the upstream Linux tree, and sometimes even Debian or Kali specific changes.

The remainder of this section focuses on the 4.9 version of the Linux kernel, but the examples can, of course, be adapted to the particular version of the kernel that you want.

In this example, we assume that the *linux-source-4.9* binary package has been installed. Note that we install a binary package containing the upstream sources but do not retrieve the Kali source package named *linux*.

```
# apt install linux-source-4.9
Reading package lists... Done
Building dependency tree
Reading state information... Done
The following additional packages will be installed:
  bc libreadline7
Suggested packages:
  libncurses-dev | ncurses-dev libqt4-dev
The following NEW packages will be installed:
  bc libreadline7 linux-source-4.9
0 upgraded, 3 newly installed, 0 to remove and 0 not upgraded.
Need to get 95.4 MB of archives.
After this operation, 95.8 MB of additional disk space will be used.
Do you want to continue? [Y/n] y
[...]
# ls /usr/src
linux-config-4.9  linux-patch-4.9-rt.patch.xz  linux-source-4.9.tar.xz
```

Notice that the package contains /usr/src/linux-source-4.9.tar.xz, a compressed archive of the kernel sources. You must extract these files in a new directory (not directly under /usr/src/,

---
[4]https://kernel.org/

since there is no need for special permissions to compile a Linux kernel). Instead, ~/kernel/ is more appropriate.

```
$ mkdir ~/kernel; cd ~/kernel
$ tar -xaf /usr/src/linux-source-4.9.tar.xz
```

9.2.3. Configuring the Kernel

The next step consists of configuring the kernel according to your needs. The exact procedure depends on the goals.

The kernel build depends on a kernel configuration file. In most cases, you will most likely keep as close as possible to that proposed by Kali, which, like all Linux distributions, is installed in the /boot directory. In this case, rather than reconfiguring everything from scratch, it is sufficient to make a copy of the /boot/config-*version* file. (The version should be the same as that version of the kernel currently used, which can be found with the uname -r command.) Place the copy into a .config file in the directory containing the kernel sources.

```
$ cp /boot/config-4.9.0-kali1-amd64 ~/kernel/linux-source-4.9/.config
```

Alternatively, since the kernel provides default configurations in arch/*arch*/configs/*_defconfig, you can put your selected configuration in place with a command like make x86_64_defconfig (in the case of a 64-bit PC) or make i386_defconfig (in the case of a 32-bit PC).

Unless you need to change the configuration, you can stop here and skip to section 9.2.4, "Compiling and Building the Package" [page 235]. If you need to make changes or if you decide to reconfigure everything from scratch, you must take the time to configure your kernel. There are various dedicated interfaces in the kernel source directory that can be used by calling the make *target* command, where *target* is one of the values described below.

make menuconfig compiles and launches a text-mode kernel configuration interface (this is where the *libncurses5-dev* package is required), which allows navigating the many available kernel options in a hierarchical structure. Pressing the Space key changes the value of the selected option, and Enter validates the button selected at the bottom of the screen; Select returns to the selected sub-menu; Exit closes the current screen and moves back up in the hierarchy; Help will display more detailed information on the role of the selected option. The arrow keys allow moving within the list of options and buttons. To exit the configuration program, choose Exit from the main menu. The program then offers to save the changes that you have made; accept if you are satisfied with your choices.

Other interfaces have similar features but they work within more modern graphical interfaces, such as make xconfig, which uses a Qt graphical interface, and make gconfig, which uses GTK+. The former requires *libqt4-dev*, while the latter depends on *libglade2-dev* and *libgtk2.0-dev*.

Dealing with Outdated .config Files When you provide a `.config` file that has been generated with another (usually older) kernel version, you will have to update it. You can do so with `make oldconfig`, which will interactively ask you the questions corresponding to the new configuration options. If you want to use the default answer to all those questions, you can use `make olddefconfig`. With `make oldnoconfig`, it will assume a negative answer to all questions.

9.2.4. Compiling and Building the Package

Clean Up Before Rebuilding If you have already compiled a kernel in the directory and wish to rebuild everything from scratch (for example because you substantially changed the kernel configuration), you will have to run `make clean` to remove the compiled files. `make distclean` removes even more generated files, including your `.config` file, so make sure to back it up first.

Once the kernel configuration is ready, a simple `make deb-pkg` will generate up to five Debian packages in standard `.deb` format: *linux-image*-version, which contains the kernel image and the associated modules; *linux-headers*-version, which contains the header files required to build external modules; *linux-firmware-image*-version, which contains the firmware files needed by some drivers (this package might be missing when you build from the kernel sources provided by Debian or Kali); *linux-image*-version-*dbg*, which contains the debugging symbols for the kernel image and its modules; and *linux-libc-dev*, which contains headers relevant to some user-space libraries like GNU's C library (glibc).

The *version* is defined by the concatenation of the upstream version (as defined by the variables VERSION, PATCHLEVEL, SUBLEVEL, and EXTRAVERSION in the `Makefile`), of the LOCALVERSION configuration parameter, and of the LOCALVERSION environment variable. The package version reuses the same version string with an appended revision that is regularly incremented (and stored in `.version`), except if you override it with the KDEB_PKGVERSION environment variable.

```
$ make deb-pkg LOCALVERSION=-custom KDEB_PKGVERSION=$(make kernelversion)-1
[...]
$ ls ../*.deb
../linux-headers-4.9.0-kali1-custom_4.9.2-1_amd64.deb
../linux-image-4.9.0-kali1-custom_4.9.2-1_amd64.deb
../linux-image-4.9.0-kali1-custom-dbg_4.9.2-1_amd64.deb
../linux-libc-dev_4.9.2-1_amd64.deb
```

To actually use the built kernel, the only step left is to install the required packages with `dpkg -i file.deb`. The "linux-image" package is required; you only have to install the "linux-headers" package if you have some external kernel modules to build, which is the case if you have some

"*-dkms" packages installed (check with `dpkg -l "*-dkms" | grep ^ii`). The other packages are generally not needed (Unless you know why you need them!).

9.3. Building Custom Kali Live ISO Images

Kali Linux has a ton of functionality and flexibility right out of the box. Once Kali is installed, you can perform all sorts of amazing feats with a little guidance, creativity, patience, and practice. However, you can also customize a Kali build so that it contains specific files or packages (to scale up or scale down performance and features) and can perform certain functions automatically. For example, the Kali ISO of Doom[5] and the Kali Evil Wireless Access Point[6] are both excellent projects that rely on a custom-built implementation of Kali Linux. Let's take a look at the process of rolling a custom Kali Linux ISO image.

Official Kali ISO images are built with live-build[7], which is a set of scripts that allows for the complete automation and customization of all facets of ISO image creation. The *live-build* suite uses an entire directory structure as input for its configuration. We store this configuration and some associated helper scripts in a live-build-config Git repository. We will use this repository as a basis for building customized images.

Before going further, you must know that the commands shown in this section are meant to be run on an up-to-date Kali Linux system. They are very likely to fail if run on a non-Kali system or if the system is out of date.

9.3.1. Installing Pre-Requisites

The first step is to install the packages needed and to retrieve the Git repository with the Kali *live-build* configuration:

```
# apt install curl git live-build
[...]
# git clone git://git.kali.org/live-build-config.git
[...]
# cd live-build-config
# ls
auto  build_all.sh  build.sh  kali-config  README
```

At this point, you can already create an updated (but unmodified) Kali ISO image just by running `./build.sh --verbose`. The build will take a long time to complete as it will download all the packages to include. When finished, you will find the new ISO image in the `images` directory.

---

[5]https://www.offensive-security.com/kali-linux/kali-linux-iso-of-doom
[6]https://www.offensive-security.com/kali-linux/kali-linux-evil-wireless-access-point/
[7]http://debian-live.alioth.debian.org/live-build/

9.3.2. Building Live Images with Different Desktop Environments

The `build.sh` live-build wrapper that we provide is responsible for setting up the `config` directory that `live-build` expects to find. It can put in place different configurations depending on its --variant option.

The wrapper creates the `config` directory by combining files from `kali-config/common` and `kali-config/variant-X`, where X is the name of a variant given with the --variant parameter. When the option is not explicitly given, it uses default as the name of the variant.

The `kali-config` directory contains directories for the most common desktop environments:

- `e17` for Enlightenment;
- `gnome` for GNOME;
- `i3wm` for the corresponding window manager;
- `kde` for KDE;
- `lxde` for LXDE;
- `mate` for the Mate Desktop Environment;
- `xfce` for XFCE.

The `light` variant is a bit special; it is based on XFCE[8] and is used to generate the official "light" ISO images that contain a reduced set of applications.

You can easily create a Kali live image using KDE as desktop environment with this single command:

```
# ./build.sh --variant kde --verbose
```

This concept of *variant* allows for some high-level pre-defined customizations but if you take the time to read through the Debian Live System Manual[9], you will discover many other ways to customize the images, just by changing the content of the appropriate sub-directory of `kali-config`. The following sections will provide some examples.

9.3.3. Changing the Set of Installed Packages

Once launched, `live-build` installs all the packages listed in `package-lists/*.list.chroot` files. The default configuration that we provide includes a `package-lists/kali.list.chroot` file, which lists *kali-linux-full* (the main meta-package pulling all the Kali packages to include). You can comment out this package and put another meta-package of your choice or include a precise set of other packages. You can also combine both approaches by starting with a meta-package and adding supplementary packages of your choice.

---

[8] https://www.xfce.org/
[9] http://debian-live.alioth.debian.org/live-manual/unstable/manual/html/live-manual.en.html

With `package-lists`, you can only include packages that are already available in the official Kali repository. But if you have custom packages, you can include them in the live image by placing the `.deb` files in a `packages.chroot` directory (for example `kali-config/config-gnome/packages.chroot` if you build the GNOME variant).

Meta-packages are empty packages whose sole purpose is to have many dependencies on other packages. They make it easier to install sets of packages that you often want to install together. The kali-meta source package builds all the meta-packages provided by Kali Linux:

- kali-linux: the base system (it is pulled by all the other meta-packages)
- kali-linux-full:the default Kali Linux installation
- kali-linux-all: meta-package of all the meta-packages and other packages (almost everything that Kali provides so it is really huge!)
- kali-linux-sdr: Software Defined Radio (SDR) tools
- kali-linux-gpu: GPU-powered tools (tools making use of the computing power available in your graphical card)
- kali-linux-wireless: wireless assessment and analysis tools
- kali-linux-web: web applications assessment tools
- kali-linux-forensic: forensic tools (finding evidence of what happened)
- kali-linux-voip: Voice Over IP tools
- kali-linux-pwtools: password cracking tools
- kali-linux-top10: the ten most popular tools
- kali-linux-rfid: RFID tools

You can leverage these meta-packages when you create custom package lists for `live-build`. The full list of available meta-packages and the tools they include can be found at `http://tools.kali.org/kali-metapackages`

| Debconf Preseeding of Installed Packages | You can provide Debconf preseed files (see section 4.3.2, "Creating a Preseed File" [page 93] for explanations) as `preseed/*.cfg` files. They will be used to configure the packages installed in the live file system. |

9.3.4. Using Hooks to Tweak the Contents of the Image

`live-build` offers hooks that can be executed at different steps of the build process. Chroot hooks are executable scripts that you install as `hooks/live/*.chroot` files in your config tree and that are executed within the chroot. While `chroot` is the command that lets you temporarily changes the operating system's root directory to a directory of your choice, it is also used by extension to designate a directory hosting a full (alternate) file system tree. This is the case here with `live-build`, where the chroot directory is the directory where the live file system is being prepared. Since applications started in a chroot can't see outside of that directory, the same goes with the chroot hooks: you can only use and modify anything available in that chroot environment. We rely on those hooks to perform multiple Kali specific customizations (see `kali-config/common/hooks/live/kali-hacks.chroot`).

Binary hooks (`hooks/live/*.binary`) are executed in the context of the build process (and not chrooted anywhere) at the end of the process. You can modify the content of the ISO image built but not of the live file system since at this point, it has already been generated. We use this feature in Kali to make some changes to the default isolinux configuration generated by live-build. For example, see `kali-config/common/hooks/live/persistence.binary` where we add the boot menu entries enabling persistence.

9.3.5. Adding Files in the ISO Image or in the Live Filesystem

Another very common customization is to add files either in the live file system or in the ISO image.

You can add files to the live file system by putting them at their expected location below the `includes.chroot` config directory. For example, we provide `kali-config/common/includes.chroot/usr/lib/live/config/0031-root-password`, which ends up as `/usr/lib/live/config/0031-root-password` in the live file system.

> **Live-Boot Hooks** Scripts installed as `/lib/live/config/XXXX-name` are executed by the init script of the live-boot package. They reconfigure many aspects of the system to be suited for a live system. You can add scripts of your own to customize your live system at run-time: it's notably used to implement a custom boot parameter for example.

You can add files to the ISO image by putting them at their expected location below the `includes.binary` config directory. For example, we provide `kali-config/common/includes.binary/isolinux/splash.png` to override the background image used by the Isolinux bootloader (which is stored in `/isolinux/splash.png` in the filesystem of the ISO image).

9.4. Adding Persistence to the Live ISO with a USB Key

9.4.1. The Persistence Feature: Explanations

Next, we will discuss the steps required to add persistence to a Kali USB key. The nature of a live system is to be ephemeral. All data stored on the live system and all the changes made are lost when you reboot. To remedy this, you can use a feature of *live-boot* called persistence, which is enabled when the boot parameters include the persistence keyword.

Since modifying the boot menu is a non-trivial task, Kali includes two menu entries by default that enable persistence: Live USB Persistence and Live USB Encrypted Persistence, as shown in Figure 9.1, "Persistence Menu Entries" [page 240].

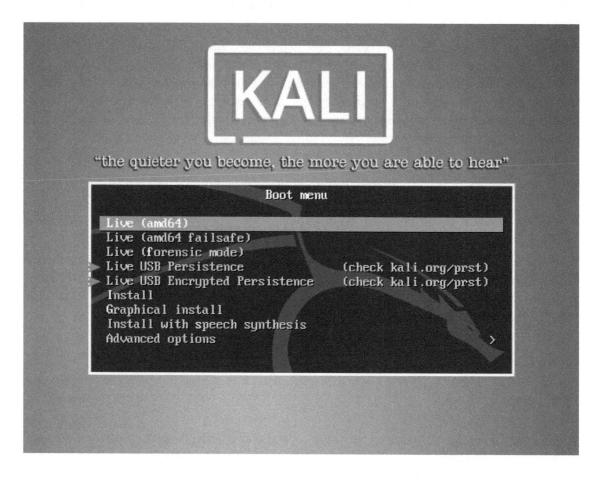

Figure 9.1 *Persistence Menu Entries*

When this feature is enabled, *live-boot* will scan all partitions looking for file systems labeled persistence (which can be overridden with the persistence-label=*value* boot parameter) and the installer will set up persistence of the directories which are listed in the `persistence.conf` file found in that partition (one directory per line). The special value "/ union" enables full persistence of all directories with a *union mount*, an overlay that stores only the changes when compared to the underlying file system. The data of the persisted directories are stored in the file system that contains the corresponding `persistence.conf` file.

9.4.2. Setting Up Unencrypted Persistence on a USB Key

In this section, we assume that you have prepared a Kali Live USB Key by following the instructions at section 2.1.4, "Copying the Image on a DVD-ROM or USB Key" [page 19] and that you have used a USB key big enough to hold the ISO image (roughly 3 GB) and the data of the directories that you want to persist. We also assume that the USB key is recognized by Linux as /dev/sdb and that it only contains the two partitions that are part of the default ISO image (/dev/sdb1 and /dev/sdb2). Be very careful when performing this procedure. You can easily destroy important data if you re-partition the wrong drive.

To add a new partition, you must know the size of the image that you copied so that you can make the new partition start after the live image. Then use `parted` to actually create the partition. The commands below analyze the ISO image named `kali-linux-2016.1-amd64.iso`, which is assumed to be present on the USB key as well:

```
# parted /dev/sdb print
Model: SanDisk Cruzer Edge (scsi)
Disk /dev/sdb: 32,0GB
Sector size (logical/physical): 512B/512B
Partition Table: msdos
Disk Flags:

Number  Start    End     Size    Type     File system  Flags
 1      32,8kB   2852MB  2852MB  primary               boot, hidden
 2      2852MB   2945MB  93,4MB  primary
# start=$(du --block-size=1MB kali-linux-2016.1-amd64.iso | awk '{print $1}')
# echo "Size of image is $start MB"
Size of image is 2946 MB
# parted -a optimal /dev/sdb mkpart primary "${start}MB" 100%
Information: You may need to update /etc/fstab.

# parted /dev/sdb print
Model: SanDisk Cruzer Edge (scsi)
Disk /dev/sdb: 32,0GB
Sector size (logical/physical): 512B/512B
Partition Table: msdos
Disk Flags:

Number  Start    End     Size    Type     File system  Flags
 1      32,8kB   2852MB  2852MB  primary               boot, hidden
 2      2852MB   2945MB  93,4MB  primary
 3      2946MB   32,0GB  29,1GB  primary
```

With the new /dev/sdb3 partition in place, format it with an ext4 filesystem labelled "persistence" with the help of the mkfs.ext4 command (and its -L option to set the label). The partition is then mounted on the /mnt directory and you add the required persistence.conf configuration file. As always, use caution when formatting any disk. You could lose valuable information if you format the wrong disk or partition.

```
# mkfs.ext4 -L persistence /dev/sdb3
mke2fs 1.43-WIP (15-Mar-2016)
Creating filesystem with 7096832 4k blocks and 1777664 inodes
Filesystem UUID: dede20c4-5239-479a-b115-96561ac857b6
Superblock backups stored on blocks:
        32768, 98304, 163840, 229376, 294912, 819200, 884736, 1605632, 2654208,
        4096000

Allocating group tables: done
Writing inode tables: done
Creating journal (32768 blocks): done
Writing superblocks and filesystem accounting information: done
# mount /dev/sdb3 /mnt
# echo "/ union" >/mnt/persistence.conf
# ls -l /mnt
total 20
drwx------ 2 root root 16384 May 10 13:31 lost+found
-rw-r--r-- 1 root root     8 May 10 13:34 persistence.conf
# umount /mnt
```

The USB key is now ready and can be booted with the "Live USB Persistence" boot menu entry.

9.4.3. Setting Up Encrypted Persistence on a USB Key

live-boot is also able to handle persistence file systems on encrypted partitions. You can thus protect the data of your persistent directories by creating a LUKS encrypted partition holding the persistence data.

The initial steps are the same up to the creation of the partition but instead of formatting it with an ext4 file system, use cryptsetup to initialize it as a LUKS container. Then open that container and setup the ext4 file system in the same way as in the non-encrypted setup, but instead of using the /dev/sdb3 partition, use the virtual partition created by cryptsetup. This virtual partition represents the decrypted content of the encrypted partition, which is available in /dev/mapper under the name that you assigned it. In the example below, we will use the name kali_persistence. Again, ensure that you are using the correct drive and partition.

```
# cryptsetup --verbose --verify-passphrase luksFormat /dev/sdb3

WARNING!
========
This will overwrite data on /dev/sdb3 irrevocably.

Are you sure? (Type uppercase yes): YES
```

```
Enter passphrase:
Verify passphrase:
Command successful.
# cryptsetup luksOpen /dev/sdb3 kali_persistence
Enter passphrase for /dev/sdb3:
# mkfs.ext4 -L persistence /dev/mapper/kali_persistence
mke2fs 1.43-WIP (15-Mar-2016)
Creating filesystem with 7096320 4k blocks and 1774192 inodes
Filesystem UUID: 287892c1-00bb-43cb-b513-81cc9e6fa72b
Superblock backups stored on blocks:
        32768, 98304, 163840, 229376, 294912, 819200, 884736, 1605632, 2654208,
        4096000

Allocating group tables: done
Writing inode tables: done
Creating journal (32768 blocks): done
Writing superblocks and filesystem accounting information: done

# mount /dev/mapper/kali_persistence /mnt
# echo "/ union" >/mnt/persistence.conf
# umount /mnt
# cryptsetup luksClose /dev/mapper/kali_persistence
```

9.4.4. Using Multiple Persistence Stores

If you have multiple use-cases for your Kali live system, you can use multiple filesystems with different labels and indicate on the boot command line which (set of) filesystems should be used for the persistence feature: this is done with the help of the persistence-label=*label* boot parameter.

Let's assume that you are a professional pen-tester. When you work for a customer, you use an encrypted persistence partition to protect the confidentiality of your data in case the USB key is stolen or compromised. At the same time, you want to be able to showcase Kali and some promotional material stored in an unencrypted partition of the same USB key. Since you don't want to manually edit the boot parameters on each boot, you want to build a custom live image with dedicated boot menu entries.

The first step is to build the custom live ISO (following section 9.3, "Building Custom Kali Live ISO Images" [page 236] and in particular section 9.3.4, "Using Hooks to Tweak the Contents of the Image" [page 238]). The main customization is to modify kali-config/common/hooks/live/persistence-menu.binary to make it look like this (note the persistence-label parameters):

```
#!/bin/sh

if [ ! -d isolinux ]; then
    cd binary
```

```
fi

cat >>isolinux/live.cfg <<END

label live-demo
    menu label ^Live USB with Demo Data
    linux /live/vmlinuz
    initrd /live/initrd.img
    append boot=live username=root hostname=kali persistence-label=demo persistence

label live-work
    menu label ^Live USB with Work Data
    linux /live/vmlinuz
    initrd /live/initrd.img
    append boot=live username=root hostname=kali persistence-label=work persistence-
        ➥ encryption=luks persistence

END
```

Next, we will build our custom ISO and copy it to the USB key. Then we will create and initialize the two partitions and files ystems that will be used for persistence. The first partition is unencrypted (labeled "demo"), and the second is encrypted (labeled "work"). Assuming /dev/sdb is our USB key and the size of our custom ISO image is 3000 MB, it would look like this:

```
# parted /dev/sdb mkpart primary 3000 MB 55%
# parted /dev/sdb mkpart primary 55% 100%
# mkfs.ext4 -L demo /dev/sdb3
[...]
# mount /dev/sdb3 /mnt
# echo "/ union" >/mnt/persistence.conf
# umount /mnt
# cryptsetup --verbose --verify-passphrase luksFormat /dev/sdb4
[...]
# cryptsetup luksOpen /dev/sdb4 kali_persistence
[...]
# mkfs.ext4 -L work /dev/mapper/kali_persistence
[...]
# mount /dev/mapper/kali_persistence /mnt
# echo "/ union" >/mnt/persistence.conf
# umount /mnt
# cryptsetup luksClose /dev/mapper/kali_persistence
```

And that's all. You can now boot the USB key and select from the new boot menu entries as needed!

| **Adding a Nuke Password for Extra Safety** | Kali has modified `cryptsetup` to implement a new feature: you can set a *nuke password* which—when used—will destroy all keys used to manage the encrypted partition. |

This can be useful when you travel a lot and need a quick way to ensure your data cannot be recovered. When booting, just type the nuke password instead of the real one and it will then be impossible for anyone (including you) to access your data.

Before using that feature, it is thus wise to make a backup copy of your encryption keys and keep them at some secure place.

Following the example in this section, you could add a nuke password with this command:

```
# cryptsetup luksAddNuke /dev/sdb4
Enter any existing passphrase:
Enter new passphrase for key slot:
Verify passphrase:
```

More information about this feature can be found in the following tutorial:

➡ https://www.kali.org/tutorials/nuke-kali-linux-luks/

9.5. Summary

In this chapter, we learned about modifying Kali source packages, which are the basic building blocks of all applications shipped in Kali. We also discovered how to customize and install the Kali kernel. Then we discussed the live-build environment and discussed how to build a customized Kali Linux ISO. We also demonstrated how to create both encrypted and unencrypted Kali USB installs.

9.5.1. Summary Tips for Modifying Kali Packages

Modifying Kali packages is usually a task for Kali contributors and developers, but you might have specific needs not fulfilled by the official packages and knowing how to build a modified package can be very valuable, especially if you want to share your changes, deploy them internally, or cleanly roll the software back to a previous state.

When you need to modify a piece of software, it might be tempting to download the source, make the changes, and use the modified software. However, if your application requires a system-wide setup (e.g. with a `make install` step), then it will *pollute* your file system with files unknown to `dpkg` and will soon create problems that cannot be caught by package dependencies. In addition, this type of software modification is more tedious to share.

When creating a modified package, the general process is always the same: grab the source package, extract it, make your changes, and then build the package. For each step, there are often multiple tools that can handle each task.

To start rebuilding a Kali package, first download the source package, which is composed of a `*.dsc` (*Debian Source Control*) file and of additional files referenced from that control file.

Source packages are stored on HTTP-accessible mirrors. The most efficient way to obtain them is with `apt source source-package-name`, which requires that you add a deb-src line to the `/etc/apt/sources.list` file and update the index files with `apt update`.

Additionally, you can use `dget` (from the *devscripts* package) to download a `.dsc` file directly together with its accompanying files. For Kali-specific packages whose sources are hosted in a Git repository on git.kali.org[10], you can retrieve the sources with `git clone git://git.kali.org/packages/source-package` (if you don't see anything in your repository, try switching to the kali/master branch with `git checkout kali/master`).

After downloading sources, install the packages listed in the source package's build dependencies with `sudo apt build-dep ./`. This command must be run from the package's source directory.

Updates to a source package consist of a combination of some of the following steps:

- The required first step is changing the version number to distinguish your package from the original with `dch --local version-identifier`, or modify other package details with `dch`.

- Applying a patch with `patch -p1 < patch-file` or modifying `quilt`'s patch series.

- Tweaking build options, usually found in the package's `debian/rules` file, or other files in the `debian/` directory.

After modifying a source package, you can build the binary package with `dpkg-buildpackage -us -uc -b` from the source directory, which will generate an unsigned binary package. The package can then be installed with `dpkg -i package-name_version_arch.deb`.

9.5.2. Summary Tips for Recompiling the Linux Kernel

As an advanced user, you may wish to recompile the Kali kernel. You may want to slim down the standard Kali kernel, which is loaded with many features and drivers, add non-standard drivers or features, or apply kernel patches. Beware though: a misconfigured kernel may destabilize your system and you must be prepared to accept that Kali cannot ensure security updates for your custom kernel.

For most kernel modifications, you will need to install a few packages with `apt install build-essential libncurses5-dev fakeroot`.

---

[10]http://git.kali.org

The command `apt-cache search ^linux-source` should list the latest kernel version packaged by Kali, and `apt install linux-source-version-number` installs a compressed archive of the kernel source into `/usr/src`.

The source files should be extracted with `tar -xaf` into a directory other than `/usr/src` (such as `~/kernel`).

When the time comes to configure your kernel, keep these points in mind:

- Unless you are an advanced user, you should first populate a kernel configuration file. The preferred method is to borrow Kali's standard configuration by copying `/boot/config-version-string` to `~/kernel/linux-source-version-number/.config`. Alternatively, you can use `make architecture_defconfig` to get a reasonable configuration for the given architecture.

- The text-based `make menuconfig` kernel configuration tool will read the `.config` file and present you all the configuration items in a huge menu that you can navigate. Selecting an item shows you its documentation, its possible values, and permits you to enter a new value.

When run from your kernel source directory, `make clean` will remove previously-compiled files and `make deb-pkg` will generate up to five Debian packages. The *linux-image*-version `.deb` file contains the kernel image and the associated modules.

To actually use the built kernel, install the required packages with `dpkg -i file.deb`. The "linux-image" package is required; you only have to install the "linux-headers" package if you have some external kernel modules to build, which is the case if you have some "*-dkms" packages installed (check with `dpkg -l "*-dkms" | grep ^ii`). The other packages are generally not needed (unless you know why you need them!).

9.5.3. Summary Tips for Building Custom Kali Live ISO Images

Official Kali ISO images are built with live-build[11], which is a set of scripts that allows for the complete automation and customization of all facets of ISO image creation.

Your Kali system must be completely up-to-date before using live-build.

The Kali live-build configuration can be retrieved from Kali's Git repositories with two commands: `apt install curl git live-build` followed by `git clone git://git.kali.org/live-build-config.git`

To generate an updated but unmodified Kali ISO image, simply run `./build.sh --verbose`. The build will take a long time to complete as it will download all the packages to include. When finished, you will find the new ISO image in the `images` directory. If you add `--variant variant` to the command line, it will build the given variant of the Kali ISO image. The various variants

---

[11]http://debian-live.alioth.debian.org/live-build/

are defined by their configuration directories `kali-config/variant-*`. The main image is the gnome variant.

There are several ways to customize your ISO by modifying live-build's configuration directory:

- Packages can be added to (or removed from) a live ISO by modifying `package-lists/*.list.chroot` files.

- Custom packages can be included in the live image by placing the `.deb` files in a `packages.chroot` directory. Their installation can be preseeded with `preseed/*.cfg` files.

- You can add files to the live filesystem by putting them at their expected location below the `includes.chroot` config directory.

- You can execute scripts during the live system's chroot setup process by installing them as `hooks/live/*.chroot` files. You can also execute scripts at boot time of the generated live image: you must arrange for them to be installed in `/usr/lib/live/config/`*XXXX-name*, for example by relying on the `includes.chroot` config directory.

- The Debian Live Systems Manual[12] is an excellent reference for live-build configuration and testing.

Setting up encrypted and unencrypted persistence on a USB key: it's fairly simple to create a standard Kali Live USB installation. Although the process may seem syntactically complex, it is relatively straight-forward to add both encrypted and unencrypted persistence to your portable installation to significantly extend its functionality.

In the next chapter, we will discuss how Kali scales to the enterprise. We will discuss configuration management and show you how to extend and customize Kali Linux in a way that is easy to deploy whether you have a pair of machines, or several thousand.

---

[12]`http://debian-live.alioth.debian.org/live-manual/unstable/manual/html/live-manual.en.html`

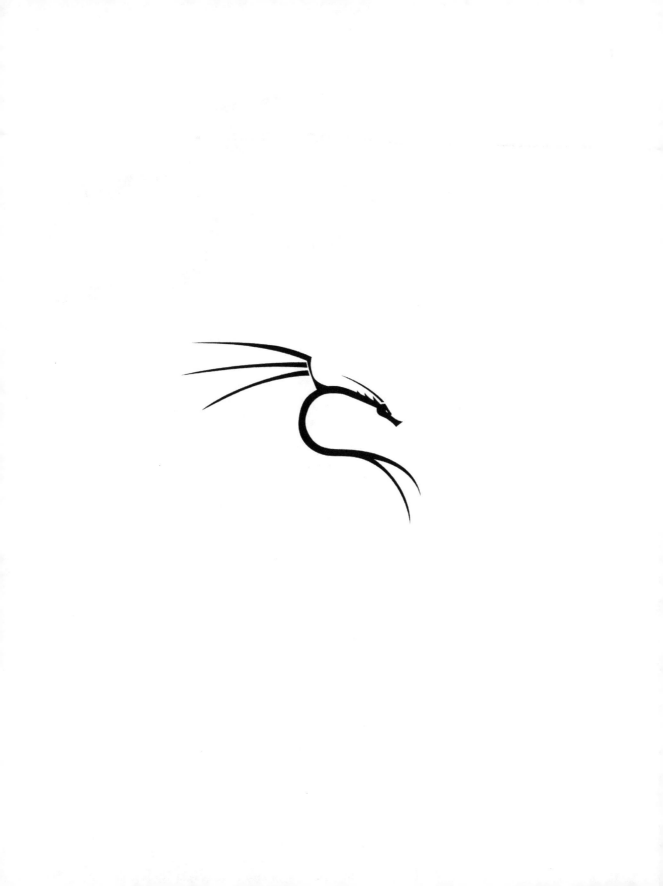

Keywords

PXE installation
Configuration
management
Saltstack
Forking Kali packages
Configuration
packages
Package repository

Chapter

Kali Linux in the Enterprise

10

Contents

So far, we have seen that Kali is an extremely capable and secure Debian derivative providing industrial-strength security and encryption features, advanced package management, multi-platform capability, and (what it is most-known for) an arsenal of world-class tools for the security professional. What might not be obvious is how Kali scales beyond the desktop to medium or large scale deployments and even to the enterprise level. In this chapter, we will show you how well Kali can scale beyond the desktop, providing centralized management and enterprise-level control over multiple Kali Linux installations. In short, after reading this chapter you will be able to quickly deploy highly secure Kali systems preconfigured for your specific needs and keep them synchronized thanks to Kali's (semi-automatic) installation of package updates.

This level of scale requires several steps, including initiating a PXE network boot, use of an advanced configuration management tool (SaltStack), the ability to fork and customize packages, and the deployment of a package repository. We will cover each step in detail, show you how to get the "heavy lifting" out of the way, and deploy, manage, and maintain multitudes of custom Kali Linux installations with relative ease. As if that were not enough, we will throw in a crowd of minions to assist you in running your empire.

10.1. Installing Kali Linux Over the Network (PXE Boot)

As we have seen in previous chapters, the basic Kali Linux installation process is straightforward once you know your way around. But if you have to install Kali on multiple machines, the standard setup can be quite tedious. Thankfully, you can start the Kali installation procedure by booting a computer over the network. This allows you to install Kali quickly and easily on many machines at a time.

First, you will need to boot your target machine from the network. This is facilitated by the Pre-boot eXecution Environment (PXE), a client/server interface designed to boot any networked machine from the network even if it does not have an operating system installed. Setting up PXE network boot requires that you configure at least a trivial file transfer protocol (TFTP) server and a DHCP/BOOTP server. You will also need a web server if you want to host a *debconf* preseeding file that will be automatically used in the installation process.

Fortunately, *dnsmasq* handles both DHCP and TFTP so that you can rely on a single service to set up everything you need. And the Apache web server is installed (but not enabled) by default on Kali systems.

Separate DHCP and TFTP daemons   For more complex setups, *dnsmasq*'s feature set might be too limited or you might want to enable PXE booting on your main network that already runs a DHCP daemon. In both cases, you will then have to configure separate DHCP and TFTP daemons.

The Debian installation manual covers the setup of *isc-dhcp-server* and *tftpd-hpa* for PXE booting.

➡ https://www.debian.org/releases/stable/amd64/ch04s05.html

In order to set up *dnsmasq*, you must first configure it through /etc/dnsmasq.conf. A basic configuration consists of only a few key lines:

```
# Network interface to handle
interface=eth0
# DHCP options
# IP range to allocate
dhcp-range=192.168.101.100,192.168.101.200,12h
# Gateway to announce to clients
dhcp-option=option:router,192.168.101.1
# DNS servers to announce to clients
dhcp-option=option:dns-server,8.8.8.8,8.8.4.4
# Boot file to announce to clients
dhcp-boot=pxelinux.0
# TFTP options
enable-tftp
# Directory hosting files to serve
tftp-root=/tftpboot/
```

With /etc/dnsmasq.conf configured, you will need to place the installation boot files in the /tftpboot/ directory. Kali Linux provides a file archive dedicated to this purpose that can be directly unpacked into /tftpboot/. Simply select between 32-bit (i386) and 64-bit (amd64) and standard or graphical (gtk) install methods for your target machine and choose the appropriate archive:

➡ http://http.kali.org/dists/kali-rolling/main/installer-amd64/current/images/netboot/gtk/netboot.tar.gz

➡ http://http.kali.org/dists/kali-rolling/main/installer-amd64/current/images/netboot/netboot.tar.gz

➡ http://http.kali.org/dists/kali-rolling/main/installer-i386/current/images/netboot/gtk/netboot.tar.gz

➡ http://http.kali.org/dists/kali-rolling/main/installer-i386/current/images/netboot/netboot.tar.gz

Once you have selected the archive, create /tftpboot/, download the archive, and unpack it into that directory:

```
# mkdir /tftpboot
# cd /tftpboot
# wget http://http.kali.org/dists/kali-rolling/main/installer-amd64/current/images/
    ➡ netboot/netboot.tar.gz
# tar xf netboot.tar.gz
# ls -l
total 25896
drwxrwxr-x 3 root root    4096 May  6 04:43 debian-installer
```

```
lrwxrwxrwx 1 root root          47 May  6 04:43 ldlinux.c32 -> debian-installer/amd64/boot
    ➡ -screens/ldlinux.c32
-rw-r--r-- 1 root root 26507247 May  6 04:43 netboot.tar.gz
lrwxrwxrwx 1 root root          33 May  6 04:43 pxelinux.0 -> debian-installer/amd64/
    ➡ pxelinux.0
lrwxrwxrwx 1 root root          35 May  6 04:43 pxelinux.cfg -> debian-installer/amd64/
    ➡ pxelinux.cfg
-rw-rw-r-- 1 root root          71 May  6 04:43 version.info
```

The unpacked files include the *pxelinux* bootloader, which uses the same configuration files as *syslinux* and *isolinux*. Because of this, you can tweak the boot files in debian-installer/amd64/boot-screens/ as you would when generating custom Kali Linux Live ISO images.

For example, assuming that you have picked the textual installer, you can add boot parameters to preseed the language, country, keymap, hostname, and domainname values. You can also point the installer to an external preseed URL and configure the timeout so that the boot happens automatically if no key is pressed within 5 seconds. To accomplish this, you would first modify the debian-installer/amd64/txt.cfg file:

```
label install
        menu label ^Install
        kernel debian-installer/amd64/linux
        append vga=788 initrd=debian-installer/amd64/initrd.gz --- quiet language=en
            ➡ country=US keymap=us hostname=kali domain= url=http://192.168.101.1/
            ➡ preseed.cfg
```

Then, you would modify the debian-installer/amd64/syslinux.cfg file to adjust the timeout:

```
# D-I config version 2.0
# search path for the c32 support libraries (libcom32, libutil etc.)
path debian-installer/amd64/boot-screens/
include debian-installer/amd64/boot-screens/menu.cfg
default debian-installer/amd64/boot-screens/vesamenu.c32
prompt 0
timeout 50
```

Armed with the ability to boot any machine from the network via PXE, you can take advantage of all the features outlined in section 4.3, "Unattended Installations" [page 91], enabling you to do full booting, preseeding, and unattended installation on multiple computers without physical boot media. Also, don't forget the flexibility of the boot parameter preseed/url=http://*server*/preseed.cfg (nor the use of the url alias), which allows you to set a network-based preseed file.

10.2. Leveraging Configuration Management

With the ability to install Kali on multiple computers very quickly, you will need some help in managing those machines post-installation. You can leverage configuration management tools to manage machines or configure replacement computers to any desired state.

Kali Linux contains many popular configuration management tools that you might want to use (*ansible, chef, puppet, saltstack*, etc.) but in this section, we will only cover *SaltStack*.

➡ https://saltstack.com

10.2.1. Setting Up SaltStack

SaltStack is a centralized configuration management service: a *salt master* manages many *salt minions*. You should install the *salt-master* package on a server that is reachable by all the hosts that you want to manage and *salt-minion* on the hosts that you wish to manage. Each minion must be told where to find their master. Simply edit /etc/salt/minion and set the master key to the DNS name (or IP address) of the Salt master. Note that Salt uses YAML as format for its configuration files.

```
minion# vim /etc/salt/minion
minion# grep ^master /etc/salt/minion
master: 192.168.122.105
```

Each minion has a unique identifier stored in /etc/salt/minion_id, which defaults to its hostname. This minion identifier will be used in the configuration rules and as such, it is important to set it properly before the minion opens its connection to the master:

```
minion# echo kali-scratch >/etc/salt/minion_id
minion# systemctl enable salt-minion
minion# systemctl start salt-minion
```

When the *salt-minion* service is running, it will try to connect to the Salt master to exchange some cryptographic keys. On the master side, you have to accept the key that the minion is using to identify itself to let the connection proceed. Subsequent connections will be automatic:

```
master# systemctl enable salt-master
master# systemctl start salt-master
master# salt-key --list all
Accepted Keys:
Denied Keys:
Unaccepted Keys:
kali-scratch
Rejected Keys:
master# salt-key --accept kali-scratch
The following keys are going to be accepted:
```

```
Unaccepted Keys:
kali-scratch
Proceed? [n/Y] y
Key for minion kali-scratch accepted.
```

10.2.2. Executing Commands on Minions

As soon as minions are connected, you can execute commands on them from the master:

```
master# salt '*' test.ping
kali-scratch:
    True
kali-master:
    True
```

This command asks all minions (the '*' is a wildcard targeting all minions) to execute the ping function from the test execution module. This function returns a True value on success and is a simple way to ensure that the connection is working between the master and the various minions.

You can also target a specific minion by giving its identifier in the first parameter, or possibly a subset of minions by using a less-generic wildcard (such as '*-scratch' or 'kali-*'). Here is an example of how to execute an arbitrary shell command on the kali-scratch minion:

```
master# salt kali-scratch cmd.shell 'uptime; uname -a'
kali-scratch:
    05:25:48 up 44 min,  2 users,  load average: 0.00, 0.01, 0.05
    Linux kali-scratch 4.5.0-kali1-amd64 #1 SMP Debian 4.5.3-2kali1 (2016-05-09) x86_64
    ➥   GNU/Linux
```

Salt Module Reference There are many execution modules available for all sorts of use cases. We won't cover them all here, but the full list is available at https://docs.saltstack.com/en/latest/ref/modules/all/index.html. You can also obtain a description of all the execution modules and their available functions on a given minion with the salt *minion* sys.doc command. Running this command returns a very long list of functions, but you can filter the list by passing the name of a function or module prefixed by its parent module as a parameter:

```
master# salt kali-scratch sys.doc disk.usage
disk.usage:

    Return usage information for volumes mounted on this
    ➥   minion
```

One of the most useful modules is pkg, which is a package manager abstraction relying on the appropriate package manager for the system (apt-get for Debian and its derivatives like Kali).

The pkg.refresh_db command updates the package list (that is, it performs apt-get update) while pkg.upgrade installs all the available updates (it performs apt-get upgrade or apt-get dist-upgrade, depending on the options received). The pkg.list_upgrades command lists the pending upgrade operations (that would be performed by the pkg.upgrade dist_upgrade=True command).

The service module is an abstraction of the service manager (systemd in the case of Kali), which lets you perform all the usual systemctl operations: service.enable, service.disable, service.start, service.stop, service.restart, and service.reload:

```
master# salt '*' service.enable ssh
kali-scratch:
    True
kali-master:
    True
master# salt '*' service.start ssh
kali-master:
    True
kali-scratch:
    True
master# salt '*' pkg.refresh_db
kali-scratch:
    ----------
kali-master:
    ----------
master# salt '*' pkg.upgrade dist_upgrade=True
kali-scratch:
    ----------
    changes:
        ----------
        base-files:
            ----------
            new:
                1:2016.2.1
            old:
                1:2016.2.0
[...]
        zaproxy:
            ----------
            new:
                2.5.0-0kali1
            old:
                2.4.3-0kali3
    comment:
    result:
        True
```

As a more concrete sample, you could easily set up a distributed *Nmap* scan with *dnmap*. After having installed the package on all the minions, you start the server in a first terminal:

```
server# salt '*' pkg.install dnmap
[...]
server# vim dnmap.txt
server# dnmap_server -f dnmap.txt
```

Assuming that the server IP is 1.2.3.4, you can next tell all minions to start a client process that connects to the server:

```
server# salt '*' cmd.run_bg template=jinja 'dnmap_client -s 1.2.3.4 -a {{ grains.id }}'
kali-scratch:
    ----------
    pid:
        17137
[...]
```

Note that the example uses cmd.run_bg to run the dnmap_client command in the background. Don't wait until it finishes, since it is a long-running process. Unfortunately, it doesn't kill itself properly when you interrupt the server so you might have to clean it up:

```
server# salt '*' cmd.shell 'pkill -f dnmap_client'
```

10.2.3. Salt States and Other Features

While remote execution is an important building block, it is only a tiny fraction of what SaltStack can do.

When setting up a new machine, you often run many commands and tests to determine the details of the system prior to installation. These operations can be formalized in re-usable configuration templates called *state files.* The operations described in state files can then be performed with a single state.apply salt command.

To save some time, you can rely on many ready-to-use state files that have been created by the community and which are distributed in "Salt formulas":

➡ https://docs.saltstack.com/en/latest/topics/development/conventions/formulas.html

There are many other features that can be combined:

- Scheduled execution of actions
- Defining actions in response to events triggered by minions
- Collecting data out of minions

- Orchestration of a sequence of operations across multiple minions

- Applying states over SSH without installing the salt-minion service

- Provisioning systems on cloud infrastructures and bringing them under management

- And more

SaltStack is quite vast and we can't possibly cover all the features here. In fact, there are books dedicated entirely to SaltStack and the online documentation is very extensive as well. Check it out if you want to learn more about its features:

➡ https://docs.saltstack.com/en/latest/

If you manage a significant number of machines, you would be well advised to learn more about SaltStack as you can save a significant amount of time when deploying new machines and you will be able to maintain a coherent configuration throughout your network.

To give you a taste of what it looks like to work with state files, we will cover a simple example: how to enable the APT repository and install a package that you create in section 10.3.3, "Creating a Package Repository for APT" [page 269] and section 10.3.2, "Creating Configuration Packages" [page 263]. You will also register a SSH key in root's account so that you can login remotely in case of problems.

By default, state files are stored in /srv/salt on the master; they are YAML structured files with a .sls extension. Just like for running commands, applying a state relies on many state modules:

➡ https://docs.saltstack.com/en/latest/topics/tutorials/starting_states.html

➡ https://docs.saltstack.com/en/latest/ref/states/all/

Your /srv/salt/offsec.sls file will call three of those modules:

```
offsec_repository:
  pkgrepo.managed:
    - name: deb http://pkgrepo.offsec.com offsec-internal main
    - file: /etc/apt/sources.list.d/offsec.list
    - key_url: salt://offsec-apt-key.asc
    - require_in:
      - pkg: offsec-defaults

offsec-defaults:
  pkg.installed

ssh_key_for_root:
  ssh_auth.present:
    - user: root
    - name: ssh-rsa AAAAB3NzaC1yc2...89C4N rhertzog@kali
```

The offsec_repository state relies on the pkgrepo state module. The example uses the managed function in that state module to register a package repository. With the key_url attribute, you let salt know that the (ASCII armored) GPG key required to verify the repository's signature can be fetched from /srv/salt/offsec-apt-key.asc on the salt master. The require_in attribute ensures that this state is processed before the offsec-defaults, since the latter needs the repository correctly configured to be able to install the package.

The offsec-defaults state installs the package of the same name. This shows that the name of the key is often an important value for states, although it can always be overridden with a name attribute (as done for the former state). For simple-cases like this one, this is both readable and concise.

The last state (ssh_key_for_root) adds the SSH key given in the name attribute to /root/.ssh/ authorized_keys (the target user is set in the user attribute). Note that we have shortened the key for readability here, but you should put the full key in the name attribute.

This state file can next be applied to a given minion:

```
server# salt kali-scratch state.apply offsec
kali-scratch:
----------
          ID: offsec_repository
    Function: pkgrepo.managed
        Name: deb http://pkgrepo.offsec.com offsec-internal main
      Result: True
     Comment: Configured package repo 'deb http://pkgrepo.offsec.com offsec-internal
       ➥ main'
     Started: 06:00:15.767794
    Duration: 4707.35 ms
     Changes:
              ----------
              repo:
                  deb http://pkgrepo.offsec.com offsec-internal main
----------
          ID: offsec-defaults
    Function: pkg.installed
      Result: True
     Comment: The following packages were installed/updated: offsec-defaults
     Started: 06:00:21.325184
    Duration: 19246.041 ms
     Changes:
              ----------
              offsec-defaults:
                  ----------
                  new:
                      1.0
                  old:
----------
          ID: ssh_key_for_root
    Function: ssh_auth.present
```

```
      Name: ssh-rsa AAAAB3NzaClyc2...89C4N rhertzog@kali
    Result: True
   Comment: The authorized host key AAAAB3NzaClyc2...89C4N for user root was added
   Started: 06:00:40.582539
  Duration: 62.103 ms
   Changes:
            ----------
            AAAAB3NzaClyc2...89C4N:
                New

Summary for kali-scratch
------------
Succeeded: 3 (changed=3)
Failed:    0
------------
Total states run:     3
Total run time:   24.015 s
```

It can also be permanently associated to the minion by recording it in the /srv/salt/top.sls file, which is used by the state.highstate command to apply all relevant states in a single pass:

```
server# cat /srv/salt/top.sls
base:
  kali-scratch:
    - offsec
server# salt kali-scratch state.highstate
kali-scratch:
----------
          ID: offsec_repository
    Function: pkgrepo.managed
        Name: deb http://pkgrepo.offsec.com offsec-internal main
      Result: True
     Comment: Package repo 'deb http://pkgrepo.offsec.com offsec-internal main' already
          ➡   configured
     Started: 06:06:20.650053
    Duration: 62.805 ms
     Changes:
----------
          ID: offsec-defaults
    Function: pkg.installed
      Result: True
     Comment: Package offsec-defaults is already installed
     Started: 06:06:21.436193
    Duration: 385.092 ms
     Changes:
----------
          ID: ssh_key_for_root
```

```
   Function: ssh_auth.present
       Name: ssh-rsa AAAAB3NzaC1yc2...89C4N rhertzog@kali
     Result: True
    Comment: The authorized host key AAAAB3NzaC1yc2...89C4N is already present for
        ➡ user root
    Started: 06:06:21.821811
   Duration: 1.936 ms
    Changes:

Summary for kali-scratch
------------
Succeeded: 3
Failed:    0
------------
Total states run:     3
Total run time: 449.833 ms
```

10.3. Extending and Customizing Kali Linux

Sometimes you need to modify Kali Linux to make it fit your local needs. The best way to achieve this is to maintain your own package repository hosting the modified versions of the Kali packages that you had to fork, as well as supplementary packages providing custom configuration and extra software (not provided by Kali Linux).

10.3.1. Forking Kali Packages

Please refer to section 9.1, "Modifying Kali Packages" [page 222] for explanations about this topic.

All packages can be forked if you have a good reason but you must be aware that forking a package has a cost, since you have to update it every time that Kali publishes an update. Here are some reasons why you might want to fork a package:

- To add a patch to fix a bug or add a new feature. Although in most cases, you will want to submit that patch to the upstream developers so that the bug is fixed or the feature is added at the source.

- To compile it with different options (assuming that there are good reasons why Kali did not compile it with those options; otherwise it might be best to discuss this with Kali developers to see if they can enable the desired options).

By contrast, here are some bad reasons to fork a package along with suggestions of how to handle your problem:

- To modify a configuration file. You have multiple, better options like using configuration management to automatically install a modified configuration file or installing a configuration package that will put a file in a configuration directory (when available) or that will divert the original configuration file.

- To update to a newer upstream version. Again, it is better to work with developers to update the package directly in Debian or Kali. With the rolling release model, updates are rather quick to reach end users.

Among all the available packages, there are some that are building blocks of Kali Linux and that could be interesting to fork in some situations:

- *kali-meta*: this source package builds all the kali-linux-* meta packages and notably *kali-linux-full*, which defines what packages are installed in the default Kali Linux ISO image.

- *desktop-base*: This source package contains various miscellaneous files that are used by default in desktop installations. Consider forking this package if you would like to show your organization's brand in the default background or change the theme of the desktop.

- *kali-menu*: this package defines the structure of the Kali menu and provides `.desktop` files for all applications that should be listed in the Kali menu.

10.3.2. Creating Configuration Packages

Now that we have touched on PXE booting and discussed configuration management with SaltStack as well as package forking, it is time to wrap these processes up into a practical example and extend the scenario by creating a custom configuration package to deploy a custom configuration to multiple machines semi-automatically.

In this example, you will create a custom package that sets up and utilizes your own package repository and GnuPG signing key, distributes a SaltStack configuration, pushes a custom background, and provides default desktop settings in a unified way to all your Kali installations.

This may seem like a daunting task (especially if you glance through the Debian New Maintainer Guide[1]) but fortunately for us, a configuration package is mainly a sophisticated file archive and turning it into a package is rather easy.

Looking into a Sample Package	If you want to look into a real package that is basically a configuration package, consider the *kali-defaults* package. It is not as simple as the sample in this section but it has all the relevant characteristics and even uses some advanced techniques (like `dpkg-divert`) to replace files already provided by other packages.

---

[1] `https://www.debian.org/doc/manuals/maint-guide/`

The *offsec-defaults* package will contain a few files:

- /etc/apt/sources.list.d/offsec.list: a sources.list entry for APT, enabling the company's internal package repository

- /etc/apt/trusted.gpg.d/offsec.gpg: the GnuPG key used to sign the company's internal package repository

- /etc/salt/minion.d/offsec.conf: a SaltStack configuration file to indicate where to find the Salt master

- /usr/share/images/offsec/background.png: a nice background image with the Offensive Security logo

- /usr/share/glib-2.0/schemas/90_offsec-defaults.gschema.override: a file providing alternate default settings for the GNOME desktop

First, create an offsec-defaults-1.0 directory and put all the files in that directory. Then run dh_make --native (from the *dh-make* package) to add Debian packaging instructions, which will be stored in a debian sub-directory:

```
$ mkdir offsec-defaults-1.0; cd offsec-defaults-1.0
$ dh_make --native
Type of package: (single, indep, library, python)
[s/i/l/p]? i
Email-Address          : buxy@kali.org
License                : gpl3
Package Name           : offsec-defaults
Maintainer Name        : Raphaël Hertzog
Version                : 1.0
Package Type           : indep
Date                   : Thu, 16 Jun 2016 18:04:21 +0200
Are the details correct? [Y/n/q] y
Currently there is not top level Makefile. This may require additional tuning
Done. Please edit the files in the debian/ subdirectory now.
```

First, you are prompted for a package type. In the example, we selected *indep*, which indicates that this source package will generate a single binary package that can be shared across all architectures (Architecture: all). *single* acts as a counterpart, and produces a single binary package that is dependent on the target architecture (Architecture: any). In this case, *indep* is more relevant, since the package only contains text files and no binary programs, so that it can be used similarly on computers of all architectures. The *library* type is useful for shared libraries, since they need to follow strict packaging rules. In a similar fashion, *python* should be restricted to Python modules.

The dh_make command created a debian subdirectory containing many files. Some are required, in particular rules, control, changelog, and copyright. Files with the .ex extension are example files that can be used by modifying them and removing the extension. When they are not needed, we recommend removing them. The compat file should be kept, since it is required for the correct functioning of the *debhelper* suite of programs (all beginning with the dh_ prefix) used at various stages of the package build process.

The copyright file must contain information about the authors of the documents included in the package, and the related license. If the default license selected by dh_make does not suit you, then you must edit this file. Here is the modified version of the copyright file:

```
Format: https://www.debian.org/doc/packaging-manuals/copyright-format/1.0/
Upstream-Name: offsec-defaults

Files: *
Copyright: 2016 Offensive Security
License: GPL-3.0+

License: GPL-3.0+
 This program is free software: you can redistribute it and/or modify
 it under the terms of the GNU General Public License as published by
 the Free Software Foundation, either version 3 of the License, or
 (at your option) any later version.
 .
 This package is distributed in the hope that it will be useful,
 but WITHOUT ANY WARRANTY; without even the implied warranty of
 MERCHANTABILITY or FITNESS FOR A PARTICULAR PURPOSE.  See the
 GNU General Public License for more details.
 .
 You should have received a copy of the GNU General Public License
 along with this program. If not, see <https://www.gnu.org/licenses/>.
 .
 On Debian systems, the complete text of the GNU General
 Public License version 3 can be found in "/usr/share/common-licenses/GPL-3".
```

The default `changelog` file is generally appropriate; replacing the "Initial release" with a more verbose explanation should be enough:

```
offsec-defaults (1.0) unstable; urgency=medium

  * Add salt minion's configuration file.
  * Add an APT's sources.list entry and an APT's trusted GPG key.
  * Override the gsettings schema defining the background picture.

 -- Raphaël Hertzog <buxy@kali.org>  Thu, 16 Jun 2016 18:04:21 +0200
```

In the example, we will make changes to the `control` file. We will change the Section field to *misc* and remove the Homepage, Vcs-Git, and Vcs-Browser fields. Lastly, we will fill in the Description field:

```
Source: offsec-defaults
Section: misc
Priority: optional
Maintainer: Raphaël Hertzog <buxy@kali.org>
Build-Depends: debhelper (>= 9)
Standards-Version: 3.9.8

Package: offsec-defaults
Architecture: all
Depends: ${misc:Depends}
Description: Default settings for Offensive Security
 This package contains multiple files to configure computers
 owned by Offensive Security.
 .
 It notably modifies:
  - APT's configuration
  - salt-minion's configuration
  - the default desktop settings
```

The `rules` file usually contains a set of rules used to configure, build, and install the software in a dedicated subdirectory (named after the generated binary package). The contents of this subdirectory are then archived within the Debian package as if it were the root of the filesystem. In this case, files will be installed in the `debian/offsec-defaults/` subdirectory. For example, to end up with a package installing `/etc/apt/sources.list.d/offsec.list`, install the file in `debian/offsec-defaults/etc/apt/sources.list.d/offsec.list`. The rules file is used as a `Makefile`, with a few standard targets (including clean and binary, used respectively to clean the source directory and generate the binary package).

What is a Makefile file? You may have noticed the message concerning the missing `Makefile` at the end of the `dh_make` output and the mention of its similarity to the `rules` file. A `Makefile` is a script file used by the make program; it describes rules for how to build a set of files from each other in a tree of dependencies. For instance, a program can be built from a set of source files. The `Makefile` file describes these rules in the following format:

```
target: source1 source2 ...
        command1
        command2
```

The interpretation of such a rule is as follows: if one of the `source*` files is more recent than the `target` file, then the target needs to be generated, using `command1` and `command2`.

Note that the command lines must start with a tab character; also note that when a command line starts with a dash character (-), failure of the command does not interrupt the whole process.

Although this file is the heart of the process, it contains only the bare minimum for running a standard set of commands provided by the `debhelper` tool. Such is the case for files generated by `dh_make`. To install most of your files, we recommend configuring the behavior of the `dh_install` command by creating the following `debian/offsec-defaults.install` file:

```
apt/offsec.list etc/apt/sources.list.d/
apt/offsec.gpg etc/apt/trusted.gpg.d/
salt/offsec.conf etc/salt/minion.d/
images/background.png usr/share/images/offsec/
```

You could also use this to install the gsettings override file but debhelper provides a dedicated tool for this (`dh_installgsettings`) so you can rely on it. First, put your settings in `debian/offsec-defaults.gsettings-override`:

```
[org.gnome.desktop.background]
picture-options='zoom'
picture-uri='file:///usr/share/images/offsec/background.png'
```

Next, override the `dh_installgsettings` call in `debian/rules` to increase the priority to the level expected for an organization override (which is 90 according to the manual page):

```
#!/usr/bin/make -f

%:
        dh $@

override_dh_installgsettings:
        dh_installgsettings --priority=90
```

At this point, the source package is ready. All that is left to do is to generate the binary package with the same method used previously for rebuilding packages: run the dpkg-buildpackage -us -uc command from within the offsec-defaults-1.0 directory:

```
$ dpkg-buildpackage -us -uc
dpkg-buildpackage: info: source package offsec-defaults
dpkg-buildpackage: info: source version 1.0
dpkg-buildpackage: info: source distribution unstable
dpkg-buildpackage: info: source changed by Raphaël Hertzog <buxy@kali.org>
dpkg-buildpackage: info: host architecture amd64
 dpkg-source --before-build offsec-defaults-1.0
 fakeroot debian/rules clean
dh clean
   dh_testdir
   dh_auto_clean
   dh_clean
 dpkg-source -b offsec-defaults-1.0
dpkg-source: info: using source format '3.0 (native)'
dpkg-source: info: building offsec-defaults in offsec-defaults_1.0.tar.xz
dpkg-source: info: building offsec-defaults in offsec-defaults_1.0.dsc
 debian/rules build
dh build
   dh_testdir
   dh_update_autotools_config
   dh_auto_configure
   dh_auto_build
   dh_auto_test
 fakeroot debian/rules binary
dh binary
   dh_testroot
   dh_prep
   dh_auto_install
   dh_install
   dh_installdocs
   dh_installchangelogs
   debian/rules override_dh_installgsettings
make[1]: Entering directory '/home/rhertzog/kali/kali-book/samples/offsec-defaults-1.0'
dh_installgsettings --priority=90
make[1]: Leaving directory '/home/rhertzog/kali/kali-book/samples/offsec-defaults-1.0'
   dh_perl
   dh_link
   dh_strip_nondeterminism
   dh_compress
   dh_fixperms
   dh_installdeb
   dh_gencontrol
   dh_md5sums
```

```
  dh_builddeb
dpkg-deb: building package 'offsec-defaults' in '../offsec-defaults_1.0_all.deb'.
 dpkg-genchanges  >../offsec-defaults_1.0_amd64.changes
dpkg-genchanges: info: including full source code in upload
 dpkg-source --after-build offsec-defaults-1.0
dpkg-buildpackage: info: full upload; Debian-native package (full source is included)
```

10.3.3. Creating a Package Repository for APT

Now that you have a custom package, you can distribute it through an APT package repository.
Use reprepro to create the desired repository and to fill it. This tool is rather powerful and its
manual page is certainly worth reading.

A package repository is typically hosted on a server. To properly separate it from other services
running on the server, it is best to create a user dedicated to this service. In the dedicated user
account, you will be able to host the repository files and also the GnuPG key that will be used to
sign the package repository:

```
# apt install reprepro gnupg
[...]
# adduser --system --group pkgrepo
Adding system user 'pkgrepo' (UID 136) ...
Adding new group 'pkgrepo' (GID 142) ...
Adding new user 'pkgrepo' (UID 136) with group 'pkgrepo' ...
Creating home directory '/home/pkgrepo' ...
# chown pkgrepo $(tty)
# su - -s /bin/bash pkgrepo
$ gpg --gen-key
gpg (GnuPG) 2.1.11; Copyright (C) 2016 Free Software Foundation, Inc.
This is free software: you are free to change and redistribute it.
There is NO WARRANTY, to the extent permitted by law.

gpg: directory '/home/pkgrepo/.gnupg' created
gpg: new configuration file '/home/pkgrepo/.gnupg/dirmngr.conf' created
gpg: new configuration file '/home/pkgrepo/.gnupg/gpg.conf' created
gpg: keybox '/home/pkgrepo/.gnupg/pubring.kbx' created
Note: Use "gpg --full-gen-key" for a full featured key generation dialog.

GnuPG needs to construct a user ID to identify your key.

Real name: Offensive Security Repository Signing Key
Email address: repoadmin@offsec.com
You selected this USER-ID:
    "Offensive Security Repository Signing Key <repoadmin@offsec.com>"
```

```
Change (N)ame, (E)mail, or (O)kay/(Q)uit? o
We need to generate a lot of random bytes. It is a good idea to perform
some other action (type on the keyboard, move the mouse, utilize the
disks) during the prime generation; this gives the random number
generator a better chance to gain enough entropy.
[...]
gpg: /home/pkgrepo/.gnupg/trustdb.gpg: trustdb created
gpg: key B4EF2D0D marked as ultimately trusted
gpg: directory '/home/pkgrepo/.gnupg/openpgp-revocs.d' created
gpg: revocation certificate stored as '/home/pkgrepo/.gnupg/openpgp-revocs.d/
   ➡ F8FE22F74F1B714E38DA6181B27F74F7B4EF2D0D.rev'
public and secret key created and signed.

gpg: checking the trustdb
gpg: marginals needed: 3  completes needed: 1  trust model: PGP
gpg: depth: 0  valid:   1  signed:   0  trust: 0-, 0q, 0n, 0m, 0f, 1u
pub   rsa2048/B4EF2D0D 2016-06-17 [S]
      Key fingerprint = F8FE 22F7 4F1B 714E 38DA  6181 B27F 74F7 B4EF 2D0D
uid          [ultimate] Offensive Security Repository Signing Key <repoadmin@offsec.com>
sub   rsa2048/38035F38 2016-06-17 []
```

Note that when you are prompted for a passphrase, you should enter an empty value (and confirm that you don't want to protect your private key) as you want to be able to sign the repository non-interactively. Note also that gpg requires write access to the terminal to be able to securely prompt for a passphrase: that is why you changed the ownership of the virtual terminal (which is owned by root since you initially connected as that user) before starting a shell as pkgrepo.

Now you can start setting up the repository. A dedicated directory is necessary for reprepro and inside that directory you have to create a conf/distributions file documenting which distributions are available in the package repository:

```
$ mkdir -p reprepro/conf
$ cd reprepro
$ cat >conf/distributions <<END
Codename: offsec-internal
AlsoAcceptFor: unstable
Origin: Offensive Security
Description: Offsec's Internal packages
Architectures: source amd64 i386
Components: main
SignWith: F8FE22F74F1B714E38DA6181B27F74F7B4EF2D0D
END
```

The required fields are Codename, which gives the name of the distribution, Architectures, which indicates which architectures will be available in the distribution (and accepted on the input side), and Components, which indicates the various components available in the distribution (components are a sort of sub-section of the distribution, which can be enabled separately in APT's sources.list). The Origin and Description fields are purely informative and they are copied as-is in the Release file. The SignWith field asks reprepro to sign the repository with the GnuPG key whose identifier is listed (put the full fingerprint here to ensure you use the correct key, and not another one colliding on the short identifier). The AlsoAcceptFor setting is not required but makes it possible to process .changes files whose Distribution field has a value listed here (without this, it would only accept the distribution's codename in that field).

With this basic setup in place, you can let reprepro generate an empty repository:

```
$ reprepro export
Exporting indices...
$ find .
.
./db
./db/version
./db/references.db
./db/contents.cache.db
./db/checksums.db
./db/packages.db
./db/release.caches.db
./conf
./conf/distributions
./dists
./dists/offsec-internal
./dists/offsec-internal/Release.gpg
./dists/offsec-internal/Release
./dists/offsec-internal/main
./dists/offsec-internal/main/source
./dists/offsec-internal/main/source/Release
./dists/offsec-internal/main/source/Sources.gz
./dists/offsec-internal/main/binary-amd64
./dists/offsec-internal/main/binary-amd64/Packages
./dists/offsec-internal/main/binary-amd64/Release
./dists/offsec-internal/main/binary-amd64/Packages.gz
./dists/offsec-internal/main/binary-i386
./dists/offsec-internal/main/binary-i386/Packages
./dists/offsec-internal/main/binary-i386/Release
./dists/offsec-internal/main/binary-i386/Packages.gz
./dists/offsec-internal/InRelease
```

As you can see, reprepro created the repository meta-information in a dists sub-directory. It also initialized an internal database in a db sub-directory.

It is now time to add your first package. First, copy the files generated by the build of the offsec-defaults package (offsec-defaults_1.0.dsc, offsec-defaults_1.0.tar.xz, `offsec-defaults_1.0_all.deb`, and `offsec-defaults_1.0_amd64.changes`) into `/tmp` on the server hosting the package repository and ask `reprepro` to include the package:

```
$ reprepro include offsec-internal /tmp/offsec-defaults_1.0_amd64.changes
Exporting indices...
$ find pool
pool
pool/main
pool/main/o
pool/main/o/offsec-defaults
pool/main/o/offsec-defaults/offsec-defaults_1.0.dsc
pool/main/o/offsec-defaults/offsec-defaults_1.0.tar.xz
pool/main/o/offsec-defaults/offsec-defaults_1.0_all.deb
```

As you can see, it added the files into its own package pool in a `pool` sub-directory.

The `dists` and `pool` directories are the two directories that you need to make (publicly) available over HTTP to finish the setup of your APT repository. They contain all the files that APT will want to download.

Assuming that you want to host this on a virtual host named pkgrepo.offsec.com, you could create the following Apache configuration file, save it to `/etc/apache2/sites-available/pkgrepo.offsec.com.conf`, and enable it with `a2ensite pkgrepo.offsec.com`):

```
<VirtualHost *:80>
    ServerName pkgrepo.offsec.com
    ServerAdmin repoadmin@offsec.com

    ErrorLog /var/log/apache2/pkgrepo.offsec.com-error.log
    CustomLog /var/log/apache2/pkgrepo.offsec.com-access.log "%h %l %u %t \"%r\" %>s %O"

    DocumentRoot /home/pkgrepo/reprepro

    <Directory "/home/pkgrepo/reprepro">
        Options Indexes FollowSymLinks MultiViews
        Require all granted
        AllowOverride All
    </Directory>
</VirtualHost>
```

And the corresponding `sources.list` entry to add on machines that need packages from this repository would look like this:

```
deb http://pkgrepo.offsec.com offsec-internal main

# Enable next line if you want access to source packages too
# deb-src http://pkgrepo.offsec.com offsec-internal main
```

Your package is now published and should be available to your networked hosts.

Although this has been a lengthy setup, the "heavy lifting" is now completed. You can boot your networked machines via PXE, install a customized version of Kali Linux without interaction thanks to a network-delivered preseed, configure SaltStack to manage your configurations (and control minions!), create forked custom packages, and distribute those packages through your own package repository. This provides centralized management and enterprise-level control over multiple Kali Linux installations. In short, you can now quickly deploy highly secure Kali systems preconfigured for your specific needs and keep them synchronized thanks to Kali's (semi-automatic) installation of all package updates.

10.4. Summary

Kali Linux scales beyond the desktop to medium or large scale deployments and even to the enterprise level. In this chapter, we covered how to centralize management of multiple Kali installations with SaltStack, allowing you to quickly deploy highly secure Kali systems preconfigured for your specific needs. We also revealed how you can keep them synchronized thanks to Kali's (semi-automatic) installation of package updates.

We discussed package forking, which allows you to create your own customized distributable source packages.

In summary, let's review the major steps required to establish Salt masters and minions, which allow you remote control and configuration of remote hosts.

Summary Tips:

- Boot machine from the network with PXE, with at least a TFTP file server, a DHCP/BOOTP server (and a web server for debconf preseeding). *dnsmasq* handles both DHCP and TFTP, and the *apache2* web server comes pre-installed (but disabled) on Kali.

- The Debian installation manual covers the setup of *isc-dhcp-server* and *tftpd-hpa* for PXE booting:

  ➡ https://www.debian.org/releases/stable/amd64/ch04s05.html

- *dnsmasq* is configured through /etc/dnsmasq.conf. A basic configuration consists of only a few key lines:

```
# Network interface to handle
interface=eth0
# DHCP options
# IP range to allocate
dhcp-range=192.168.101.100,192.168.101.200,12h
# Gateway to announce to clients
dhcp-option=option:router,192.168.101.1
# DNS servers to announce to clients
dhcp-option=option:dns-server,8.8.8.8,8.8.4.4
# Boot file to announce to clients
```

```
dhcp-boot=pxelinux.0
# TFTP options
enable-tftp
# Directory hosting files to serve
tftp-root=/tftpboot/
```

- Unpack 32-bit (i386), 64-bit (amd64), standard or graphical (gtk) installation boot files from the Kali archive into /tftpboot/. The archives can be found here:

  ➡   http://http.kali.org/dists/kali-rolling/main/installer-amd64/current/images/netboot/gtk/netboot.tar.gz

  ➡   http://http.kali.org/dists/kali-rolling/main/installer-amd64/current/images/netboot/netboot.tar.gz

  ➡   http://http.kali.org/dists/kali-rolling/main/installer-i386/current/images/netboot/gtk/netboot.tar.gz

  ➡   http://http.kali.org/dists/kali-rolling/main/installer-i386/current/images/netboot/netboot.tar.gz

```
# mkdir /tftpboot
# cd /tftpboot
# wget http://http.kali.org/dists/kali-rolling/main/installer-amd64/current/
   ➡ images/netboot/netboot.tar.gz
# tar xf netboot.tar.gz
```

- Optionally modify txt.cfg to preseed parameters or custom timeouts. See section 4.3, "Unattended Installations" [page 91]. Next, you can leverage configuration management tools to manage machines or configure remote computers to any desired state.

- SaltStack is a centralized configuration management service: a Salt master manages many Salt minions. Install the *salt-master* package on a reachable server and *salt-minion* on managed hosts.

- Edit the /etc/salt/minion YAML-formatted config file and set the master key to the DNS name (or IP address) of the Salt master.

- Set minion's unique identifier in /etc/salt/minion_id:

```
minion# echo kali-scratch >/etc/salt/minion_id
minion# systemctl enable salt-minion
minion# systemctl start salt-minion
```

- Key exchange will follow. On the master, accept minion's identification key. Subsequent connections will be automatic:

```
master# systemctl enable salt-master
master# systemctl start salt-master
master# salt-key --list all
```

```
Accepted Keys:
Denied Keys:
Unaccepted Keys:
kali-scratch
Rejected Keys:
master# salt-key --accept kali-scratch
The following keys are going to be accepted:
Unaccepted Keys:
kali-scratch
Proceed? [n/Y] y
Key for minion kali-scratch accepted.
```

- Once minions are connected, you can execute commands on them from the master. Examples:

```
master# salt '*' test.ping
kali-scratch:
True
kali-master:
True
master# salt kali-scratch cmd.shell 'uptime; uname -a'
master# salt kali-scratch sys.doc'
master# salt '*' service.enable ssh
[...]
master# salt '*' service.start ssh
[...]
master# salt '*' pkg.refresh_db
[...]
master# salt '*' pkg.upgrade dist_upgrade=True
server# salt '*' cmd.shell 'pkill -f dnmap_client'
```

- The full list of execution modules can be found at https://docs.saltstack.com/en/latest/ref/modules/all/index.html.

- Use Salt state files (re-usable configuration templates) to schedule actions, collect data, orchestrate sequences of operations on multiple minions, provision cloud systems and bring them under management, and more. Save time with pre-defined Salt formulas:

➡   https://docs.saltstack.com/en/latest/topics/development/conventions/formulas.html

- When it comes time to fork a package, first decide if it is a task that you need to tackle. There are significant advantages and disadvantages. Review them carefully. The *kali-meta*, *desktop-base*, and *kali-menu* packages are interesting, probable choices. The process of forking a package can be daunting and is difficult to summarize.

Now that we have covered all the bases in terms of installation, configuration, customization, and deployment of Kali Linux, let's turn towards the role of Kali Linux in the field of Information Security.

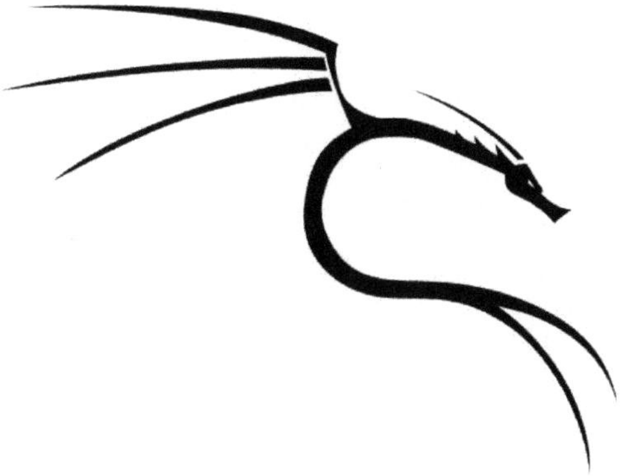

Keywords

Types of assessments
Vulnerability
assessment
Compliance
penetration test
Traditional
penetration test
Application
assessment
Types of attacks
Denial of service
Memory corruption
Web vulnerabilities
Password attacks
Client-side attacks

KALI LINUX
REVEALED

Chapter

11

Introduction to Security Assessments

Contents

We have covered many Kali Linux-specific features up to this point so you should have a strong understanding of what makes Kali special and how to accomplish a number of complex tasks.

Before putting Kali to use however, there are a few concepts relating to security assessments that you should understand. In this chapter, we will introduce these concepts to get you started and provide references that will help if you need to use Kali to perform a security assessment.

To start with, it is worth taking some time to explore exactly what "security" means when dealing with information systems. When attempting to secure an information system, you focus on three primary attributes of the system:

- *Confidentiality*: can actors who should not have access to the system or information access the system or information?

- *Integrity*: can the data or the system be modified in some way that is not intended?

- *Availability*: are the data or the system accessible when and how it is intended to be?

Together, these concepts make up the CIA (Confidentiality, Integrity, Availability) triad and in large part, are the primary items that you will focus on when securing a system as part of standard deployment, maintenance, or assessment.

It is also important to note that in some cases, you may be far more concerned with one aspect of the CIA triad than others. For instance, if you have a personal journal that contains your most secret thoughts, the confidentiality of the journal may be far more important to you than the integrity or the availability. In other words, you may not be as concerned about whether someone can write to the journal (as opposed to reading it) or whether or not the journal is always accessible. On the other hand, if you are securing a system that tracks medical prescriptions, the integrity of the data will be most critical. While it is important to prevent other people from reading what medications someone uses and it is important that you can access this list of medications, if someone were able to change the contents of the system (altering the integrity), it could lead to life-threatening results.

When you are securing a system and an issue is discovered, you will have to consider which of these three concepts, or which combination of them, the issue falls into. This helps you understand the problem in a more comprehensive manner and allows you to categorize the issues and respond accordingly. It is possible to identify vulnerabilities that impact a single, or multiple items from the CIA triad. To use a web application with a SQL injection vulnerability as an example:

- *Confidentiality*: a SQL injection vulnerability that allows an attacker to extract the full contents of the web application, allowing them to have full access to read all the data, but no ability to change the information or disable access to the database.

- *Integrity*: a SQL injection vulnerability that allows an attacker to change the existing information in the database. The attacker can't read the data or prevent others from accessing the database.

- *Availability*: a SQL injection vulnerability that initiates a long-running query, consuming a large amount of resources on the server. This query, when initiated multiple times, leads to a denial of service (DoS) situation. The attacker has no ability to access or change data but can prevent legitimate users from accessing the web application.

- *Multiple*: a SQL injection vulnerability leads to full interactive shell access to the host operating system running the web application. With this access, the attacker can breach the confidentiality of the system by accessing data as they please, compromise the integrity of the system by altering data, and if they so choose, destroy the web application, leading to a compromise of the availability of the system.

The concepts behind the CIA triad are not overly complicated, and realistically are items that you are working with intuitively, even if you don't recognize it. However, it is important to mindfully interact with the concept as it can help you recognize where to direct your efforts. This conceptual foundation will assist you with the identification of the critical components of your systems and the amount of effort and resources worth investing in correcting identified problems.

Another concept that we will address in detail is *risk*, and how it is made up of *threats* and *vulnerabilities*. These concepts are not too complex, but they are easy to get wrong. We will cover these concepts in detail later on, but at a high level, it is best to think of *risk* as what you are trying to prevent from happening, *threat* as who would do it to you, and *vulnerability* as what allows them to do it. Controls can be put in place to address the threat or vulnerability, with the goal of mitigating the risk.

For example, when visiting some parts of the world, you may be at substantial *risk* of catching malaria. This is because the *threat* of mosquitoes is very high in some areas, and you are almost certainly not immune to malaria. Fortunately, you can control the *vulnerability* with medication and attempt to control the *threat* with the use of bug repellent and mosquito nets. With controls in place addressing both the *threat* and the *vulnerability*, you can help ensure the *risk* does not actualize.

11.1. Kali Linux in an Assessment

When preparing to use Kali Linux in the field, you must first ensure you have a clean, working installation. A common mistake that many novice security professionals make is using a single installation across multiple assessments. This is a problem for two primary reasons:

- Over the course of an assessment, you will often manually install, tweak, or otherwise change your system. These one-off changes may get you up and running quickly or solve a particular problem, but they are difficult to keep track of; they make your system more difficult to maintain; and they complicate future configurations.

- Each security assessment is unique. Leaving behind notes, code, and other changes can lead to confusion, or worse — cross-contamination of client data.

That is why starting with a clean Kali installation is highly recommended and why having a pre-customized version of Kali Linux that is ready for automated installation quickly pays off. Be sure to refer back to section 9.3, "Building Custom Kali Live ISO Images" [page 236] and section 4.3, "Unattended Installations" [page 91] on how to do this, since the more you automate today, the less time you waste tomorrow.

Everyone has different requirements when it comes to how they like Kali Linux configured when they are in the field, but there are some universal recommendations that you really want to follow. First, consider using an encrypted installation as documented in section 4.2.2, "Installation on a Fully Encrypted File System" [page 85]. This will protect your data on the physical machine, which is a life-saver if your laptop is ever stolen.

For extra safety during travel, you might want to nuke the decryption key (see "Adding a Nuke Password for Extra Safety" [page 245]) after having sent an (encrypted) copy of the key to a co-worker in the office. That way, your data are secure until you get back to the office where you can restore the laptop with the decryption key.

Another item that you should double-check is the list of packages that you have installed. Consider what tools you might need for the work you are setting out to accomplish. For example, if you are embarking on a wireless security assessment, you may consider installing the *kali-linux-wireless* metapackage, which contains all of the wireless assessment tools available in Kali Linux, or if a web application assessment is coming up, you can install all of the available web application testing tools with the *kali-linux-web* metapackage. It is best to assume that you will not have easy access to the Internet while conducting a security assessment, so be sure to prepare as much as possible in advance.

For the same reason, you might want to review your network settings (see section 5.1, "Configuring the Network" [page 104] and section 7.3, "Securing Network Services" [page 153]). Double-check your DHCP settings and review the services that are listening on your assigned IP address. These settings might make a critical impact to your success. You can't assess what you can't see and excessive listening services might flag your system and get you shut down before you get started.

If your role involves investigating network intrusions, paying close attention to your network settings is even more important and you need to avoid altering the impacted systems. A customized version of Kali with the *kali-linux-forensic* metapackage booted up in forensics mode will not automatically mount disks or use a swap partition. In this way, you can help maintain the integrity of the system under analysis while making use of the many forensics tools available in Kali Linux.

It is critical that you properly prepare your Kali Linux installation for the job. You will find that a clean, efficient, and effective Kali environment will always make everything that follows much smoother.

11.2. Types of Assessments

Now that you have ensured that your Kali environment is ready, the next step is defining exactly what sort of assessment you are conducting. At the highest level, we may describe four types of assessments: a *vulnerability assessment*, a *compliance test*, a *traditional penetration test*, and an *application assessment*. An engagement may involve various elements of each type of assessment but it is worth describing them in some detail and explaining their relevance to your Kali Linux build and environment.

Before delving into the different types of assessments, it is important to first note the difference between a vulnerability and an exploit.

A *vulnerability* is defined as a flaw that, when taken advantage of, will compromise the confidentiality, integrity, or availability of an information system. There are many different types of vulnerabilities that can be encountered, including:

- File Inclusion: File inclusion vulnerabilities[1] in web applications allow you to *include* the contents of a local or remote file into the computation of a program. For example, a web application may have a "Message of the day" function that reads the contents of a file and includes it in the web page to display it to the user. When this type of feature is programmed incorrectly, it can allow an attacker to modify their web request to force the site to include the contents of a file of their choosing.

- SQL Injection: A SQL injection[2] attack is one where the input validation routines for the program are bypassed, allowing an attacker to provide SQL commands for the targeted program to execute. This is a form of command execution that can lead to potential security issues.

- Buffer Overflow: A buffer overflow[3] is a vulnerability that bypasses input validation routines to write data into a buffer's adjacent memory. In some cases, that adjacent memory location may be critical to the operation of the targeted program and control of code execution can be obtained through careful manipulation of the overwritten memory data.

- Race Conditions: A race condition[4] is a vulnerability that takes advantage of timing dependencies in a program. In some cases, the workflow of a program depends on a specific sequence of events to occur. If you can alter this sequence of events, that may lead to a vulnerability.

An *exploit*, on the other hand, is software that, when used, takes advantage of a specific vulnerability, although not all vulnerabilities are exploitable. Since an exploit must change a running process, forcing it to make an unintended action, exploit creation can be complex. Furthermore, there are a number of anti-exploit technologies in modern computing platforms that have been

---

[1]https://en.wikipedia.org/wiki/File_inclusion_vulnerability
[2]https://en.wikipedia.org/wiki/SQL_injection
[3]https://en.wikipedia.org/wiki/Buffer_overflow
[4]https://en.wikipedia.org/wiki/Race_condition

designed to make it harder to exploit vulnerabilities, such as Data Execution Prevention[5] (DEP) and Address Space Layout Randomization[6] (ASLR). However, just because there is no publicly-known exploit for a specific vulnerability, that does not mean that one does not exist (or that one can not be created). For example, many organizations sell commercialized exploits that are never made public, so all vulnerabilities must be treated as potentially exploitable.

11.2.1. Vulnerability Assessment

A *vulnerability* is considered a weakness that could be used in some manner to compromise the confidentiality, integrity, or availability of an information system. In a vulnerability assessment, your objective is to create a simple inventory of discovered vulnerabilities within the *target environment*. This concept of a target environment is extremely important. You must be sure to stay within the scope of your client's target network and required objectives. Creeping outside the scope of an assessment can cause an interruption of service, a breach of trust with your client, or legal action against you and your employer.

Due to its relative simplicity, a vulnerability test is often completed in more mature environments on a regular basis as part of demonstrating their due diligence. In most cases, an automated tool, such as the ones in the Vulnerability Analysis[7] and Web Applications[8] categories of the Kali Tools site and Kali desktop Applications menu, is used to discover live systems in a target environment, identify listening services, and enumerate them to discover as much information as possible such as the server software, version, platform, and so on.

This information is then checked for known signatures of potential issues or vulnerabilities. These signatures are made up of data point combinations that are intended to represent known issues. Multiple data points are used, because the more data points you use, the more accurate the identification. A very large number of potential data points exist, including but not limited to:

- Operating System Version: It is not uncommon for software to be vulnerable on one operating system version but not on another. Because of this, the scanner will attempt to determine, as accurately as possible, what operating system version is hosting the targeted application.

- Patch Level: Many times, patches for an operating system will be released that do not increase the version information, but still change the way a vulnerability will respond, or even eliminate the vulnerability entirely.

- Processor Architecture: Many software applications are available for multiple processor architectures such as Intel x86, Intel x64, multiple versions of ARM, UltraSPARC, and so on.

---

[5]https://en.wikipedia.org/wiki/Executable_space_protection#Windows
[6]https://en.wikipedia.org/wiki/Address_space_layout_randomization
[7]http://tools.kali.org/category/vulnerability-analysis
[8]http://tools.kali.org/category/web-applications

In some cases, a vulnerability will only exist on a specific architecture, so knowing this bit of information can be critical for an accurate signature.

- Software Version: The version of the targeted software is one of the basic items that needs to be captured to identify a vulnerability.

These, and many other data points, will be used to make up a signature as part of a vulnerability scan. As expected, the more data points that match, the more accurate the signature will be. When dealing with signature matches, you can have a few different potential results:

- True Positive: The signature is matched and it captures a true vulnerability. These results are the ones you will need to follow up on and correct, as these are the items that malicious individuals can take advantage of to hurt your organization (or your client's).

- False Positive: The signature is matched; however the detected issue is not a true vulnerability. In an assessment, these are often considered noise and can be quite frustrating. You never want to dismiss a true positive as a false positive without more extensive validation.

- True Negative: The signature is not matched and there is no vulnerability. This is the ideal scenario, verifying that a vulnerability does not exist on a target.

- False Negative: The signature is not matched but there is an existing vulnerability. As bad as a false positive is, a false negative is much worse. In this case, a problem exists but the scanner did not detect it, so you have no indication of its existence.

As you can imagine, the accuracy of the signatures is extremely important for accurate results. The more data that are provided, the greater the chance there is to have accurate results from an automated signature-based scan, which is why authenticated scans are often so popular.

With an authenticated scan, the scanning software will use provided credentials to authenticate to the target. This provides a deeper level of visibility into a target than would otherwise be possible. For instance, on a normal scan you may only detect information about the system that can be derived from listening services and the functionality they provide. This can be quite a bit of information sometimes but it can't compete with the level and depth of data that will be obtained if you authenticate to the system and comprehensively review all installed software, applied patches, running processes, and so on. This breadth of data is useful for detecting vulnerabilities that otherwise may not have been discovered.

A well-conducted vulnerability assessment presents a snapshot of potential problems in an organization and provides metrics to measure change over time. This is a fairly lightweight assessment, but even still, many organizations will regularly perform automated vulnerability scans in off-hours to avoid potential problems during the day when service availability and bandwidth are most critical.

As previously mentioned, a vulnerability scan will have to check many different data points in order to get an accurate result. All of these different checks can create load on the target system as well as consume bandwidth. Unfortunately, it is difficult to know exactly how many resources will be consumed on the target as it depends on the number of open services and the types of checks that would be associated with those services. This is the cost of doing a scan; it is going to occupy system resources. Having a general idea of the resources that will be consumed and how much load the target system can take is important when running these tools.

Scanning Threads Most vulnerability scanners include an option to set *threads per scan*, which equates to the number of concurrent checks that occur at one time. Increasing this number will have a direct impact on the load on the assessment platform as well as the networks and targets you are interacting with. This is important to keep in mind as you use these scanners. It is tempting to increase the threads in order to complete scans faster but remember the substantial load increase associated with doing so.

When a vulnerability scan is finished, the discovered issues are typically linked back to industry standard identifiers such as CVE number[9], EDB-ID[10], and vendor advisories. This information, along with the vulnerabilities CVSS score[11], is used to determine a risk rating. Along with false negatives (and false positives), these arbitrary risk ratings are common issues that need to be considered when analyzing the scan results.

Since automated tools use a database of signatures to detect vulnerabilities, any slight deviation from a known signature can alter the result and likewise the validity of the perceived vulnerability. A false positive incorrectly flags a vulnerability that does not exist, while a false negative is effectively blind to a vulnerability and does not report it. Because of this, a scanner is often said to only be as good as its signature rule base. For this reason, many vendors provide multiple signature sets: one that might be free to home users and another fairly expensive set that is more comprehensive, which is generally sold to corporate customers.

The other issue that is often encountered with vulnerability scans is the validity of the suggested risk ratings. These risk ratings are defined on a generic basis, considering many different factors such as privilege level, type of software, and pre- or post-authentication. Depending on your environment, these ratings may or may not be applicable so they should not be accepted blindly. Only those well-versed in the systems and the vulnerabilities can properly validate risk ratings.

While there is no universally defined agreement on risk ratings, NIST Special publication 800-30[12] is recommended as a baseline for evaluation of risk ratings and their accuracy in your environment. NIST SP 800-30 defines the true risk of a discovered vulnerability as *a combination of the likelihood of occurrence and the potential impact.*

---

[9]https://cve.mitre.org
[10]https://www.exploit-db.com/about/
[11]https://www.first.org/cvss
[12]http://csrc.nist.gov/publications/PubsSPs.html#800-30

Likelihood of Occurrence

According to the National Institute of Standards and Technology (NIST), the likelihood of occurrence is based on the probability that a particular threat is capable of exploiting a particular vulnerability, with possible ratings of Low, Medium, or High.

- High: the potential adversary is highly skilled and motivated and the measures that have been put in place to protect against the vulnerability are insufficient.

- Medium: the potential adversary is motivated and skilled but the measures put in place to protect against the vulnerability may impede their success.

- Low: the potential adversary is unskilled or lacks motivation and there are measures in place to protect against the vulnerability that are partially or completely effective.

Impact

The level of impact is determined by evaluating the amount of harm that could occur if the vulnerability in question were exploited or otherwise taken advantage of.

- High: taking advantage of the vulnerability could result in very significant financial losses, serious harm to the mission or reputation of the organization, or even serious injury, including loss of life.

- Medium: taking advantage of the vulnerability could lead to financial losses, harm to the mission or reputation of the organization, or human injury.

- Low: taking advantage of the vulnerability could result in some degree of financial loss or impact to the mission and reputation of the organization.

Overall Risk

Once the likelihood of occurrence and impact have been determined, you can then determine the overall risk rating, which is defined as a function of the two ratings. The overall risk can be rated Low, Medium, or High, which provides guidance to those responsible for securing and maintaining the systems in question.

- High: There is a strong requirement for additional measures to be implemented to protect against the vulnerability. In some cases, the system may be allowed to continue operating but a plan must be designed and implemented as soon as possible.

- Medium: There is a requirement for additional measures to be implemented to protect against the vulnerability. A plan to implement the required measures must be done in a timely manner.

- Low: The owner of the system will determine whether to implement additional measures to protect against the vulnerability or they can opt to accept the risk instead and leave the system unchanged.

In Summary

With so many factors making up the true risk of a discovered vulnerability, the pre-defined risk ratings from tool output should only be used as a starting point to determine the true risk to the overall organization.

Competently-created reports from a vulnerability assessment, when analyzed by a professional, can provide an initial foundation for other assessments, such as compliance penetration tests. As such, it is important to understand how to get the best results possible from this initial assessment.

Kali makes an excellent platform for conducting a vulnerability assessment and does not need any special configuration. In the Kali Applications menu, you will find numerous tools for vulnerability assessments in the Information Gathering, Vulnerability Analysis, and Web Application Analysis categories. Several sites, including the aforementioned Kali Linux Tools Listing[13], The Kali Linux Official Documentation[14] site, and the free Metasploit Unleashed[15] course provide excellent resources for using Kali Linux during a vulnerability assessment.

11.2.2. Compliance Penetration Test

The next type of assessment in order of complexity is a compliance-based penetration test. These are the most common penetration tests as they are government- and industry-mandated requirements based on a compliance framework the entire organization operates under.

While there are many industry-specific compliance frameworks, the most common would likely be Payment Card Industry Data Security Standard[16] (PCI DSS), a framework dictated by payment card companies that retailers processing card-based payments must comply with. However, a number of other standards exist such as the Defense Information Systems Agency Security Technical Implementation Guides[17] (DISA STIG), Federal Risk and Authorization Management Program[18] (FedRAMP), Federal Information Security Management Act[19] (FISMA), and others. In some cases, a corporate client may request an assessment, or ask to see the results of the most recent assessment for various reasons. Whether ad-hoc or mandated, these sorts of assessments are collectively

---

[13]http://tools.kali.org/tools-listing
[14]http://docs.kali.org
[15]https://www.offensive-security.com/metasploit-unleashed/
[16]https://www.pcisecuritystandards.org/documents/Penetration_Testing_Guidance_March_2015.pdf
[17]http://iase.disa.mil/stigs/Pages/index.aspx
[18]https://www.fedramp.gov/about-us/about/
[19]http://csrc.nist.gov/groups/SMA/fisma/

called compliance-based penetration tests, or simply "compliance assessments" or "compliance checks".

A compliance test often begins with a vulnerability assessment. In the case of PCI compliance auditing[20], a vulnerability assessment, when performed properly, can satisfy several of the base requirements, including: "2. Do not use vendor-supplied defaults for system passwords and other security parameters" (for example, with tools from the Password Attacks menu category), "11. Regularly test security systems and processes" (with tools from the Database Assessment category) and others. Some requirements, such as "9. Restrict physical access to cardholder data" and "12. Maintain a policy that addresses information security for all personnel" don't seem to lend themselves to traditional tool-based vulnerability assessment and require additional creativity and testing.

Despite the fact that it might not seem straight-forward to use Kali Linux for some elements of a compliance test, the fact is that Kali is a perfect fit in this environment, not just because of the wide range of security-related tools, but because of the open-source Debian environment it is built on, allowing for the installation of a wide range of tools. Searching the package manager with carefully chosen keywords from whichever compliance framework you are using is almost certain to turn up multiple results. As it stands, many organizations use Kali Linux as the standard platform for these exact sorts of assessments.

11.2.3. Traditional Penetration Test

A traditional penetration test has become a difficult item to define, with many working from different definitions, depending on the space they operate in. Part of this market confusion is driven by the fact that the term "Penetration Test" has become more commonly used for the previously mentioned compliance-based penetration test (or even a vulnerability assessment) where, by design, you are not delving too deep into the assessment because that would go beyond the minimum requirements.

For the purposes of this section, we will side-step that debate and use this category to cover assessments that go beyond the minimum requirements; assessments that are designed to actually improve the overall security of the organization.

As opposed to the previously-discussed assessment types, penetration tests don't often start with a scope definition, but instead a goal such as, "simulate what would happen if an internal user is compromised" or, "identify what would happen if the organization came under focused attack by an external malicious party." A key differentiator of these sorts of assessments is that they don't just find and validate vulnerabilities, but instead leverage identified issues to uncover the worst-case scenario. Instead of relying solely on heavy vulnerability scanning toolsets, you must follow up with validation of the findings through the use of exploits or tests to eliminate false positives and do your best to detect hidden vulnerabilities or false negatives. This often involves exploiting

---

[20]https://www.pcisecuritystandards.org/documents/PCIDSS_QRGv3_2.pdf

vulnerabilities discovered initially, exploring the level of access the exploit provides, and using this increased access as leverage for additional attacks against the target.

This requires critical review of the target environment along with manual searching, creativity, and outside-the-box thinking to discover other avenues of potential vulnerability and ultimately using other tools and tests outside those found by the heavier vulnerability scanners. Once this is completed, it is often necessary to start the whole process over again multiple times to do a full and complete job.

Even with this approach, you will often find that many assessments are composed of different phases. Kali makes it easy to find programs for each phase by way of the Kali Menu:

- Information Gathering: In this phase, you focus on learning as much as possible about the target environment. Typically, this activity is non-invasive and will appear similar to standard user activity. These actions will make up the foundation of the rest of the assessment and therefore need to be as complete as possible. Kali's Information Gathering category has dozens of tools to uncover as much information as possible about the environment being assessed.

- Vulnerability Discovery: This will often be called "active information gathering", where you don't attack but engage in non-standard user behavior in an attempt to identify potential vulnerabilities in the target environment. This is where the previously-discussed vulnerability scanning will most often take place. The programs listed in the Vulnerability Analysis, Web Application Analysis, Database Assessment, and Reverse Engineering categories will be useful for this phase.

- Exploitation: With the potential vulnerabilities discovered, in this phase you try to exploit them to get a foothold into the target. Tools to assist you in this phase can be found in the Web Application Analysis, Database Assessment, Password Attacks, and Exploitation Tools categories.

- Pivoting and Exfiltration: Once the initial foothold is established, further steps have to be completed. These are often escalating privileges to a level adequate to accomplish your goals as an attacker, pivoting into other systems that may not have been previously accessible to you, and exfiltrating sensitive information from the targeted systems. Refer to the Password Attacks, Exploitation Tools, Sniffing & Spoofing, and Post Exploitation categories to help with this phase.

- Reporting: Once the active portion of the assessment is completed, you then have to document and report on the activities that were conducted. This phase is often not as technical as the previous phases, however it is highly important to ensure your client gets full value from the work completed. The Reporting Tools category contains a number of tools that have proven useful in the reporting phase.

In most cases, these assessments will be very unique in their design as every organization will operate with different threats and assets to protect. Kali Linux makes a very versatile base for these sorts of assessments and this is where you can really take advantage of the many Kali Linux customization features. Many organizations that conduct these sorts of assessments will maintain highly customized versions of Kali Linux for internal use to speed up deployment of systems before a new assessment.

Customizations that organizations make to their Kali Linux installations will often include:

- Pre-installation of commercial packages with licensing information. For instance, you may have a package such as a commercial vulnerability scanner that you would like to use. To avoid having to install this package with each build, you can do it once[21] and have it show up in every Kali deployment you do.

- Pre-configured connect-back virtual private networks (VPN). These are very useful in leave-behind devices that allow you to conduct "remote internal" assessments. In most cases, these systems will connect back to an assessor-controlled system, creating a tunnel that the assessor can use to access internal systems. The Kali Linux ISO of Doom[22] is an example of this exact type of customization.

- Pre-installed internally-developed software and tools. Many organizations will have private toolsets, so setting these up once in a customized Kali install[23] saves time.

- Pre-configured OS configurations such as host mappings, desktop wallpaper, proxy settings, etc. Many Kali users have specific settings[24] they like to have tweaked just so. If you are going to do a re-deployment of Kali on a regular basis, capturing these changes makes a lot of sense.

11.2.4. Application Assessment

While most assessments have a broad scope, an application assessment is a specialty that is narrowly focused on a single application. These sorts of assessments are becoming more common due to the complexity of mission-critical applications that organizations use, many of which are built in-house. An application assessment is usually added on to a broader assessment, as required. Applications that may be assessed in this manner include, but are not limited to:

- Web applications: The most common externally-facing attack surface, web applications make great targets simply because they are accessible. Often, standard assessments will find basic problems in web applications, however a more focused review is often worth the time to identify issues relating to the workflow of the application. The *kali-linux-web* meta-package has a number of tools to help with these assessments.

- Compiled desktop applications: Server software is not the only target; desktop applications also make up a wonderful attack surface. In years past, many desktop applications such as

---

[21]http://docs.kali.org/kali-dojo/02-mastering-live-build

[22]https://www.offensive-security.com/kali-linux/kali-rolling-iso-of-doom/

[23]http://docs.kali.org/development/live-build-a-custom-kali-iso

[24]https://www.offensive-security.com/kali-linux/kali-linux-recipes/

PDF readers or web-based video programs were highly targeted, forcing them to mature. However, there are still a wide number of desktop applications that are a wealth of vulnerabilities when properly reviewed.

- Mobile applications: As mobile devices become more popular, mobile applications will become that much more of a standard attack surface in many assessments. This is a fast moving target and methodologies are still maturing in this area, leading to new developments practically every week. Tools related to the analysis of mobile applications can be found in the Reverse Engineering menu category.

Application assessments can be conducted in a variety of different ways. As a simple example, an application-specific automated tool can be run against the application in an attempt to identify potential issues. These tools will use application-specific logic in an attempt to identify unknown issues rather than just depending on a set of known signatures. These tools must have a built-in understanding of the application's behavior. A common example of this would be a web application vulnerability scanner such as Burp Suite[25], directed against an application that first identifies various input fields and then sends common SQL injection attacks to these fields while monitoring the application's response for indications of a successful attack.

In a more complex scenario, an application assessment can be conducted interactively in either a *black box* or *white box* manner.

- Black Box Assessment: The tool (or assessor) interacts with the application with no special knowledge or access beyond that of a standard user. For instance, in the case of a web application, the assessor may only have access to the functions and features that are available to a user that has not logged into the system. Any user accounts used would be ones where a general user can self-register the account. This would prevent the attacker from being able to review any functionality that is only available to users that need to be created by an administrator.

- White Box Assessment: The tool (or assessor) will often have full access to the source code, administrative access to the platform running the application, and so on. This ensures that a full and comprehensive review of all application functionality is completed, regardless of where that functionality lives in the application. The trade-off with this is that the assessment is in no way a simulation of actual malicious activity.

There are obviously shades of grey in between. Typically, the deciding factor is the goal of the assessment. If the goal is to identify what would happen in the event that the application came under a focused external attack, a black box assessment would likely be best. If the goal is to identify and eliminate as many security issues as possible in a relatively short time period, a white box approach may be more efficient.

---

[25]https://portswigger.net/burp/

In other cases, a hybrid approach may be taken where the assessor does not have full access to the application source code of the platform running the application, but user accounts are provisioned by an administrator to allow access to as much application functionality as possible.

Kali is an ideal platform for all manner of application assessments. On a default installation, a range of different application-specific scanners are available. For more advanced assessments, a range of tools, source editors, and scripting environments exist. You may find the Web Application[26] and Reverse Engineering[27] sections of the Kali Tools[28] website helpful.

11.3. Formalization of the Assessment

With your Kali environment ready and the type of assessment defined, you are almost ready to start working. Your last step is to formalize the work to be done. This is critically important, as this defines what the expectations for the work will be, and grants you permission to conduct what might otherwise be illegal activity. We will cover this at a high level, but this is a very complex and important step so you will likely want to check with your organization's legal representative for assistance.

As part of the formalization process, you will need to define the rules of engagement for the work. This covers items such as:

- What systems are you allowed to interact with? It is important to ensure you don't accidentally interfere with anything that is critical to business operations.
- What time of day and over what attack window is the assessment allowed to occur? Some organizations like to limit the times that the assessment work can be conducted.
- When you discover a potential vulnerability, are you allowed to exploit it? If not, what is the approval process? There are some organizations that take a very controlled approach to each exploitation attempt, whereas others would like a more realistic approach. It is best to define these expectations clearly before work begins.
- If a significant issue is discovered, how should it be handled? Sometimes, organizations want to be informed right away, otherwise it is typically addressed at the end of the assessment.
- In case of emergency, who should you contact? It is always important to know who to contact when a problem of any sort occurs.
- Who will know about the activity? How will it be communicated to them? In some cases, organizations will want to test their incident response and detection performance as part of the assessment. It is always a good idea to know this beforehand, so you know if you should take any degree of stealth in the approach to the assessment.

---

[26]http://tools.kali.org/category/web-applications
[27]http://tools.kali.org/category/reverse-engineering
[28]http://tools.kali.org

- What are the expectations at the end of the assessment? How will results be communicated? Know what all parties expect at the end of the assessment. Defining the deliverable is the best way to keep everyone happy after the work is completed.

While not complete, this listing gives you an idea of the details that should be covered. However, you should realize that there is no substitute for good legal representation. Once these items are defined, you need to acquire proper authorization to perform the assessment, since much of the activity that you will do in the course of an assessment may not be legal without proper authority from someone with the authority to give that permission.

With all that in place, there is still one last step you will want to take before starting work: validation. Never trust the scope that you are provided—always validate it. Use multiple information sources to confirm that the systems within scope are in fact owned by the client and that they are operated by the client as well. With the prevalence of cloud services, an organization may forget that they don't actually own the systems providing them service. You may find that you have to obtain special permission from a cloud service provider before starting work. In addition, always validate IP address blocks. Don't count on an organization's assumption that they own entire IP blocks, even if they sign off on them as viable targets. For example, we have seen examples of organizations that request an assessment of an entire class C network range when, in fact, they only owned a subset of those addresses. By attacking the entire class C address space, we would have ended up attacking the organization's network neighbors. The OSINT Analysis sub-category of the Information Gathering menu contains a number of tools that can assist you with this validation process.

11.4. Types of Attacks

Once the work is taking place, what are some of the specific sorts of attacks that you will be conducting? Each type of vulnerability[29] has its own associated exploitation techniques. This section will cover the various classes of vulnerabilities that you will interact with most often.

No matter what category of vulnerability you are looking at, Kali makes these tools and exploits easy to find. The Kali menu on your graphical user interface is divided up into categories to help make the right tool easier to find. In addition, the Kali Tools website[30] has comprehensive listings of the various tools available in Kali, organized by category and tagged for easy browsing. Each entry contains detailed information about the tool as well as example usage.

---

[29]https://www.cvedetails.com/vulnerabilities-by-types.php
[30]http://tools.kali.org/tools-listing

11.4.1. Denial of Service

Denial of service attacks leverage a vulnerability to create a loss of service, often by crashing the vulnerable process. The Stress Testing category of the Kali Linux menu contains a number of tools for this purpose.

When many people hear the term "denial of service attack", they immediately think of resource consumption attacks that are sent out from multiple sources at once against a single target. These would be a *distributed* denial of services attack, or DDoS. These sorts of attacks are rarely part of a professional security assessment.

Instead, a singular denial of service attack is most often the result of an improper attempt to exploit a vulnerability. If an exploit writer releases partially functional, or proof-of-concept (PoC) code and it is used in the field, this could create a denial of service condition. Even a properly-coded exploit may only work under very specific circumstances but cause a denial of service under lesser circumstances. It may seem that the solution is to only use safe and tested exploit code, or to write your own. Even with this solution, there are no guarantees and this severely limits the assessor, causing undue constraints, which results in a lesser assessment. Instead, the key is compromise. Avoid PoC code and untested exploits in the field and always make sure a lawyer has you covered for other mishaps.

Typically, denial of service attacks are not launched intentionally. Most automated vulnerability tools will declare denial of service vulnerabilities as lower risk due to the fact that while you can remove a service from operation, that service can't be exploited for code execution. However, it is important to remember that not all exploits are released publicly and a denial of service vulnerability may mask a deeper, more serious threat. A code execution exploit for a known denial of service may exist but not be public. The point is, pay attention to denial of service vulnerabilities and encourage your customer to get them patched regardless of their (often low) threat rating.

11.4.2. Memory Corruption

A memory corruption happens when a location within the memory space of a process is accidentally modified due to programming mistakes. Memory corruption bugs usually lead to unpredictable program behavior, however in many cases, these bugs allow process memory manipulation in such a way that the program execution flow can be controlled, allowing attacker-defined activity.

These attacks are typically referred to as buffer overflows, although this term is an over-simplification. The most common types of memory corruption are vastly different from one another and have their own tactics and techniques required for successful exploitation.

- Stack Buffer Overflow: When a program writes more data to a buffer on the stack than there is space available for it, adjacent memory can be corrupted, often causing the program to crash.

- Heap Corruption: Heap memory is allocated at run- time and usually contains data from the running program. Heap corruptions occur by manipulating the data to overwrite through the linked list of heap memory pointers.

- Integer Overflow: These overflows occur when an application tries to create a numeric value that can't be contained within its allocated storage space.

- Format String: When a program accepts user input and formats it without checking it, memory locations can be revealed or overwritten, depending on the format tokens that are used.

11.4.3. Web Vulnerabilities

Due to the fact that modern web sites are no longer static pages, but instead dynamically generated for the user, the average website is quite complex. Web vulnerabilities take advantage of this complexity in an effort to attack either the back end page generation logic or the presentation to the visitor of the site.

These sorts of attacks are extremely common, as many organizations have reached the point where they have very few externally facing services. Two of the most prevalent web application attack types[31] are SQL injection and cross-site scripting (XSS).

- SQL injection: These attacks take advantage of improperly-programmed applications that do not properly sanitize user input, leading to the ability to extract information from the database or even the complete takeover of the server.

- Cross-site scripting: As with SQL injection, XSS attacks result from improper sanitization of user input, allowing attackers to manipulate the user or site into executing code in the context of their own browser session.

Complex, rich, and complicated web applications are very common, presenting a welcome attack surface for malicious parties. You will find a large number of useful tools in the Web Application Analysis menu category and the *kali-linux-web* metapackage.

11.4.4. Password Attacks

Password attacks are attacks against the authentication system of a service. These attacks are often broken into online password attacks and offline password attacks, which you will find reflected in the Password Attacks menu category. In an online password attack, multiple passwords are attempted against a running system. In an offline password attack, the hashed or encrypted values of the passwords are obtained and the attacker attempts to obtain the clear text values. The protection against this sort of attack is the fact that it is computationally expensive to work through this process, limiting the number of attempts per second you can generate. However,

---

[31]https://www.owasp.org/index.php/Top_10_2013-Top_10

workarounds for this do exist, such as using graphic processor units (GPUs) to accelerate the number of attempts that can be made. The *kali-linux-gpu* metapackage contains a number of tools that tap into this power.

Most commonly, password attacks target vendor-supplied default passwords. As these are well-known values, attackers will scan for these default accounts, hoping to get lucky. Other common attacks include custom dictionary attacks where a wordlist is created that has been tailored to the target environment and then an online password attack against common, default, or known accounts is conducted where each word is attempted in sequence.

In an assessment, it is very important to understand the potential consequences of this sort of attack. First, they are often very noisy due to the repeated authentication attempts. Secondly, these attacks can often result in an account lock out situation after too many invalid attempts are performed against a single account. Finally, the performance of these attacks is often quite slow, resulting in difficulty when attempting to use a comprehensive wordlist.

11.4.5. Client-Side Attacks

Most attacks are conducted against servers, but as services have become harder to attack, easier targets have been selected. Client-side attacks are a result of this, where an attacker will target the various applications installed on the workstation of an employee within a target organization. The Social Engineering Tools menu category has a number of excellent applications that can help conduct these types of attacks.

This sort of attack is best exploited by the Flash, Acrobat Reader, and Java attacks that were very common in the early 2000s. In these cases, attackers would try to solicit a target to visit a malicious web page. These pages would contain specialized code that would trigger vulnerabilities in these client-side applications, resulting in the ability to run malicious code on the targets system.

Client-side attacks are incredibly difficult to prevent, requiring a great deal of user education, constant application updates, and network controls to effectively mitigate the risk.

11.5. Summary

In this chapter, we took a brief look at Kali's role in the field of information security. We discussed the importance of a clean, working installation and the use of encryption before heading out to the field in order to protect your client's information, and the importance of legal representation to protect you and your client's interests.

The components of the CIA (confidentiality, integrity, availability) triad are the primary items that you will focus on when securing a system as part of standard deployment, maintenance, or assessment. This conceptual foundation will assist you with the identification of the critical components of your systems and the amount of effort and resources worth investing into correcting identified problems.

We discussed several types of vulnerabilities including file inclusion, SQL injection, buffer overflows, and race conditions.

The accuracy of the signatures is extremely important to get useful vulnerability assessment results. The more data that are provided, the higher chance there is to have accurate results from an automated signature-based scan, which is why authenticated scans are often so popular.

Since automated tools use a database of signatures to detect vulnerabilities, any slight deviation from a known signature can alter the result and likewise the validity of the perceived vulnerability.

We also discussed the four types of assessments: the *vulnerability assessment, compliance test, traditional penetration test*, and the *application assessment.* Even though each type of assessment leverages a core set of tools, many of the tools and techniques overlap.

The vulnerability assessment is relatively simple in comparison to the other assessment types and often consists of an automated inventory of discovered issues within a target environment. In this section, we discussed that a vulnerability is a flaw that, when exploited, will compromise the confidentiality, integrity, or availability of an information system. Since it is signature-based, this type of assessment relies on accurate signatures and can present false positives and negatives. You will find the core tools for this type of assessment in the Vulnerability Analysis and Exploitation Tools menu categories of Kali Linux.

Compliance tests are based on government- and industry-mandated requirements (such as PCI DSS, DISA STIG, and FISMA), which are in turn based on a compliance framework. This test usually begins with a vulnerability assessment.

A traditional penetration test is a thorough security assessment that is designed to improve the overall security posture of an organization based on certain real-world threats. This type of test involves several steps (mirrored by the Kali Linux menu structure) and culminates in exploitation of vulnerabilities and pivoting access to other machines and networks within the target scope.

Application assessments (usually white- or black-box) focus on a single application and use specialized tools such as those found in the Web Application Analysis, Database Assessment, Reverse Engineering, and Exploitation Tools menu categories.

Several types of attacks were discussed including: denial of service, which breaks the behavior of an application and makes it inaccessible; memory corruption, which leads to manipulation of process memory, often allowing an attacker code execution; web attacks, which attack web services using techniques like SQL injection and XSS attacks; and password attacks, which often leverage password lists to attack service credentials.

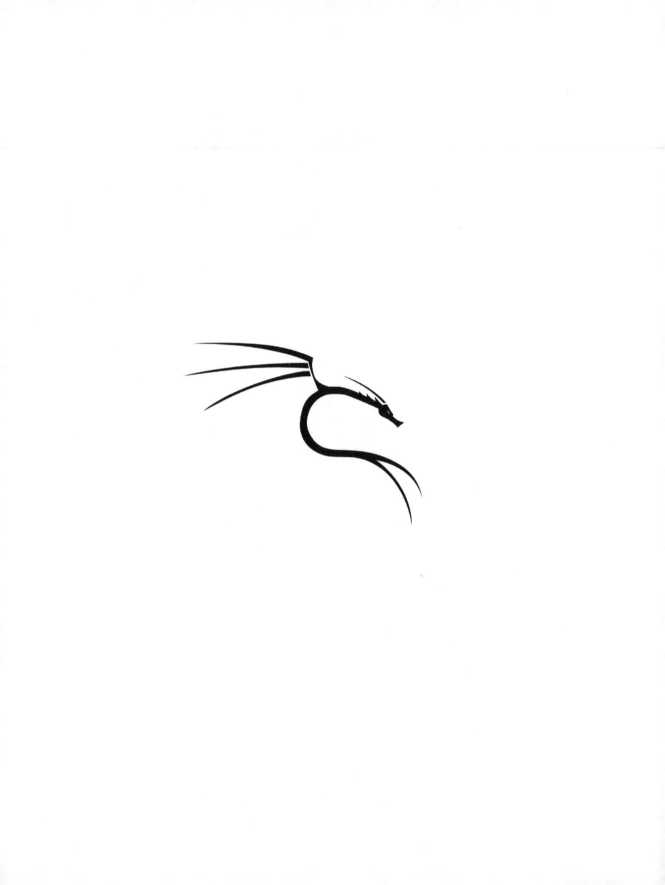

Keywords

Constant changes
Certifications
Trainings

Conclusion: The Road Ahead

Contents

Congratulations! Hopefully you should now be more familiar with your Kali Linux system and you should not be afraid of using it for any experiment that you can think of. You have discovered its most interesting features but you also know its limits and various ways to work around those limitations.

If you have not put all features into practice, keep this book around for reference purposes and refresh your memory when you are about to try a new feature. Remember that there is nothing better than practice (and perseverance) to develop new skills. Try Harder[1], as the Offensive Security trainers keep repeating.

12.1. Keeping Up with Changes

With a constantly-changing distribution like *kali-rolling*, some parts of the book will necessarily become obsolete. We will do our best to keep it up to date (at least for the online version) but for most parts we tried to provide generic explanations that should be useful for a long time to come.

That said, you should be ready to embrace changes and to find out solutions to any problem that might pop up. With the better understanding of Kali Linux and its relationship to Debian, you can rely on both the Kali and Debian communities and their numerous resources (bug trackers, forums, mailing lists, etc.) when you are getting stuck.

Don't be afraid to file bugs (see section 6.3, "Filing a Good Bug Report" [page 129])! If you are like me, by the time you have completed the steps involved in filing a good bug report (and it takes some time), you will have solved the problem or at least found a good work-around. And by actually filing the bug, you will be helping others who are affected by the issue.

12.2. Showing Off Your Newly Gained Knowledge

Are you proud of your new Kali Linux skills? Would you like to ensure that you remember the really important things? If you answer yes to one of those questions, then you should consider applying for the Kali Linux Certified Professional program.

It is a comprehensive certification that will ensure that you know how to deploy and use Kali Linux in many realistic use cases. It is a nice addition to your resume and it also proves that you are ready to go further.

12.3. Going Further

This book taught you a lot of things that any Kali Linux user should know, but we made some hard choices to keep it short, and there are many topics that were not covered.

---

[1]https://www.offensive-security.com/offsec/say-try-harder/

12.3.1. Towards System Administration

If you want to learn more about system administration, then we can only recommend that you check out the Debian Administrator's Handbook:

➡ https://debian-handbook.info/get/

You will find there many supplementary chapters covering common Unix services that we have entirely skipped in this book. And even for chapters that have been reused in the Kali book, you will find plenty of supplementary tips, notably on the packaging system (which is also covered more extensively at its lowest level).

The Debian book obviously presents more deeply the Debian community and the way it is organized. While this knowledge is not vital, it is really useful when you have to interact with Debian contributors, for example through bug reports.

12.3.2. Towards Penetration Testing

You probably noticed by now that this book did not teach you penetration testing. But the things you learned are still important. You are now ready to fully exploit the power of Kali Linux, the best penetration testing framework. And you have the basic Linux skills required to participate in Offensive Security's training.

If you feel that you are not yet ready for a paid course, you can start by following the Metasploit Unleashed[2] free online training. Metasploit is a very popular penetration testing tool and you have to know it if you are serious about your plans to learn penetration testing.

The next logical step would then be to follow the Penetration Testing with Kali Linux[3] online course leading the path to the famous "Offensive Security Certified Professional" certification. This online course can be followed at your own pace but the certification is actually a difficult, 24h long, real-word, hands-on penetration test which takes place in an isolated VPN network.

Are you up to the challenge?

---

[2]https://www.offensive-security.com/metasploit-unleashed/
[3]https://www.offensive-security.com/information-security-training/

Index

D

database assessment, 6
database server, 111
dch, 226
dd, 22
debconf, 214
debconf-get, 97
debconf-get-selections, 94
debconf-set, 97
DEBEMAIL, 265
DEBFULLNAME, 265
Debian
    relationship with Kali Linux, 4
Debian Administrator's Handbook, 303
Debian Free Software Guidelines, 5
Debian GNU/Linux, 2
Debian Policy, 5
debian-archive-keyring, 203
debian-kernel-handbook, 232
debian/changelog, 226, 266
debian/control, 266
debian/copyright, 265
debian/patches, 225
debian/rules, 229, 267
debuild, 231
default passwords, 153
default.target, 117
deletion of a group, 109
delgroup, 109
denial of service, 295
dependency, 207
Depends, header field, 207
desktop environment, 3
    choice during build of live ISO, 237
desktop-base, 263
detecting changes on the filesystem, 162
device file, 49
df, 60
dh-make, 264
dh_install, 267
DHCP, 252

dictionary attacks, 296
directives, Apache, 115, 116
DirectoryIndex, Apache directive, 115
disable an account, 109
disk preseed, 93
Disks (program), 20
diskutil, 23
distribution, Linux, 2
dm-crypt, 86
dmesg, 60
DNAT, 155
dnsmasq, 252
docs.kali.org, 127
documentation, 124, 126
download
    ISO image, 14
    the sources, 223
dpkg, 170
    database, 212
    dpkg --verify, 162
    internal operation, 213
dpkg-buildpackage, 230
dpkg-deb, 231
dpkg-source --commit, 227
drive, USB drive, 19
DROP, 155
dropdb, 112
dropuser, 112
dual boot, 84

E

echo, 54
editor, 56
encrypted partition, 85
encrypted persistence, 242
engineering
    reverse, 6
    social engineering, 7
Enhances, header field, 208
environment
    environment variable, 54
ExecCGI, Apache directive, 115

owner
    group, 57
    user, 57

About the Authors

A Debian developer for more than 20 years and author of the *Debian Administrator's Handbook*, Raphaël Hertzog is the Debian guru in the Kali team. When he isn't working with Kali, he offers his Debian expertise through Freexian, a company he founded. He helps others by building derivatives and custom installers, packaging software for Debian, improving existing packages (by fixing bugs and adding new features), and more.

Mati Aharoni is an infosec dinosaur with more than a decade of active involvement in the infosec community. Aharoni has founded projects like the BackTrack and Kali Linux Open Source distributions, and the Exploit Database, as well as Offensive Security – a leading infosec company, well-known for its industry-defining security certifications and training. Between exploit writing and cataloging, penetration testing, Kali development and tinkering with hardware, Aharoni enjoys the evangelical role of convincing anyone who will listen about the virtues of Kali Linux.

Jim O'Gorman is the president of Offensive Security's US-based services. Jim has more than a decade of experience conducting penetration tests on heavily defended environments across the globe. Additionally, Jim is the lead instructor for the Penetration with Kali Linux Offensive Security course.

CPSIA information can be obtained
at www.ICGtesting.com
Printed in the USA
BVHW011005160221
600245BV00007B/192

9 780997 615609